BUSH
v.
GORE

BUSH V. GORE

The Court Cases and the Commentary

E.J. DIONNE JR.
WILLIAM KRISTOL

EDITORS

BROOKINGS INSTITUTION PRESS
Washington, D.C.

Copyright © 2001
THE BROOKINGS INSTITUTION
1775 Massachusetts Avenue, N.W., Washington, D.C. 20036
www.brookings.edu

Library of Congress Cataloging-in-Publication data
Bush v. Gore : the court cases and the commentary /
E. J. Dionne Jr. and William Kristol, editors.
    p.   cm.
Includes index.
  ISBN 0-8157-0107-1 (alk. paper)
1. Bush, George W. (George Walker), 1946—Trials, litigation, etc.
2. Gore, Albert, 1948—Trials, litigation, etc. 3. Contested
elections—United States. 4. Contested elections—Florida.
5. Presidents—United States—Election—2000. I. Title: Bush versus Gore.
II. Dionne, E. J. III. Kristol, William.
  KF5074.2 .B87 2001   2001000721
  342.73'075—dc21   CIP

9 8 7 6 5 4 3

The paper used in this publication meets minimum requirements of the American National Standard for Information Sciences—Permanence of Paper for Printed Library Materials: ANSI Z39.48-1992.

Typeset in Adobe Garamond

Composition by Oakland Street Publishing
Arlington, Virginia

Printed by R. R. Donnelley and Sons
Harrisonburg, Virginia

Contents

COMMENTARY
NOVEMBER 7–21, 2000

COMMENTARY
NOVEMBER 22–DECEMBER 9, 2000

COMMENTARY
DECEMBER 10–13, 2000

COMMENTARY
DECEMBER 14, 2000 . . .

Chronology

NOVEMBER 7–DECEMBER 18, 2000

R	5	6	7	8	9	10	11	
E	12	13	14	15	16	17	18	
B	19	20	21	22	23	24	25	
M	26	27	28	29	30	1	2	
E	3	4	5	6	7	8	9	D
V	10	11	12	13	14	15	16	E
O	17	18	19	20	21	22	23	C
N	24	25	26	27	28	29	30	E M B E R

NOVEMBER

7 Election Day.

8 Original tally of election results. Gore leads in national popular vote by narrow margin. Florida, Oregon, and New Mexico too close to call. Thirty-seven electoral votes are at issue, including twenty-five Florida electors.

Florida Division of Elections reports that Bush leads state by 1,784 votes (2,909,135 to 2,907,351).

9 Unofficial (AP) returns give Gore 218, 441 vote lead over Bush nationally (49,244,746 to 49,026,305).

Machine recount required under Florida Election Code narrows Bush's lead to 327 votes (2,910,198 to 2,909,871).

Gore seeks hand recounts in Volusia, Palm Beach, Broward, and Miami-Dade counties.

Florida Secretary of State Katherine Harris declines to waive statutory November 14 deadline for submission of county vote totals.

11 Bush petitions U.S. District Court for the Southern District of Florida to block manual recounts of disputed tallies.

13 District Court refuses to grant Bush request to block hand recounts.

14 Leon County Circuit Court judge Terry Lewis rules that statutory seven-day recount deadline is mandatory, but that Volusia board may amend its returns at later date; authorizes Secretary to exercise discretion in whether to accept late amended returns in statewide certification. [pages 19–23]

Secretary certifies county totals excluding absentee ballots.

Secretary issues criteria for accepting late filings and orders counties seeking to file late returns to submit written statements justifying facts and circumstances by 2:00 p.m., November 15.

15 Bush appeals district court ruling to U.S. Court of Appeals for the Eleventh Circuit. Court agrees to hear Bush request for injunction blocking further recounts.

Florida Supreme Court denies Secretary's request to block recounts; accepts Palm Beach County's request for clarification of dispute between Secretary and Florida Attorney General on legality of recount.

Volusia, Palm Beach, Miami-Dade, and Broward counties submit statements requesting late returns; Secretary determines that none justify extension of filing deadline.

16 Florida Supreme Court rules 7-0 that Palm Beach and Broward counties may continue hand recount.

Gore and Florida Democrats seek emergency ruling from Leon County Circuit Court judge Terry Lewis to find Secretary in contempt of November 14 order and compel Secretary to accept amended returns.

Florida Supreme Court stays Secretary's certification to hear case for hand recounts; allows manual processing of overseas ballots and hand recounts of ballots.

Local Democrats sue Seminole County Canvassing Board in County Circuit Court alleging fraudulent absentee ballot practices.

17 Judge Terry Lewis denies Gore's November 14 motion for emergency ruling, finding that Secretary has "exercised her reasoned judgment to determine what relevant factors and criteria should be considered. . . ."

18 Overseas ballots counted, increasing Bush's lead to 930 votes.

20 Florida Supreme Court hears oral arguments.

21 Florida Supreme Court backs hand recounts in selected counties; imposes November 26, 5:00 p.m deadline for return of ballot counts; orders Secretary to accept manual recounts submitted before deadline. [pages 24–47]

22 Bush petitions U.S. Supreme Court for writ of certiorari to Florida Supreme Court.

23 Florida Supreme Court refuses to compel Miami-Dade County to resume manual recount.

24 U.S. Supreme Court agrees to hear Bush appeal of Florida Supreme Court ruling.

26 Florida Elections Canvassing Commission (which includes Secretary) certifies election results, finding Bush lead of 537 votes (2,912,790 to 2,912,253), and declares Bush winner of Florida's twenty-five electoral votes.

27 Gore files suit contesting certification in Leon County Circuit Court (Judge N. Sanders Sauls); at issue are votes in Nassau, Miami-Dade, and Palm Beach counties.

30 Palm Beach ballots delivered by truck to Leon County Circuit Court.

DECEMBER

1 Oral arguments in U.S. Supreme Court.

Florida Supreme Court rejects Gore petition for immediate recount of Palm Beach County ballots.

2-3 Oral arguments in Leon County Circuit Court (Judge N. Sanders Sauls)

4 U.S. Supreme Court declines (9-0) to review federal questions asserted in Bush petition; vacates November 21 Florida Supreme Court order and remands case for further consideration. [pages 48–52]

Leon County Circuit Court judge N. Sanders Sauls rules that Gore has failed to prove "reasonable probability" that election would have turned out differently if not for problems counting ballots. [pages 53–57]

5 Florida Democrats file suit alleging balloting irregularities in Seminole and Martin counties; request discarding of approximately 15,000 absentee ballots.

6 U.S. Court of Appeals for the Eleventh Circuit rejects Bush request to bar manual recounts.

Republican leaders of Florida Legislature call for special session on December 8.

7 Florida Supreme Court hears oral argument in Gore's appeal of Leon County Circuit Court ruling.

8 Florida Supreme Court backs (4-3) Gore appeal: orders Leon County Circuit Court to hand-tabulate 9,000 ballots in Miami-Dade County; orders Secretary to include in certified result 215 Palm Beach County votes and 168 Miami-Dade County votes for Gore; directs Palm Beach County Circuit Court to resolve Bush assertion that Gore's net gain in Palm Beach totals 176 votes. [pages 58–96]

Bush appeals Florida Supreme Court ruling to U.S. Supreme Court.

9 U.S. Supreme Court stays (5-4) Florida Supreme Court December 8 ruling. [pages 97–99]

11 Oral arguments in U.S. Supreme Court.

Florida Supreme Court (on remand by December 4 U.S. Supreme Court order) issues order reversing holdings of Leon County Circuit Court judges that Secretary acted within her discretion in rejecting late filings of Palm Beach and Volusia counties.

12 U.S. Supreme Court reverses (5-4) Florida Supreme Court December 11 ruling; bars further counting of disputed ballots; remands case to Florida Supreme Court. [pages 100–43]

Florida Legislature appoints Bush electors.

Florida Supreme Court rejects (6-0, 1 abstention) appeals of Seminole and Martin counties; upholds opinions of Leon County Circuit Court judges Terry Lewis and Nikki Clark finding no evidence of fraud or intentional misconduct.

13 Gore ends campaign; concedes election.

14 Florida Supreme Court dismisses case remanded from U.S. Supreme Court, finding that Florida Election Code does not provide the elements necessary for resolution of the disputed issues. [pages 144–61]

18 Electoral College votes; Bush receives 271 votes, Gore 266.

Introduction

The Florida Moment

E.J. DIONNE JR.
WILLIAM KRISTOL

Our nation has never decided a presidential contest the way it decided the election of 2000. Never before has an election hung on the judgment of the United States Supreme Court, let alone on a decision that split the court into bitter camps and was settled by a single vote. Not in 124 years has a presidential election result been so disputed. Never in all those years have so many Americans believed that the winner of the White House actually lost the election. Nor in all those years has the winning side been so convinced that the losing candidate was intent on "stealing the election." Rarely in our history have Americans been so divided on basic issues of democracy: how the votes should be counted, whether the electoral system was fair, and which legal bodies should decide the winner.

The editors of this book are friends who disagree on what should have happened in the extraordinary five weeks following Election Day 2000. We agree that the judiciary played a much larger role in the result than is proper in a democratic republic. But we disagree, as our own essays in this volume make clear, about which court decided wrongly. We disagree as well about whether or not the Florida legislature had a role to play in determining which candidate should have received that state's 25 electoral votes. We disagree over the merits of the United States Supreme Court's 5-to-4 ruling in favor of Bush.

But we both believe that what might be called The Florida Moment was an important moment—even a touchstone—in our nation's politics and history. This collection is built around that premise. It will be, we hope, of immediate interest to the many citizens who became passionately involved in the great national debate about the Florida recount and the very mechanisms of democracy.

But we hope and suspect that this book might also be of long-term interest to students of American politics (in classrooms and lecture halls, to be sure, but not just there), because the debate surrounding the Five Week Recount War engaged fundamental issues of American politics. These include the obligations of fairness and equality, the requirements of a democratic system, the roles of elected bodies and the courts in interpreting and vindicating the Constitution, the best means of ensuring racial justice at the polls, the value of openness and public disclosure. During the Florida battle, we argued about everything from how (and if) ballots should be recounted to the ways in which some voting mechanisms treated some voters more fairly than others. And we argued about court decisions—especially the Supreme Court's final ruling in *Bush* v. *Gore*, which will be debated in the coming months and years as intently as many other famously controversial court cases.

The first half of the volume gathers what we and the editors at the Brookings Institution Press believe to be the most important legal documents in the Bush-Gore confrontation. Although written by lawyers for legal purposes, most of these documents are surprisingly accessible to those without formal legal training (a group that includes us). Their readability may reflect the fact that almost all of them dealt with more than legal technicalities. They engaged some of the most basic issues in our democracy.

The book begins with the early advisory rulings on the recounts by Florida's state officials. It moves on to the intermediate court rulings and ends with the critical decisions in early December by the Florida Supreme Court and the United States Supreme Court. We have included the dissents in all the major cases. As is often the case with dissents, they provided some of the most eloquent statements of principle in the entire controversy.

Readers interested in other legal documents relating to the Florida election cases, including oral and written arguments, will be able to find them on a web site established as a companion to this book, at www.brookings. edu/bushvgore. In some instances, court decisions reprinted here have been edited to cut out long, distracting, parenthetical, references to other cases. The full texts can be found on the website.

The second half of the book consists of contemporaneous commentaries on the controversy. These include columns, magazine articles, editorials and also a few news stories that shed important light on the issues at stake.

Whatever else people make of this controversy in the future, it's fair to say that it generated a rather high level of discussion at the time—much of it produced on very short deadlines. We believe that many of these articles (we don't pretend to know for certain which ones) will remain illuminating many years from now as powerful testimony to the issues that mattered at a crucial moment in our country's political history. Philosophers, law professors, political scientists, and political commentators understood rather quickly the significance of what was transpiring, and they were moved to place the controversy in a larger context—without, as you'll see, putting aside their own commitments, principles, and passions.

Yes, there was also a fair amount of invective, directed especially (and, in the view of one editor but not the other, unfairly) at Al Gore, and also at the courts. But for better or worse, invective is also part of the political debate—and what may look like invective to one person may look like reasoned argument to another. In the end, the reader can decide which was which.

We have tried to minimize the level of invective by selecting articles that highlight what we see as particularly important issues raised by The Florida Moment. These include judicial activism (on both sides); the right of voters to have their ballots counted; the role of the political branches of government in deciding political contests; the right of all Americans to know how Florida actually voted; the obligations of political candidates in close races to the common good; the vices and virtues of the electoral college; the right of all voters to cast their ballots free from intimidation; and the proper reading of what our Constitution says about how presidential elections should be decided.

We also warn readers that, to keep this volume to a manageable size, we have left out much fine writing about the Florida struggle. In the final stages of editing, we had to cut commentaries that one or both of us admired, because we had run out of space. We do think that the writers included here are broadly representative   and among the best representatives—of the range of opinions offered during The Florida Moment. We tried to make the best judgment we could about which article, of several candidates, best presented a particular aspect of the case. But we understand—and hope readers, and those writers not included here, will understand—that such judgments can be subjective. On certain issues, especially on the U.S. Supreme Court's final ruling, we decided to run the risk of including overlapping arguments because the questions at stake were of particular interest.

This collection leans toward commentary rather than reportage. Many good journalists will continue to report on what happened in Florida, and several comprehensive accounts will no doubt be published in the coming months and years. That also means we have left out much of the fine work done by Florida newspapers during the recount struggle. We hope and suspect that the efforts of Florida journalists will be captured in other volumes.

Our purpose here is to present the arguments raised by the recount battle and to explore the issues behind the controversy. Virtually all the commentaries we have chosen are short, pungent, and aimed at a general audience. Many of them are by distinguished scholars who joined the national debate on op-ed pages and in magazines. Readers who believe that some important article or comment was excluded should contact us through the Brookings Institution Press. If we ever put together a second edition of this book, we'll be grateful for the advice.

As best as we could, we organized the commentaries in chronological order so readers could follow the arguments from the beginning of the controversy to the end. We have included dates on all the pieces. But dates on magazine articles can be misleading, since magazines often date themselves for the end of their newsstand sale period rather than by the date of actual publication. In ordering the commentaries, we have tried to follow the real time of publication, not the magazine cover dates.

We confess to having included several of our own pieces here. It would be perfectly just to accuse us of having a bias in our own favor, but those pieces might at least help explain why each of us believes The Florida Moment was so important and enlightening. We'd also note that some of our own articles were among those that hit the cutting room floor and didn't make the book.

Both editors stand behind the book as a whole, but there was a division of labor. Dionne was primarily responsible for selecting the pieces that were sympathetic to the idea of carrying the recount forward, opposed to the Florida legislature's effort to insinuate itself in the battle, and critical of the United States Supreme Court's decision. Kristol was primarily responsible for selecting those critical of the Florida Supreme Court's rulings in favor of further recounts, supportive of a role for the Florida legislature, and favorable toward the U.S. Supreme Court decision. It should be said, though, that in a fair number of cases we agreed on what were the best arguments presented, even against our respective sides. We also tried to include commentaries that did not strictly represent one side of the argument or the other, though we did lean toward pieces that sharpened and, we hope, might clarify the debate.

Readers will note that some writers have identifications under their articles—about what they do, where they teach, and the like—and others do not. We generally followed what originally appeared in print. Writers without identification are editors, staff writers, or columnists for the publication listed, or well-known syndicated columnists.

This volume would have been impossible absent the remarkable work on a demanding schedule by a long list of very able and very generous people at the Brookings Institution Press. Robert Faherty, the director, and Becky Clark, marketing director, saw that a collection of this sort might be appealing to readers, useful to teachers and students, and helpful in furthering the debate unleashed by The Florida Moment. They went to work immediately and with great skill and good cheer.

They enlisted virtually the whole staff of the press. Chris Kelaher searched, searched, and searched again for the various commentaries. It is not an exaggeration to say this book could not have happened without him. Tin-Ming Hsu and Chris were extraordinarily thoughtful in helping to choose the commentaries. Charles Dibble did a superb job editing and organizing the cases. Lawrence Converse, Janet Walker, Susan Woollen, and Tanjam Jacobson handled design, editing, and production and did amazing things on an extremely condensed schedule. Tom Parsons restructured the Brookings catalogue to allow us to announce this book.

Cynthia Strauss-Ortiz ably did the very onerous and essential work of gaining permissions to reprint the pieces here. And for help on so many tasks, great thanks also to Colin Johnson, Nicole Pagano, Christopher O'Brien, and Isha Wilkerson.

This book would have been impossible to produce if a large number of publications and columnists' syndicates had not granted us permission, on a very timely basis, to reprint work published elsewhere. We acknowledge them elsewhere in the book, but we are grateful to them all.

Shortly after the votes—or at least most of them—were counted, the conservative writer Terry Teachout suggested in *Commentary* magazine that the results of the election showed our country divided into two nations. He called them "Republican Nation" and "Democratic Nation." Most striking, Teachout argued, were the divisions along the lines of region and culture.

Although it's possible to argue that the divisions in the country are not quite as stark as Teachout suggests—a fact he acknowledges himself—his argument is compelling. And it is dead on when it comes to the country's reaction to The Florida Moment.

Millions of Democrats will believe for the rest of their lives that George W. Bush became president through illegitimate means. They will believe he won only because his campaign blocked and obstructed recounts in Florida—and because this cynical strategy was ratified by a narrow, partisan U.S. Supreme Court majority that abused its power to install its preferred choice in the White House.

Millions of Republicans will forever resent Democrats for not acknowledging the legitimacy of Bush's election. They will always see the recount as an unprincipled ploy by the Gore campaign—supported by a narrow Florida Supreme Court majority—to add into the state's totals as many questionable ballots in selected counties as might be necessary to grant Gore victory.

A difference of this sort is not easily forgotten and the wounds it creates are not easily healed. This book proposes not to settle the argument but to document it. It shows how intelligent Americans came to disagree so profoundly and so passionately not only on which candidate should become our president, but also on how he should be chosen.

Court Cases

The Florida election gave rise to, by a rough count, no fewer than thirty separate (and often simultaneous) proceedings in three federal courts and five state courts. We have selected what we believe to be the most important of the rulings. Inevitably, there are omissions; George Bush, for example, petitioned the federal courts for an injunction to halt the manual recount of disputed tallies in several Florida counties, and the Court of Appeals for the Eleventh Circuit answered with a carefully argued, 100+ page opinion denying relief, but these proceedings were overshadowed by the disputes between (and within) the Florida Supreme Court and the U.S. Supreme Court. What we've reprinted here are the most closely watched, and as the commentary attests, vigorously discussed cases.

Most of the opinions are presented in their entirety. In a few instances, for the sake of readability, we have deleted long strings of citations and extended quotations whose omission does not detract from the arguments presented; these deletions and our interpolations (such as cross-references) are signaled with brackets. The full text of these and other opinions related to the Florida election, as well as filings by the various parties to the proceedings, appears on the Brookings Institution website (www.brookings.edu/bushvgore).

Florida Department of State
Division of Elections

Advisory Opinion DE 00-10:
Deadline for Certification on County Results

November 13, 2000

§§ 102.111 and 102.112, Fla. Stat.

The Honorable Charles E. Burton, Chairperson
Palm Beach County Canvassing Board
West Palm Beach, Florida

Dear Judge Burton:

This is in response to your request for an opinion relating to sections 102.111 and 102.112, Florida Statutes. You are chairperson of the Palm Beach County Canvassing Boards and pursuant to section 106.23(2), Florida Statutes, the Division of Elections has the authority to issue an opinion to you.

You state that the Palm Beach County Canvassing Board voted to have a manual recount of all ballots cast in the presidential election. Further, you state that the manual recount will not be completed by 5:00 p.m. of the seventh day following the election as provided in sections 102.11 and 102.112, Florida Statutes. Essentially you ask:

1. What effect will the provisions of section 102.111, Florida Statutes, when read in conjunction with section 102.112, Florida Statutes, have on the votes cast in the presidential election by the citizens of Palm Beach County?
2. May the board certify all other election results to the Department of State while the manual recount continues for the Presidential election?

In response to your first question, if the Palm Beach County Canvassing Board fails to certify the county returns to the Elections Canvassing Commission by 5:00 p.m. of the seventh day following the election, the votes cast in Palm Beach County will not be counted in the certification of the statewide results.

Section 102.111, Florida Statutes, is explicitly mandatory. It provides, "[i]f the county returns are not received by the Department of State by

5 p.m. on the 7th day following an election, all missing counties shall be ignored, and the results shown by the returns on file shall be certified."

Section 102.112, Florida Statutes, provides in pertinent part that returns must be filed by 5 p.m. on the seventh day following the first primary and general election. Further, if the returns are not received by the department by the time specified, such returns may be ignored and the results on file at the time may be certified by the department. This section contemplates unforeseen circumstances not specifically contemplated by the legislature. Such unforeseen circumstances might include a natural disaster such as Hurricane Andrew, where compliance with the law would be impossible. But a close election, regardless of the identity of the candidates, is not such a circumstance. The legislature obviously specifically contemplated close elections in that the law provides for automatic recounts, protests, and manual recounts. It also plainly states when this process must end.

Therefore, absent such unforeseen circumstances, returns from the county must be received by the Elections Canvassing Commission by 5 p.m. on the seventh day following the election in order to be included in the certification of the statewide results.

The answer to your second question is yes, the county canvassing board may certify other election results to the Department of State while the manual recount continues for the presidential election.

SUMMARY

Absent such unforeseen circumstances such as a natural disaster, returns from the county must be received by the Elections Canvassing Commission by 5 p.m. on the seventh day following the election in order to be included in the certification of the statewide results. The county canvassing board may certify other election results to the Department of State while the manual recount continues for the presidential election.

Sincerely,

L. CLAYTON ROBERTS
Director, Division of Elections

Prepared by:

KRISTI REID BRONSON
Assistant General Counsel

Advisory Opinion DE 00-11:
Definitions of Errors in Vote Tabulation

November 13, 2000

§ 102.166(5), Fla. Stat.

Mr. Al Cardenas, Chairman
Republican Party of Florida
Post Office Box 311
Tallahassee, Florida 32302

Dear Mr. Cardenas:

This is in response to your request for an opinion relating to section 102.166(5), Florida Statutes. You are the Chairman for the Republican Party of Florida and pursuant to section 106.23(2), Florida Statutes, the Division of Elections has authority to issue an opinion to you.

You ask:

1. What is the meaning of the term "error in the vote tabulation" as used in section 102.166(5), Florida Statutes?
2. What is the meaning of "affecting the outcome of the election" as used in section 102.166(5), Florida Statutes?
3. What manner of "error" and what type and/or degree of effect on the outcome would serve as a lawful predicate for a manual recount of all ballots under section 102.166(5)(c), Florida Statutes?

Your questions involve the interpretation of election laws and can be answered with an advisory opinion. Section 102.166(5), Florida Statutes, provides in pertinent part that if the manual recount indicates an error in the vote tabulation which could affect the outcome of the election, the county canvassing board shall: (a) correct the error and recount the remaining precincts with the vote tabulation system; (b) request the Department of State to verify the tabulation software; or (c) manually recount all ballots.

An "error in the vote tabulation" means a counting error in which the vote tabulation system fails to count properly marked marksense or properly punched punchcard ballots. Such an error could result from incorrect election parameters, or an error in the vote tabulation and reporting software of the voting system. The inability of a voting systems to read an improperly marked marksense or improperly punched punchcard ballot is not a "error in the vote tabulation" and would not trigger the requirement for the county canvassing board to take one of the actions specified in subsections 102.155(5)(a) through (c), Florida Statutes. An error that could "affect the outcome of the election" is an error of a magnitude sufficient to make a difference as to which candidate wins the election.

SUMMARY

An "error in the vote tabulation," means a counting error in which the vote tabulation system fails to count properly marked marksense or properly punched punchcard ballots. An error that could "affect the outcome of the election" is an error of a magnitude sufficient to make a difference as to which candidate wins the election.

Sincerely,

L. CLAYTON ROBERTS
Director, Division of Elections

Prepared by:

KRISTI REID BRONSON
Assistant General Counsel

Advisory Opinion DE 00-13:
Manual Recount Procedures and
Partial Certification of County Returns

November 13, 2000

§§ 102.166(5) and 102.151, Fla. Stat.

The Honorable Charles E. Burton, Chairperson
Palm Beach County Canvassing Board
Palm Beach County Courthouse
West Palm Beach, Florida 33401

Dear Judge Burton:

This is in response to your request for an opinion. You are chairperson of the Palm Beach County Canvassing Board and pursuant to section 106.23(2), Florida Statutes, the Division of Elections has the authority to issue an opinion to you. Essentially, you ask:

1. Would a discrepancy between the number of votes determined by a tabulation system and by a manual recount of four precincts be con-

sidered an "error in voting tabulation" that could affect the outcome of an election within the meaning of section 102.166(5), Florida Statutes, thereby enabling the canvassing board to manually recount ballots for the entire county?

2. May a county canvassing board do a partial certification of the votes pursuant to section 102.151, Florida Statutes, for the November 7, 2000 election that excludes the votes for the candidates of the presidential election?

With regard to your first question, section 102.166(5), Florida Statutes, provides that if the manual recount indicates an error in the vote tabulation which could affect the outcome of the election, the county canvassing board shall: (a) correct the error and recount the remaining precincts with the vote tabulation system; (b) request the Department of State to verify the tabulation software; or (c) manually recount all ballots.

An "error in the vote tabulation" means a counting error in which the vote tabulation system fails to count properly marked marksense or properly punched punchcard ballots. Such an error could result from incorrect election parameters, or an error in the vote tabulation and reporting software of the voting system. Therefore, unless the discrepancy between the number of votes determined by the tabulation system and by the manual recount of four precincts is caused by incorrect election parameters or software errors, the county canvassing board is not authorized to manually recount ballots for the entire county nor perform any action specified in section 102.166(5)(a) and (b), Florida Statutes.

With regard to your second question, the answer is yes. The county canvassing board may do a partial certification of the votes pursuant to section 102.151, Florida Statutes, for the November 7, 2000 election that excludes the results of the presidential election.

SUMMARY

An "error in the vote tabulation" means a counting error in which the vote tabulation system fails to count properly marked markedsense or properly punched punchcard ballots. Such an error could result from incorrect election parameters, or an error in the vote tabulation and reporting software of the voting system. Therefore, unless the discrepancy between the number of votes determined by the tabulation system and by the manual recount of four precincts is caused by incorrect election parameters or software errors, the county canvassing board is not authorized to manually recount ballots for the entire county nor perform any action specified in section 102.166(5)(a) and (b), Florida Statutes. The county canvassing board may do a partial certification of the votes pursuant to section 102.151, Florida Statutes, for the November 7, 2000 election that excludes the results for the presidential election.

Sincerely,

L. CLAYTON ROBERTS
Director, Division of Elections

Prepared by:

KRISTI REID BRONSON
Assistant General Counsel

Florida Attorney General
Advisory Legal Opinion

AGO 2000-65

November 14, 2000

Subject: Manual recount of ballots, error in voter tabulation

The Honorable Charles E. Burton
Chair, Palm Beach County Canvassing Board
County Courthouse
West Palm Beach, Florida 33401

Dear Judge Burton:

On behalf of the Palm Beach County Canvassing Board, you have asked this office's opinion as to the meaning of "error in voting tabulation which could affect the outcome of" an election as that phrase is used in section 102.166(5), Florida Statutes.

I am answering your request fully mindful that just yesterday the Division of Elections rendered Division of Elections Opinion 00-11 to the Chairman of the Republican Party, interpreting the duties of a county canvassing board pursuant to section 102.166(5), Florida Statutes.[1] Because

1. The validity of the opinion of the Division of Elections is questionable since it appears to exceed the authority granted to the division by Florida law. Section 106.23(2),

the Division of Elections opinion is so clearly at variance with the existing Florida statutes and case law, and because of the immediate impact this erroneous opinion could have on the on-going recount process, I am issuing this advisory opinion.

Section 102.166(4), Florida Statutes, permits a local canvassing board, upon request of a candidate or political party, to authorize a manual recount to include at least three precincts and at least 1 percent of the total votes cast for such candidate.[2] Section 102.166(5), Florida Statutes, provides "[i]f the manual recount indicates an error in vote tabulation which could affect the outcome of the election, the county canvassing board shall" among other options, manually recount all ballots.

Division of Election Opinion 00-11 concludes that the language "error in the vote tabulation" in section 102.166(5), Florida Statutes, refers only to a counting error in the vote tabulation system. The opinion concludes that the inability of a voting system to read an "improperly marked marksense or improperly punched punchcard ballot" is not an "error in the voter tabulation system" and would not, therefore, trigger a recount of all ballots.

The division's opinion is wrong in several respects.

The opinion ignores the plain language of the statute which refers not to an error in the vote tabulation system but to an error in the vote tabulation. The Legislature has used the terms "vote tabulation system" and "automatic tabulating equipment" elsewhere in section 102.166, Florida Statutes, when it intended to refer to the system rather than the vote count. Yet the division, by reading "vote tabulation" and "vote tabulation system" as synonymous, blurs the distinctions that the Legislature clearly delineated in section 102.166.[3]

The error in vote tabulation might be caused by a mechanical malfunction in the operation of the vote counting system, but the error might also result from the failure of a properly functioning mechanical system to discern the choices of the voters as revealed by the ballots. The fact that both possi-

---

Florida Statutes, provides the division with the authority to render advisory opinions interpreting the election code to, among others, a political party relating to actions such party has taken or proposes to take. Division of Elections Opinion 00-11, however, erroneously seeks to advise a political party about the responsibilities of the supervisor of elections and local canvassing board under section 102.166(5).

2. See, §102.166(4)(d), Fla. Stat., stating that the person requesting the recount "shall choose three precincts to be recounted."

3. See, e.g., Department of Professional Regulation, Board of Medical Examiners v. Durrani, 455 So. 2d 515 (Fla. 1st DCA 1984) (legislative use of different terms in different portions of same statute is strong evidence that different meanings were intended).

bilities are contemplated is evidenced by section 102.166(7) and (8), Florida Statutes. While subsection (8) addresses verification of tabulation software, subsection (7) provides procedures for an examination of the ballot by the canvassing board and counting teams to determine the voter's intent.

The division's opinion, without authority or support, effectively nullifies the language of section 102.166(7), Florida Statutes. Nothing in subsection (7) limits its application to the recount of all ballots. Rather, the procedures for a manual recount in subsection (7) equally apply to the initial sampling manual recount authorized in section 102.166(4)(d). Section 102.166(7)(b) states:

> If a counting team is unable to determine a voter's intent in casting a ballot, the ballot shall be presented to the county canvassing board for it to determine the voter's intent.

Yet under the division's interpretation, such language is rendered superfluous. It is fundamental principle of statutory construction that statutory language is not to be assumed to be surplusage; rather a statute is to be construed to give meaning to all words and phrases contained within [the] statute.[4]

Section 102.166(7) clearly recognizes that an examination by a person of the ballot will occur to determine whether the voter complied with the statutory requirement, *i.e.,* marked the marksense or punched the punchcard ballot. The statutes do not specify how a punchcard must be punched. Clearly, there may be instances where a punchcard or marksense ballot was not punched or marked in a manner in which the electronic or electromechanical equipment was able to read the ballot. Such a deficiency in the equipment in no way compromises the voter's intent or the canvassing board's ability to review the ballot and determine the voter's intent. In fact, section 101.5614(5) and (6), Florida Statutes, contemplate that such an examination will occur. Section 101.5614(6) provides that the ballot will not be counted if it is impossible to determine the elector's choice or the elector marks more than one name than there are persons to be elected.

Clearly, the manual count of the sampling precincts which reveals a discrepancy between votes counted by the automatic tabulating equipment and valid ballots which were not properly read by the equipment but which constitute ballots in which the voter complied with the statutory require-

---

4. *See, Terrinoni v. Westward Ho!,* 418 So. 2d 1143 (Fla. 1st DCA 1982); *Pinellas County v. Woolley,* 189 So. 2d 217 (Fla. 2d DCA 1966); Ops. Att'y Gen. Fla. 95-27 (1995); 91-16 (1991) (operative language in a statute may not be regarded as surplusage); 91-11 (1991) (statute must be construed so as to give meaning to all words and phrases contained within that statute).

ments and in which the voter's intent may be ascertained, constitutes an "error in vote tabulation." If the error is sufficient that it could affect the outcome of the election, then a manual recount of all ballots may be ordered by the county canvassing board.

The division's opinion fails to acknowledge the longstanding case law in Florida which has held that the intent of the voters as shown by their ballots should be given effect. Where a ballot is marked so as to plainly indicate the voter's choice and intent, it should be counted as marked unless some positive provision of law would be violated.[5]

As the state has moved toward electronic voting, nothing in this evolution has diminished the standards first articulated in such decisions as *State ex rel. Smith v. Anderson*[6] and *State ex rel. Nuccio v. Williams*[7] that the intent of the voter is of paramount concern and should be given effect if the voter has complied with the statutory requirement and that intent may be determined. For example, if a voter has clearly, physically penetrated a punchcard ballot, the canvassing board has the authority to determine that the voter's intention is clearly expressed even though such puncture is not sufficient to be read by automatic tabulating equipment.

In *State ex rel. Carpenter v. Barber*,[8] the Court stated:

> "The intention of the voter should be ascertained from a study of the ballot and the vote counted, if the will and intention of the voter can be determined, even though the cross mark 'X' appears before or after the name of said candidate. See, *Wiggins, Co. Judge, v. State ex rel. Drane*, 106 Fla. 793, 144 So. 62; *Nuccio v. Williams*, 97 Fla. 159, 120 So. 310; *State ex rel. Knott v. Haskell*, 72 Fla. 176, 72 So. 651."

The Florida Statutes contemplate that where electronic or electromechanical voting systems are used, no vote is to be declared invalid or void if there is a clear indication of the intent of the voter as determined by the county canvassing board.[9]

5. *See, State ex rel. Smith v. Anderson*, 8 So. 1 (Fla. 1890); *Darby v. State*, 75 So. 411 (Fla. 1917); *State ex rel. Nuccio v. Williams*, 120 So. 310 (Fla. 1929) (in performing their duty of counting, tabulating, and making due return of ballots cast in an election, the inspectors may, in some cases of ambiguity or apparent uncertainty in the name voted for, determine, from the fact of the ballot as cast, the person for whom a vote was intended by the voter).

6. 8 So. 1 (Fla. 1890).

7. 120 So. 310 (Fla. 1929).

8. 198 So. 49, 51 (Fla. 1940).

9. *See, Wiggins v. State ex rel. Drane*, 144 So. 62, 63 (Fla. 1932) (separate tabulation and return of what may be deemed regular ballots does not mean that only regular bal-

In light of the plain language of section 102.166(5), Florida Statutes, authorizing a manual recount of all ballots when the sampling manual recount indicates an error in vote tabulation which could affect the outcome of the election and the general principles of election law, I must express my disagreement with the conclusions reached in Division of Election Opinion 00-11. Rather I am of the opinion that the term "error in voter tabulation" encompasses a discrepancy between the number of votes determined by a voter tabulation system and the number of votes determined by a manual count of a sampling of precincts pursuant to section 102.166(4), Florida Statutes.

Sincerely,

ROBERT A. BUTTERWORTH
Attorney General

---

lots are to be counted; if the marking of the ballot should be irregular, but the voter casting such ballot has clearly indicated by an X-mark the candidate of his choice, the ballot should be counted as intended).

In the Circuit Court of the Second Judicial Circuit, in and for Leon County, Florida

Case No. CV 00-2700

Michael McDermott, Ann Mcfall, and Patricia Northey, as the Canvassing Board for Volusia County, Florida, Canvassing Board for Palm Beach County, Florida, Democratic Party of Florida, and Vice President Albert Gore, Plaintiffs,

v.

Honorable Katherine Harris, as Secretary of State, State of Florida, and Honorable Katherine Harris, Honorable Bob Crawford, and Honorable Laurence C. Roberts, as the Elections Canvassing Commission, Governor George W. Bush, and Matt Butler, Defendants.

November 14, 2000

Order Granting in Part and Denying in Part Motion for Temporary Injunction

This declaratory judgment action is before me on the Motion of the Canvassing Board for Volusia County for a temporary injunction against the Secretary of State and the Elections Canvassing Commission. By motion and agreement of the parties, the Florida Democratic Party, Candidate Al Gore, and the Canvassing Board of Palm Beach County have intervened as Party Plaintiffs, and Candidate George W. Bush and Elector Matt Butler have intervened as Party Defendants.

The heart of the issue raised by the motion is this: Section 102.166, *Florida Statutes,* contemplates that upon request a county canvassing board may authorize a manual recount of votes cast in an election. Both Volusia and Palm Beach Counties have so authorized, and are in the process of conducting, a manual recount. The Boards are concerned that the manual recounts may not be completed by 5:00 p.m. today, November 14, 2000, which is the deadline imposed upon them by Section 102.112, *Florida Statutes,* to certify and report the election returns to the Secretary of State. This Section provides that if the returns are not received by the deadline, such returns *may* be ignored by the Secretary in her certification of results statewide.

The Plaintiffs insist that the Secretary of State *must* consider the certified results from Volusia and Palm Beach Counties, even if they are filed late, if they are still engaged in the manual recount of the votes. The Secretary of State insists that, absent an Act of God such as hurricane, any returns not received by the statutory deadline *will not* be counted in the statewide tabulations and certification of the election results. For the reasons set forth below, I find that the county Canvassing Boards must certify and file what election returns they have by the statutory deadline of 5:00 p.m. on November 14, 2000, with due notification to the Secretary of State of any pending manual recounts, and may thereafter file supplemental or corrective returns. The Secretary of State may ignore such late filed returns, but may not do so arbitrarily, rather only by the proper exercise of discretion after consideration of all appropriate facts and circumstances.

The Secretary of State takes the position that the law requires the County Canvassing Boards to certify and report the results of elections in their counties no later than 5:00 p.m., November 14, 2000, that there are no exceptions to this mandate, and that the Secretary is likewise required by law to ignore any untimely received returns unless the untimeliness is caused by a hurricane or other Act of God.[1] I give great deference to the interpretation by the Secretary of the election laws, and I agree that the Canvassing Boards must file their returns by 5:00 p.m. today. I disagree, however that the Secretary is required to ignore any late filed returns absent an Act of God. There are several reasons for my conclusion.

1. A reading of the entire Election Code suggests a legislative intent to balance the desire for accuracy with the desire for finality. By concentrating on the deadline imposed by Section 102.112, *Florida Statutes,* the secretary has come down hard on the side of finality. This interpretation ignores, however, Section 102.166, *Florida Statutes,* which gives to the County Canvassing Boards the authority to authorize a manual recount. A request for such recount may be made within three days of the election. If a manual recount of at least three precincts and at least one percent (1%) of the total votes indicates an error in vote tabulation which could effect the outcome of the election, the Canvassing Board *shall* either (a) correct

---

1. The Secretary of State acknowledges that Section 102.112, rather than Section 102.111, *Florida Statutes,* prevails as to the question of whether the Department has any discretion in whether to ignore late filed results.

the error and recount the remaining precincts with the vote tabulation system, (b) request the Department of State to verify the tabulation software, or (c) manually recount all ballots.

Depending on when a request is made and then acted upon, it is easy to imagine a situation where a manual recount could be lawfully authorized, commenced, but not completed within seven days of the election. The Secretary of State responds that the authority to authorize a manual recount is subject to the requirement that such recount be done and the results certified no later than the deadline imposed by Section 102.112, *Florida Statutes.* This would mean, however, that only in sparsely populated counties could a Canvassing Board safely exercise what the Legislature has clearly intended to be an option where the Board has a real question as to the accuracy of a vote.

2. Section 102.166, *Florida Statutes* gives any candidate, or a qualified elector, the right to protest the returns of a County Canvassing Board by filing a sworn written protest, and that protest may be filed within five (5) days of the election or anytime before the Canvassing Board certifies the results, *whichever occurs later.* This suggests that the Canvassing Board might be in a position of having to address a protest of its returns the day before, or hours before, it was to certify the results pursuant to the deadline in Section 102.112 *Florida Statutes*, thus making it impossible to correct any error before the deadline. It is unlikely that the Legislature would give the right to protest returns, but make it meaningless because it could not be acted upon.

3. Section 102.168 provides for the contesting of an election by an unsuccessful candidate or qualified elector, by filing a complaint in Circuit Court within ten (10) days after the Canvassing Board certifies the result of an election or within five (5) days after the Canvassing Board certifies the results of an election following a protest pursuant to Section 102.166 (1), *Florida Statutes, whichever occurs later.* This provision suggests that certifications of the results in an election might occur later than usual if there is a protest of the returns.

4. The Secretary of State acknowledges that, by consent decree with the Federal Government, the absentee ballots of overseas electors must be counted if received up to ten (10) days after the election (three days beyond the deadline imposed by Section 102.112, *Florida Statutes*). The county Canvassing Board cannot report final returns, nor can the Election Canvassing Commission determine a winner of the election until all of

these overseas absentee ballots are counted. The Secretary explains this anomaly by inferring a requirement to do one certification of results seven (7) days after the election and a "supplemental certification" ten (10) days after the election. There is, however, no statutory provision that provides for such supplemental certification. Instead, Section 102.111, *Florida Statutes*, which deals specifically with the duty of the Elections Canvassing Commission, requires the Commission to "as soon as the official results are compiled from all Counties, certify the returns of the election and *determine and declare who has been selected for each office. . . ."*

5. As noted earlier, the Secretary acknowledge that Section 102.112, *Florida Statutes*, uses the discretionary term "may," instead of the mandatory term "shall" as to whether late returns are to be ignored by the Secretary in certifying the results of the election. That the Secretary *may* ignore late filed returns necessarily means that the Secretary *does not have to* ignore such returns. It is, as the Secretary acknowledges, within her discretion.

To determine ahead of time that such returns *will* be ignored, however, unless caused by some Act of God, is not the exercise of discretion. It is the abdication of that discretion. An Act of God has long been considered to excuse even the most mandatory of requirements. Rather, the exercise of discretion, by its nature, contemplates a decision based upon a weighing and a consideration of all attendant facts and circumstances.

The Florida Supreme Court has stated that substantial compliance is sufficient to comply with such mandatory filing deadlines. See *Chappel v. Martinez*, 536 So. 2d 1007 (Fla. 1988). If the returns are received from a County at 5:05 p.m. on November 14, 2000, should the results be ignored? What about fifteen minutes? An hour? What if there was an electrical power shortage? Some other malfunction of the transmitting equipment? More particularly related to this case, when was the request for recount made? What were the reasons given? When did the Canvassing Board decide to do a manual recount? What was the basis for determination that such a recount was the appropriate action? How late were the results?

Obviously, the list of scenarios is almost endless and the questions that would need to be asked in properly exercising discretion as to whether to ignore or not ignore late filed returns are numerous. The Secretary may, and should, consider all of the facts and circumstances.

The County Canvassing Boards are, indeed, mandated to certify and file their returns with the Secretary of State by 5:00 p.m today, November 14, 2000. There is nothing, however, to prevent the County Canvassing Boards from filing with the Secretary of State further returns after completing a manual recount. It is then up to the Secretary of State, as the Chief Election Officer, to determine whether any such corrective or supplemental returns filed after 5:00 p.m today, are to be ignored. Just as the County Canvassing Boards have the authority to exercise discretion in determining whether a manual recount should be done, the Secretary of State has the authority to exercise her discretion in reviewing that decision, considering all attendant facts and circumstances, and decide whether to include or to ignore the late filed returns in certifying the election results and declaring a winner.

Just as the Secretary cannot decide ahead of time what late returns should or should not be ignored, it would not be proper for me to do so by injunction. I can lawfully direct the Secretary to properly exercise her discretion in making a decision on the returns, but I cannot enjoin the Secretary to make a particular decision, nor can I rewrite the Statute which, by its plain meaning, mandates the filing of returns by the Canvassing Boards by 5:00 p.m. on November 14, 2000.

I also note that although the Canvassing Boards cannot properly contest an election, an unsuccessful candidate, or any qualified Elector, may file, pursuant to Section 102.168, *Florida Statutes,* a complaint in Circuit Court contesting the election results. One of the specific itemized grounds for such a challenge is the "rejection of a number of legal votes sufficient to change or place in doubt the result of the election."

Accordingly it is

ORDERED AND ADJUDGED that the Secretary of State is directed to withhold determination as to whether or not to ignore late filed returns, if any, from Plaintiff Canvassing Boards, until due consideration of all relevant facts and circumstances consistent with the sound exercise of discretion. In all other respects, the Motion for Temporary injunction is denied.

DONE AND ORDERED in Chambers at Tallahassee, Leon County, Florida, this 14th day of November, 2000.

TERRY P. LEWIS
Circuit Judge

Supreme Court of Florida

Nos. SC00-2346, SC00-2348 & SC00-2349

Palm Beach County Canvassing Board, Petitioner, *v.*
Katherine Harris, ETC., ET AL. Respondents.

Volusia County Canvassing Board, ET AL., Appellants, *v.*
Katherine Harris, ETC., ET AL., Appellees.

Florida Democratic Party, Appellant, *v.*
Katherine Harris, ETC., ET AL., Appellees.

November 21, 2000

PER CURIAM
We have for review two related trial court orders appealed to the First District Court of Appeal, which certified the orders to be of great public importance requiring immediate resolution by this Court (Case Numbers SC00-2348 and SC00-2349). We have jurisdiction under article V, section 3(b)(5) of the Florida Constitution. For the reasons set forth in this opinion, we reverse the orders of the trial court.[1]

I. FACTS
A. The Election
On Tuesday, November 7, 2000, the State of Florida, along with the rest of the United States, conducted a general election for the President of the United States. The Division of Elections ("Division") reported on Wednesday, November 8, that George W. Bush, the Republican candidate, had received 2,909,135 votes, and Albert Gore Jr., the Democratic candidate, had

---

1. The Palm Beach County Canvassing Board has filed in this Court an "Emergency Petition for Extraordinary Writ" against Secretary of State Katherine Harris and others (Case Number SC00-2346). We have examined our jurisdiction under article V, section 3(b)(8) of the Florida Constitution. However, because the issue raised by that separate petition can be disposed of in our pending case and because we have previously stated in our order of November 16, 2000, that there was "no legal impediment" to the manual recounts continuing, we deem it unnecessary to determine if we have a separate basis of jurisdiction for entertaining the writ. Accordingly, by separate order we dismiss the petition.

received 2,907,351 votes. Because the overall difference in the total votes cast for each candidate was less than one-half of one percent of the total votes cast for that office (i.e., the difference was 1,784 votes), an automatic recount was conducted pursuant to section 102.141(4), Florida Statutes.[2]

In light of the closeness of the election, the Florida Democratic Executive Committee on Thursday, November 9, requested that manual recounts be conducted in Broward, Palm Beach, and Volusia Counties pursuant to section 102.166, Florida Statutes (2000).[3] Pursuant to section 102.166 (4)(d), the county canvassing boards of these counties conducted a sample manual recount of at least one percent of the ballots cast. Initial manual recounts demonstrated the following: In Broward County, a recount of one percent of the ballots indicated a net increase of four votes for Gore; and in Palm Beach County, a recount of four sample precincts yielded a net increase of nineteen votes for Gore. Based on these recounts, several of the county canvassing boards determined that the manual recounts conducted indicated "an error in the vote tabulation which could affect the outcome of the election." Based on this determination, several canvassing boards voted to conduct countywide manual recounts pursuant to section 102.166(5)(c).

B. The Appeal Proceedings

Concerned that the recounts would not be completed prior to the deadline set forth in section 102.111(1), Florida Statutes (2000), requiring that all county returns be certified by 5 p.m. on the seventh day after an election, the Palm Beach County Canvassing Board, pursuant to section 106.23, Florida Statutes (2000), sought an advisory opinion from the Division of Elections, requesting an interpretation of the deadline set forth in sections 102.111 and 102.112. The Division of Elections responded by issuing Advisory Opinion DE 00-10 [pages 9–10], stating that absent unforeseen circumstances, returns from the county must be received by 5 p.m. on the

2. The recount resulted in a substantially reduced figure for the overall difference between the two candidates. Section 102.141(4), Florida Statutes (2000), provides in pertinent part:

(4) If the returns for any office reflect that a candidate was defeated or eliminated by one-half of a percent or less of the votes cast for such office . . . the board responsible for certifying the results of the vote on such race or measure shall order a recount of the votes cast with respect to such office or measure.

3. We have not discussed the events in Miami-Dade County because Miami-Dade is not a party nor has it sought to intervene in this case.

seventh day following the election in order to be included in the certification of the statewide results.

Relying upon this advisory opinion, the Florida Secretary of State (the Secretary) issued a statement on Monday, November 13, 2000, that she would ignore returns of the manual recounts received by the Florida Department of State (the Department) after Tuesday, November 14, 2000, at 5:00 p.m. The Volusia County Canvassing Board (the Volusia Board) on Monday, November 13, 2000, filed suit in the Circuit Court of the Second Judicial Circuit in Leon County, Florida, seeking declaratory and injunctive relief, and the candidates and the Palm Beach County Canvassing Board (the Palm Beach Board), among others, were allowed to intervene. In its suit, the Volusia Board sought a declaratory judgment that it was not bound by the November 14, 2000, deadline and also sought an injunction barring the Secretary from ignoring election returns submitted by the Volusia Board after that date.

The trial court ruled on Tuesday, November 14, 2000, that the deadline was mandatory but that the Volusia Board may amend its returns at a later date and that the Secretary, after "considering all attendant facts and circumstances," may exercise her discretion in determining whether to ignore the amended returns.[4] Later that day, the Volusia Board filed a notice of appeal of this ruling to the First District Court of Appeal, and the Palm Beach Board filed a notice of joinder in the appeal.

Subsequent to the circuit court's order, the Secretary announced that she was in receipt of certified returns (i.e., the returns resulting from the initial recount) from all counties in the State. The Secretary then instructed Florida's Supervisors of Elections (Supervisors) that they must submit to her by 2 p.m., Wednesday, November 15, 2000, a written statement of "the facts and circumstances" justifying any belief on their part that they should be allowed to amend the certified returns previously filed. Four counties submitted their statements on time. After considering the reasons in light of specific criteria,[5] the Secretary on Wednesday, November 15, 2000, re-

4. [*Eds:* The court quotes the trial court order in *McDermott v. Harris,* above, pages 22–23]

5 The criteria considered by the Secretary are as follows [*Eds.*: citations omitted]:
    Facts & Circumstances Warranting Waiver of Statutory Deadline
    1. Where there is proof of voter fraud that affects the outcome of the election. [. . .] 2. Where there has been a substantial noncompliance with statutory election procedures, and reasonable doubt exists as to whether the certified results expressed the will of the voters. [. . .] 3. Where election officials have made a good faith effort to comply with the statutory deadline and are

jected the reasons and again announced that she would not accept the amended returns but rather would rely on the earlier certified totals for the four counties. The Secretary further stated that after she received the certified returns of the overseas absentee ballots from each county, she would certify the results of the presidential election on Saturday, November 18, 2000.

On Thursday, November 16, 2000, the Florida Democratic Party and Albert Gore filed a motion in Circuit Court of the Second Judicial Circuit in Leon County, Florida, seeking to compel the Secretary to accept amended returns. After conducting a hearing, the court denied relief in a brief order dated Friday, November 17, 2000.[6] That day, both the Democratic Party and Gore appealed to the First District Court of Appeal, which consolidated the appeals with the Volusia Board's appeal already pending there, and certified both of the underlying trial court orders to this Court based on the Court's "pass-through" jurisdiction.[7] By orders dated Friday, November 17, 2000, this Court accepted jurisdiction, set an expedited briefing schedule, and enjoined the Secretary and the Elections Canvass-

---

prevented from timely complying with their duties as a result of an act of God, or extenuating circumstances beyond their control, by way of example, an electrical power outage, a malfunction of the transmitting equipment, or a mechanical malfunction of the voting tabulation system. [. . .]
Facts & Circumstances Not Warranting Waiver of Statutory Deadline
1. Where there has been substantial compliance with statutory election procedures and the contested results relate to voter error, and there exists a reasonable expectation that the certified results expressed the will of the voters. [. . .]
2. Where there exists a ballot that may be confusing because of the alignment and location of the candidates' names, but is otherwise in substantial compliance with the election laws. [. . .]
3. Where there is nothing "more than a mere possibility that the outcome of the election would have been effected." [. . .]
Letter from Katherine Harris to Palm Beach County Canvassing Board (Nov. 15, 2000).
6. The court's order reads in part:
On the limited evidence presented, it appears that the Secretary has exercised her reasoned judgment to determine what relevant factors and criteria should be considered, applied them to the facts and circumstances pertinent to the individual counties involved, and made her decision. My order requires nothing more.
McDermott v. Harris, No. 00-2700, unpublished order at 2 (Fla. 2d Cir. Ct., Nov. 17, 2000).
7. See Art. V, § 3(b)(5), Fla. Const. ("[The Court may] review any order or judgment of a trial court certified by the district court of appeal in which an appeal is pending to be of great public importance . . . and certified to require immediate resolution by the supreme court.").

ing Commission (Commission) from certifying the results of the presidential election until further order of this Court.[8]

II. GUIDING PRINCIPLES

Twenty-five years ago, this Court commented that the will of the people, not a hyper-technical reliance upon statutory provisions, should be our guiding principle in election cases:

> [T]he real parties in interest here, not in the legal sense but in realistic terms, are the voters. They are possessed of the ultimate interest and it is they whom we must give primary consideration. The contestants have direct interests certainly, but the office they seek is one of high public service and of utmost importance to the people, thus subordinating their interest to that of the people. Ours is a government of, by and for the people. Our federal and state constitutions guarantee the right of the people to take an active part in the process of that government, which for most of our citizens means participation via the election process. *The right to vote is the right to participate; it is also the right to speak, but more importantly the right to be heard.* We must tread carefully on that right or we risk the unnecessary and unjustified muting of the public voice. By refusing to recognize an otherwise valid exercise of the right of a citizen to vote for the sake of sacred, unyielding adherence to statutory scripture, we would in effect nullify that right.

Boardman v. Esteva, 323 So. 2d 259, 263 (Fla. 1975) (emphasis added). We consistently have adhered to the principle that the will of the people is the paramount consideration.[9] Our goal today remains the same as it was a quarter of a century ago, i.e., to reach the result that reflects the will of the voters, whatever that might be. This fundamental principle, and our traditional rules of statutory construction, guide our decision today.

8. Subsequently, the Volusia Board moved to voluntarily dismiss its appeal in this Court. The Court granted the motion, but indicated that the case style would remain the same and that Gore and the Palm Beach Board "would continue as intervenors/appellants in this action."

9. See *State ex rel. Chappell v. Martinez,* 536 So. 2d 1007, 1009 (Fla. 1988) (holding that disenfranchisement of voters is not proper where there has been substantial compliance with the election statute and the intent of voter can be ascertained); *Beckstrom v. Volusia County Canvassing Bd.,* 707 So. 2d 720, 726 (Fla. 1998) (holding that courts should not frustrate will of voters if that will can be determined).

III. ISSUES

The questions before this Court include the following: Under what circumstances may a Board authorize a countywide manual recount pursuant to section 102.166(5); must the Secretary and Commission accept such recounts when the returns are certified and submitted by the Board after the seven day deadline set forth in sections 102.111 and 102.112?[10]

IV. LEGAL OPINION OF THE DIVISION OF ELECTIONS

The first issue this Court must resolve is whether a County Board may conduct a countywide manual recount where it determines there is an error in vote tabulation that could affect the outcome of the election. Here, the Division issued opinion DE 00-13 [pages 12–14], which construed the language "error in vote tabulation" to exclude the situation where a discrepancy between the original machine return and sample manual recount is due to the manner in which a ballot has been marked or punched.

Florida courts generally will defer to an agency's interpretation of statutes and rules the agency is charged with implementing and enforcing.[11] Florida courts, however, will not defer to an agency's opinion that is contrary to law.[12] We conclude that the Division's advisory opinion regarding vote tabulation is contrary to law because it contravenes the plain meaning of section 102.166(5).

Pursuant to section 102.166(4)(a), a candidate who appears on a ballot, a political committee that supports or opposes an issue that appears on a ballot, or a political party whose candidate's name appeared on the ballot may file a written request with the County Board for a manual recount. This request must be filed with the Board before the Board certifies the election results or within seventy-two hours after the election, whichever occurs later.[13] Upon filing the written request for a manual recount, the canvassing board may authorize a manual recount.[14] The decision whether to conduct a manual recount is vested in the sound discretion of the Board.[15] If the canvassing board decides to authorize the manual recount,

10. Neither party has raised as an issue on appeal the constitutionality of Florida's election laws.

11. See Donato v. American Tel. & Tel. Co., 767 So. 2d 1146, 1153 (Fla. 2000); Smith v. Crawford, 645 So. 2d 513, 521 (Fla. 1st DCA 1994).

12. See Donato, 767 So. 2d at 1153; Nikolits v. Nicosia, 682 So. 2d 663, 666 (Fla. 4th DCA 1996).

13. § 102.166(4)(b), Fla. Stat. (2000).

14. § 102.166(4)(c), Fla. Stat. (2000).

15. See Broward County Canvassing Bd. v. Hogan, 607 So. 2d 508, 510 (Fla. 4th DCA 1992).

the recount must include at least three precincts and at least one percent of the total votes cast for each candidate or issue, with the person who requested the recount choosing the precincts to be recounted.[16] If the manual recount indicates an "error in the vote tabulation which could affect the outcome of the election," the county canvassing board "shall":

(a) Correct the error and recount the remaining precincts with the vote tabulation system;

(b) Request the Department of State to verify the tabulation software; or

(c) Manually recount all ballots.

§ 102.166(5)(a)–(c), Fla. Stat. (2000) (emphasis added).

The issue in dispute here is the meaning of the phrase "error in the vote tabulation" found in section 102.166(5). The Division opines that an "error in the vote tabulation" only means a counting error resulting from incorrect election parameters or an error in the vote tabulating software. We disagree.

The plain language of section 102.166(5) refers to an error in the vote tabulation rather than the vote tabulation system. On its face, the statute does not include any words of limitation; rather, it provides a remedy for any type of mistake made in tabulating ballots. The Legislature has utilized the phrase "vote tabulation system" and "automatic tabulating equipment" in section 102.166 when it intended to refer to the voting system rather than the vote count. Equating "vote tabulation" with "vote tabulation system" obliterates the distinction created in section 102.166 by the Legislature.

Sections 101.5614(5) and (6) also support the proposition that the "error in vote tabulation" encompasses more than a mere determination of whether the vote tabulation system is functioning. Section 101.5614(5) provides that "no vote shall be declared invalid or void if there is a clear indication of the intent of the voter as determined by the canvassing board." Conversely, section 101.5614(6) provides that any vote in which the Board cannot discern the intent of the voter must be discarded. Taken together, these sections suggest that "error in the vote tabulation" includes errors in the failure of the voting machinery to read a ballot and not simply errors resulting from the voting machinery.

Moreover, section 102.141(4), which outlines the Board's responsibility in the event of a recount, states that the Board "shall examine the counters on the machines or the tabulation of the ballots cast in each precinct in which the office or issue appeared on the ballot and determine whether the

16. See § 102.166(4)(d), Fla. Stat. (2000).

returns *correctly* reflect the votes cast." § 102.141, Fla. Stat. (2000) (emphasis added). Therefore, an "error in the vote tabulation" includes a discrepancy between the number of votes determined by a voter tabulation system and the number of voters determined by a manual count of a sampling of precincts pursuant to section 102.166(4).

Although error cannot be completely eliminated in any tabulation of the ballots, our society has not yet gone so far as to place blind faith in machines. In almost all endeavors, including elections, humans routinely correct the errors of machines. For this very reason Florida law provides a human check on both the malfunction of tabulation equipment and error in failing to accurately count the ballots. Thus, we find that the Division's opinion DE 00-13 regarding the ability of county canvassing boards to authorize a manual recount is contrary to the plain language of the statute.

Having concluded that the county canvassing boards have the authority to order countywide manual recounts, we must now determine whether the Commission[17] must accept a return after the seven-day deadline set forth in sections 102.111 and 102.112 under the circumstances presented.

V. APPLICABLE LAW

The abiding principle governing all election law in Florida is set forth in article I, section 1, Florida Constitution:

> Section 1. Political power. All political power is inherent in the people. The enunciation herein of certain rights shall not be construed to deny or impair others retained by the people.

Art. I, § 1, Fla. Const. The constitution further provides that elections shall be regulated by law:

> Section 1. Regulation of elections. All elections by the people shall be by direct and secret vote. General elections shall be determined by a plurality of votes cast. *Registration and elections shall, and political party functions may, be regulated by law*; however, the requirements for a candidate with no party affiliation or for a candidate of a minor party for placement of the candidate's name on the ballot shall be no greater

17. The Commission is composed of the Secretary of State, the Director of the Division of Elections, and the Governor. See § 102.111, Fla. Stat. In this instance, Florida Governor Jeb Bush has removed himself from the Commission because his brother, Texas Governor George W. Bush, is the Republican candidate for President of the United States. Robert Crawford, Florida Commissioner or Agriculture, has been appointed to replace Florida Governor Jeb Bush. See § 102.111, Fla. Stat.

than the requirements for a candidate of the party having the largest
number of registered voters.

Art. VI, § 1, Fla. Const. (emphasis added).

The Florida Election Code ("Code"), contained in chapters 97–106,
Florida Statutes (2000), sets forth specific criteria regulating elections. The
Florida Secretary of State is the chief election officer of the state and is
charged with general oversight of the election system.[18] The Supervisor of
Elections ("Supervisor") in each county is an elected official[19] and is
charged with appointing two Election Boards for each precinct within the
county prior to an election.[20] Each Election Board is composed of inspectors and clerks,[21] all of whom must be residents of the county,[22] and is
charged with conducting the voting in the election, counting the votes,[23]
and certifying the results to the Supervisor[24] by noon of the day following
the election.[25] The County Canvassing Board ("Canvassing Board" or
"Board"), which is composed of the Supervisor, a county court judge, and
the chair of the board of county commissioners,[26] then canvasses the returns countywide,[27] reviews the certificates,[28] and transmits the returns for
state and federal officers to the Florida Department of State ("Department")
by 5:00 p.m. of the seventh day following the election.[29] No deadline is set
for filing corrected, amended, or supplemental returns.

The Elections Canvassing Commission ("Canvassing Commission" or
"Commission"), which is composed of the Governor, the Secretary of State,
and the Director of the Division of Elections, canvasses the returns
statewide, determines and declares who has been elected for each office,
and issues a certificate of election for each office as soon as the results are
compiled.[30] If any returns appear to be irregular or false and the Commission is unable to determine the true vote for a particular office, the Com-

18. § 97.012, Fla. Stat. (2000).
19. § 98.015, Fla. Stat. (2000).
20. § 102.012(1), Fla. Stat. (2000).
21. § 102.012(1), Fla. Stat. (2000).
22. § 102.012(2), Fla. Stat. (2000).
23. § 102.012(4), Fla. Stat. (2000).
24. § 102.071, Fla. Stat. (2000).
25. § 102.141(3), Fla. Stat. (2000).
26. § 102.141(1), Fla. Stat. (2000).
27. § 102.141(2), Fla. Stat. (2000).
28. § 102.141 (3), Fla. Stat. (2000).
29. §§ 102.111–.112, Fla. Stat. (2000).
30. §§ 102.111, .121, Fla. Stat. (2000).

mission certifies that fact and does not include those returns in its canvass.[31] In determining the true vote, the Commission has no authority to look beyond the county's returns.[32] A candidate or elector can "protest" the returns of an election as being erroneous by filing a protest with the appropriate County Canvassing Board.[33] And finally, a candidate, elector, or taxpayer can "contest" the certification of election results by filing a post-certification action in circuit court within certain time limits[34] and setting forth specific grounds.[35]

VI. STATUTORY AMBIGUITY

The provisions of the Code are ambiguous in two significant areas. First, the time frame for conducting a manual recount under section 102.166(4) is in conflict with the time frame for submitting county returns under sections 102.111 and 102.112. Second, the mandatory language in section 102.111 conflicts with the permissive language in 102.112.

A. The Recount Conflict

Section 102.166(1) states that "[a]ny candidate for nomination or election, or any elector qualified to vote in the election related to such candidacy, shall have the right to protest the returns of the election as being erroneous

---

31. § 102.131, Fla. Stat. (2000) ("If any returns shall appear to be irregular or false so that the Elections Canvassing Commission is unable to determine the true vote for any office . . . the commission shall so certify and shall not include the returns in its determination, canvass, and declaration.").

32. § 102.131, Fla. Stat. (2000) ("The Elections Canvassing Commission in determining the true vote shall not have authority to look beyond the county returns.").

33. § 102.166, Fla. Stat. (2000).

34. See § 102.168(2), Fla. Stat. (2000) (explaining that the action must be filed within ten days after the last Board certifies its returns or within five days after the last Board certifies its returns following a protest).

35. The grounds for contesting an election are set forth in section 102.168(3), Florida Statutes (2000):

   (a) Misconduct, fraud, or corruption . . . sufficient to change or place in doubt the result of the election.
   (b) Ineligibility of the successful candidate . . . .
   (c) Receipt of a number of illegal votes or rejection of a number of legal votes sufficient to change or place in doubt the result of the election.
   (d) Proof that any elector, election official or canvassing board member was given or offered a bribe . . . .
   (e) Any other cause or allegation which, if sustained, would show that a person other than the successful candidate was the person duly nominated or elected to the office in question.

by filing with the appropriate canvassing board a sworn, written protest."
The time period for filing a protest is "prior to the time the canvassing
board certifies the results for the office being protested or within 5 days after midnight of the date the election is held, whichever occurs later."

Section 102.166(4)(a), the operative subsection in this case, further provides that, in addition to any protest, "any candidate whose name appeared
on the ballot . . . or any political party whose candidates' names appeared
on the ballot may file a written request with the county canvassing board
for a manual recount" accompanied by the "reason that the manual recount
is being requested." Section 102.166(4)(b) further provides that the written request may be made prior to the time the Board certifies the returns
or within seventy-two hours after the election, whichever occurs later:[36]

> (4)(a) Any candidate whose name appeared on the ballot, any po-
> litical committee that supports or opposes an issue which appeared
> on the ballot, or any political party whose candidates' names appeared
> on the ballot may file a written request with the county canvassing
> board for a manual recount. The written request shall contain a state-
> ment of the reason the manual recount is being requested.
>
> (b) *Such request must be filed with the canvassing board prior to the
> time the canvassing board certifies the results for the office being protested
> or within 72 hours after midnight of the date the election was held,
> whichever occurs later.*

§ 102.166, Fla. Stat. (2000) (emphasis added).

36. As discussed in *Siegel v. Lepore,* [120 F. Supp. 2d 1041] (S.D. Fla. 2000):
On its face, the manual recount provision does not limit candidates' access
to the ballot or interfere with voters' right to associate or vote. Instead the
manual recount provision is intended to safeguard the integrity and reliability of the electoral process by providing a structural means of detecting
and correcting clerical or electronic tabulating errors in the counting of election ballots. While discretionary in its application, the provision is not
wholly standardless. Rather, the central purpose of the scheme, as evidenced
by its plain language, is to remedy 'an error in the vote tabulation which
could affect the outcome of the election.' Fla. Stat. § 102.166(5). In this
pursuit, the provision strives to strengthen rather than dilute the right to
vote by securing, as nearly as humanly possible, an accurate and true reflection of the will of the electorate. Notably, the four county canvassing
boards [that were] challenged in this suit have reported various anomalies
in the initial automated count and recount. The state manual recount provision therefore serves important governmental interests.

A Board "may" authorize a manual recount[37] and such a recount must include at least three precincts and at least one percent of the total votes cast for the candidate.[38] The following procedure then applies:

(5) If the manual recount indicates an error in the vote tabulation which could affect the outcome of the election, the county canvassing board shall:

(a) Correct the error and recount the remaining precincts with the vote tabulation system;

(b) Request the Department of State to verify the tabulation software; or

(c) Manually recount all ballots.

(6) Any manual recount shall be open to the public.

(7) Procedures for a manual recount are as follows:

(a) The county canvassing board shall appoint as many counting teams of at least two electors as is necessary to manually recount the ballots. A counting team must have, when possible, members of at least two political parties. A candidate involved in the race shall not be a member of the counting team.

(b) If a counting team is unable to determine a voter's intent in casting a ballot, the ballot shall be presented to the county canvassing board for it to determine the voter's intent.

§ 102.166, Fla. Stat. (2000).

Under this scheme, a candidate can request a manual recount at any point prior to certification by the Board and such action can lead to a full recount of all the votes in the county. Although the Code sets no specific deadline by which a manual recount must be completed, logic dictates that the period of time required to complete a full manual recount may be substantial, particularly in a populous county, and may require several days. The protest provision thus conflicts with section 102.111 and 102.112, which state that the Boards "must" submit their returns to the Elections Canvassing Commission by 5:00 p.m. of the seventh day following the election or face penalties. For instance, if a party files a pre-certification protest on the sixth day following the election and requests a manual recount and the initial manual recount indicates that a full countywide re-

37. The statute does not set forth any criteria for determining when a manual recount is appropriate. See § 102.166(4)(c), Fla. Stat. (2000) ("The county canvassing board may authorize a manual recount.").

38. § 102.166(4)(d), Fla. Stat. (2000).

count is necessary, the recount procedure in most cases could not be completed by the deadline in sections 102.111 and 102.112, i.e., by 5:00 p.m. of the seventh day following the election.

B. The "Shall" and "May" Conflict

In addition to the conflict in the above statutes, sections 102.111 and 102.112 contain a dichotomy. Section 102.111, which sets forth general criteria governing the State Canvassing Commission, was enacted in 1951 as part of the Code and provides as follows:

> 102.111 Elections Canvassing Commission.
> (1) Immediately after certification of any election by the county canvassing board, the results shall be forwarded to the Department of State concerning the election of any federal or state officer. The Governor, the Secretary of State, and the Director of the Division of Elections shall be the Elections Canvassing Commission. The Elections Canvassing Commission shall, as soon as the official results are compiled from all counties, certify the returns of the election and determine and declare who has been elected for each office. In the event that any member of the Elections Canvassing Commission is unavailable to certify the returns of any election, such member shall be replaced by a substitute member of the Cabinet as determined by the Director of the Division of Elections. *If the county returns are not received by the Department of State by 5 p.m. of the seventh day following an election, all missing counties shall be ignored,* and the results shown by the returns on file shall be certified.

§ 102.111, Fla. Stat. (2000) (emphasis added).

The Legislature in 1989 revised chapter 102 to include section 102.112, which provides that returns not received after a certain date "may" be ignored and that members of the County Board "shall" be fined:

> 102.112 Deadline for submission of county returns to the Department of State; penalties.
> (1) The county canvassing board or a majority thereof shall file the county returns for the election of a federal or state officer with the Department of State immediately after the certification of the election results. Returns must be filed by 5 p.m. on the 7th day following the first primary and general election and by 3 p.m. on the 3rd day following the second primary. *If the returns are not received by the department by the time specified, such returns may be ignored* and the re-

sults on file at that time may be certified by the department.

(2) The department shall fine each board member $ 200 for each day such returns are late, the fine to be paid only from the board member's personal funds. Such fines shall be deposited into the Election Campaign Financing Trust fund, created by s. 106.32.

(3) Members of the county canvassing board may appeal such fines to the Florida Elections Commission, which shall adopt rules for such appeals.

§ 102.112, Fla. Stat. (2000) (emphasis added).

The above statutes conflict. Whereas section 102.111 is mandatory, section 102.112 is permissive. While it is clear that the Boards must submit returns by 5 p.m. of the seventh day following the election or face penalties, the circumstances under which penalties may be assessed are unclear.

VII. LEGISLATIVE INTENT

Legislative intent — as always — is the polestar that guides a court's inquiry into the provisions of the Florida Election Code.[39] Where the language of the Code is clear and amenable to a reasonable and logical interpretation, courts are without power to diverge from the intent of the Legislature as expressed in the plain language of the Code.[40]As noted above, however, chapter 102 is unclear concerning both the time limits for submitting the results of a manual recount and the penalties that may be assessed by the Secretary. In light of this ambiguity, the Court must resort to traditional rules of statutory construction in an effort to determine legislative intent.[41]

First, it is well settled that where two statutory provisions are in conflict, the specific statute controls the general statute.[42] In the present case, whereas section 102.111 in its title and text addresses the general makeup and duties of the Elections Canvassing Commission, the statute only tangentially addresses the penalty for returns filed after the statutory date, noting that such returns "shall" be ignored by the Department. Section 102.112, on the other hand, directly addresses in its title and text both the "deadline" for submitting returns and the "penalties" for submitting returns after a certain date; the statute expressly states that such returns "may" be ignored and that dilatory Board members "shall" be fined. Based on the

---

39. *See, e.g., Florida Birth-Related Neurological Injury Compensation Ass'n v. Florida Div. of Admin. Hearings,* 686 So. 2d 1349 (Fla. 1997).

40. *See, e.g., Starr Tyme, Inc. v. Cohen,* 659 So. 2d 1064 (Fla. 1995).

41. *See, e.g., Capers v. State,* 678 So. 2d 330 (Fla. 1996).

42. *See, e.g., State ex rel. Johnson v. Vizzini,* 227 So. 2d 205 (Fla. 1969).

precision of the title and text, section 102.112 constitutes a specific penalty statute that defines both the deadline for filing returns and the penalties for filing returns thereafter and section 102.111 constitutes a non-specific statute in this regard. The specific statute controls the non-specific statute.

Second, it also is well settled that when two statutes are in conflict, the more recently enacted statute controls the older statute.[43] In the present case, the provision in section 102.111 stating that the Department "shall" ignore returns was enacted in 1951 as part of the Code. On the other hand, the penalty provision in section 102.112 stating that the Department "may" ignore returns was enacted in 1989 as a revision to chapter 102. The more recently enacted provision may be viewed as the clearest and most recent expression of legislative intent.

Third, a statutory provision will not be construed in such a way that it renders meaningless or absurd any other statutory provision.[44] In the present case, section 102.112 contains a detailed provision authorizing the assessment of fines against members of a dilatory County Canvassing Board. The fines are personal and substantial, i.e., $ 200 for each day the returns are not received. If, as the Secretary asserts, the Department were required to ignore all returns received after the statutory date, the fine provision would be meaningless. For example, if a Board simply completed its count late and if the returns were going to be ignored in any event, what would be the point in submitting the returns? The Board would simply file no returns and avoid the fines. But, on the other hand, if the returns submitted after the statutory date would not be ignored, the Board would have good reason to submit the returns and accept the fines. The fines thus serve as an alternative penalty and are applicable only if the Department may count the returns.

Fourth, related statutory provisions must be read as a cohesive whole.[45] As stated in *Forsythe v. Longboat Key Beach Erosion Control Dist.*, 604 So. 2d 452, 455 (Fla. 1992), "all parts of a statute must be read together in order to achieve a consistent whole. Where possible, courts must give effect to all statutory provisions and construe related statutory provisions in harmony with another." In this regard we consider the provisions of section 102.166 and 102.168.

Section 102.166 states that a candidate, political committee, or political party may request a manual recount any time before the County Canvassing Board certifies the results to the Department and, if the initial

43. *See, e.g., McKendry v. State*, 641 So. 2d 45 (Fla. 1994).
44. *See, e.g., Amente v. Newman*, 653 So. 2d 1030 (Fla. 1995).
45. *See, e.g., Sun Ins. Office, Ltd. v. Clay*, 133 So. 2d 735 (Fla. 1961).

manual recount indicates a significant error, the Board "shall" conduct a countywide manual recount in certain cases. Thus, if a protest is filed on the sixth day following an election and a full manual recount is required, the Board, through no fault of its own, will be unable to submit its returns to the Department by 5:00 p.m. on the seventh day following the election. In such a case, if the mandatory provision in section 102.111 were given effect, the votes of the county would be ignored for the simple reason that the Board was following the dictates of a different section of the Code. The Legislature could not have intended to penalize County Canvassing Boards for following the dictates of the Code.

And finally, when the Legislature enacted the Code in 1951, it envisioned that all votes cast during a particular election, including absentee ballots, would be submitted to the Department at one time and would be treated in a uniform fashion. Section 97.012(1) states that it is the Secretary's responsibility to "[o]btain and maintain uniformity in the application, operation, and interpretation of the election laws." Chapter 101 provides that all votes, including absentee ballots, must be received by the Supervisor no later than 7 p.m. on the day of the election. Section 101.68(2)(d) expressly states that "[t]he votes on absentee ballots shall be included in the total vote of the county." Chapter 102 requires that the Board submit the returns by 5 p.m. on the seventh day following the election.

The Legislature thus envisioned that when returns are submitted to the Department, the returns "shall" embrace all the votes in the county, including absentee ballots. This, of course, is not possible because our state statutory scheme has been superseded by federal law governing overseas voters;[46] overseas ballots must be counted if received no later than ten days following the election (i.e., the ballots do *not* have to be received by 7 p.m. of the day of the election, as provided by state law).[47] In light of the fact that overseas ballots cannot be counted until after the seven day deadline

46. According to the Secretary, this matter is governed by consent decree with the federal government.

47. *See* Fla. Admin. Code R.1S-2.013 (1998), which provides in relevant part:

(7) With respect to the presidential preference primary and the general election, any absentee ballot cast for a federal office by an overseas elector which is postmarked or signed and dated no later than the date of the Federal election shall be counted if received no later than 10 days from the date of the Federal election so long as such absentee ballot is otherwise proper. Overseas electors shall be informed by the supervisors of elections of the provisions of this rule, i.e., the ten day extension provision for the presidential preference primary and the general election, and the provision for voting for the second primary.

has expired, the mandatory language in section 102.111 has been supplanted by the permissive language of section 102.112.

Further, although county returns must be received by 5 p.m. on the seventh day following an election, the "official results" that are to be compiled in order to certify the returns and declare who has been elected must be construed in pari materia with section 101.5614(8), which specifies that "write-in, absentee *and manually counted results* shall constitute the official return of the election." (Emphasis added.)

Under this statutory scheme, the County Canvassing Boards are required to submit their returns to the Department by 5 p.m. of the seventh day following the election. The statutes make no provision for exceptions following a manual recount. If a Board fails to meet the deadline, the Secretary is not required to ignore the county's returns but rather is permitted to ignore the returns within the parameters of this statutory scheme. To determine the circumstances under which the Secretary may lawfully ignore returns filed pursuant to the provisions of section 102.166 for a manual recount, it is necessary to examine the interplay between our statutory and constitutional law at both the state and federal levels.

VIII. THE RIGHT TO VOTE

The text of our Florida Constitution begins with a Declaration of Rights, a series of rights so basic that the founders accorded them a place of special privilege.[48] The Court long ago noted the venerable role the Declaration plays in our tripartite system of government in Florida:

> It is significant that our Constitution thus commences by specifying those things which the state government must not do, before specifying certain things that it may do. These Declarations of Rights . . . have cost much, and breathe the spirit of that sturdy and self-reliant philosophy of individualism which underlies and supports our entire system of government. No race of hothouse plants could ever have produced and compelled the recognition of such a stalwart set of basic principles, and no such race can preserve them. They say to arbitrary and autocratic power, from whatever official quarter it may advance to invade these vital rights of personal liberty and private property, "Thus far shalt thou come, but no farther."

State v. City of Stuart, 97 Fla. 69, 120 So. 335, 347 (Fla. 1929). Courts must attend with special vigilance whenever the Declaration of Rights is in issue.

48. *Traylor v. State,* 596 So. 2d 957, 963 (Fla. 1992).

The right of suffrage is the preeminent right contained in the Declaration of Rights, for without this basic freedom all others would be diminished. The importance of this right was acknowledged by the authors of the Constitution, who placed it first in the Declaration. The very first words in the body of the constitution are as follows:

Section 1. Political power. *All political power is inherent in the people. The* enunciation herein of certain rights shall not be construed to deny or impair others retained by the people.

Art. I., § 1, Fla. Const. (emphasis added). The framers thus began the constitution with a declaration that all political power inheres in the people and only they, the people, may decide how and when that power may be given up.[49]

To the extent that the Legislature may enact laws regulating the electoral process, those laws are valid only if they impose no "unreasonable or unnecessary" restraints on the right of suffrage:

The declaration of rights expressly states that "all political power is inherent in the people." Article I, Section 1, Florida Constitution. The right of the people to select their own officers is their sovereign right, and the rule is against imposing unnecessary and unreasonable [restraints on that right]. . . . *Unreasonable or unnecessary* restraints on the elective process are prohibited.

Treiman v. Malmquist, 342 So. 2d 972, 975 (Fla. 1977) (emphasis added).[50]

Because election laws are intended to facilitate the right of suffrage, such laws must be liberally construed in favor of the citizens' right to vote:

Generally, the courts, in construing statutes relating to elections, hold that the same should receive a liberal construction in favor of the citizen whose right to vote they tend to restrict and in so doing to prevent disfranchisement of legal voters and the intention of the voters should prevail when counting ballots. . . . It is the intention of the law to obtain an honest expression of the will or desire of the voter.

49. *See* Talbot D'Alemberte, *Commentary,* 25A Fla. Stat. Ann., Art. I, § 1, Fla. Const. (West 1991).

50. *See also Pasco v. Heggen,* 314 So. 2d 1, 3 (Fla. 1975) ("We have also stated that only unreasonable or unnecessary restraints on the elective process are prohibited.").

State ex rel. Carpenter v. Barber, 144 Fla. 159, 198 So. 49, 51 (Fla. 1940).[51] Courts must not lose sight of the fundamental purpose of election laws: The laws are intended to facilitate and safeguard the right of each voter to express his or her will in the context of our representative democracy.[52] Technical statutory requirements must not be exalted over the substance of this right.[53]

Based on the foregoing, we conclude that the authority of the Florida Secretary of State to ignore amended returns submitted by a County Canvassing Board may be lawfully exercised only under limited circumstances as we set forth in this opinion. The clear import of the penalty provision of section 102.112 is to deter Boards from engaging in dilatory conduct contrary to statutory authority that results in the late certification of a county's returns. This deterrent purpose is achieved by the fines in section 102.112, which are substantial and personal and are levied on each member of a Board. The alternative penalty, i.e., ignoring the county's returns, punishes not the Board members themselves but rather the county's electors, for it in effect disenfranchises them.[54]

Ignoring the county's returns is a drastic measure and is appropriate only if the returns are submitted to the Department so late that their inclusion will compromise the integrity of the electoral process in either of two ways: (1) by precluding a candidate, elector, or taxpayer from contesting the certification of an election pursuant to section 102.168; or (2) by precluding Florida voters from participating fully in the federal electoral process.[55] In either case, the Secretary must explain to the Board her reason for ignoring the returns and her action must be adequately supported by the law. To disenfranchise electors in an effort to deter Board members, as the Sec-

---

51. *See also State ex rel. Whitley v. Rinehart,* 140 Fla. 645, 192 So. 819, 823 (Fla. 1939) ("Election laws should be construed liberally in favor of the right to vote. . . .").

52. *See, e.g., State ex rel. Landis v. Dyer,* 109 Fla. 33, 148 So. 201, 203 (Fla. 1933) ("The right to vote, though not inherent, is a constitutional right in this state. The Legislature may impose reasonable rules and regulations for its governance, but it cannot under the guise of such regulation unduly subvest [*Eds.*: subvert] or restrain this right.").

53. *See, e.g., Boardman v. Esteva,* 323 So. 2d 259, 269 (Fla. 1975) ("In summary, we hold that the primary consideration in an election contest is whether the will of the people has been effected.").

54. *Cf. Boardman v. Esteva,* 323 So. 2d 259, 268–69 (Fla. 1975) ("When the voters have done all that the statute has required them to do, they will not be disfranchised solely on the basis of the failure of the election officials to observe directory statutory instructions.").

55. See 3 U.S.C. §§ 1–10 (1994).

retary in the present case proposes, is unreasonable, unnecessary, and violates longstanding law.

Allowing the manual recounts to proceed in an expeditious manner, rather than imposing an arbitrary seven-day deadline, is consistent not only with the statutory scheme but with prior United States Supreme Court pronouncements:

> Indiana has found, along with many other States, that one procedure necessary to guard against irregularity and error in the tabulation of votes is the availability of a recount. Despite the fact that a certificate of election may be issued to the leading candidate within 30 days after the election, the results are not final if a candidate's option to compel a recount is exercised. A recount is an integral part of the Indiana electoral process and is within the ambit of the broad powers delegated to the States by Art. I, s 4.

Roudebush v. Hartke, 405 U.S. 15, 25 (1972) (footnotes omitted).

In addition, an accurate vote count is one of the essential foundations of our democracy. The words of the Supreme Court of Illinois are particularly apt in this case:

> The purpose of our election laws is to obtain a correct expression of the intent of the voters. Our courts have repeatedly held that, where the intention of the voter can be ascertained with reasonable certainty from his ballot, that intention will be given effect even though the ballot is not strictly in conformity with the law. . . . The legislature authorized the use of electronic tabulating equipment to expedite the tabulating process and to eliminate the possibility of human error in the counting process, not to create a technical obstruction which defeats the rights of qualified voters. This court should not, under the appearance of enforcing the election laws, defeat the very object which those law are intended to achieve. To invalidate a ballot which clearly reflects the voter's intent, simply because a machine cannot read it, would subordinate substance to form and promote the means at the expense of the end.

> The voters here did everything which the Election Code requires when they punched the appropriate chad with the stylus. These voters should not be disfranchised where their intent may be ascertained with reasonable certainty, simply because the chad they punched did not completely dislodge from the ballot. Such a failure may be attributable to the fault of the election authorities, for failing to pro-

vide properly perforated paper, or it may be the result of the voter's disability or inadvertence. Whatever the reason, where the intention of the voter can be fairly and satisfactorily ascertained, that intention should be given effect.

Pullen v. Mulligan, 561 N.E.2d 585 (Ill. 1990) (citations omitted).

IX. THE PRESENT CASE

The trial court below properly concluded that the County Canvassing Boards are required to submit their returns to the Department by 5:00 p.m. of the seventh day following the election and that the Department is not required to ignore the amended returns but rather may count them. The court, however, erred in holding that the Secretary acted within her discretion in prematurely rejecting any amended returns that would be the result of ongoing manual recounts. The Secretary's rationale for rejecting the Board's returns was as follows:

> The Board has not alleged any facts or circumstances that suggest the existence of voter fraud. The Board has not alleged any facts or circumstances that suggest that there has been substantial noncompliance with the state's statutory election procedures, coupled with reasonable doubt as to whether the certified results expressed the will of the voters. The Board has not alleged any facts or circumstances that suggest that Palm Beach County has been unable to comply with its election duties due to an act of God, or other extenuating circumstances that are beyond its control. The Board has alleged the *possibility* that the results of the manual recount *could* affect the outcome of the election if certain results obtain. However, absent an assertion that there has been substantial noncompliance with the law, I do not believe that the *possibility* of affecting the outcome of the election is enough to justify ignoring the statutory deadline. Furthermore, I find that the facts and circumstances alleged, standing alone, do not rise to the level of extenuating circumstances that justify a decision on my part to ignore the statutory deadline imposed by the Florida Legislature.

Letter from Katherine Harris to Palm Beach Canvassing Board (Nov. 15, 2000) (emphasis added).

We conclude that, consistent with the Florida election scheme, the Secretary may reject a Board's amended returns only if the returns are submitted so late that their inclusion will preclude a candidate from contesting the certification or preclude Florida's voters from participating fully in the federal electoral process. The Secretary in the present case has made no claim that either of these conditions apply at this point in time.

The above analysis is consistent with *State ex rel. Chappell v. Martinez,* 536 So. 2d 1007 (Fla. 1988), wherein the Court addressed a comparable recount issue. There, the total votes cast for each of two candidates for a seat in the United States House of Representatives were separated by less than one-half of one percent; the county conducted a mandatory recount; the Board's certification of results was not received by the Department until two days after the deadline, although the Board had telephoned the results to the Department prior to the deadline; and the unsuccessful candidate sued to prevent the Department from counting the late votes. The Court concluded that the will of the electors supersedes any technical statutory requirements:

> [T]he electorate's effecting its will through its balloting, not the hypertechnical compliance with statutes, is the object of holding an election. "There is no magic in the statutory requirements. If they are complied with to the extent that the duly responsible election officials can ascertain that the electors whose votes are being canvassed are qualified and registered to vote, and that they do so in a proper manner, then who can be heard to complain the statute has not been literally and absolutely complied with?"

Chappell, 536 So. 2d at 1008–09 (quoting *Boardman v. Esteva,* 323 So. 2d 259, 267 (Fla. 1975)).

X. CONCLUSION

According to the legislative intent evinced in the Florida Election Code, the permissive language of section 102.112 supersedes the mandatory language of section 102.111. The statutory fines set forth in section 102.112 offer strong incentive to County Canvassing Boards to submit their returns in a timely fashion. However, when a Board certifies its returns after the seven-day period because the Board is acting in conformity with other provisions of the Code or with administrative rules or for other good cause, the Secretary may impose no fines. It is unlikely that the Legislature would have intended to punish a Board for complying with the dictates of the Code or some other law.

Because the right to vote is the pre-eminent right in the Declaration of Rights of the Florida Constitution, the circumstances under which the Secretary may exercise her authority to ignore a county's returns filed after the initial statutory date are limited. The Secretary may ignore such returns only if their inclusion will compromise the integrity of the electoral process in either of two ways: (1) by precluding a candidate, elector, or taxpayer from contesting the certification of election pursuant to section 102.168; or (2) by precluding Florida voters from participating fully in the federal electoral process. In either such case, this drastic penalty must be both reasonable and necessary. But to allow the Secretary to summarily disenfranchise innocent electors in an effort to punish dilatory Board members, as she proposes in the present case, misses the constitutional mark. The constitution eschews punishment by proxy.

As explained above, the Florida Election Code must be construed as a whole. Section 102.166 governs manual recounts and appears to conflict with sections 102.111 and 102.112, which set a seven-day deadline by which County Boards must submit their returns. Further, section 102.111, which provides that the Secretary "shall" ignore late returns, conflicts with section 102.112, which provides that the Secretary "may" ignore late returns. In the present case, we have used traditional rules of statutory construction to resolve these ambiguities to the extent necessary to address the issues presented here. We decline to rule more expansively, for to do so would result in this Court substantially rewriting the Code. We leave that matter to the sound discretion of the body best equipped to address it— the Legislature.

Because of the unique circumstances and extraordinary importance of the present case, wherein the Florida Attorney General and the Florida Secretary of State have issued conflicting advisory opinions concerning the propriety of conducting manual recounts, and because of our reluctance to rewrite the Florida Election Code, we conclude that we must invoke the equitable powers of this Court to fashion a remedy that will allow a fair and expeditious resolution of the questions presented here.[56]

Accordingly, in order to allow maximum time for contests pursuant to section 102.168, amended certifications must be filed with the Elections Canvassing Commission by 5 p.m. on Sunday, November 26, 2000 and the Secretary of State and the Elections Canvassing Commission shall accept any such amended certifications received by 5 p.m. on Sunday, November 26, 2000, provided that the office of the Secretary of State, Division of Elections is open in order to allow receipt thereof. If the office is

56. At oral argument, we inquired as to whether the presidential candidates were interested in our consideration of a reopening of the opportunity to request recounts in any additional counties. Neither candidate requested such an opportunity.

not open for this special purpose on Sunday, November 26, 2000, then any amended certifications shall be accepted until 9 a.m. on Monday, November 27, 2000. The stay order entered on November 17, 2000, by this Court shall remain in effect until the expiration of the time for accepting amended certifications set forth in this opinion. The certificates made and signed by the Elections Canvassing Commission pursuant to section 102.121 shall include the amended returns accepted through the dates set forth in this opinion.

It is so ordered. No motion for rehearing will be allowed.

CHIEF JUSTICE WELLS, and JUSTICES SHAW, HARDING, ANSTEAD, PARIENTE, LEWIS, and QUINCE, JJ., concur.

Supreme Court of the United States

No. 00-836

George W. Bush, Petitioner *v.*
Palm Beach County Canvassing Board ET AL.

ON WRIT OF CERTIORARI TO THE FLORIDA SUPREME COURT

December 4, 2000

PER CURIAM

The Supreme Court of the State of Florida interpreted its elections statutes in proceedings brought to require manual recounts of ballots, and the certification of the recount results, for votes cast in the quadrennial Presidential election held on November 7, 2000. Governor George W. Bush, Republican candidate for the Presidency, filed a petition for certiorari to review the Florida Supreme Court decision. We granted certiorari on two of the questions presented by petitioner: whether the decision of the Florida Supreme Court, by effectively changing the State's elector appointment procedures after election day, violated the Due Process Clause or 3 U. S. C. § 5, and whether the decision of that court changed the manner in which the State's electors are to be selected, in violation of the legislature's power to designate the manner for selection under Art. II, §1, cl. 2 of the United States Constitution.

On November 8, 2000, the day following the Presidential election, the Florida Division of Elections reported that Governor Bush had received 2,909,135 votes, and respondent Democrat Vice President Albert Gore, Jr., had received 2,907,351, a margin of 1,784 in Governor Bush's favor. Under Fla. Stat. § 102.141(4) (2000), because the margin of victory was equal to or less than one-half of one percent of the votes cast, an automatic machine recount occurred. The recount resulted in a much smaller margin of victory for Governor Bush. Vice President Gore then exercised his statutory right to submit written requests for manual recounts to the canvassing board of any county. See § 102.166. He requested recounts in four counties: Volusia, Palm Beach, Broward, and Miami-Dade.

The parties urged conflicting interpretations of the Florida Election Code respecting the authority of the canvassing boards, the Secretary of State (hereinafter Secretary), and the Elections Canvassing Commission. On November 14, in an action brought by Volusia County, and joined by the Palm Beach County Canvassing Board, Vice President Gore, and the Florida Democratic Party, the Florida Circuit Court ruled that the statutory 7-day deadline was mandatory, but that the Volusia board could amend its returns at a later date [pages 22–23]. The court further ruled that the Secretary, after "considering all attendant facts and circumstances," [page 23] could exercise her discretion in deciding whether to include the late amended returns in the statewide certification.

The Secretary responded by issuing a set of criteria by which she would decide whether to allow a late filing. The Secretary ordered that, by 2 p.m. the following day, November 15, any county desiring to forward late returns submit a written statement of the facts and circumstances justifying a later filing. Four counties submitted statements and, after reviewing the submissions, the Secretary determined that none justified an extension of the filing deadline. On November 16, the Florida Democratic Party and Vice President Gore filed an emergency motion in the state court, arguing that the Secretary had acted arbitrarily and in contempt of the court's earlier ruling. The following day, the court denied the motion, ruling that the Secretary had not acted arbitrarily and had exercised her discretion in a reasonable manner consistent with the court's earlier ruling. The Democratic Party and Vice President Gore appealed to the First District Court of Appeal, which certified the matter to the Florida Supreme Court. That court accepted jurisdiction and *sua sponte* entered an order enjoining the Secretary and the Elections Canvassing Commission from finally certifying the results of the election and declaring a winner until further order of that court.

The Supreme Court, with the expedition requisite for the controversy, issued its decision on November 21. *Palm Beach County Canvassing Bd. v. Harris,* Nos. SC00-2346, SC00-2348, and SC00-2349 (Nov. 21, 2000), [pages 24–47] As the court saw the matter, there were two principal questions: whether a discrepancy between an original machine return and a sample manual recount resulting from the way a ballot has been marked or punched is an "error in vote tabulation" justifying a full manual recount; and how to reconcile what it spoke of as two conflicts in Florida's election laws: (a) between the time frame for conducting a manual recount under Fla. Stat. § 102.166 (2000) and the time frame for submitting county returns under §§ 102.111 and 102.112, and (b) between § 102.111, which provides that the Secretary "shall . . . ignor[e]" late election returns, and § 102.112, which provides that she "may . . . ignor[e]"such returns. With regard to the first issue, the court held that, under the plain text of the statute, a discrepancy between a sample manual recount and machine returns due to the way in which a ballot was punched or marked did constitute an "error in vote tabulation" sufficient to trigger the statutory provisions for a full manual recount.

With regard to the second issue, the court held that the "shall . . . ignor[e]" provision of § 102.111 conflicts with the "may . . . ignor[e]" provision of § 102.112, and that the "may . . . ignor[e]" provision controlled. The court turned to the questions whether and when the Secretary may ignore late manual recounts. The court relied in part upon the right to vote set forth in the Declaration of Rights of the Florida Constitution in concluding that late manual recounts could be rejected only under limited circumstances. The court then stated: "[B]ecause of our reluctance to rewrite the Florida Election Code, we conclude that we must invoke the equitable powers of this Court to fashion a remedy. . . ." [page 46]. The court thus imposed a deadline of November 26, at 5 p.m., for a return of ballot counts. The 7-day deadline of § 102.111, assuming it would have applied, was effectively extended by 12 days. The court further directed the Secretary to accept manual counts submitted prior to that deadline.

As a general rule, this Court defers to a state court's interpretation of a state statute. But in the case of a law enacted by a state legislature applicable not only to elections to state offices, but also to the selection of Presidential electors, the legislature is not acting solely under the authority given it by the people of the State, but by virtue of a direct grant of authority made under Art. II, § 1, cl. 2, of the United States Constitution. That provision reads:

"Each State shall appoint, in such Manner as the Legislature thereof may direct, a Number of Electors, equal to the whole Number of Senators and Representatives to which the State may be entitled in the Congress. . . ."

Although we did not address the same question petitioner raises here, in *McPherson v. Blacker*, 146 U.S. 1, 25 (1892), we said:

"[Art. II, § 1, cl. 2] does not read that the people or the citizens shall appoint, but that 'each State shall'; and if the words 'in such manner

as the legislature thereof may direct,' had been omitted, it would
seem that the legislative power of appointment could not have been
successfully questioned in the absence of any provision in the state
constitution in that regard. Hence the insertion of those words, while
operating as a limitation upon the State in respect of any attempt to
circumscribe the legislative power, cannot be held to operate as a limitation on that power itself."

There are expressions in the opinion of the Supreme Court of Florida that
may be read to indicate that it construed the Florida Election Code without regard to the extent to which the Florida Constitution could, consistent with Art. II, § 1, cl. 2, "circumscribe the legislative power." The opinion states, for example, that "[t]o the extent that the Legislature may enact
laws regulating the electoral process, those laws are valid only if they impose no 'unreasonable or unnecessary' restraints on the right of suffrage"
guaranteed by the state constitution [page 41]. The opinion also states that
"[b]ecause election laws are intended to facilitate the right of suffrage, such
laws must be liberally construed in favor of the citizens' right to vote. . . ."
Ibid.

In addition, 3 U. S. C. § 5 provides in pertinent part:

"If any State shall have provided, by laws enacted prior to the day
fixed for the appointment of the electors, for its final determination
of any controversy or contest concerning the appointment of all or
any of the electors of such State, by judicial or other methods or procedures, and such determination shall have been made at least six
days before the time fixed for the meeting of the electors, such determination made pursuant to such law so existing on said day, and
made at least six days prior to said time of meeting of the electors,
shall be conclusive, and shall govern in the counting of the electoral
votes as provided in the Constitution, and as hereinafter regulated,
so far as the ascertainment of the electors appointed by such State is
concerned."

The parties before us agree that whatever else may be the effect of this section, it creates a "safe harbor" for a State insofar as congressional consideration of its electoral votes is concerned. If the state legislature has provided
for final determination of contests or controversies by a law made prior to
election day, that determination shall be conclusive if made at least six days
prior to said time of meeting of the electors. The Florida Supreme Court

cited 3 U. S. C. §§ 1–10 in a footnote of its opinion, [page 42, note 55], but did not discuss § 5. Since § 5 contains a principle of federal law that would assure finality of the State's determination if made pursuant to a state law in effect before the election, a legislative wish to take advantage of the "safe harbor" would counsel against any construction of the Election Code that Congress might deem to be a change in the law.

After reviewing the opinion of the Florida Supreme Court, we find "that there is considerable uncertainty as to the precise grounds for the decision." *Minnesota v. National Tea Co.*, 309 U. S. 551, 555 (1940). This is sufficient reason for us to decline at this time to review the federal questions asserted to be present. See *ibid.*

> "It is fundamental that state courts be left free and unfettered by us in interpreting their state constitutions. But it is equally important that ambiguous or obscure adjudications by state courts do not stand as barriers to a determination by this Court of the validity under the federal constitution of state action. Intelligent exercise of our appellate powers compels us to ask for the elimination of the obscurities and ambiguities from the opinions in such cases." *Id.*, at 557.

Specifically, we are unclear as to the extent to which the Florida Supreme Court saw the Florida Constitution as circumscribing the legislature's authority under Art. II, § 1, cl. 2. We are also unclear as to the consideration the Florida Supreme Court accorded to 3 U. S. C. § 5. The judgment of the Supreme Court of Florida is therefore vacated, and the case is remanded for further proceedings not inconsistent with this opinion.

It is so ordered.

In the Circuit Court of the Second Judicial Circuit, in and for Leon County, Florida

Case No. CV-00-2808

Albert Gore, Jr., Nominee of the Democratic Party of the United States for President of the United States, and Joseph I. Lieberman, Nominee of the Democratic Party of the United States for Vice President of the United States, Plaintiffs,

v.

Katherine Harris, as Secretary of State, State of Florida, ET AL., Defendants

Final Judgment

This action was tried before the court. The finding and conclusions in the ruling of the court from the bench in open court this day shall become a part hereof. Accordingly, it is

ORDERED AND ADJUDGED that Plaintiffs Albert Gore, Jr., and Joseph I. Lieberman shall take nothing by the action and the defendants may go hence without day [*Eds.:* for *sine die*].

DONE AND ORDERED in Chambers, this 4th day December 2000.

N. SANDERS SAULS
Circuit Judge

This is a final judgment from the Circuit Court of the Second Judicial Circuit, in and for Leon County, reprinted in its entirety.

[Transcript of Bench Ruling]

At this time, the court finds and concludes as follows: The complaint filed herein states in its first paragraph that this is an action to contest the state certification in the presidential election of 2000, asserting that the State Elections Canvassing Commission's certification on November 26, 2000, is erroneous as the vote totals wrongly include illegal votes and do not include legal votes that were improperly rejected.

Plaintiffs further contest the State of Florida's certification of the electors for George W. Bush and Richard Cheney as being elected.

Reprinted with permission of The Associated Press.

Plaintiffs further challenge and contest the election certifications of the canvassing boards of Dade, Palm Beach and Nassau Counties.

As to the Dade Canvassing Board, plaintiffs seek to compel the Dade Board to include in its certification, and the State Elections Canvassing Commission to include in the state certification, a six-vote change in favor of plaintiffs, resulting from the Board's initial test partial manual recount of 1 percent of the countywide vote total conducted with respect to three precincts designated by the plaintiffs' designees; also additional votes manually hand counted in a further partial recount total resulting from the board's discretionary decision to stop completion of a full manual recount of all of the votes in all of the precincts of Dade because of insufficiency of time to complete the same. These represent the result of the count of an additional 136 precincts of the 635 precincts in Dade County. And also the results of any court-ordered manual review and recount of some 9,000 to 10,000 voter cards or ballots, which at the plaintiffs' request have been separated or were separated as alleged undervotes by the Dade Canvassing Board or the Dade supervisor of elections as a result of all of the countywide ballots being processed through the counting machines a third time and being nonreadable by the machine.

As to the Palm Beach Canvassing Board, plaintiffs seek to compel the Palm Beach Board to include in its certification, and the state Elections Canvassing Commission to include in the state certification, additional votes representing the results of an attempted partial certification of results completed before the November 26, 2000, deadline mandated by the Florida Supreme Court, as well as the additional remainder of the results of the manual recount, which was completed after the deadline and the attempted certification thereof on December 1; and in addition, the results of any court-ordered manual review and recount of some 3,300 ballots, which were objected to during the Palm Beach Board's manual recount, which plaintiffs alleged should have been counted as valid votes because that board used an improper standard.

As to Nassau, the Nassau County Canvassing Board, the plaintiffs seek to compel the Nassau Board to amend its certification, and the State Elections Canvassing Commission to amend the state certification, to reflect and include the results of the board's machine recount rather than the results of the board's original machine count, thereby resulting in a favorable net gain to plaintiffs of 51 votes.

It is the established law of Florida, as reflected in *State v. Smith* [107 Fla. 134, 144 So. 333 (1932)], that where changes or charges of irregularity of procedure or inaccuracy of returns in balloting and counting processes have been alleged, the court must find as a fact that a legal basis for ordering any recount exists before ordering such recount.

Further, it is well established, as reflected in the opinion of Judge Jonas in *Smith v. Tynes* [412 So. 2d 925 (Fla. 1st DCA 1982)], that in order to contest election results under Section 102.168 of the Florida statutes, the plaintiff must show that but for the irregularity or inaccuracy claimed, the result of the election would have been different, and he or she would have been the winner. It is not enough to show a reasonable possibility that election results could have been altered by such irregularities or inaccuracies. Rather, a reasonable probability that the results of the election would have been changed must be shown.

In this case, there is no credible statistical evidence and no other competent substantial evidence to establish by a preponderance a reasonable probability that the results of the statewide election in the State of Florida would be different from the result which has been certified by the State Elections Canvassing Commission.

The court further finds and concludes the evidence does not establish any illegality, dishonesty, gross negligence, improper influence, coercion or fraud in the balloting and counting processes.

Secondly, there is no authority under Florida law for certification of an incomplete manual recount of a portion of or less than all ballots from any county by the State Elections Canvassing Commission, nor authority to include any returns submitted past the deadline established by the Florida Supreme Court in this election.

Thirdly, although the record shows voter error and/or less than total accuracy in regard to the punch-card voting devices utilized in Dade and Palm Beach Counties, which these counties have been aware of for many years, these balloting and counting problems cannot support or effect any recounting necessity with respect to Dade County, absent the establishment of a reasonable probability that the statewide election result would be different, which has not been established in this case.

The court further finds the Dade Canvassing Board did not abuse its discretion in any of its decisions in its review and recounting processes.

Fourthly, with respect to the approximate 3,300 Palm Beach County ballots of which plaintiffs seek review, the Palm Beach Board properly exercised its discretion in its counting process and has judged those ballots which plaintiffs wish this court to again judge de novo.

All cases upon which plaintiffs rely were rendered upon mandamus prior to the modern statutory election system and remedial scheme enacted by the Legislature of the State of Florida in Section 102 of the Florida Statutes, or Chapter 102 of the Florida Statutes. The local boards have been given broad discretion, which no court may overrule absent a clear abuse of discretion. The Palm Beach County Board did not abuse its discretion in its review and recounting process. Further, it acted in full compliance with the order of the Circuit Court in and for Palm Beach County. Having done so, plaintiffs are estopped from further challenge of its process and standards. It should be noted, however, that such process and standards were changed from the prior 1990 standards, perhaps contrary to 3 U.S.C. § 5.

Furthermore, with respect to the standards utilized by the Board in its review and counting processes, the court finds that the standard utilized was in full compliance with the law, and review under another standard would not be authorized, thus creating a two-tier situation within one county as well as with respect to other counties.

The court notes that the attorney general of the State of Florida enunciated his opinion of the law with respect to this in a letter dated November 14, 2000 to the Hon. Charles E. Burton, chair of the Palm Beach County Canvassing Board [pages 14–18], which in part is as follows:

> A two-tier system would have the effect of treating voters differently depending upon what county they voted in. A voter in a county where a manual count was conducted would benefit from having a better chance of having his or her vote actually counted than a voter in a county where a hand count was halted.
>
> As the state's chief legal officer, I feel a duty to warn that if the final certified total for balloting in the State of Florida includes figures generated from this two-tier system of differing behavior by official canvassing boards, the state will incur a legal jeopardy under both the United States and State Constitutions. This legal jeopardy could potentially lead Florida to having all of its votes, in effect, disqualified, and this state being barred from the Electoral College's selection of a president.

The court finds further that the Nassau County Canvassing Board did not abuse its discretion in its certification of Nassau County's voting results. Such actions were not void or illegal and it was done within the proper exercise of its discretion upon adequate and reasonable public notice.

Further, this court would further conclude and find that the properly stated cause of action under section 102.168 of the Florida Statutes to contest a statewide federal election, the plaintiff would necessarily have to place an issue and seek as a remedy with the attendant burden of proof a review and recount of all ballots in all the counties in this state with respect to the particular alleged irregularity or inaccuracy in the balloting or counting processes alleged to have occurred.

As recently stated by Judge Klein, with the concurrence of Chief Judge Warner in the Fourth District Court of Appeal case of *Fladell v. Palm Beach Canvassing Board* [No. 4D00-4145 (November 27, 2000) (Klein, J. dissenting)], Section 102.168 provides in subsection 1 that the certification of election may be contested for presidential elections. Section 103.011 provides that "[t]he Department of State shall certify, as elected, the presidential electors of the candidates for president and vice president who receive the highest number of votes."

There is in this type of election one statewide election and one certification. Palm Beach County did not elect any person as a presidential elector, but rather the election was a winner-take-all proposition dependent on the statewide vote.

Finally, for the purpose of expedition due to the exigencies surrounding these proceedings, this court will deny those portions of the pending motions to dismiss of the various parties herein not affected by or ruled upon in these findings and conclusions with those portions consisting solely of matters of law being reviewable upon such denial.

In conclusion, the court finds that the plaintiffs have failed to carry the requisite burden of proof and judgment shall be and hereby is entered that plaintiffs shall take nothing by this action and the defendants may go hence without day.

All ballots in the custody of the clerk of this court shall remain pending review.

Supreme Court of Florida

No. SC00-243

Albert Gore, Jr., and Joseph I. Lieberman, Appellants,
v.
Katherine Harris, as Secretary, ETC., ET AL., Appellees

December 8, 2000 [as corrected December 14, 2000]

PER CURIAM.

We have for review a final judgment of a Leon County trial court certified by the First District Court of Appeal as being of great public importance and requiring immediate resolution by this Court. We have jurisdiction. *See* art. V, § 3 (b)(5), Fla. Const.[1] The final judgment under review denies all relief requested by appellants Albert Gore, Jr. and Joseph I. Lieberman, the Democratic candidates for President and Vice President of the United States, in their complaint contesting the certification of the state results in the November 7, 2000, presidential election.[2] Although we find that the appellants are entitled to reversal in part of the trial court's order and are entitled to a manual count of the Miami-Dade County undervote, we agree with the appellees that the ultimate relief would require a counting of the legal votes contained within the undervotes in all counties where the undervote has not been subjected to a manual tabulation. Accordingly, we reverse and remand for proceedings consistent with this opinion.

I. BACKGROUND

On November 26, 2000, the Florida Election Canvassing Commission (Canvassing Commission) certified the results of the election and declared Governor George W. Bush and Richard Cheney, the Republican candidates for President and Vice President, the winner of Florida's electoral votes.[3]

1. The parties have agreed that this appeal is properly before this Court.
2. The appellants have alternatively styled their request for relief as a Petition for Writ of Mandamus or Other Writs
3. See §§ 102.111 & .121, Florida Statutes (2000).

The November 26, 2000, certified results showed a 537-vote margin in favor of Bush.[4] On November 27, pursuant to the legislatively enacted "contest" provisions, Gore filed a complaint in Leon County Circuit Court contesting the certification on the grounds that the results certified by the Canvassing Commission included "a number of illegal votes" and failed to include "a number of legal votes sufficient to change or place in doubt the result of the election."[5]

Pursuant to the legislative scheme providing for an "immediate hearing" in a contest action, the trial court held a two-day evidentiary hearing on December 2 and 3, 2000, and on December 4, 2000, made an oral statement in open court denying all relief and entered a final judgment adopting the oral statement. The trial court did not make any findings as to the factual allegations made in the complaint and did not reference any of the testimony adduced in the two-day evidentiary hearing, other than to summarily state that the plaintiffs failed to meet their burden of proof. Gore appealed to the First District Court of Appeal, which certified the judgment to this Court.

The appellants' election contest is based on five instances where the official results certified involved either the rejection of a number of legal votes or the receipt of a number of illegal votes. These five instances, as summarized by the appellants' brief, are as follows:

The rejection of 215 net votes for Gore identified in a manual count by the Palm Beach Canvassing Board as reflecting the clear intent of the voters;

The rejection of 168 net votes for Gore, identified in the partial recount by the Miami-Dade County Canvassing Board.

The receipt and certification after Thanksgiving of the election night returns from Nassau County, instead of the statutorily mandated machine recount tabulation, in violation of section 102.14, Florida Statutes, resulting in an additional 51 net votes for Bush.

The rejection of an additional 3300 votes in Palm Beach County, most of which Democrat observers identified as votes for Gore but which were not included in the Canvassing Board's certified results; and

The refusal to review approximately 9000 Miami-Dade ballots, which the counting machine registered as non-votes and which have never been manually reviewed.

For the reasons stated in this opinion, we find that the trial court erred as a matter of law in not including (1) the 215 net votes for Gore identi-

4. Bush received 2,912,790 votes while Gore received 2,912,253 votes.
5. See § 102.168(3)(c), Fla. Stat. (2000).

fied by the Palm Beach County Canvassing Board[6] and (2) in not including the 168 net votes for Gore identified in a partial recount by the Miami-Dade County Canvassing Board. However, we find no error in the trial court's findings, which are mixed questions of law and fact, concerning (3) the Nassau County Canvassing Board and the (4) additional 3300 votes in Palm Beach County that the Canvassing Board did not find to be legal votes. Lastly, we find the trial court erred as a matter of law in (5) refusing to examine the approximately 9000 additional Miami-Dade ballots placed in evidence, which have never been examined manually.

II. APPLICABLE LAW

Article II, section I, clause 2 of the United States Constitution, grants the authority to select presidential electors "in such Manner as the Legislature thereof may direct." The Legislature of this State has placed the decision for election of President of the United States, as well as every other elected office, in the citizens of this State through a statutory scheme. These statutes established by the Legislature govern our decision today. We consider these statutes cognizant of the federal grant of authority derived from the United States Constitution and derived from 3 U.S.C. § 5 (1994) entitled "Determination of controversy as to appointment of electors." That section provides:

> If any State shall have provided, *by laws enacted prior to the day fixed for the appointment of the electors, for its final determination of any controversy or contest concerning the appointment of all or any of the electors of such State, by judicial or other methods or procedures,* and such determination shall have been made at least six days before the time fixed for the meeting of the electors, such determination made pursuant to such law so existing on said day, and made at least six days prior to said time of meeting of the electors, shall be conclusive, and shall govern in the counting of the electoral votes as provided in the Constitution, and as hereinafter regulated, so far as the ascertainment of the electors appointed by such State is concerned.

(Emphasis supplied).

This case today is controlled by the language set forth by the Legislature in section 102.168, Florida Statutes (2000). Indeed, an important part

6. Bush claims in his brief that the audited total is 176 votes. We make no determination as to which of these two numbers are accurate but direct the trial court to make this determination on remand.

of the statutory election scheme is the State's provision for a contest process, section 102.168, which laws were enacted by the Legislature prior to the 2000 election.[7] Although courts are, and should be, reluctant to interject

7. In a substantial and dramatic change of position after oral argument in this case, Bush contends in his "Motion for Leave To File Clarification of Argument" that section 102.168 cannot apply in the context of a presidential election. However, this position is in stark contrast to his position both in this case and in the prior appeal. In fact, in Oral Argument on December 7, 2000, counsel for Bush agreed that the contest provisions contained in the Florida Election Code have placed such proceedings within the arena for judicial determination, which includes the established procedures for appellate review of circuit court determinations. Further, Bush's counsel, Michael Carvin, in the prior Oral Argument in *Palm Beach Canvassing Board v. Harris*, in arguing against allowing manual recounts to continue in the protest phase, stated that he did not

> think there would be any problem in producing . . . *that kind of evidence in an election contest procedure* . . . instead of having every court in Florida resolving on an ad hoc basis the kinds of ballots that are valid and not valid, you would be centralizing the factual inquiry in one court in Leon County. So you would bring some orderliness to the process, and they would be able to resolve that evidentiary question. One way or another, a court's going to have resolve it.

(Emphasis supplied). Moreover, the Answer Brief of Bush in Case Nos. SC00-2346, 2348, and 2849 (Nov. 18, 2000) at page 18 states that "to implement Petitioners' desired policy of manual recounts at all costs, the Court is asked to. . . (5) substitute the certification process of Section 102.111 and Section 102.112 *for the contested election process of Section 102.168 as the means for determining the accuracy of the vote tallies."* (emphasis supplied). In addition, the December 5, 2000 brief of Amici curiae of the Florida House of Representatives and the Florida Senate, in case nos. SC00-2346, SC00-2348 & SC00-2349 (Dec. 5, 2000) at 8 "The Secretary's opinion was also consistent with the fact that the statutory protests that can lead to manual recounts are county-specific complaints about a particular county's machines, whereas *a complaint about punchcards generally undercounting votes* really raises a statewide issue that *should be pursued, if at all, only in a statewide contest."* (Emphasis supplied.) Finally the Amended Answer Brief of the Secretary of State asserted that

> [p]etitioner has confused a pre-certification election protest (section 102.166) with a post-certification contest (section 102.168). such facts and circumstances are usually discovered and raised in a contest action that cannot begin until after the election is certified. The Legislature imposed a deadline for certification because of the short time frame within which to begin and conclude an election contest. Petitioners are, in effect, asking this Court to delay the commencement of election contest actions, if any, by improperly using the protest procedures to contest the election before certification. *Because the facts and circumstances concerning voter error and ballot design in Palm Beach County are more properly raised in a contest action, these facts were not relevant to the Secretary's decision to certify the election. Her decision triggered the time for bringing any election contest actions.*

(Emphasis supplied.)

themselves in essentially political controversies, the Legislature has directed in section 102.168 that an election contest shall be resolved in a judicial forum. *See* § 102.168 (providing that election contests not pertaining to either house of the Legislature may be contested "in the circuit court"). This Court has recognized that the purpose of the election contest statute is "to afford a simple and speedy means of contesting election to stated offices." *Farmer v. Carson*, 110 Fla. 245, 251, 148 So. 557, 559 (1933).

In carefully construing the contest statute, no single statutory provision will be construed in such a way as to render meaningless or absurd any other statutory provision. *See Amente v. Newman*, 653 So. 2d 1030, 1032 (Fla. 1995). In interpreting the various statutory components of the State's election process, then, common-sense approach is required, so that the purpose of the statute is to give effect to the legislative directions ensuring that the right to vote will not be frustrated. *Cf. Firestone v. News-Press Pub. Co.*, 538 So. 2d 457, 460 (Fla. 1989) (approving common-sense implementation of valid portion of section 101.121, Florida Statutes (1985)—which broadly read, in pertinent part, that "no person who is not in line to vote may come [into] any polling place from the opening to the closing of the polls, except the officially designated watchers, the inspectors, the clerks of election, and the supervisor of elections or his deputy"—so as not to exclude persons accompanying aged or infirm voters, children of voting parents, doctors entering the building to treat voters needing emergency care, or persons bringing food or beverages to the election workers because such activities are recognized as "incidental to the voting process and . . . sometimes necessary to facilitate someone else's ability to vote").

Section 102.168(2) sets forth the procedures that must be followed in a contest proceeding, providing that the contestant file a complaint in the circuit court within ten days after certification of the election returns or five days after certification following a protest pursuant to section 102.166(1), Florida Statutes (2000), whichever occurs later. Section 102.168(3) outlines the grounds for contesting an election, and includes: "Receipt of a number of illegal votes or *rejection of a number of legal votes sufficient to change or place in doubt the result of the election.*" § 102.168(3)(c) (emphasis added). Finally, section 102.168(8) authorizes the circuit court judge to "fashion such orders as he or she deems necessary to *ensure that each allegation in the complaint is investigated, examined, or checked, to prevent or correct any alleged wrong, and to provide any relief appropriate under the circumstances.*" (Emphasis added.)

The Legislature substantially revised section 102.168 in 1999.[8] That amendment preserved existing rights of unsuccessful candidates and made important additional changes to strengthen the protections provided to unsuccessful candidates in a contest action to be determined.[9] Moreover,

8. Viewed historically, section 102.168 did not always provide for contests of the type we consider today. As originally enacted, section 102.168 simply provided a mechanism for ouster of elected local officials. Under that version of the statute, election challenges were limited to county offices, and only the person claiming to have been rightfully elected to the position could challenge the election. *See* Ch. 38, Art. 10, §§ 7, 8, 9 (1845).

9. The following language of section 102.168, Florida Statutes was changed in 1999 (words stricken are deletions; words underlined are additions):

(1) Except as provided in s. 102.171, the certification of election or nomination of any person to office, or of the result on any question submitted by referendum, may be contested in the circuit court by any unsuccessful candidate for such office or nomination thereto or by any elector qualified to vote in the election related to such candidacy, or by any taxpayer, respectively.

(2) Such contestant shall file a complaint, together with the fees prescribed in chapter 28, with the clerk of the circuit court within 10 days after midnight of the date the last county canvassing board empowered to canvass the returns certifies the results of the election being contested or within 5 days after midnight of the date the last county canvassing board empowered to canvass the returns certifies the results of that particular election following a protest pursuant to s. 102.166(1), whichever occurs later. adjourns and

(3) The complaint shall set forth the grounds on which the contestant intends to establish his or her right to such office or set aside the result of the election on a submitted referendum. The grounds for contesting an election under this section are:

Misconduct, fraud, or corruption on the part of any election official or any member of the canvassing board sufficient to change or place in doubt the result of the election.

(b) Ineligibility of the successful candidate for the nomination or office in dispute.

(c) Receipt of a number of illegal votes or rejection of a number of legal votes sufficient to change or place in doubt the result of the election.

(d) Proof that any elector, election official, or canvassing board member was given or offered a bribe or reward in money, property, or any other thing of value for the purpose of procuring the successful candidate's nomination or election or determining the result on any question submitted by referendum.

(e) Any other cause or allegation which, if sustained, would show that a person other than the successful candidate was the person duly nominated or elected to the office in question or that the outcome of the election on a question submitted by referendum was contrary to the result declared by the canvassing board or election board.

rather than restraining the actions of the trial court hearing the contest, the legislative amendment codified the grounds for contesting an election, entitled any candidate or elector to an immediate hearing and provided the circuit judge with express authority to fashion such orders as are necessary to ensure that each allegation in the complaint is investigated, examined or checked. *See* Fla. H. R. Comm. on Election Reform, HB 291 (1999) Staff Analysis (February 3, 1999).

Although the right to contest an election is created by statute, it has been a long-standing right since 1845 when the first election contest statute was enacted. *See* ch. 38, art. 10, §§ 7–9 Laws of Fla. (1845). As is well established in this State by our contest statute, "[t]he right to a correct count of the ballots in an election is a substantial right which it is the privilege of every candidate for office to insist on, in every case where there has been

---

(4) The canvassing board or election board shall be the proper party defendant, and the successful candidate shall be an indispensable party to any action brought to contest the election or nomination of a candidate.

(5) A statement of the grounds of contest may not be rejected, nor the proceedings dismissed, by the court for any want of form if the grounds of contest provided in the statement are sufficient to clearly inform the defendant of the particular proceeding or cause for which the nomination or election is contested.

(6) A copy of the complaint shall be served upon the defendant and any other person named therein in the same manner as in other civil cases under the laws of this state. Within 10 days after the complaint has been served, the defendant must file an answer admitting or denying the allegations on which the contestant relies or stating that the defendant has no knowledge or information concerning the allegations, which shall be deemed a denial of the allegations, and must state any other defenses, in law or fact, on which the defendant relies. If an answer is not filed within the time prescribed, the defendant may not be granted a hearing in court to assert any claim or objection that is required by this subsection to be stated in an answer.

(7) Any candidate. Qualified elector, or taxpayer presenting such a contest to a circuit judge is entitled to an immediate hearing. However, the court in its discretion may limit the time to be consumed in taking testimony, with a view therein to the circumstances of the matter and to the proximity of any succeeding primary or other election.

(8) The circuit judge to whom the contest is presented may fashion such orders as he or she deems necessary to ensure that each allegation in the complaint is investigated, examined, or checked, to prevent or correct any alleged wrong, and to provide any relief appropriate under such circumstances.

Ch. 99-339, § 3, Laws of Fla.

a failure to make a *proper count,* call, tally, or return of the votes as required by law, and this fact has been duly established as the basis for granting such relief." *State ex rel. Millinor v. Smith,* 107 Fla. 134, 139, 144 So. 333, 335 (1932) (emphasis added). The Staff Analysis of the 1999 legislative amendment expressly endorses this important principle. Similarly, the Florida House of Representatives Committee on Election Reform 1997 Interim Project on Election Contests and Recounts expressly declared:

> Recounts are an integral part of the election process. For one's vote, when cast, to be translated into a true message, that vote must be accurately counted, and if necessary, recounted. The moment an individual's vote becomes subject to error in the vote tabulation process, the easier it is for that vote to be diluted.
>
> Furthermore, with voting statistics tracing a decline in voter turnout and in increase in public skepticism, every effort should be made to ensure the integrity of the electoral process.
>
> Integrity is particularly crucial at the tabulation stage because many elections occur in extremely competitive jurisdictions, where very close election results are always possible. In addition, voters and the media expect rapid and accurate tabulation of election returns, regardless of whether the election is close or one sided. Nonetheless, when large numbers of votes are to be counted, it can be expected that some error will occur in tabulation or in canvassing.

Id. at 15 (footnotes omitted). It is with the recognition of these legislative realities and abiding principles that we address whether the trial court made errors of law in rendering its decision.

III. ORDER ON REVIEW

Vice President Gore claims that the trial court erred in the following three ways: (1) The trial court held that an election contest proceeding was essentially an appellate proceeding where the County Canvassing Board's decision must be reviewed with an "abuse of discretion," rather than "de novo," standard of review; (2) The court held that in a contest proceeding in a statewide election a court must review all the ballots cast throughout the state, not just the contested ballots; (3) The court failed to apply the legal standard for relief expressly set forth in section 102.168(3)(c).

A. The Trial Court's Standard of Review

The Florida Election Code sets forth a two-pronged system for challenging vote returns and election procedures. The "protest" and "contest" provisions are distinct proceedings. A protest proceeding is filed with the County Canvassing Board and addresses the validity of the vote returns. The relief that may be granted includes a manual recount. The Canvassing Board is a neutral ministerial body. *See Morse v. Dade County Canvassing Board,* 456 So. 2d 1314 (Fla 3d DCA 1984). A contest proceeding, on the other hand, is filed in circuit court and addresses the validity of the election itself. Relief that may be granted is varied and can be extensive. No appellate relationship exists between a "protest" and a "contest"; a protest is not a prerequisite for a contest. *Cf. Flack v. Carter,* 392 So. 2d 37 (Fla. 1st DCA 1980) (holding that an election protest under section 102.166 was not a condition precedent to an election contest under section 102.168). Moreover, the trial court in the contest action does not sit as an appellate court over the decisions of the Canvassing Board. Accordingly, while the Board's actions concerning the elections process may constitute evidence in a contest proceeding, the Board's decisions are not to be accorded the highly deferential "abuse of discretion" standard of review during a contest proceeding.

In the present case, the trial court erroneously applied an appellate abuse of discretion standard to the Boards' decisions. The trial court's oral order reads in relevant part:

> The local boards have been given broad discretion which no Court may overrule, absent a clear abuse of discretion.

Gore v. Harris, No. 00-2808 (Fla. 2d Cir. Ct. Dec. 4, 2000) [page 56]. The trial court further noted: "The court further finds that the Dade Canvassing Board did not abuse its discretion. . . . The Palm Beach County Board did not abuse its discretion in its review and recounting process."[10] In applying the abuse of discretion standard of review to the Boards' actions, the trial court relinquished an improper degree of its own authority to the Boards. This was error.

B. Must All the Ballots Be Counted Statewide?

Appellees contend that even if a count of the undervotes in Miami-Dade were appropriate, section 102.168, Florida Statutes (2000), requires a count of all votes in Miami-Dade County and the entire state as opposed to a selected number of votes challenged. However, the plain language of section 102.168 refutes Appellees' argument.

10. *Gore v. Harris,* No. 00-2808 (Fla. 2d Cir. Ct. Dec. 4, 2000) [pages 55–56].

Section 102.168(2) sets forth the procedures that must be followed in a contest proceeding, providing that the contestant file a complaint in the circuit court within ten days after certification of the election returns or five days after certification following a protest pursuant to section 102.166(1), whichever occurs later. Section 102.168(3) outlines the grounds for contesting an election, and includes: "Receipt of a number of illegal votes or *rejection of a number of legal votes sufficient to change or place in doubt the result of the election.*" § 102.168(3)(c) (emphasis added). Finally, section 102.168(8) authorizes the circuit court judge to "fashion such orders as he . . . deems necessary to ensure that each allegation in the complaint is investigated, examined, or checked, to prevent or correct any alleged wrong, and to provide any relief appropriate under the circumstances."

As explained above, section 102.168(3)(c) explicitly contemplates contests based upon a "rejection of a number of legal votes sufficient to change the outcome of an election." Logic dictates that to bring a challenge based upon the rejection of a specific number of legal votes under section 102.168(3)(c), the contestant must establish the "number of legal votes" which the county canvassing board failed to count This number, therefore, under the plain language of the statute, is limited to the votes identified and challenged under section 102.168(3)(c), rather than the entire county. Moreover, counting uncontested votes in a contest would be irrelevant to a determination of whether certain uncounted votes constitute legal votes that have been rejected. On the other hand, a consideration of "legal votes" contained in the category of "undervotes" identified statewide may be properly considered as evidence in the contest proceedings and, more importantly, in fashioning any relief.

We do agree, however, that it is absolutely essential in this proceeding and to any final decision, that a manual recount be conducted for all legal votes in this State, not only in Miami-Dade County, but in all Florida counties where there was an undervote, and, hence a concern that not every citizen's vote was counted. This election should be determined by a careful examination of the votes of Florida's citizens and not by strategies extraneous to the voting process. This essential principle, that the outcome of elections be determined by the will of the voters, forms the foundation of the election code enacted by the Florida Legislature and has been consistently applied by this Court in resolving elections disputes.

We are dealing with the essence of the structure of our democratic society; with the interrelationship, within that framework, between the United States Constitution and the statutory scheme established pursuant to that authority by the Florida Legislature. Pursuant to the authority extended by the United States Constitution, in section 103.011, Florida Statutes (2000), the Legislature has expressly vested in the citizens of the State of Florida the right to select the electors for President and Vice President of the United States:

> Electors of President and Vice President, known as presidential electors, shall be elected on the first Tuesday after the first Monday in November of each year the number of which is a multiple of 4. Votes cast for the actual candidates for President and Vice President shall be counted as votes cast for the presidential electors supporting such candidates. The Department of State shall certify as elected the presidential electors of the candidates for President and Vice President who receive the highest number of votes.

Id. In so doing, the Legislature has placed the election of presidential electors squarely in the hands of Florida's voters under the general election laws of Florida.[11] Hence, the Legislature has expressly recognized the will of the people of Florida as the guiding principle for the selection of all elected officials in the State of Florida, whether they be county commissioners or presidential electors.

When an election contest is filed under section 102.168, Florida Statutes (2000), the contest statute charges trial courts to:

> fashion such orders as he or she deems necessary to ensure that each allegation in the complaint is *investigated, examined, or checked,* to prevent or correct any alleged wrong, and to provide any relief appropriate under such circumstances.

Id. (emphasis added). Through this statute, the Legislature has granted trial courts broad authority to resolve election disputes and fashion appropriate relief. In turn, this Court, consistent with legislative policy, has pointed to the "will of the voters" as the primary guiding principle to be utilized by trial courts in resolving election contests:

---

11. In other words, the Legislature has prescribed a single election scheme for local, state and federal elections. The Legislature has not, beyond granting to Florida's voters the right to select presidential electors, indicated in any way that it intended that a different (and unstated) set of election rules should apply to the selection of presidential electors. Of course, because the selection and participation of Florida's electors in the presidential election process is subject to a stringent calendar controlled by federal law, the Florida election law scheme must yield in the event of a conflict.

[T]he real parties in interest here, not in the legal sense but in realistic terms, are the voters. They are possessed of the ultimate interest and it is they whom we must give primary consideration. The contestants have direct interests certainly, but the office they seek is one of high public service and of utmost importance to the people, thus subordinating their interests to that of the people. Ours is a government of, by and for the people. Our federal and state constitutions guarantee the right of the people to take an active part in the process of that government, which for most of our citizens means participation via the election process. The right to vote is the right to participate; it is also the right to speak, but more importantly *the right to be heard.*

Boardman v. Esteva, 323 So. 2d 259, 263 (Fla. 1975) (emphasis added). For example, the Legislature has mandated that no vote shall be ignored "if there is a clear indication of the intent of the voter" on the ballot, unless it is "impossible to determine the elector's choice. . . ." §101.5614(5)–(6) Fla. Stat. (2000). Section 102.166(7), Florida Statutes (2000), also provides that the focus of any manual examination of a ballot shall be to determine the voter's intent. The clear message from this legislative policy is that every citizen's vote be counted whenever possible, whether in an election for a local commissioner or an election for President of the United States.[12]

The demonstrated problem of not counting legal votes inures to any county utilizing a counting system which results in undervotes and "no registered vote" ballots. In a countywide election, one would not simply examine such categories of ballots from a single precinct to insure the reliability and integrity of the countywide vote. Similarly, in this statewide election, review should not be limited to less than all counties whose tabulation has resulted in such categories of ballots. Relief would not be "appropriate under [the] circumstances" if it failed to address the "otherwise valid exercise of the right of a citizen to vote" of all those citizens of this

---

12. In the election contest at issue here, this Court can do no more than see that every citizen's vote be counted. But it can do no less. In a scenario somewhat analogous to that presented here, and in an election contest for a seat in the United States House of Representatives, the contesting candidate sought to *exclude* some 11,000 votes from being counted because the votes were not timely reported to the Secretary of State. *See State ex rel. Chappell v. Martinez,* 536 So. 2d 1007. This Court, in a unanimous opinion authored by Justice McDonald, refused to exclude the votes and held that the contesting candidate "has presented no compelling reason for disenfranchising the 11,000 residents of Flagler County who cast their ballots on November 8." *Id.* at 1009.

State who, being similarly situated, have had their legal votes rejected. This is particularly important in a Presidential election, which implicates both State and uniquely important national interests. The contestant here satisfied the threshold requirement by demonstrating that, upon consideration of the thousands of undervote or "no registered vote" ballots presented, the number of legal votes therein were sufficient to at least place in doubt the result of the election. However, a final decision as to the result of the statewide election should only be determined upon consideration of the legal votes contained within the undervote or "no registered vote" ballots of all Florida counties, as well as the legal votes already tabulated.

C. The Plaintiff's Burden of Proof

It is immediately apparent, in reviewing the trial court's ruling here, that the trial court failed to apply the statutory standard and instead applied an improper standard in determining the contestant's burden under the contest statute. The trial court began its analysis by stating:

> [I]t is well established and reflected in the opinion of Judge Joanos and *Smith v. Tine*[13][sic], that in order to contest election results under Section 102.168 of the Florida Statutes, the Plaintiff must show that, but for the irregularity, or inaccuracy claimed, the result of the election would have been different, and he or she would have been the winner.
>
> It is not enough to show a reasonable possibility that election results could have been altered by such irregularities, or inaccuracies, rather, a reasonable probability that the results of the election would have been changed must be shown.
>
> In this case, there is no credible statistical evidence, and no other competent substantial evidence to establish by a preponderance of a reasonable probability that the results of the statewide election in the State of Florida would be different from the result which has been certified by the State Elections Canvassing Commission.

This analysis overlooks and fails to recognize the specific and material changes to the statute which the Legislature made in 1999 that control

13. *Smith v. Tynes,* 412 So. 2d 925 (Fla. 1st DCA 1982) (involving allegations of enumerated acts asserted to constitute fraud and misrepresentation to the electorate sufficient to produce a different result) (citing *Nelson v. Robinson,* 301 So. 2d 508 (Fla. 2d DCA 1974), *cert. denied,* 303 So. 2d 21 (Fla. 1974) (involving a post-election challenge to a form of ballot which listed the candidates for a single office in alphabetical order using the same color ink, but on different lines)).

these proceedings. While the earlier version, like the current version, provided that a contestant shall file a complaint setting forth "the grounds on which the contestant intends to establish his or her right to such office or set aside the result of the election," the prior version did not specifically enumerate the "grounds for contesting an election under this section." Those grounds, as contained in the 1999 statute, now explicitly include, in subsection (c), the "receipt of a number of illegal votes or rejection of a number of legal votes sufficient to change *or place in doubt* the result of the election." (Emphasis supplied.) Assuming that reasonableness is an implied component of such a doubt standard,[14] the determination of whether the plaintiff has met his or her burden of proof to establish that the result of an election is in doubt is a far different standard than the "reasonable probability" standard, which was applicable to contests under the old version of the statute, and erroneously applied and articulated as a "preponderance of a reasonable probability" standard by the trial court here. A person authorized to contest an election is required to demonstrate that there have been legal votes cast in the election that have not been counted (here characterized as "undervotes" or "no vote registered" ballots) and that available data[15] shows that a number of legal votes would be recovered from the entire pool of the subject ballots which, if cast for the unsuccessful candidate, would change or place in doubt the result of the election. Here, there has been an undisputed showing of the existence of some 9,000 " under votes" in an election contest decided by a margin measured in the hundreds. Thus, a threshold contest showing that the result of an election has been placed in doubt, warranting a manual count of all undervotes or "no vote registered" ballots, has been made.

IV. LEGAL VOTES

Having first identified the proper standard of review, we turn now to the allegations of the complaint filed in this election contest To test the sufficiency of those allegations and the proof, it is essential to understand what, under Florida law, may constitute a "legal vote," and what constitutes rejection of such vote.

Section 101.5614(5), Florida Statutes (2000), provides that "no vote shall be declared invalid or void if there is a clear indication of the intent

14. *Cf. Standard Jury Instructions in Criminal Cases,* 697 So. 2d 84, 90 (Fla. 1997) (approving standard jury instruction regarding "reasonable doubt," which is "not a mere possible doubt, a speculative, imaginary or forced doubt," and which "may arise from the evidence, conflict in the evidence or the lack of evidence").

15. In this case, the circuit court did not review the ballot presented as evidence.

of the voter as determined by the canvassing board." Section 101.5614(6) provides, conversely, that any vote in which the board cannot discern the intent of the voter must be discarded. Lastly, section 102.166(7)(b) provides that, "if a counting team is unable to determine a voter's intent in casting a ballot, the ballot shall be presented to the county canvassing board for it to determine the voter's intent." This legislative emphasis on discerning the voter's intent is mirrored in the case law of this State, and in that of other states.

This Court has repeatedly held, in accordance with the statutory law of this State, that so long as the voter's intent may be discerned from the ballot, the vote constitutes a "legal vote" that should be counted. *See McAlpin v. State ex rel. Avriett,* 155 Fla. 33, 19 So. 2d 420 (1944); *see also State ex rel. Peacock v. Latham,* 125 Fla. 69, 70, 169 So. 597, 598 (1936) (holding that the election contest statute "affords an efficient available remedy and legal procedure by which the circuit court can investigate and determine, not only the legality of the votes cast, but can correct any inaccuracies in the count of the ballots by having them brought into the court and examining the contents of the ballot boxes if properly preserved"). As the State has moved toward electronic voting, nothing in this evolution has diminished the long-standing case law and statutory law that the intent of the voter is of paramount concern and should always be given effect if the intent can be determined. *Cf. Boardman v. Esteva,* 323 So. 2d 259 (Fla. 1975), *cert. denied,* 425 U.S. 967 (1976) (recognizing the overarching principle that, where voters do all that statutes require them to do, they should not be disfranchised solely because of failure of election officials to follow directory statutes).

Not surprisingly, other states also have recognized this principle. *Cf. Delahunt v. Johnston,* 423 Mass. 731, 671 N.E.2d 1241 (Mass. 1996) (holding that a vote should be counted as a legal vote if it properly indicates the voter's intent with reasonable certainty); *Duffy v. Mortenson,* 497 N.W.2d 437 (S.D. 1993) (applying the rule that every marking found where a vote should be should be treated as an intended vote in the absence of clear evidence to the clear contrary); *Pullen v. Mulligan,* 138 Ill. 2d 21, 561 N.E.2d 585, 149 Ill. Dec. 215 (Ill. 1990) (holding that votes could be recounted by manual means to the extent that the voter's intent could be determined with reasonable certainty, despite the existence of a statute which provided that punch card ballots were to be recounted by automated tabulation equipment).

Accordingly, we conclude that a legal vote is one in which there is a "clear indication of the intent of the voter." We next address whether the term "rejection" used in section 102.168(3)(c) includes instances where the County Canvassing Board has not counted legal votes. Looking at the statutory scheme as a whole, it appears that the term "rejected" does encompass votes that may exist but have not been counted. As explained above, in 1999, the Legislature substantially revised the contest provision of the Election Code. *See* H.R. Comm. on Election Reform, HB 281 (February 3, 1999). One of the revisions to the contest provision included the codification of the grounds for contesting an election. See *id.* at 7. The House Bill noted that one of the grounds for contesting an election at common law was the "Receipt of a number of illegal votes or rejection of a number of legal votes sufficient to change or place in doubt the result of the election." As noted above, the contest statute ultimately contained this ground for contesting the results of an election.

To further determine the meaning of the term "rejection", as used by the Legislature, we may also look to Florida case law. In *State ex rel. Clark v. Klingensmith,* 121 Fla. 297, 163 So. 704 (1935), an individual who lost an election brought an action for quo warranto challenging his opponent's right to hold office. The challenger challenged twenty-two ballots, which he divided into four groups. One of these groups included three ballots that the challenger claimed had not been counted. *See* 121 Fla. at 298, 163 So. at 705. This Court concluded that "the *rejection* of votes from legal voters, not brought about by fraud, and not of such magnitude as to demonstrate that a free expression of the popular will has been suppressed," is insufficient to void an election, "at least unless it be shown that the votes rejected would have changed the result." 121 Fla. at 300, 163 So. at 705. Therefore, the Court appears to have equated a "rejection" of legal votes with the failure to count legal votes, while at the same time recognizing that a sufficient number of such votes must have been rejected to merit relief This notion of "rejected" is also in accordance with the common understanding of rejection of votes as used in other election cases. In discussing the facts in *Roudebush v. Hartke,* 405 U.S. 15 (1972), the United States Supreme Court explained:

> If a recount is conducted in any county, the voting machine tallies are checked and the sealed bags containing the paper ballots are opened. The recount commission may make new and independent determinations as to which ballots shall be counted. In other words, it may reject ballots initially counted and count ballots initially rejected. *Id.*

This also comports with cases from other jurisdictions that suggest that a legal vote will be deemed to have been "rejected" where a voting machine fails to count a ballot, which has been executed in substantial compliance with applicable voting requirements and reflects, the clear intent of the voter to express a definite choice. See *In re Matter of the Petition of Katy Gray-Sadler*, 164 N.J. 468, 753 A.2d 1101, 1105–06 (N.J. 2000); *Moffat v. Bleiman*, 142 N.J. Super. 217, 361 A.2d 74, 77 (N.J. Super. Ct. App. Div. 1976).

Here, then, it is apparent that there have been sufficient allegations made which, if analyzed pursuant to the proper standard, compel the conclusion that legal votes sufficient to place in doubt the election results have been rejected in this case.

V. THIS CASE

We must review the instances in which appellants claim that they established that legal votes were rejected or illegal voters were included in the certifications.

The refusal to review approximately 9,000 additional Miami-Dade Ballots, which the counting machine registered as non-votes and which have never been manually reviewed.

On November 9, 2000, the Miami-Dade County Democratic Party made a timely request under section 102.166 for a manual recount.[16] After first deciding against a full manual recount, the Miami-Dade County Canvassing Board voted to begin a manual recount of all ballots cast in Miami-Dade County for the Presidential election, and the manual recount began on November 19, 2000. On November 21, 2000, this Court issued its decision in *Palm Beach Canvassing Board v. Harris* (Fla. Nov. 21, 2000) [pages {000}–{000}], stating that amended certifications must be filed by 5 p.m. on Sunday, November 26, 2000. The Miami-Dade Canvassing Board thereafter suspended the manual recount and voted to use the election returns previously compiled. Earlier that day, the panel had decided to limit its recount to the 10,750 "undervotes," that is, ballots on which no vote was registered by counting machines. The Board's stated reason for the suspension of the manual recount was that it would be impossible to complete the recount before the deadline set forth by this Court. At the time that

16. On November 9, 2000, a manual recount was requested on behalf of Vice-President Gore in four counties—Miami-Dade, Broward, Palm Beach and Volusia. Broward County and Volusia County timely completed a manual recount. It is undisputed that the results of the manual recounts in Volusia County and Broward County were included in the statewide certifications.

the Board suspended the recount, approximately 9,000 of the 10,750 undervotes had not yet been reviewed. In the two days that the Board had counted ballots, the Board identified 436 additional legal votes (from 20 percent of the precincts, representing 15 percent of the votes cast) which the machines failed to register, resulting in a net vote of 168 votes for Gore. Nonetheless, in addition to suspending further recounting, the Board also determined that it would not include the additional 436 votes that had been tabulated in its partially completed recount.

Specifically as to Miami-Dade County, the trial court found:

> [A]lthough the record shows voter error, and/or less than total accuracy in regard to the punchcard voting devices utilized in Miami-Dade and Palm Beach Counties, which these counties have been aware of for many years, these balloting and counting problems cannot support or effect any recounting necessity with respect to Miami-Dade County, absent the establishment of a reasonable probability that the statewide election result would be different, which has not been established in this case.

The Court further finds that the Dade Canvassing Board did not abuse its discretion in any of its decisions in its review in [*Eds.*: for *in* read *and*] recounting processes [page 55]. This statement is incorrect as a matter of law. In fact, as the Third District determined in *Miami-Dade County Democratic Party v. Miami-Dade County Canvassing Board*, 25 Fla. L. Weekly D2723 (Fla. 3d DCA Nov. 22, 2000), the results of the sample manual recount and the actual commencement of the full manual recount triggered the Canvassing Board's "mandatory obligation to recount all of the ballots in the county." In addition, the circuit court was bound at the time it ruled to follow this appellate decision. This Court has determined the decisions of the district courts of appeal represent the law of this State unless and until they are overruled by this Court, and therefore, in the absence of interdistrict conflict, district court decisions bind all Florida trial courts. *See Pardo v. State*, 596 So. 2d 665, 666 (Fla. 1992).

However, regardless of this error, we again note the focus of the trial court's inquiry in an election contest authorized by the Legislature pursuant to the express statutory provisions of section 102.168 is not by appellate review to determine whether the Board properly or improperly failed to complete the manual recount. Rather, as expressly set out in section 102.168, the court's responsibility is to determine whether "legal votes" were rejected sufficient to change or place in doubt the results of the election. Without ever examining or investigating the ballots that the machine failed to register as a vote, the trial court in this case concluded that there was no probability of a different result. First, as we stated the trial court erred as a matter of law in utilizing the wrong standard. Second, and more importantly, by failing to examine the specifically identified group of uncounted ballots that is claimed to contain the rejected legal votes, the trial court has refused to address the issue presented. Appellants have also been denied the very evidence that they have relied on to establish their ultimate entitlement to relief.[17] The trial court has presented the plaintiffs with the ultimate Catch-22, acceptance of the only evidence that will resolve the issue but a refusal to examine such evidence. We also note that whether or not the Board could have completed the manual recount by November 26, 2000, or whether the Board should have fulfilled its responsibility and completed the full manual recount it commenced, the fact remains that the manual recount was not completed through no fault of the Appellant.[18]

3300 Votes in Palm Beach County

Appellants also contend that the trial court erred in finding that they failed to satisfy their burden of proof with respect to the 3300 votes that the Palm Beach County Canvassing Board reviewed and concluded did not constitute "legal votes" pursuant to section 102.168(3)(c). However, unlike the approximately 9000 ballots in Miami-Dade that the County Canvassing Board did not manually recount, the Palm Beach County Canvassing Board did complete a manual recount of these 3300 votes and concluded that, because the intent of the voter in these 3300 ballots was not discernible, these

17. The Miami-Dade Canvassing Board stated as its reasons that it stopped an ongoing manual recount because it determined that it could not meet this Court's certification deadline. However, nothing in this Court's prior opinion nor the statutory scheme governing manual recounts would have prevented the Board from continuing after certification the manual recount that it had properly started. The Canvassing Board is a neutral ministerial body. See *Morse v. Dade County Canvassing Board*, 456 So. 2d 1314 (Fla. 3d DCA 1984). Therefore, although the Board may have acted in a neutral fashion, the fact remains that three other Boards (Broward, Palm Beach and Volusia) completed the recounts.

18. On Thanksgiving Day, November 23, 2000, an Emergency Petition for Writ for Mandamus was filed in which Gore sought to compel the Miami-Dade Canvassing Board to continue with the manual recount. Although we denied relief on that same day, in our order denying this relief, the Court specifically stated that the denial was "without prejudice to any party raising any issue presented in the writ in any future proceeding." Accordingly, at the time that we denied mandamus relief we clearly contemplated that this claim could be raised in a contest action.

ballots did not constitute "legal votes." After a two-day trial in this case, the circuit court concluded:

[W]ith respect to the approximately 3,300 Palm Beach County ballots of which plaintiffs seek review, the Palm Beach Board properly exercised its discretion in its counting process and has judged those ballots which plaintiffs wish this court to again judge de novo. . . . The Palm Beach County board did not abuse its discretion in its review and recounting process. Further, it acted in full compliance with the order of the circuit court in and for Palm Beach County [pages 55–56].

We find no error in the trial court's determination that appellants did not establish a preliminary basis for relief as to the 3300 Palm Beach County votes because the appellants have failed to make a threshold showing that "legal votes" were rejected. Although the protest and contest proceedings are separate statutory provisions, when a manual count of ballots has been conducted by the Canvassing Board pursuant to section 102.166, the circuit court in a contest proceeding does not have the obligation de novo to simply repeat an otherwise-proper manual count of the ballots. As stated above, although the trial court does not review a Canvassing Board's actions under an abuse of discretion standard, the Canvassing Board's actions may constitute evidence that a ballot does or does not qualify as a legal vote. Because the appellants have failed to introduce any evidence to refute the Canvassing Board's determination that the 3300 ballots did not constitute "legal votes," we affirm the trial court's holding as to this issue. This reflects the proper interaction of section 102.166 governing protests and manual recounts and section 102.168 governing election contests.

Whether the vote totals must be revised to include the legal votes actually identified in the Palm Beach County and Miami-Dade County manual recounts?

Appellants claim that the certified vote totals must be amended to include legal votes identified as being for one of the presidential candidates by the County Canvassing Boards of Palm Beach County and Miami-Dade during their manual recounts. After working for a period of many days, the Palm Beach County Canvassing Board conducted and completed a full manual recount in which the Board identified a net gain of 215 votes for Gore.[19] As discussed above, the Miami-Dade Canvassing Board commenced a manual recount but did not complete the recount. During the

19. Bush asserted that the audited total is 176 votes.

partial recount it identified an additional legal votes, of which 302 were for Gore and 134 were for Bush, resulting in a net gain of 168 votes for Gore.

The circuit court concluded as to Palm Beach County that there was not any "authority to include any returns submitted past the deadline established by the Florida Supreme Court in this election." This conclusion was erroneous as a matter of law. The deadline of November 26, 2000, at 5 p.m. was established in order to allow maximum time for contests pursuant to section 102.168. The deadline was never intended to prohibit legal votes identified after that date through ongoing manual recounts to be excluded from the statewide official results in the Election Canvassing Commission's certification of the results of a recount of less than all of a county's ballots. In the same decision we held that all returns must be considered unless their filing would effectively prevent an election contest from being conducted or endanger the counting of Florida's electors in the presidential election. As to Miami-Dade County, in light of our holding that the circuit court should have counted the undervote, we agree with appellants that the partial recount results should also be included in the total legal votes for this election. Because the county canvassing boards identified legal votes and these votes could change the outcome of the election, we hold that the trial court erred in rejecting the legal votes identified in the Miami-Dade County and Palm Beach County manual recounts. These votes must be included in the certified vote totals. We find that appellants did not establish that the Nassau County Canvassing Board acted improperly.

CONCLUSION

Through no fault of appellants, a lawfully commenced manual recount in Dade County was never completed and recounts that were completed were not counted. Without examining or investigating the ballots that were not counted by the machines, the trial court concluded there was no reasonable probability of a different result. However, the proper standard required by section 102.168 was whether the results of the election were placed in doubt. On this record there can be no question that there are legal votes within the 9000 uncounted votes sufficient to place the results of this election in doubt. We know this not only by evidence of statistical analysis but also by the actual experience of recounts conducted. The votes for each candidate that have been counted are separated by no more than approximately 500 votes and may be separated by as little as approximately 100 votes. Thousands of uncounted votes could obviously make a difference. Although in all elections the Legislature and the courts have recognized that the voter's intent is paramount, in close elections the necessity for counting all legal votes becomes critical. However, the need for accuracy must be weighed against the need for finality. The need for prompt resolution and finality is especially critical in presidential elections where there is an outside deadline established by federal law. Notwithstanding, consistent with the legislative mandate and our precedent, although the time constraints are limited, we must do everything required by law to ensure that legal votes that have not been counted are included in the final election results.[20] As recognized by the Florida House of Representatives Committee on Election Reform 1997 Interim Project on Election Contests and Recounts:

> [A]ll election contests and recounts can be traced to either an actual failure in the election system or a perception that the system has failed. Public confidence in the election process is essential to our democracy. *If the voter cannot be assured of an accurate vote count,* or an election unspoiled by fraud, *they will not have faith in other parts of the political process.* Nonetheless, it is inevitable that legitimate doubts of the validity and accuracy of election outcomes will arise. It is crucial, therefore, to have clearly defined legal mechanisms for contesting or recounting election results.

Id. at 21 (emphasis supplied) (footnote omitted).

Only by examining the contested ballots, which are evidence in the election contest, can a meaningful and final determination in this election contest be made. As stated above, one of the provisions of the contest statute, section 102.168(8), provides that the circuit court judge may "fashion such orders as he . . . deems *necessary to ensure that each allegation in the complaint* is investigated, *examined* or checked, to prevent any alleged wrong, and to provide any *relief appropriate under such circumstances.* (emphasis supplied).

In addition to the relief requested by appellants to count the Miami-Dade undervote, claims have been made by the various appellees and intervenors that because this is a statewide election, statewide remedies would be called

20. This Presidential election has demonstrated the vulnerability of what we believe to be a bedrock principle of democracy: that every vote counts. While there are areas in this State which implement systems (such as the optical scanner) where the margins of error, and the ability to demonstrably verify those margins of error, are consistent with accountability in our democratic process, in these election contests based upon allegations that functioning punch-card voting machines have failed to record legal votes, the demonstrated margins of error may be so great to suggest that it is necessary to reevaluate utilization of the mechanisms employed as a viable system.

for. As we discussed in this opinion, we agree. While we recognize that time is desperately short, we cannot in good faith ignore both the appellant's right to relief as to their claims concerning the uncounted votes in Miami-Dade County nor can we ignore the correctness of the assertions that any analysis and ultimate remedy should be made on a statewide basis.[21]

We note that contest statutes vest broad discretion in the circuit court to "provide any relief appropriate under the circumstances." Section 102.168(5). Moreover, because venue of an election contest that covers more than one county lies in Leon County, see 102.1685, Florida Statutes (2000), the circuit court has jurisdiction, as part of the relief it orders, to order the Supervisor of Elections and the Canvassing Boards, as well as the necessary public officials, in all counties that have not conducted a manual recount or tabulation of the undervotes in this election to do so forthwith, said tabulation to take place in the individual counties where the ballots are located.[22]

Accordingly, for the reasons stated in this opinion, we reverse the final judgment of the trial court dated December 4, 2000, and remand this cause for the circuit court to immediately tabulate by hand the approximate 9000 Miami-Dade ballots, which the counting machine registered as non-votes, but which have never been manually reviewed, and for other relief that may thereafter appear appropriate. The circuit court is directed to enter such orders as are necessary to add any legal votes to the total statewide certifications and to enter any orders necessary to ensure the inclusion of the ad-

21. The dissents would have us throw up our hands and say that because of looming deadlines and practical difficulties we should give up any attempt to have the election of the presidential electors rest upon the vote of Florida citizens as mandated by the Legislature. While we agree that practical difficulties may well end up controlling the outcome of the election we vigorously disagree that we should therefore abandon our responsibility to resolve this election dispute under the rule of law. We can only do the best we can to carry out our sworn responsibilities to the justice system and its role in this process. We, and our dissenting colleagues, have simply done the best we can, and remain confident that others charged with similar heavy responsibilities will also do the best they can to fulfill their duties as they see them.

22. We are mindful of the fact that due to the time constraints, the count of the undervotes places demands on the public servants throughout the State to work over this week-end. However, we are confident that with the cooperation of the officials in all the counties, the remaining undervotes in these counties can be accomplished within the required time frame. We note that public officials in many counties have worked diligently over the past thirty days in dealing with exigencies that have occurred because of this unique historical circumstance arising from the presidential election of 2000. We commend those dedicated public servants for attempting to make this election process truly reflect the vote of all Floridians.

ditional legal votes for Gore in Palm Beach County[23] and the 168 additional legal votes from Miami-Dade County.

Because time is of the essence, the circuit court shall commence the tabulation of the Miami-Dade ballots immediately. The circuit court is authorized, in accordance with the provisions of section 102.168(8), to be assisted by the Leon County Supervisor of Elections or its sworn designees. Moreover, since time is also of the essence in any statewide relief that the circuit court must consider, any further statewide relief should also be ordered forthwith and simultaneously with the manual tabulation of the Miami-Dade undervotes.

In tabulating the ballots and in making a determination of what is a "legal" vote, the standards to be employed is that established by the Legislature in our Election Code which is that the vote shall be counted as a "legal" vote if there is "clear indication of the intent of the voter." Section 101.5614(5), Florida Statutes (2000).

It is so ordered.

Justices Anstead, Pariente, Lewis, and Quince concur.
Chief Justice Wells dissents with an opinion.
Justice Harding dissents with an opinion, in which Justice Shaw concurs.

NO MOTION FOR REHEARING WILL BE ALLOWED.

Chief Justice Wells dissenting.

I join Justice Harding's dissenting opinion except as to his conclusions with regard to error by Judge Sauls and his conclusions as to the separateness of section 102.166 and 102.168, Florida Statutes (2000). I write separately to state my additional conclusions and concerns.

I want to make it clear at the outset of my separate opinion that I do not question the good faith or honorable intentions of my colleagues in the majority. However, I could not more strongly disagree with their decision to reverse the trial court and prolong this judicial process. I also believe that the majority's decision cannot withstand the scrutiny which will certainly immediately follow under the United States Constitution.

My succinct conclusion is that the majority's decision to return this case to the circuit court for a count of the under-votes from either Miami-Dade County or all counties has no foundation in the law of Florida as it existed on November 7, 2000, or at any time until the issuance of this opinion. The majority returns the case to the circuit court for this partial recount of un-

---

23. *See* discussion *supra* note 6.

der-votes on the basis of unknown or, at best, ambiguous standards with
authority to obtain help from others, the credentials, qualifications, and ob-
jectivity of whom are totally unknown. That is but a first glance at the im-
ponderable problems the majority creates.

Importantly to me, I have a deep and abiding concern that the prolonging of judicial process in this counting contest propels this country and
this state into an unprecedented and unnecessary constitutional crisis. I
have to conclude that there is a real and present likelihood that this constitutional crisis will do substantial damage to our country, our state, and
to this Court as an institution.

On the basis of my analysis of Florida law as it existed on November 7,
2000, I conclude that the trial court's decision can and should be affirmed.
Under our law, of course, a decision of a trial court reaching a correct result will be affirmed if it is supportable under any theory, even if an appellate court disagrees with the trial court's reasoning. *Dade County School
Bd. v. Radio Station WQBA*, 731 So. 2d 638, 644–45 (Fla. 1999). I conclude that there are more than enough theories to support this trial court's
decision. There are two fundamental and historical principles of Florida
law that this Court has recognized which are relevant here. First, at common law, there was no right to contest an election; thus, any right to contest an election must be construed to grant only those rights that are explicitly set forth by the Legislature. *See McPherson v. Flynn*, 397 So. 2d 665,
668 (Fla. 1981). In *Flynn*, we held that, "at common law, except for limited application of quo warranto, there was no right to contest in court any
public election, because such a contest is political in nature and therefore
outside the judicial power." *Id.* at 667. Second, this Court gives deference
to decisions made by executive officials charged with implementing
Florida's election laws. See *Krivanek v. Take Back Tampa Political Committee*, 625 So. 2d 840 (Fla 1993). In *Krivanek,* we said:

> We acknowledge that election laws should generally be liberally
> construed in favor of an elector. However, the judgment of officials
> duly charged with carrying out the election process should be pre-
> sumed correct if reasonable and not in derogation of the law. *Board-
> man v. Esteva*, 323 So. 2d 259 (Fla. 1975), *cert. denied*, 425 U.S. 967
> (1976). As noted in *Boardman:*
>
>> The election process is subject to legislative prescription and
>> constitutional command and is committed to the executive
>> branch of government through duly designated officials all

charged with specific duties. . . . [The] judgments [of those officials] are entitled to be regarded by the courts as presumptively correct and if rational and not clearly outside legal requirements should be upheld rather than substituted by the impression a particular judge or panel of judges might deem more appropriate. It is certainly the intent of the constitution and the legislature that the results of elections are to be efficiently, honestly and promptly ascertained by election officials to whom some latitude of judgment is accorded, and that courts are to overturn such determinations only for compelling reasons when there are clear, substantial departures from essential requirements of law.

Id. at 844–45 (alterations in original). These two concepts are the foundation of my analysis of the present case.

At the outset, I note that, after an evidentiary hearing, the trial court expressly found no dishonesty, gross negligence, improper influence, coercion, or fraud in the balloting and counting processes based upon the evidence presented. I conclude this finding should curtail this Court's involvement in this election through this case and is a substantial basis for affirming the trial court. Historically, this Court has only been involved in elections when there have been substantial allegations of fraud and then only upon a high threshold because of the chill that a hovering judicial involvement can put on elections. This to me is the import of this Court's decision in *Boardman v. Esteva*, 323 So. 2d 259 (Fla. 1975). We lowered that threshold somewhat in *Beckstrom v. Volusia County Canvassing Board*, 707 So. 2d 720 (Fla. 1998), but we continued to require a substantial noncompliance with election laws. That must be the very lowest threshold for a court's involvement. Otherwise, we run a great risk that every election will result in judicial testing. Judicial restraint in respect to elections is absolutely necessary because the health of our democracy depends on elections being decided by voters— not by judges. We must have the self-discipline not to become embroiled in political contests whenever a judicial majority subjectively concludes to do so because the majority perceives it is "the right thing to do." Elections involve the other branches of government. A lack of self-discipline in being involved in elections, especially by a court of last resort, always has the potential of leading to a crisis with the other branches of government and raises serious separation-of-powers concerns.

I find that the trial judge correctly concluded that plaintiffs were not entitled to a manual recount. Petitioners filed this current election contest after protests in Palm Beach and Miami-Dade Counties. Section 102.168, Florida Statutes, in its present form is a new statute adopted by the Legislature in 1999. I conclude that the present statutory scheme contemplates that protests of returns[24] and requests for manual recounts[25] are first to be presented to the county canvassing boards. See § 102.166, Fla. Stat. This naturally follows from the fact that, even with the adoption of the 1999 amendments to section 102.168, the only procedures for manual recounts are in the protest statute. Once a protest has been filed, a county canvassing board then has the discretion, in accordance with the procedures set forth in section 102.166(4), Florida Statutes, whether to order a sample limited manual recount. See § 102.166(4)(c), Fla. Stat. (2000). Once the sample recount is complete and the county canvassing board concludes that there was an error in the vote tabulation that could affect the outcome of the election, section 102.166(5) instructs what must then be done. One option is to manually recount all ballots. See § 102.166(5)(c), Fla. Stat. (2000).[26]

I believe that the contest and protest statutes must logically be read together. The contest statute has significant references to the protest statute. If there is a protest, a party authorized by the statute to file a contest must file a complaint "within 5 days after midnight of the date the last county canvassing board empowered to canvass the returns certifies the results of that particular election following a protest pursuant to s. 102.166(1)." § 102.168(2), Fla. Stat. (2000). In the election contest, the canvassing board is the proper party defendant under section 102.168(4). Further, under section 102.168(8), the circuit judge to whom the contest is presented may fashion such orders as he or she deems necessary to ensure that the allegations upon which the complaint is brought are investigated, examined, or checked.

24. See § 102.166(1), Fla. Stat. (2000).
25. See § 102.166(4)(b), Fla. Stat. (2000).
26. Also problematic with the majority's analysis is that the majority only requires that the "under-votes" are to be counted. How about the "over-votes?" Section 101.5614(6) provides that a ballot should not be counted "if an elector marks more names than there are persons to be elected to an office," meaning the voter voted for more than one person for president. The underlying premise of the majority's rationale is that in such a close race a manual review of ballots rejected by the machines is necessary to ensure that all legal votes cast are counted. The majority, however, ignores the over-votes. Could it be said, without reviewing the over-votes, that the machine did not err in not counting them?

It seems patently erroneous to me to assume that the vote-counting machines can err when reading under-votes but not err when reading over-votes. Can the majority say, without having the over-votes looked at, that there are no legal votes among the over-votes?

I find correct the analysis undertaken in *Broward County Canvassing Board v. Hogan*, 607 So. 2d 508 (Fla. 4th DCA 1992), a case recently cited by this Court in *Palm Beach County Canvassing Board v. Harris* (Fla. Nov. 21, 2000). In *Hogan*, the Fourth District Court of Appeal reversed the trial court's order granting a manual recount, in contravention of the county canvassing board's decision noting that:

> Although section 102.168 grants the right of contest, it does not change the discretionary aspect of the review procedures outlined in section 102.166. The statute clearly leaves the decision whether or not to hold a manual recount of the votes as a matter to be decided within the discretion of the canvassing board.

Id. at 510. I do not believe there is any sound reason to conclude that the Legislature's adoption of revised section 102.168 in 1999 intended to change this and provide for a duplicative recount by an individual circuit judge.

I also agree with the trial judge's conclusion that in a statewide election the only way a court can order a manual recount of ballots that were allegedly not counted because of some irregularity or inaccuracy in the balloting or counting process is to order that the votes in all counties in which those processes were used be recounted. I do not find any legal basis for the majority of this Court to simply cast aside the determination by the trial judge made on the proof presented at a two-day evidentiary hearing that the evidence did not support a statewide recount. To the contrary, I find the majority's decision in that regard quite extraordinary.

Section 102.168(3), Florida Statues (2000), states in pertinent part:

> The *grounds* for contesting an election under this section are:
> . . .
> (c) Receipt of a number of illegal votes or rejection of a number of legal votes sufficient to change or place in doubt the result of the election.

(Emphasis added.) In other words, to establish a cause of action, plaintiff must allege an irregularity that places in doubt the result of the election. First, to "contest" simply means to challenge. *See Webster's Dictionary* 250 (10th ed. 1994). Second, section 102.168(5), provides:

> A statement of the *grounds of contest* may not be rejected, nor the proceedings dismissed, by the court for any want of form if the grounds of contest provided in the statement *are sufficient to clearly inform the defendant of the particular proceeding or cause for which the nomination or election is* contested.

(Emphasis added.) Upon my reading of the statute, I conclude that the language "grounds of contest" unambiguously means: a basis upon which a plaintiff can establish a cause of action. This standard is simply the threshold that must be met to bring forth the contest action. Thus, this standard is *not* the standard that the judge must use in deciding whether a plaintiff who brings the contest has *successfully* met his or her burden to order a recount or set aside election results. Although it is unclear from case law what standard must be satisfied in order to grant appropriate relief, it undoubtedly cannot be a low standard. Recently, in *Beckstrom*, this Court declined to invalidate an election despite a finding that the canvassing board was grossly negligent and in substantial noncompliance with the absentee voting statutes. See *Beckstrom*. Thus, merely stating the cause of action under the contest statute does not entitle a party to a recount or require the court to set aside an election. More must be required. This is especially true here, where, as in *Beckstrom*, the trial judge found no dishonesty, gross negligence, improper influence, coercion, or fraud in the balloting and counting processes. Thus, a plaintiff's burden in establishing grounds on which a circuit judge could order relief of any kind was simply not met. It is illogical to interpret section 102.168(3)(c) to set such a low standard where a plaintiff merely has to allege a cause of action to successfully carry the contest.[27]

Furthermore, even conceding that the trial judge at the outset applied an erroneous "probability of doubt" standard in deciding that plaintiffs failed to meet their burden of establishing a cause of action, the trial judge faced a conundrum that must be adequately explained. Plaintiffs asked the trial judge to grant the very remedy—a recount of the undervotes—they prayed for without first establishing that remedy was warranted. Before any relief is granted, a plaintiff must allege that enough legal votes were rejected to place in doubt the results of the election. However, in order for the plaintiffs to meet this burden, the under-vote ballots must be preliminarily manually recounted. Following this logic to its conclusion would require a circuit court to order partial manual recounts upon the mere filing of a contest. This proposition plainly has no basis in law.

As I have stated, I conclude in the case at bar that sections 102.166 and 106.168 must be read in pari materia. My analysis in this regard is bolstered

27. In addition, under a protest the threshold that must be met to order a recount must be lower than that under a contest, which action can only be brought after certification of the returns. Therefore, the threshold to successfully carry a contest must be higher than that of a mere protest.

in situations, as here, where there was an initial protest filed in a county pursuant to section 102.166 and a subsequent contest of that same county's return pursuant to section 102.168. It appears logical to me that a circuit judge in a section 102.168 contest should review a county canvassing board's determinations in a section 102.166 protest under an abuse-of-discretion standard. I see no other reason why the county canvassing board would be a party defendant if the circuit court is not intended to evaluate the canvassing board's decisions with respect to manual recount decisions made in a section 102.166 protest. Finally, it is plain to me that it is only in section 102.166 that there are any procedures for manual recounts which address the logistics of a recount, including who is to conduct the count, that it is to take place in public, and what is to be recounted.[28]

The majority quotes section 101.5614(5) for the proposition of settling how a county canvassing board should count a vote. The majority states that "no vote shall be declared invalid or void if there is a clear indication of the intent of the voter as determined by the canvassing board." §101.5614(5), Fla. Stat. (2000). Section 101.5614(5), however, is a statute that authorizes the creation of a duplicate ballot where a "ballot card . . . is damaged or defective so that it cannot properly be counted by the automatic tabulating equipment." There is no basis in this record that suggests that the approximately 9000 ballots from Miami-Dade County were damaged or defective.

Laying aside this problem and assuming the majority is correct that section 101.5614(5) correctly annunciates the standard by which a county canvassing board should judge a questionable ballot, section 101.5614(5) utterly fails to provide any meaningful standard. There is no doubt that every vote should be counted where there is a "clear indication of the intent of the voter." The problem is how a county canvassing board translates that directive to these punch cards. Should a county canvassing board count or not count a "dimpled chad" where the voter is able to successfully dislodge the chad in every other contest on that ballot? Here, the county canvassing boards disagree. Apparently, some do and some do not. Continuation of this system of county-by-county decisions regarding how a dimpled chad is counted is fraught with equal protection concerns which will even-

---

28. I am persuaded that even with these procedures manual recounts by the canvassing board are constitutionally suspect. See *Touchston v. McDermott*, No. 00-15985 (U.S. 11th Cir. Dec. 6, 2000) (Tjoflat, J., dissenting). This would be compounded by giving that power to an individual circuit judge and providing him or her, with no standards.

tually cause the election results in Florida to be stricken by the federal courts or Congress.[29]

Based upon this analysis and adhering to the interpretation of the 1992 *Hogan* case, I conclude the circuit court properly looked at what the county canvassing boards have done and found that they did not abuse their discretion, Regarding Miami-Dade County, I find that the trial judge properly concluded that the Miami-Dade Canvassing Board did not abuse its discretion in deciding to discontinue the manual recount begun on November 19, 2000. Evidence presented at trial indicated that the Miami-Dade Board made three different decisions in respect to manual recounts. The first decision was not to count, the second was to count, and the third was not to count. The third decision was based upon the determination by the Miami-Dade Board that it could not make the November 26,2000, deadline set by this Court in *Harris* and that it did not want to jeopardize disenfranchising a segment of its voters. The law does not require futile acts. See *Haimovitz v. Robb,* 130 Fla. 844; 178 So. 827 (1937). Section 102.166(5)(c) *requires that, if there is a manual recount, all of the ballots have to be recounted.* I cannot find that the Miami-Dade Board's decision that *all* the ballots could not be manually recounted between November 22 and November 26, 2000, to be anything but a decision based upon reality. Moreover, not to count all of the ballots if any were to be recounted would plainly be changing the rules after the election and would be unfairly discriminatory against votes in the precincts in which there was no manual recount. Thus, I agree with the trial court that the Miami-Dade Board did not abuse its discretion in discontinuing the manual recount.

In respect to the Palm Beach County Canvassing Board, I likewise find that the trial judge did not err in finding that the Palm Beach Board was within its discretion in rejecting the approximately 3300 votes in which it could not discern voter intent. As set forth in *Boardman,* the county canvassing boards are vested with the responsibility to make judgments on the validity of ballots, and its determinations will be overturned *only* for compelling reasons when there are clear, substantial departures from essential requirements of law. See *Boardman,* 323 So. 2d at 268 n 5. Petitioners have not met this burden.

I also agree with the trial judge that the Election Canvassing Commission (Commission) did not abuse its discretion in refusing to accept either an amended return reflecting the results of a partial manual recount or a late amended return filed by the Palm Beach Board. I conclude that it is

29. *See supra* note 28.

plain error for the majority to hold that the Commission abused its discretion in enforcing a deadline set by this Court that recounts be completed and certified by November 26, 2000. I conclude that this not only changes a rule after November 7, 2000, but it also changes a rule this Court made on November 26, 2000.

As I stated at the outset, I conclude that this contest simply must end. Directing the trial court to conduct a manual recount of the ballots violates article II, section 1, clause 2 of the United States Constitution, in that neither this Court nor the circuit court has the authority to create the standards by which it will count the under-voted ballots. The Constitution reads in pertinent part: "Each State shall appoint, in such Manner as the Legislature thereof may direct, a Number of Electors." Art. II, § 1, cl. 2, U.S. Const. The Supreme Court has described this authority granted to the state legislatures as "plenary." See *McPherson v. Blacker*, 146 U.S. 1, 7 (1892). "Plenary" is defined as "full, entire, complete, absolute, perfect, [and] unqualified." *Black's Law Dictionary* 1154 (6th ed. 1990).

The Legislature has given to the county canvassing boards—and only these boards—the authority to ascertain the intent of the voter. *See* §102.166(7)(b), Fla. Stat. (2000). Just this week, the United States Supreme Court reminded us of the teachings from Blacker when it said:

> "[Art. II, § 1, cl. 2] does not read that the people or the citizens shall appoint, but that 'each State shall'; and if the words 'in such manner as the legislature thereof may direct,' had been omitted, it would seem that the legislative power of appointment could not have been successfully questioned in the absence of any provision in the state constitution in that regard. Hence the insertion of those words, while operating as a limitation upon the State in respect of any attempt to circumscribe the legislative power, cannot be held to operate as a limitation on that power itself."

Bush v. Palm Beach Canvassing Bd. (U.S. Dec. 4, 2000) [pages 50–51] (quoting *Blacker*, 146 U.S. at 25). Clearly, in a presidential election, the Legislature has not authorized the courts of Florida to order partial recounts, either in a limited number of counties or statewide. This Court's order to do so appears to me to be in conflict with the United States Supreme Court decision.

Laying aside the constitutional infirmities of this Court's action today, what the majority actually creates is an overflowing basket of practical problems. Assuming the majority recognizes a need to protect the votes of

Florida's presidential electors,[30] the entire contest must be completed "at least six days before" December 18, 2000, the date the presidential electors meet to vote. *See* 3 U.S.C. § 5 (1994). The safe harbor deadline day is December 12, 2000. Today is Friday, December 8, 2000. Thus, under the majority's time line, all manual recounts must be completed in five days, assuming the counting begins today.

In that time frame, all questionable ballots must be reviewed by the judicial officer appointed to discern the intent of the voter in a process open to the public.[31] Fairness dictates that a provision be made for either party to object to how a particular ballot is counted. Additionally, this short time period must allow for judicial review. I respectfully submit this cannot be completed without taking Florida's presidential electors outside the safe harbor provision, creating the very real possibility of disenfranchising those nearly six million voters who were able to correctly cast their ballots on election day.

Another significant problem is that the majority returns this case to the circuit court for a recount with no standards. I do not, and neither will the trial judge, know whether to count or not count ballots on the criteria used by the canvassing boards, what those criteria are, or to do so on the basis of standards divined by Judge Sauls. A continuing problem with these manual recounts is their reliability. It only stands to reason that many times a reading of a ballot by a human will be subjective, and the intent gleaned from that ballot is only in the mind of the beholder. This subjective counting is only compounded where no standards exist or, as in this statewide contest, where there are no statewide standards for determining voter intent by the various canvassing boards, individual judges, or multiple unknown counters who will eventually count these ballots.

I must regrettably conclude that the majority ignores the magnitude of its decision. The Court fails to make provision for: (1) the qualifications of those who count; (2) what standards are used in the count—are they the same standards for all ballots statewide or a continuation of the county-by-county constitutionally suspect standards; (3) who is to observe the count; (4) how one objects to the count; (5) who is entitled to object to the

---

30. As the Supreme Court recently noted, 3 U.S.C § 5 creates a safe harbor provision regarding congressional consideration of a state's electoral votes should all contests and controversies be resolved at least six days prior to December 18, 2000, if made pursuant to the state of the law as it existed on election day. *See Bush* [pages 51–52]. There is no legislative suggestion that the Florida Legislature did not want to take advantage of this safe harbor provision.

31. *See* § 102.166(6), Fla. Stat. (2000).

count; (6) whether a person may object to a counter; (7) the possible lack of personnel to conduct the count; (8) the fatigue of the counters; and (9) the effect of the differing intra-county standards.

This Court's responsibility must be to balance the contest allegations against the rights of all Florida voters who are not involved in election contests to have their votes counted in the electoral college. To me, it is inescapable that there is no practical way for the contest to continue for the good of this country and state.

I am persuaded that Justice Terrell was correct in 1936 when he said:

> This court is committed to the doctrine that extraordinary relief will not be granted in case where it plainly appears that although the complaining party may be ordinarily entitled to it, *if the granting of such relief in the particular case will result in confusion and disorder* and will produce an injury to the public which outweighs the individual right of the complainant to have the relief he seeks.

State ex rel. Pooser v. Wester, 126 Fla. 49, 54, 170 So. 736, 738–39 (1936) (emphasis added).

For a month, Floridians have been working on this problem. At this point, I am convinced of the following.

First, there have been an enormous number of citizens who have expended heroic efforts as members of canvassing boards, counters, and observers, and as legal counsel who have in almost all instances, in utmost good faith attempted to bring about a fair resolution of this election. I know that, regardless of the outcome, all of us are in their debt for their efforts on behalf of representative democracy.

Second, the local election officials, state election officials, and the courts have been attempting to resolve the issues of this election with an election code which any objective, frank analysis must conclude never contemplated this circumstance. Only to state a few of the incongruities, the time limits of sections 102.112, 102.166, and 102.168 and 3 U.S.C. §§ 1, 5, and 7 simply do not coordinate in any practical way with a presidential election in Florida in the year 2000. Therefore, section 102.168, Florida Statues, is inconsistent with the remedy being sought here because it is unclear in a presidential election as to: (1) whether the candidates or the presidential electors should be party to this election contest; (2) what the possible remedy would be; and (3) what standards to apply in counting the ballots statewide.

Third, under the United States Supreme Court's analysis in *Bush v. Palm Beach County Canvassing Board,* wherein the Supreme Court calls to our attention *McPherson v. Blacker*, 146 U.S. 1 (1892), there is uncertainty as to whether the Florida Legislature has even given the courts of Florida any power to resolve contests or controversies in respect to presidential elections.

Fourth, there is no available remedy for the petitioners on the basis of these allegations. Quite simply, courts cannot fairly continue to proceed without jeopardizing the votes and rights of other citizens through a further count of these votes.

I must take seriously the counsel of the Supreme Court in *Bush:*

> Since [3 U.S.C.] § 5 contains a principle of federal law that would assure finality of the State's determination if made pursuant to a state law in effect before the election, a legislative wish to take advantage of the "safe harbor" would counsel against any construction of the Election Code that Congress might deem to be a change in the law.

[page 52].

This case has reached the point where finality must take precedence over continued judicial process. I agree with the view attributed to John Allen Paulos, a professor of mathematics at Temple University, who was quoted as saying, "The margin of error in this election is far greater than the margin of victory, no matter who wins."[32] Further judicial process will not change this self-evident fact and will only result in confusion and disorder. Justice Terrell and this Court wisely counseled against such a course of action sixty-four years ago. I would heed that sound advice and affirm Judge Sauls.

Justice Harding, dissenting.

I would affirm Judge Sauls' order because I agree with his ultimate conclusion in this case, namely that the Appellants failed to carry their requisite burden of proof and thus are not entitled to relief. However, in reaching his conclusion, Judge Sauls applied erroneous standards in two instances. First, in addressing the Appellants' challenges of the election certifications in Miami-Dade and Palm Beach Counties, the judge stated that "the local boards have been given broad discretion, which no court may overrule, absent a clear abuse of discretion." Applying this standard, the judge concluded that the Miami-Dade County Canvassing Board did not

32. Philip Gailey, *The Election Is a Tie, So Let's Get On With It*, St. Petersburg Times, Dec. 3, 2000, at 3D (quoting David Remnick, *Comment: Decisions, Decisions*, The New Yorker, Dec. 4, 2000, at 35.

abuse its discretion in any of its decisions in the review and recounting process. While abuse of discretion is the proper standard for assessing a canvassing board's actions in a section 102.166 protest proceeding, it is not applicable to this section 102.168 contest proceeding. Judge Sauls improperly intertwined these two proceedings and the standards applicable to each.

In 1999, the Florida Legislature extensively amended the contest statute to specify the grounds authorized for contesting an election and to set up a time frame for contests. *See* ch. 99-339, § 3, at 3547–49, Laws of Fla. The Legislature also amended the protest statute by eliminating the role of the circuit courts in protest proceedings. *See id.,* § 1, at 3546. The county canvassing boards have been granted discretion to authorize a manual recount when requested by a candidate, political party, or political committee who seeks to protest the returns of an election as being erroneous. *See* §102.166(4)(c), Fla. Stat. (2000) ("The county canvassing board *may* authorize a manual recount.") (emphasis added).

In contrast, a contest proceeding involves a legal challenge to the outcome of an election. The circuit judge is statutorily charged with three tasks in a contest proceeding: (1) to ensure that each allegation in the contestant's complaint is investigated, examined, or checked; (2) to prevent or correct any alleged wrong; and (3) to provide any relief appropriate under such circumstances. See § 102.168(8), Fla. Stat. (2000). Where a contestant alleges that the canvassing board has rejected a number of legal votes "sufficient to change or place in doubt the result of the election" due to the board's decision to curtail or deny a manual recount, the circuit judge should examine this issue de novo and not under an abuse of discretion standard. § 102.168(3)(c), Fla. Stat. (2000)

Second, Judge Sauls erred in concluding that a contestant under section 102.168(3)(c) must show a "reasonable probability that the results of the election would have been changed." Judge Sauls cited the First District Court of Appeal's decision in *Smith v. Tynes,* 412 So. 2d 925, 926 (Fla. 1st DCA 1982), as establishing this standard for election contests. However, as discussed above, when the Legislature amended section 102.168 in 1999, it specified five grounds for contesting an election, including the receipt of a number of illegal votes or rejection of a number of legal votes *sufficient to change or place in doubt the result of the election."* (Emphasis added.) *Smith v. Tynes,* which was decided in 1982, addressed the pre-amendment statute which did not specify the grounds for a contest. Thus, the current statutory standard controls here.

While I disagree with Judge Sauls on the standards applicable to this election contest, I commend him for the way that he conducted the proceedings below under extreme time constraints and pressure. Further, I believe that Judge Sauls properly concluded that there was no authority to include the Palm Beach County returns filed after the explicit deadline established by this Court.

I conclude that the application of the erroneous standards is not determinative in this case. I agree with Judge Sauls that the Appellants have not carried their burden of showing that the number of legal votes rejected by the canvassing boards is sufficient to change or place in doubt the result of this *statewide* election. That failure of proof controls the outcome here. Moreover, as explained below, I do not believe that an adequate remedy exists under the circumstances of this case.

I conclude that Judge Sauls properly found that the evidence presented by Appellants, even if believed, was insufficient to warrant any remedy under section 102.168.

The basis for Appellants claim for relief under section 102.168 is that there is a "no-vote" problem, i.e., ballots which, although counted by machines at least once, allegedly have not been counted in the presidential election. The evidence showed that this no-vote problem, to the extent it exists, is a statewide problem.[33] Appellants ask that only a subset of these no-votes be counted.

In a presidential election, however, section 102.168, by its title, is an "Election" contest and, as such, it is not a local contest seeking to define the correct winner of the popular vote in any individual county. The action is to determine whether the Secretary of State certified the correct winner for the entire State of Florida. By its plain language, section 102.168(1) provides that only the "unsuccessful candidate" may contest an election. If this contest provision may be invoked as to individual county results, as argued by Appellants, then Vice President Gore's choice of the three particular counties was improper because he was not "unsuccessful" in those counties. I read the statute as applying to *statewide results* in statewide elections. Thus, Vice President Gore, as the unsuccessful candidate statewide, could contest the election results. However, in this contest proceeding, Appellants had an obligation to show, by a preponderance of the evidence, that the

33. No-votes (ballots for which the no vote for Presidential electors was recorded) exist throughout the state, not just in the counties selected by Appellants. Of the 177,655 no-votes in the November 7, 2000, election in Florida, 28,492 occurred in Miami-Dade County and 29,366 occurred in Palm Beach County. *See* Division of Elections, Voter Turnout Report, S-DX 41; Division of Elections, General Election Results, S-DX 40.

outcome of the statewide election would likely be changed by the relief they sought.

Appellants failed, however, to provide any meaningful statistical evidence that the outcome of the Florida election would be different if the "no-vote" in other counties had been counted; their proof that the outcome of the vote in two counties would likely change the results of the election was insufficient. It would be improper to permit Appellants to carry their burden in a statewide election by merely demonstrating that there were a sufficient number of no-votes that could have changed the returns in isolated counties. Recounting a subset of counties selected by the Appellants does not answer the ultimate question of whether a sufficient number of uncounted legal votes could be recovered from the statewide "no-votes" to change the result of the statewide election. At most, such a procedure only demonstrates that the losing candidate would have had greater success in the subset of counties most favorable to that candidate.

Moreover, assuming that there may be some shortfall in counting the votes cast with punch card ballots, such a problem is only properly considered as being systemic with the punch card system itself and any remedy would have had to be statewide. Any other remedy would disenfranchise tens of thousands of other Florida voters, as I have serious concerns that Appellant's interpretation of 102.168 would violate other voters' rights to due process and equal protection of the law under the Fifth and Fourteenth Amendments to the United States Constitution.

As such, I would find that the selective recounting requested by Appellant is not available under the election contest provisions of section 102.168. Such an application does not provide for a more accurate reflection of the will of the voters but, rather, allows for an unfair distortion of the statewide vote. It is patently unlawful to permit the recount of "no-votes" in a single county to determine the outcome of the November 7, 2000, election for the next President of the United States. We are a nation of laws, and we have survived and prospered as a free nation because we have adhered to the rule of law. Fairness is achieved by following the rules.

Finally, even if I were to conclude that the Appellant's allegations and evidence were sufficient to warrant relief, I do not believe that the rules permit an adequate remedy under the circumstances of this case. This Court, in its prior opinion, and all of the parties agree that election controversies and contests must be finally and conclusively determined by December 12, 2000. *See* 3 U.S.C. § 5. This Court is "not required to do a useless act nor are we required to act if it is impossible for us to grant effectual relief." *State v. Strasser,* 445 So. 2d 322, 322 (Fla. 1983). See also *Hoshaw v. State,* 533

So. 2d 886, 887 (Fla. 3d DCA 1988) ("The law does not require futile acts."); *International Fidelity Ins. Co. v. Prestige Rent-A-Car, Inc.*, 715 So. 2d 1025, 1028 (Fla. 5th DCA 1998) ("Florida law does not require trial courts to enter orders which are impossible to execute or which require parties to perform acts that cannot be of any force or effect."). Clearly, the only remedy authorized by law would be a statewide recount of more than 170,000 "no-vote" ballots by December 12. Even if such a recount were possible, speed would come at the expense of accuracy, and it would be difficult to put any faith or credibility in a vote total achieved under such chaotic conditions. In order to undertake this unprecedented task, the majority has established standards for manual recounts—a step that this Court refused to take in an earlier case,[34] presumably because there was no authority for such action and nothing in the record to guide the Court in setting such standards. The same circumstances exist in this case. All of the parties should be afforded an opportunity to be heard on this very important issue.

While this Court must be ever mindful of the Legislature's plenary power to appoint presidential electors, *see* U.S. Const. art. II, § 1, cl. 2, I am more concerned that the majority is departing from the essential requirements of the law by providing a remedy which is impossible to achieve and which will ultimately lead to chaos. In giving Judge Sauls the direction to order a statewide recount, the majority permits a remedy which was not prayed for, which is based upon a premise for which there is no evidence, and which presents Judge Sauls with directions to order entities (i.e. local canvassing boards) to conduct recounts when they have not been served, have not been named as parties, but, most importantly, have not had the opportunity to be heard. In effect, the majority is allowing the results of the statewide election to be determined by the manual recount in Miami-Dade County because a statewide recount will be impossible to accomplish. Even if by some miracle a portion of the statewide recount is completed by December 12, a partial recount is not acceptable. The uncertainty of the outcome of this election will be greater under the remedy afforded by the majority than the uncertainty that now exists.

The circumstances of this election call to mind a quote from football coaching legend Vince Lombardi: "We didn't lose the game, we just ran out of time."

JUSTICE SHAW concurs.

---

34. *See Palm Beach County Canvassing Bd. v. Harris,* Nos. SC00-2346, SC00-2348, SC00-2349 (Fla., Nov. 21, 2000) [pages 24–47], *vacated by Bush v. Palm Beach Canvassing Bd.* (U.S., Dec. 4, 2000) [pages 48–52] .

Supreme Court of the United States

No. 00-949 (00A504)

George W. Bush, ET AL., Petitioners *v.*
Albert Gore, Jr., ET AL.

ON APPLICATION FOR STAY

December 9, 2000

The application for stay presented to Justice Kennedy and by him referred to the Court is granted, and it is ordered that the mandate of the Florida Supreme Court, case No. SC00-2431, is hereby stayed pending further order of the Court. In addition, the application for stay is treated as a petition for a writ of certiorari, and the petition for a writ of certiorari is granted. [. . .] The case is set for oral argument on Monday, December 11, 2000 at 11 a.m., and a total of 1½ hours is allotted for oral argument.

JUSTICE SCALIA, concurring.

Though it is not customary for the court to issue an opinion in connection with its grant of a stay, I believe a brief response is necessary to Justice Stevens' dissent. I will not address the merits of the case, since they will shortly be before us in the petition for certiorari that we have granted. It suffices to say that the issuance of the stay suggests that a majority of the Court, while not deciding the issues presented, believe that the petitioner has a substantial probability of success.

On the question of irreparable harm, however, a few words are appropriate. The issue is not, as the dissent puts it, whether "[c]ounting every legally cast vote ca[n] constitute irreparable harm." One of the principal issues in the appeal we have accepted is precisely whether that votes that have been ordered to be counted are, under a reasonable interpretation of Florida law, "legally cast vote[s]." The counting of votes that are of questionable legality does in my view threaten irreparable harm to petitioner, and to the country, by casting a cloud upon what he claims to be the legitimacy of his election. Count first, and rule upon legality afterwards, is not a recipe for producing election results that have the public acceptance democratic stability requires. Another issue in the case, moreover, is the propriety, indeed the constitutionality of letting the standard for determination of voters' intent—dimpled chads, hanging chads, etc.—vary from county to county, as the Florida Supreme Court opinion, as interpreted by the Circuit Court, permits. If petitioner is correct that counting in this fashion is unlawful, permitting the count to proceed on that erroneous basis will prevent an accurate recond from being conducted on a proper basis later, since it is generally agreed that each manual recount produces a degradation of the ballots, which renders a subsequent count inaccurate.

For these reasons, I have joined the Court's issuance of stay, with a highly accelerated timetable for resolving this case on the merits.

JUSTICE STEVENS, with whom JUSTICE SOUTER, JUSTICE GINSBURG, and JUSTICE BREYER join, dissenting.

To stop the counting of legal votes, the majority today departs from three venerable rules of judicial restraint that have guided the Court throughout its history. On questions of state law, we have consistently respected the opinions of the highest courts of the States. On questions whose resolution is committed at least in large measure to another branch of the Federal Government, we have construed our own jurisdiction narrowly and exercised it cautiously. On federal constitutional questions that were not fairly presented to the court whose judgment is being reviewed, we have prudently declined to express an opinion. The majority has acted unwisely.

Time does not permit a full discussion of the merits. It is clear, however, that a stay should not be granted unless an applicant makes a substantial showing of a likelihood of irreparable harm. In this case, applicants have failed to carry that heavy burden. Counting every legally cast vote cannot constitute irreparable harm. On the other hand, there is a danger that a stay may cause irreparable harm to the respondents—and, more importantly, the public at large—because of the risk that "the entry of the stay would be tantamount to a decision on the merits in favor of the applicants." *National Socialist Party of America v. Skokie*, 434 U. S. 1327, 1328 (1977) (Stevens, J. in chambers). Preventing the recount from being completed will inevitably cast a cloud on the legitimacy of the election.

It is certainly not clear that the Florida decision violated federal law. The Florida Code provides elaborate procedures for ensuring that ever eligible voter has a full and fair opportunity to case a ballot and that every ballot so cast is counted. See, *e.g.,* Fla. Stat. §§ 101.5614(5), 102.166 (2000). In its opinion, the Florida Supreme Court gave weight to that legislative command. Its ruling was consistent with earlier Florida cases that have repeatedly described the interest in correctly ascertaining the will of the voters as paramount. See *State ex rel Chappell v. Martinez,* 563 So. 2d 1007 (1998); *Boardman v. Estreva,* 323 So. 2d 259 (1976); *McAlpin v. State ex rel. Avriett,* 19 So 2d 420 (1944); *State ex rel. Peacock v. Latham,* 169 So. 597, 598; *State ex rel. Carpenter v. Barber,* 198 So. 49 (1940). Its ruling also appears to be consistent with the prevailing view in other states. See, *e.g., Pullen v. Milligan,* 561 N.E. 2d 585, 611 (Ill. 1990). As a more fundamental matter, the Florida court's ruling reflects the basic principle, inherent in our Constitution and our democracy, that every legal vote should be counted. See *Reynolds v. Sims,* 377 U.S. 533, 544–555 (1964); cf. *Hardke v. Roudebush,* 321 F. Supp. 1370, 1378–1379 (S.D. Ind. 1970) (Stevens, J., dissenting); accord *Roudebush v. Hartke,* 405 U.S. 15 (1972).

Accordingly, I respectfully dissent.

Supreme Court of the United States

No. 00-949

George W. Bush, ET AL., Petitioners *v.*
Albert Gore, Jr., ET AL.

ON WRIT OF CERTIORARI TO
THE FLORIDA SUPREME COURT

December 12, 2000

PER CURIAM

I

On December 8, 2000, the Supreme Court of Florida ordered that the Circuit Court of Leon County tabulate by hand 9,000 ballots in Miami-Dade County. It also ordered the inclusion in the certified vote totals of 215 votes identified in Palm Beach County and 168 votes identified in Miami-Dade County for Vice President Albert Gore, Jr., and Senator Joseph Lieberman, Democratic Candidates for President and Vice President. The Supreme Court noted that petitioner, Governor George W. Bush asserted that the net gain for Vice President Gore in Palm Beach County was 176 votes, and directed the Circuit Court to resolve that dispute on remand. The court further held that relief would require manual recounts in all Florida counties where so-called "undervotes" had not been subject to manual tabulation. The court ordered all manual recounts to begin at once. Governor Bush and Richard Cheney, Republican Candidates for the Presidency and Vice Presidency, filed an emergency application for a stay of this mandate. On December 9, we granted the application, treated the application as a petition for a writ of certiorari, and granted certiorari.

The proceedings leading to the present controversy are discussed in some detail in our opinion in *Bush v. Palm Beach County Canvassing Bd.,* [pages 48–52] *(per curiam) (Bush I).* On November 8, 2000, the day following the Presidential election, the Florida Division of Elections reported that petitioner, Governor Bush, had received 2,909,135 votes, and respondent, Vice

President Gore, had received 2,907,351 votes, a margin of 1,784 for Governor Bush. Because Governor Bush's margin of victory was less than "one-half of a percent . . . of the votes cast," an automatic machine recount was conducted under § 102.141(4) of the election code, the results of which showed Governor Bush still winning the race but by a diminished margin. Vice President Gore then sought manual recounts in Volusia, Palm Beach, Broward, and Miami-Dade Counties, pursuant to Florida's election protest provisions. Fla. Stat. § 102.166 (2000). A dispute arose concerning the deadline for local county canvassing boards to submit their returns to the Secretary of State (Secretary). The Secretary declined to waive the November 14 deadline imposed by statute. §§ 102.111, 102.112. The Florida Supreme Court, however, set the deadline at November 26. We granted certiorari and vacated the Florida Supreme Court's decision, finding considerable uncertainty as to the grounds on which it was based. *Bush I,* [page 52]. On December 11, the Florida Supreme Court issued a decision on remand reinstating that date.

On November 26, the Florida Elections Canvassing Commission certified the results of the election and declared Governor Bush the winner of Florida's 25 electoral votes. On November 27, Vice President Gore, pursuant to Florida's contest provisions, filed a complaint in Leon County Circuit Court contesting the certification. Fla. Stat. § 102.168 (2000). He sought relief pursuant to § 102.168(3)(c), which provides that "receipt of a number of illegal votes or rejection of a number of legal votes sufficient to change or place in doubt the result of the election" shall be grounds for a contest. The Circuit Court denied relief, stating that Vice President Gore failed to meet his burden of proof. He appealed to the First District Court of Appeal, which certified the matter to the Florida Supreme Court.

Accepting jurisdiction, the Florida Supreme Court affirmed in part and reversed in part. *Gore v. Harris,* [pages 59–60, 78–81]. The court held that the Circuit Court had been correct to reject Vice President Gore's challenge to the results certified in Nassau County and his challenge to the Palm Beach County Canvassing Board's determination that 3,300 ballots cast in that county were not, in the statutory phrase, "legal votes."

The Supreme Court held that Vice President Gore had satisfied his burden of proof under § 102.168(3)(c) with respect to his challenge to Miami-Dade County's failure to tabulate, by manual count, 9,000 ballots on which the machines had failed to detect a vote for President ("undervotes") [page 67]. Noting the closeness of the election, the Court explained that "[o]n this record, there can be no question that there are legal votes within the 9,000 uncounted votes sufficient to place the results of this election in doubt." *Id.,* at [page 78]. A "legal vote," as determined by the Supreme Court, is "one in which there is a 'clear indication of the intent of the voter.'" *Id.,* at [page 72]. The court therefore ordered a hand recount of the 9,000 ballots in Miami-Dade County. Observing that the contest provisions vest broad discretion in the circuit judge to "provide any relief appropriate under such circumstances," Fla. Stat. § 102.168(8) (2000), the Supreme Court further held that the Circuit Court could order "the Supervisor of Elections and the Canvassing Boards, as well as the necessary public officials, in all counties that have not conducted a manual recount or tabulation of the undervotes . . . to do so forthwith, said tabulation to take place in the individual counties where the ballots are located" [page 80].

The Supreme Court also determined that both Palm Beach County and Miami-Dade County, in their earlier manual recounts, had identified a net gain of 215 and 168 legal votes, respectively, for Vice President Gore. *Id.,* at [pages 77–78]. Rejecting the Circuit Court's conclusion that Palm Beach County lacked the authority to include the 215 net votes submitted past the November 26 deadline, the Supreme Court explained that the deadline was not intended to exclude votes identified after that date through ongoing manual recounts. As to Miami-Dade County, the Court concluded that although the 168 votes identified were the result of a partial recount, they were "legal votes [that] could change the outcome of the election." *Id.,* at [page 78]. The Supreme Court therefore directed the Circuit Court to include those totals in the certified results, subject to resolution of the actual vote total from the Miami-Dade partial recount.

The petition presents the following questions: whether the Florida Supreme Court established new standards for resolving Presidential election contests, thereby violating Art. II, § 1, cl. 2, of the United States Constitution and failing to comply with 3 U.S.C. § 5, and whether the use of standardless manual recounts violates the Equal Protection and Due Process Clauses. With respect to the equal protection question, we find a violation of the Equal Protection Clause.

II
A

The closeness of this election, and the multitude of legal challenges which have followed in its wake, have brought into sharp focus a common, if heretofore unnoticed, phenomenon. Nationwide statistics reveal that an estimated 2% of ballots cast do not register a vote for President for whatever reason, including deliberately choosing no candidate at all or some voter error, such as voting for two candidates or insufficiently marking a ballot. See Ho, More Than 2M Ballots Uncounted, AP Online (Nov. 28, 2000); Kelley, Balloting Problems Not Rare But Only In A Very Close Election Do Mistakes And Mismarking Make A Difference, Omaha World-Herald (Nov. 15, 2000). In certifying election results, the votes eligible for inclusion in the certification are the votes meeting the properly established legal requirements.

This case has shown that punch card balloting machines can produce an unfortunate number of ballots which are not punched in a clean, complete way by the voter. After the current counting, it is likely legislative bodies nationwide will examine ways to improve the mechanisms and machinery for voting.

B

The individual citizen has no federal constitutional right to vote for electors for the President of the United States unless and until the state legislature chooses a statewide election as the means to implement its power to appoint members of the Electoral College. U.S. Const., Art. II, § 1. This is the source for the statement in *McPherson v. Blacker*, 146 U.S. 1, 35 (1892), that the State legislature's power to select the manner for appointing electors is plenary; it may, if it so chooses, select the electors itself, which indeed was the manner used by State legislatures in several States for many years after the Framing of our Constitution. *Id.*, at 28–33. History has now favored the voter, and in each of the several States the citizens themselves vote for Presidential electors. When the state legislature vests the right to vote for President in its people, the right to vote as the legislature has prescribed is fundamental; and one source of its fundamental nature lies in the equal weight accorded to each vote and the equal dignity owed to each voter. The State, of course, after granting the franchise in the special context of Article II, can take back the power to appoint electors. See *id.*, at 35 ("[T]here is no doubt of the right of the legislature to resume the power at any time, for it can neither be taken away nor abdicated") (quoting S. Rep. No. 395, 43d Cong., 1st Sess.).

The right to vote is protected in more than the initial allocation of the franchise. Equal protection applies as well to the manner of its exercise. Having once granted the right to vote on equal terms, the State may not, by later arbitrary and disparate treatment, value one person's vote over that of another. See, *e.g., Harper v. Virginia Bd. of Elections,* 383 U.S. 663, 665 (1966) ("[O]nce the franchise is granted to the electorate, lines may not be drawn which are inconsistent with the Equal Protection Clause of the Fourteenth Amendment"). It must be remembered that "the right of suffrage can be denied by a debasement or dilution of the weight of a citizen's vote just as effectively as by wholly prohibiting the free exercise of the franchise." *Reynolds v. Sims,* 377 U.S. 533, 555 (1964).

There is no difference between the two sides of the present controversy on these basic propositions. Respondents say that the very purpose of vindicating the right to vote justifies the recount procedures now at issue. The question before us, however, is whether the recount procedures the Florida Supreme Court has adopted are consistent with its obligation to avoid arbitrary and disparate treatment of the members of its electorate.

Much of the controversy seems to revolve around ballot cards designed to be perforated by a stylus but which, either through error or deliberate omission, have not been perforated with sufficient precision for a machine to count them. In some cases a piece of the card—a chad—is hanging, say by two corners. In other cases there is no separation at all, just an indentation.

The Florida Supreme Court has ordered that the intent of the voter be discerned from such ballots. For purposes of resolving the equal protection challenge, it is not necessary to decide whether the Florida Supreme Court had the authority under the legislative scheme for resolving election disputes to define what a legal vote is and to mandate a manual recount implementing that definition. The recount mechanisms implemented in response to the decisions of the Florida Supreme Court do not satisfy the minimum requirement for non-arbitrary treatment of voters necessary to secure the fundamental right. Florida's basic command for the count of legally cast votes is to consider the "intent of the voter." *Gore v. Harris,* [page 81]. This is unobjectionable as an abstract proposition and a starting principle. The problem inheres in the absence of specific standards to ensure its equal application. The formulation of uniform rules to determine intent based on these recurring circumstances is practicable and, we conclude, necessary.

The law does not refrain from searching for the intent of the actor in a multitude of circumstances; and in some cases the general command to ascertain intent is not susceptible to much further refinement. In this instance, however, the question is not whether to believe a witness but how to interpret the marks or holes or scratches on an inanimate object, a piece of cardboard or paper which, it is said, might not have registered as a vote during the machine count. The factfinder confronts a thing, not a person. The search for intent can be confined by specific rules designed to ensure uniform treatment.

The want of those rules here has led to unequal evaluation of ballots in various respects. See *Gore v. Harris,* [page 87] (Wells, J., dissenting) ("Should a county canvassing board count or not count a 'dimpled chad' where the voter is able to successfully dislodge the chad in every other contest on that ballot? Here, the county canvassing boards disagree"). As seems to have been acknowledged at oral argument, the standards for accepting or rejecting contested ballots might vary not only from county to county but indeed within a single county from one recount team to another.

The record provides some examples. A monitor in Miami-Dade County testified at trial that he observed that three members of the county canvassing board applied different standards in defining a legal vote. 3 Tr. 497, 499 (Dec. 3, 2000). And testimony at trial also revealed that at least one county changed its evaluative standards during the counting process. Palm Beach County, for example, began the process with a 1990 guideline which precluded counting completely attached chads, switched to a rule that considered a vote to be legal if any light could be seen through a chad, changed back to the 1990 rule, and then abandoned any pretense of a *per se* rule, only to have a court order that the county consider dimpled chads legal. This is not a process with sufficient guarantees of equal treatment.

An early case in our one person, one vote jurisprudence arose when a State accorded arbitrary and disparate treatment to voters in its different counties. *Gray v. Sanders,* 372 U.S. 368 (1963). The Court found a constitutional violation. We relied on these principles in the context of the Presidential selection process in *Moore v. Ogilvie,* 394 U.S. 814 (1969), where we invalidated a county-based procedure that diluted the influence of citizens in larger counties in the nominating process. There we observed that "the idea that one group can be granted greater voting strength than another is hostile to the one man, one vote basis of our representative government." *Id.,* at 819.

The State Supreme Court ratified this uneven treatment. It mandated that the recount totals from two counties, Miami-Dade and Palm Beach, be included in the certified total. The court also appeared to hold *sub silentio* that the recount totals from Broward County, which were not completed until after the original November 14 certification by the Secretary of State, were to be considered part of the new certified vote totals even though the county certification was not contested by Vice President Gore. Yet each of the counties used varying standards to determine what was a legal vote. Broward County used a more forgiving standard than Palm Beach County, and uncovered almost three times as many new votes, a result markedly disproportionate to the difference in population between the counties.

In addition, the recounts in these three counties were not limited to so-called undervotes but extended to all of the ballots. The distinction has real consequences. A manual recount of all ballots identifies not only those ballots which show no vote but also those which contain more than one, the so-called overvotes. Neither category will be counted by the machine. This is not a trivial concern. At oral argument, respondents estimated there are as many as 110,000 overvotes statewide. As a result, the citizen whose ballot was not read by a machine because he failed to vote for a candidate in a way readable by a machine may still have his vote counted in a manual recount; on the other hand, the citizen who marks two candidates in a way discernable by the machine will not have the same opportunity to have his vote count, even if a manual examination of the ballot would reveal the requisite indicia of intent. Furthermore, the citizen who marks two candidates, only one of which is discernable by the machine, will have his vote counted even though it should have been read as an invalid ballot. The State Supreme Court's inclusion of vote counts based on these variant standards exemplifies concerns with the remedial processes that were under way.

That brings the analysis to yet a further equal protection problem. The votes certified by the court included a partial total from one county, Miami-Dade. The Florida Supreme Court's decision thus gives no assurance that the recounts included in a final certification must be complete. Indeed, it is respondent's submission that it would be consistent with the rules of the recount procedures to include whatever partial counts are done by the time of final certification, and we interpret the Florida Supreme Court's decision to permit this. See [page 80], n. 21) (noting "practical difficulties" may control outcome of election, but certifying partial Miami-Dade total nonetheless). This accommodation no doubt results from the truncated contest period established by the Florida Supreme Court in *Bush I*, at respondents' own urging. The press of time does not diminish the constitutional concern. A desire for speed is not a general excuse for ignoring equal protection guarantees.

In addition to these difficulties the actual process by which the votes were to be counted under the Florida Supreme Court's decision raises further concerns. That order did not specify who would recount the ballots.

The county canvassing boards were forced to pull together ad hoc teams comprised of judges from various Circuits who had no previous training in handling and interpreting ballots. Furthermore, while others were permitted to observe, they were prohibited from objecting during the recount.

The recount process, in its features here described, is inconsistent with the minimum procedures necessary to protect the fundamental right of each voter in the special instance of a statewide recount under the authority of a single state judicial officer. Our consideration is limited to the present circumstances, for the problem of equal protection in election processes generally presents many complexities.

The question before the Court is not whether local entities, in the exercise of their expertise, may develop different systems for implementing elections. Instead, we are presented with a situation where a state court with the power to assure uniformity has ordered a statewide recount with minimal procedural safeguards. When a court orders a statewide remedy, there must be at least some assurance that the rudimentary requirements of equal treatment and fundamental fairness are satisfied.

Given the Court's assessment that the recount process underway was probably being conducted in an unconstitutional manner, the Court stayed the order directing the recount so it could hear this case and render an expedited decision. The contest provision, as it was mandated by the State Supreme Court, is not well calculated to sustain the confidence that all citizens must have in the outcome of elections. The State has not shown that its procedures include the necessary safeguards. The problem, for instance, of the estimated 110,000 overvotes has not been addressed, although Chief Justice Wells called attention to the concern in his dissenting opinion. See [page 84], n. 26.

Upon due consideration of the difficulties identified to this point, it is obvious that the recount cannot be conducted in compliance with the requirements of equal protection and due process without substantial additional work. It would require not only the adoption (after opportunity for argument) of adequate statewide standards for determining what is a legal vote, and practicable procedures to implement them, but also orderly judicial review of any disputed matters that might arise. In addition, the Secretary of State has advised that the recount of only a portion of the ballots requires that the vote tabulation equipment be used to screen out undervotes, a function for which the machines were not designed. If a recount of overvotes were also required, perhaps even a second screening would be necessary. Use of the equipment for this purpose, and any new software developed for it, would have to be evaluated for accuracy by the Secretary of State, as required by Fla. Stat. § 101.015 (2000).

The Supreme Court of Florida has said that the legislature intended the State's electors to "participate fully in the federal electoral process," as provided in 3 U.S.C. § 5. [. . .]; see also *Palm Beach Canvassing Bd. v. Harris* (Fla., Dec 11, 2000) [slip op. at 27]. That statute, in turn, requires that any controversy or contest that is designed to lead to a conclusive selection of electors be completed by December 12. That date is upon us, and there is no recount procedure in place under the State Supreme Court's order that comports with minimal constitutional standards. Because it is evident that any recount seeking to meet the December 12 date will be unconstitutional for the reasons we have discussed, we reverse the judgment of the Supreme Court of Florida ordering a recount to proceed.

Seven Justices of the Court agree that there are constitutional problems with the recount ordered by the Florida Supreme Court that demand a remedy. See *post*, at [pages 124–25] (Souter, J., dissenting); *post*, at [page 133, 142] (Breyer, J. , dissenting). The only disagreement is as to the remedy. Because the Florida Supreme Court has said that the Florida Legislature intended to obtain the safe-harbor benefits of 3 U.S.C. § 5, Justice Breyer's proposed remedy— remanding to the Florida Supreme Court for its ordering of a constitutionally proper contest until December 18—contemplates action in violation of the Florida election code, and hence could not be part of an "appropriate" order authorized by Fla. Stat. § 102.168(8) (2000).

* * *

None are more conscious of the vital limits on judicial authority than are the members of this Court, and none stand more in admiration of the Constitution's design to leave the selection of the President to the people, through their legislatures, and to the political sphere. When contending parties invoke the process of the courts, however, it becomes our unsought responsibility to resolve the federal and constitutional issues the judicial system has been forced to confront.

The judgment of the Supreme Court of Florida is reversed, and the case is remanded for further proceedings not inconsistent with this opinion. Pursuant to this Court's Rule 45.2, the Clerk is directed to issue the mandate in this case forthwith.

It is so ordered.

CHIEF JUSTICE REHNQUIST, with whom JUSTICE SCALIA
and JUSTICE THOMAS join, concurring.

We join the *per curiam* opinion. We write separately because we believe
there are additional grounds that require us to reverse the Florida Supreme
Court's decision.

I

We deal here not with an ordinary election, but with an election for the
President of the United States. In *Burroughs v. United States,* 290 U.S. 534,
545 (1934), we said:

> "While presidential electors are not officers or agents of the fed-
> eral government (*In re Green,* 134 U.S. 377, 379), they exercise fed-
> eral functions under, and discharge duties in virtue of authority con-
> ferred by, the Constitution of the United States. The President is
> vested with the executive power of the nation. The importance of his
> election and the vital character of its relationship to and effect upon
> the welfare and safety of the whole people cannot be too strongly
> stated."

Likewise, in *Anderson v. Celebrezze,* 460 U.S. 780, 794–795 (1983) (footnote omitted), we said: "[I]n the context of a Presidential election, state-
imposed restrictions implicate a uniquely important national interest. For
the President and the Vice President of the United States are the only
elected officials who represent all the voters in the Nation."

In most cases, comity and respect for federalism compel us to defer to
the decisions of state courts on issues of state law. That practice reflects our
understanding that the decisions of state courts are definitive pronouncements of the will of the States as sovereigns. Cf. *Erie R. Co. v. Tompkins,* 304
U.S. 64 (1938). Of course, in ordinary cases, the distribution of powers
among the branches of a State's government raises no questions of federal
constitutional law, subject to the requirement that the government be republican in character. See U.S. Const., Art. IV, § 4. But there are a few exceptional cases in which the Constitution imposes a duty or confers a power
on a particular branch of a State's government. This is one of them. Article
II, § 1, cl. 2, provides that "[e]ach State shall appoint, in such Manner as
the *Legislature* thereof may direct," electors for President and Vice President.
(Emphasis added.) Thus, the text of the election law itself, and not just its
interpretation by the courts of the States, takes on independent significance.

In *McPherson v. Blacker*, 146 U.S. 1 (1892), we explained that Art. II, § 1, cl. 2, "conveys the broadest power of determination" and "leaves it to the legislature exclusively to define the method" of appointment. *Id.*, at 27. A significant departure from the legislative scheme for appointing Presidential electors presents a federal constitutional question.

3 U.S.C. § 5 informs our application of Art. II, § 1, cl. 2, to the Florida statutory scheme, which, as the Florida Supreme Court acknowledged, took that statute into account. Section 5 provides that the State's selection of electors "shall be conclusive, and shall govern in the counting of the electoral votes" if the electors are chosen under laws enacted prior to election day, and if the selection process is completed six days prior to the meeting of the electoral college. As we noted in *Bush v. Palm Beach County Canvassing Bd., ante*, [page 52],

> "Since § 5 contains a principle of federal law that would assure finality of the State's determination if made pursuant to a state law in effect before the election, a legislative wish to take advantage of the 'safe harbor' would counsel against any construction of the Election Code that Congress might deem to be a change in the law."

If we are to respect the legislature's Article II powers, therefore, we must ensure that postelection state-court actions do not frustrate the legislative desire to attain the "safe harbor" provided by § 5.

In Florida, the legislature has chosen to hold statewide elections to appoint the State's 25 electors. Importantly, the legislature has delegated the authority to run the elections and to oversee election disputes to the Secretary of State (Secretary), Fla. Stat. § 97.012(1) (2000), and to state circuit courts, §§ 102.168(1), 102.168(8). Isolated sections of the code may well admit of more than one interpretation, but the general coherence of the legislative scheme may not be altered by judicial interpretation so as to wholly change the statutorily provided apportionment of responsibility among these various bodies. In any election but a Presidential election, the Florida Supreme Court can give as little or as much deference to Florida's executives as it chooses, so far as Article II is concerned, and this Court will have no cause to question the court's actions. But, with respect to a Presidential election, the court must be both mindful of the legislature's role under Article II in choosing the manner of appointing electors and deferential to those bodies expressly empowered by the legislature to carry out its constitutional mandate.

In order to determine whether a state court has infringed upon the legislature's authority, we necessarily must examine the law of the State as it existed prior to the action of the court. Though we generally defer to state courts on the interpretation of state law—*see, e.g., Mullaney v. Wilbur,* 421 U.S. 684 (1975)—there are of course areas in which the Constitution requires this Court to undertake an independent, if still deferential, analysis of state law.

For example, in *NAACP v. Alabama ex rel. Patterson,* 357 U.S. 449 (1958), it was argued that we were without jurisdiction because the petitioner had not pursued the correct appellate remedy in Alabama's state courts. Petitioners had sought a state-law writ of certiorari in the Alabama Supreme Court when a writ of mandamus, according to that court, was proper. We found this state-law ground inadequate to defeat our jurisdiction because we were "unable to reconcile the procedural holding of the Alabama Supreme Court" with prior Alabama precedent. *Id.,* at 456. The purported state-law ground was so novel, in our independent estimation, that "petitioner could not fairly be deemed to have been apprised of its existence." *Id.,* at 457. Six years later we decided *Bouie v. City of Columbia,* 378 U.S. 347 (1964), in which the state court had held, contrary to precedent, that the state trespass law applied to black sit-in demonstrators who had consent to enter private property but were then asked to leave. Relying upon *NAACP,* we concluded that the South Carolina Supreme Court's interpretation of a state penal statute had impermissibly broadened the scope of that statute beyond what a fair reading provided, in violation of due process. See 378 U.S. at 361–362. What we would do in the present case is precisely parallel: Hold that the Florida Supreme Court's interpretation of the Florida election laws impermissibly distorted them beyond what a fair reading required, in violation of Article II.[1]

1. Similarly, our jurisprudence requires us to analyze the "background principles" of state property law to determine whether there has been a taking of property in violation of the Takings Clause. That constitutional guarantee would, of course, afford no protection against state power if our inquiry could be concluded by a state supreme court holding that state property law accorded the plaintiff no rights. See *Lucas v. South Carolina Coastal Council,* 505 U.S. 1003 (1992). In one of our oldest cases, we similarly made an independent evaluation of state law in order to protect federal treaty guarantees. In *Fairfax's Devisee v. Hunter's Lessee,* 7 Cranch 603 (1813), we disagreed with the Supreme Court of Appeals of Virginia that a 1782 state law had extinguished the property interests of one Denny Fairfax, so that a 1789 ejectment order against Fairfax supported by a 1785 state law did not constitute a future confiscation under the 1783 peace treaty with Great Britain. See *id.,* at 623; *Hunter v. Fairfax's Devisee,* 1 Munf. 218 (Va. 1809).

This inquiry does not imply a disrespect for state courts but rather a re-spect for the constitutionally prescribed role of state legislatures. To attach definitive weight to the pronouncement of a state court, when the very question at issue is whether the court has actually departed from the statu-tory meaning, would be to abdicate our responsibility to enforce the ex-plicit requirements of Article II.

II

Acting pursuant to its constitutional grant of authority, the Florida Legis-lature has created a detailed, if not perfectly crafted, statutory scheme that provides for appointment of Presidential electors by direct election. Fla. Stat. § 103.011 (2000). Under the statute, "votes cast for the actual candi-dates for President and Vice President shall be counted as [v]otes cast for the presidential electors supporting such candidates." *Ibid.* The legislature has designated the Secretary of State as the "chief election officer," with the responsibility to "[o]btain and maintain uniformity in the application, op-eration, and interpretation of the election laws." § 97.012. The state legis-lature has delegated to county canvassing boards the duties of administer-ing elections. § 102.141. Those boards are responsible for providing results to the state Elections Canvassing Commission, comprising the Governor, the Secretary of State, and the Director of the Division of Elections. § 102.111. Cf. *Boardman v. Esteva*, 323 So. 2d 259, 268, n. 5 (1975) ("The election process . . . is committed to the executive branch of government through duly designated officials all charged with specific duties . . . . [The] judgments [of these officials] are entitled to be regarded by the courts as presumptively correct . . . ").

After the election has taken place, the canvassing boards receive returns from precincts, count the votes, and in the event that a candidate was de-feated by .5% or less, conduct a mandatory recount. Fla. Stat. § 102.141(4) (2000). The county canvassing boards must file certified election returns with the Department of State by 5 p.m. on the seventh day following the election. § 102.112(1). The Elections Canvassing Commission must then certify the results of the election. § 102.111(1).

The state legislature has also provided mechanisms both for protesting election returns and for contesting certified election results. Section 102.166 governs protests. Any protest must be filed prior to the certifica-tion of election results by the county canvassing board. § 102.166(4)(b). Once a protest has been filed, "the county canvassing board may authorize a manual recount." § 102.166(4)(c). If a sample recount conducted pursuant to § 102.166(5) "indicates an error in the vote tabulation which could affect the outcome of the election," the county canvassing board is instructed to: "(a) Correct the error and recount the remaining precincts with the vote tabulation system; (b) Request the Department of State to verify the tabulation software; or (c) Manually recount all ballots," § 102.166(5). In the event a canvassing board chooses to conduct a manual recount of all ballots, § 102.166(7) prescribes procedures for such a recount.

Contests to the certification of an election, on the other hand, are controlled by § 102.168. The grounds for contesting an election include "receipt of a number of illegal votes or rejection of a number of legal votes sufficient to change or place in doubt the result of the election." §102.168(3)(c). Any contest must be filed in the appropriate Florida circuit court, Fla. Stat. § 102.168(1), and the canvassing board or election board is the proper party defendant, § 102.168(4). Section 102.168(8) provides that "the circuit judge to whom the contest is presented may fashion such orders as he or she deems necessary to ensure that each allegation in the complaint is investigated, examined, or checked, to prevent or correct any alleged wrong, and to provide any relief appropriate under such circumstances." In Presidential elections, the contest period necessarily terminates on the date set by 3 U.S.C. § 5 for concluding the State's "final determination" of election controversies."

In its first decision, *Palm Beach Canvassing Bd. v. Harris* (Nov. 21, 2000) (*Harris I*) [pages 24–47], the Florida Supreme Court extended the 7-day statutory certification deadline established by the legislature.[2] This modification of the code, by lengthening the protest period, necessarily shortened the contest period for Presidential elections. Underlying the extension of the certification deadline and the shortchanging of the contest period was, presumably, the clear implication that certification was a matter of significance: The certified winner would enjoy presumptive validity, making a contest proceeding by the losing candidate an uphill battle. In its latest opinion, however, the court empties certification of virtually all legal consequence during the contest, and in doing so departs from the provisions enacted by the Florida Legislature.

The court determined that canvassing boards' decisions regarding whether to recount ballots past the certification deadline (even the certification deadline established by *Harris I*) are to be reviewed de novo, although the election code clearly vests discretion whether to recount in the

2. We vacated that decision and remanded that case; the Florida Supreme Court reissued the same judgment with a new opinion on December 11, 2000.

boards, and sets strict deadlines subject to the Secretary's rejection of late tallies and monetary fines for tardiness. See Fla. Stat. § 102.112 (2000). Moreover, the Florida court held that all late vote tallies arriving during the contest period should be automatically included in the certification regardless of the certification deadline (even the certification deadline established by *Harris I*), thus virtually eliminating both the deadline and the Secretary's discretion to disregard recounts that violate it.[3]

Moreover, the court's interpretation of "legal vote," and hence its decision to order a contest-period recount, plainly departed from the legislative scheme. Florida statutory law cannot reasonably be thought to require the counting of improperly marked ballots. Each Florida precinct before election day provides instructions on how properly to cast a vote, § 101.46; each polling place on election day contains a working model of the voting machine it uses, § 101.5611; and each voting booth contains a sample ballot, § 101.46. In precincts using punch-card ballots, voters are instructed to punch out the ballot cleanly:

AFTER VOTING, CHECK YOUR BALLOT CARD TO BE SURE YOUR VOTING SELECTIONS ARE CLEARLY AND CLEANLY PUNCHED AND THERE ARE NO CHIPS LEFT HANGING ON THE BACK OF THE CARD.

Instructions to Voters, quoted in *Touchston v. McDermott,* 2000 WL 1781942, *6 & n. 19 (CA11) (Tjoflat, J., dissenting). No reasonable person would call it "an error in the vote tabulation," Fla. Stat. § 102.166(5), or a "rejection of legal votes," Fla. Stat. § 102.168(3)(c),[4] when electronic or electromechanical equipment performs precisely in the manner designed, and fails to count those ballots that are not marked in the manner that these voting instructions explicitly and prominently specify. The scheme that the Florida Supreme Court's opinion attributes to the legislature is one in which machines are *required* to be "capable of correctly counting votes," § 101.5606(4), but which nonetheless regularly produces elections in which legal votes are predictably *not* tabulated, so that in close elections manual recounts are regularly required. This is of course absurd. The Secretary of State, who is authorized by law to issue binding interpre-

3. Specifically, the Florida Supreme Court ordered the Circuit Court to include in the certified vote totals those votes identified for Vice President Gore in Palm Beach County and Miami-Dade County.

4. It is inconceivable that what constitutes a vote that must be counted under the "error in the vote tabulation" language of the protest phase is different from what constitutes a vote that must be counted under the "legal votes" language of the contest phase.

tations of the election code, §§ 97.012, 106.23, rejected this peculiar read-ing of the statutes. See DE 00-13 (opinion of the Division of Elections [pages 12–14]). The Florida Supreme Court, although it must defer to the Secretary's interpretations, see *Krivanek v. Take Back Tampa Political Committee,* 625 So. 2d 840, 844 (Fla. 1993), rejected her reasonable interpre-tation and embraced the peculiar one. See *Palm Beach County Canvassing Board v. Harris,* No. SC00-2346 (Dec. 11, 2000) (*Harris III*).

But as we indicated in our remand of the earlier case, in a Presidential election the clearly expressed intent of the legislature must prevail. And there is no basis for reading the Florida statutes as requiring the counting of improperly marked ballots, as an examination of the Florida Supreme Court's textual analysis shows. We will not parse that analysis here, except to note that the principal provision of the election code on which it relied, § 101.5614(5), was, as the Chief Justice pointed out in his dissent from *Harris II,* entirely irrelevant. See *Gore v. Harris,* No. SC00-2431, [page 87] (Dec. 8, 2000). The State's Attorney General (who was supporting the Gore challenge) confirmed in oral argument here that never before the present election had a manual recount been conducted on the basis of the con-tention that "undervotes" should have been examined to determine voter intent. Tr. of Oral Arg. in *Bush v. Palm Beach County Canvassing Bd.,* 39–40 (Dec. 1, 2000); cf. *Broward County Canvassing Board v. Hogan,* 607 So. 2d 508, 509 (Fla. Ct. App. 1992) (denial of recount for failure to count bal-lots with "hanging paper chads"). For the court to step away from this es-tablished practice, prescribed by the Secretary of State, the state official charged by the legislature with "responsibility to . . . [o]btain and main-tain uniformity in the application, operation, and interpretation of the elec-tion laws," § 97.012(1), was to depart from the legislative scheme.

III

The scope and nature of the remedy ordered by the Florida Supreme Court jeopardizes the "legislative wish" to take advantage of the safe harbor pro-vided by 3 U.S.C. § 5. *Bush v. Palm Beach County Canvassing Bd., ante* [page 52]. December 12, 2000, is the last date for a final determination of the Florida electors that will satisfy § 5. Yet in the late afternoon of De-cember 8th—four days before this deadline—the Supreme Court of Florida ordered recounts of tens of thousands of so-called "undervotes" spread through 64 of the State's 67 counties. This was done in a search for elusive—perhaps delusive—certainty as to the exact count of 6 million votes. But no one claims that these ballots have not previously been tabulated; they were initially read by voting machines at the time of the election, and thereafter reread by virtue of Florida's automatic recount provision. No one claims there was any fraud in the election. The Supreme Court of Florida ordered this additional recount under the provision of the election code giving the circuit judge the authority to provide relief that is "appropriate under such circumstances." Fla. Stat. § 102.168(8) (2000).

Surely when the Florida Legislature empowered the courts of the State to grant "appropriate" relief, it must have meant relief that would have become final by the cut-off date of 3 U.S.C. § 5. In light of the inevitable legal challenges and ensuing appeals to the Supreme Court of Florida and petitions for certiorari to this Court, the entire recounting process could not possibly be completed by that date. Whereas the majority in the Supreme Court of Florida stated its confidence that "the remaining undervotes in these counties can be [counted] within the required time frame," ([page 80], n. 22), it made no assertion that the seemingly inevitable appeals could be disposed of in that time. Although the Florida Supreme Court has on occasion taken over a year to resolve disputes over local elections, see, *e.g., Beckstrom v. Volusia County Canvassing Bd.*, 707 So. 2d 720 (1998) (resolving contest of sheriff's race 16 months after the election), it has heard and decided the appeals in the present case with great promptness. But the federal deadlines for the Presidential election simply do not permit even such a shortened process.

As the dissent noted:

"In [the four days remaining], all questionable ballots must be reviewed by the judicial officer appointed to discern the intent of the voter in a process open to the public. Fairness dictates that a provision be made for either party to object to how a particular ballot is counted. Additionally, this short time period must allow for judicial review. I respectfully submit this cannot be completed without taking Florida's presidential electors outside the safe harbor provision, creating the very real possibility of disenfranchising those nearly 6 million voters who are able to correctly cast their ballots on election day." [page 90] (Wells, C. J., dissenting).

The other dissenters echoed this concern: "The majority is departing from the essential requirements of the law by providing a remedy which is impossible to achieve and which will ultimately lead to chaos." *Id.*, at [page 96] (Harding, J., dissenting, Shaw, J. concurring).

Given all these factors, and in light of the legislative intent identified by the Florida Supreme Court to bring Florida within the "safe harbor" provision of 3 U.S.C. § 5, the remedy prescribed by the Supreme Court of Florida cannot be deemed an "appropriate" one as of December 8. It significantly departed from the statutory framework in place on November 7, and authorized open-ended further proceedings which could not be completed by December 12, thereby preventing a final determination by that date.

For these reasons, in addition to those given in the *per curiam*, we would reverse.

JUSTICE STEVENS, with whom JUSTICE GINSBURG
and JUSTICE BREYER join, dissenting.

The Constitution assigns to the States the primary responsibility for determining the manner of selecting the Presidential electors. See Art. II, § 1, cl. 2. When questions arise about the meaning of state laws, including election laws, it is our settled practice to accept the opinions of the highest courts of the States as providing the final answers. On rare occasions, however, either federal statutes or the Federal Constitution may require federal judicial intervention in state elections. This is not such an occasion.

The federal questions that ultimately emerged in this case are not substantial. Article II provides that "[e]ach *State* shall appoint, in such Manner as the Legislature thereof may direct, a Number of Electors." *Ibid.* (emphasis added). It does not create state legislatures out of whole cloth, but rather takes them as they come—as creatures born of, and constrained by, their state constitutions. Lest there be any doubt, we stated over 100 years ago in *McPherson v. Blacker*, 146 U.S. 1, 25 (1892), that "[w]hat is forbidden or required to be done by a State" in the Article II context "is forbidden or required of the legislative power under state constitutions as they exist." In the same vein, we also observed that "[t]he [State's] legislative power is the supreme authority except as limited by the constitution of the State." *Ibid.*; cf. *Smiley v. Holm*, 285 U.S. 355, 367 (1932).[1] The legislative

1. "Wherever the term 'legislature' is used in the Constitution it is necessary to consider the nature of the particular action in view." 285 U.S. at 367. It is perfectly clear that the meaning of the words "Manner" and "Legislature" as used in Article II, § 1, parallels the usage in Article I, § 4, rather than the language in Article V. *U.S. Term Limits, Inc. v. Thornton*, 514 U.S. 779, 805 (1995). Article I, § 4, and Article II, § 1, both call upon legislatures to act in a lawmaking capacity whereas Article V simply calls on the legislative body to deliberate upon a binary decision. As a result, petitioners' reliance on *Leser v. Garnett*, 258 U.S. 130 (1922), and *Hawke v. Smith (No. 1)*, 253 U.S. 221 (1920), is misplaced.

power in Florida is subject to judicial review pursuant to Article V of the Florida Constitution, and nothing in Article II of the Federal Constitution frees the state legislature from the constraints in the state constitution that created it. Moreover, the Florida Legislature's own decision to employ a unitary code for all elections indicates that it intended the Florida Supreme Court to play the same role in Presidential elections that it has historically played in resolving electoral disputes. The Florida Supreme Court's exercise of appellate jurisdiction therefore was wholly consistent with, and indeed contemplated by, the grant of authority in Article II.

It hardly needs stating that Congress, pursuant to 3 U.S.C. § 5, did not impose any affirmative duties upon the States that their governmental branches could "violate." Rather, § 5 provides a safe harbor for States to select electors in contested elections "by judicial or other methods" established by laws prior to the election day. Section 5, like Article II, assumes the involvement of the state judiciary in interpreting state election laws and resolving election disputes under those laws. Neither § 5 nor Article II grants federal judges any special authority to substitute their views for those of the state judiciary on matters of state law.

Nor are petitioners correct in asserting that the failure of the Florida Supreme Court to specify in detail the precise manner in which the "intent of the voter," Fla. Stat. § 101.5614(5) (Supp. 2001), is to be determined rises to the level of a constitutional violation.[2] We found such a violation when individual votes within the same State were weighted unequally, see, e.g., *Reynolds v. Sims,* 377 U.S. 533, 568 (1964), but we have never before called into question the substantive standard by which a State determines that a vote has been legally cast. And there is no reason to think that the guidance provided to the factfinders, specifically the various canvassing boards, by the "intent of the voter" standard is any less sufficient—or will lead to results any less uniform—than, for example, the

---

2. The Florida statutory standard is consistent with the practice of the majority of States, which apply either an "intent of the voter" standard or an "impossible to determine the elector's choice" standard in ballot recounts. The following States use an "intent of the voter" standard: [*Eds.*: citations to state statutes are omitted] [Arizona; Connecticut; Indiana; Maine; Maryland; Massachusetts; Michigan; Missouri; Texas; Utah; Vermont; Washington; Wyoming]. The following States employ a standard in which a vote is counted unless it is "impossible to determine the elector's [or voter's] choice": [*Eds.* citations to state statutes are omitted] [Alabama; Arizona; California; Colorado; Delaware; Idaho; Illinois; Iowa; Maine; Minnesota; Montana; Nevada; New York; North Carolina; North Dakota; Ohio; Oklahoma; Oregon; South Carolina; South Dakota; Tennessee; West Virginia].

"beyond a reasonable doubt" standard employed everyday by ordinary citizens in courtrooms across this country.[3]

Admittedly, the use of differing substandards for determining voter intent in different counties employing similar voting systems may raise serious concerns. Those concerns are alleviated—if not eliminated—by the
fact that a single impartial magistrate will ultimately adjudicate all objections arising from the recount process. Of course, as a general matter, "the
interpretation of constitutional principles must not be too literal. We must
remember that the machinery of government would not work if it were not
allowed a little play in its joints." *Bain Peanut Co. of Tex. v. Pinson*, 282 U.S.
499, 501 (1931) (Holmes, J.). If it were otherwise, Florida's decision to
leave to each county the determination of what balloting system to employ—despite enormous differences in accuracy[4]—might run afoul of
equal protection. So, too, might the similar decisions of the vast majority
of state legislatures to delegate to local authorities certain decisions with
respect to voting systems and ballot design.

Even assuming that aspects of the remedial scheme might ultimately be
found to violate the Equal Protection Clause, I could not subscribe to the
majority's disposition of the case. As the majority explicitly holds, once a
state legislature determines to select electors through a popular vote, the
right to have one's vote counted is of constitutional stature. As the majority further acknowledges, Florida law holds that all ballots that reveal the
intent of the voter constitute valid votes. Recognizing these principles, the
majority nonetheless orders the termination of the contest proceeding before all such votes have been tabulated. Under their own reasoning, the appropriate course of action would be to remand to allow more specific procedures for implementing the legislature's uniform general standard to be
established.

In the interest of finality, however, the majority effectively orders the disenfranchisement of an unknown number of voters whose ballots reveal their
intent—and are therefore legal votes under state law—but were for some

3. Cf. *Victor v. Nebraska*, 511 U.S. 1, 5 (1994) ("The beyond a reasonable doubt standard is a requirement of due process, but the Constitution neither prohibits trial courts
from defining reasonable doubt nor requires them to do so").

4. The percentage of nonvotes in this election in counties using a punch-card system
was 3.92%; in contrast, the rate of error under the more modern optical-scan systems was
only 1.43%. *Siegel v. LePore*, No. 00-15981, 2000 WL 1781946, *31, *32, *43 (charts C
and F) (CA11, Dec. 6, 2000). Put in other terms, for every 10,000 votes cast, punch-card
systems result in 250 more nonvotes than optical-scan systems. A total of 3,718,305 votes
were cast under punch-card systems, and 2,353,811 votes were cast under optical-scan
systems. *Ibid.*

reason rejected by ballot-counting machines. It does so on the basis of the deadlines set forth in Title 3 of the United States Code. *Ante,* at [page 107]. But, as I have already noted, those provisions merely provide rules of decision for Congress to follow when selecting among conflicting slates of electors. *Supra,* at [p. 118]. They do not prohibit a State from counting what the majority concedes to be legal votes until a bona fide winner is determined. Indeed, in 1960, Hawaii appointed two slates of electors and Congress chose to count the one appointed on January 4, 1961, well after the Title 3 deadlines. See Josephson & Ross, Repairing the Electoral College, 22 J. Legis. 145, 166, n. 154 (1996).[5] Thus, nothing prevents the majority, even if it properly found an equal protection violation, from ordering relief appropriate to remedy that violation without depriving Florida voters of their right to have their votes counted. As the majority notes, "[a] desire for speed is not a general excuse for ignoring equal protection guarantees." *Ante,* at [page 106].

Finally, neither in this case, nor in its earlier opinion in *Palm Beach County Canvassing Bd. v. Harris* (Fla., Nov. 21, 2000) [pages 24–27], did the Florida Supreme Court make any substantive change in Florida electoral law.[6] Its decisions were rooted in long-established precedent and were consistent with the relevant statutory provisions, taken as a whole. It did what courts do[7]—it decided the case before it in light of the legislature's intent to leave no legally cast vote uncounted. In so doing, it relied on the sufficiency of the general "intent of the voter" standard articulated by the state legislature, coupled with a procedure for ultimate review by an impartial judge, to resolve the concern about disparate evaluations of contested ballots. If we assume—as I do—that the members of that court and

5. Republican electors were certified by the Acting Governor on November 28, 1960. A recount was ordered to begin on December 13, 1960. Both Democratic and Republican electors met on the appointed day to cast their votes. On January 4, 1961, the newly elected Governor certified the Democratic electors. The certification was received by Congress on January 6, the day the electoral votes were counted. Josephson & Ross, 22 J. Legis., at 166, n. 154.

6. When, for example, it resolved the previously unanswered question whether the word "shall" in Fla. Stat. § 102.111 or the word "may" in § 102.112 governs the scope of the Secretary of State's authority to ignore untimely election returns, it did not "change the law." Like any other judicial interpretation of a statute, its opinion was an authoritative interpretation of what the statute's relevant provisions have meant since they were enacted. *Rivers v. Roadway Express, Inc.,* 511 U.S. 298, 312–313 (1994).

7. "It is emphatically the province and duty of the judicial department to say what the law is." *Marbury v.* Madison, 1 Cranch 137 (1803).

the judges who would have carried out its mandate are impartial, its decision does not even raise a colorable federal question.

What must underlie petitioners' entire federal assault on the Florida election procedures is an unstated lack of confidence in the impartiality and capacity of the state judges who would make the critical decisions if the vote count were to proceed. Otherwise, their position is wholly without merit. The endorsement of that position by the majority of this Court can only lend credence to the most cynical appraisal of the work of judges throughout the land. It is confidence in the men and women who administer the judicial system that is the true backbone of the rule of law. Time will one day heal the wound to that confidence that will be inflicted by today's decision. One thing, however, is certain. Although we may never know with complete certainty the identity of the winner of this year's Presidential election, the identity of the loser is perfectly clear. It is the Nation's confidence in the judge as an impartial guardian of the rule of law.

I respectfully dissent.

JUSTICE SOUTER, with whom JUSTICE BREYER joins, and with whom JUSTICE STEVENS and JUSTICE GINSBURG join with regard to all but Part C, dissenting.

The Court should not have reviewed either *Bush v. Palm Beach County Canvassing Bd., ante,* [pages 48–52] (*per curiam*), or this case, and should not have stopped Florida's attempt to recount all undervote ballots, see *ante* at [page 52], by issuing a stay of the Florida Supreme Court's orders during the period of this review, see *Bush v. Gore,* [page 97] If this Court had allowed the State to follow the course indicated by the opinions of its own Supreme Court, it is entirely possible that there would ultimately have been no issue requiring our review, and political tension could have worked itself out in the Congress following the procedure provided in 3 U.S.C. § 15. The case being before us, however, its resolution by the majority is another erroneous decision. As will be clear, I am in substantial agreement with the dissenting opinions of Justice Stevens, Justice Ginsburg and Justice Breyer. I write separately only to say how straightforward the issues before us really are.

There are three issues: whether the State Supreme Court's interpretation of the statute providing for a contest of the state election results somehow violates 3 U.S.C. § 5; whether that court's construction of the state statutory provisions governing contests impermissibly changes a state law from what the State's legislature has provided, in violation of Article II, § 1, cl.

2, of the national Constitution; and whether the manner of interpreting markings on disputed ballots failing to cause machines to register votes for President (the undervote ballots) violates the equal protection or due process guaranteed by the Fourteenth Amendment. None of these issues is difficult to describe or to resolve.

A

The 3 U.S.C. § 5 issue is not serious. That provision sets certain conditions for treating a State's certification of Presidential electors as conclusive in the event that a dispute over recognizing those electors must be resolved in the Congress under 3 U.S.C. § 15. Conclusiveness requires selection under a legal scheme in place before the election, with results determined at least six days before the date set for casting electoral votes. But no State is required to conform to § 5 if it cannot do that (for whatever reason); the sanction for failing to satisfy the conditions of § 5 is simply loss of what has been called its "safe harbor." And even that determination is to be made, if made anywhere, in the Congress.

B

The second matter here goes to the State Supreme Court's interpretation of certain terms in the state statute governing election "contests," Fla. Stat. § 102.168 (2000); there is no question here about the state court's interpretation of the related provisions dealing with the antecedent process of "protesting" particular vote counts, § 102.166, which was involved in the previous case, *Bush v. Palm Beach County Canvassing Board.* The issue is whether the judgment of the state supreme court has displaced the state legislature's provisions for election contests: is the law as declared by the court different from the provisions made by the legislature, to which the national Constitution commits responsibility for determining how each State's Presidential electors are chosen? See U.S. Const., Art. II, § 1, cl. 2. Bush does not, of course, claim that any judicial act interpreting a statute of uncertain meaning is enough to displace the legislative provision and violate Article II; statutes require interpretation, which does not without more affect the legislative character of a statute within the meaning of the Constitution. Brief for Petitioners 48, n. 22, in *Bush v. Palm Beach County Canvassing Bd., et al.,* 531 U.S. ___ (2000). What Bush does argue, as I understand the contention, is that the interpretation of § 102.168 was so unreasonable as to transcend the accepted bounds of statutory interpretation, to the point of being a nonjudicial act and producing new law untethered to the legislative act in question. The starting point for evaluating the claim that the Florida Supreme Court's interpretation effectively rewrote § 102.168 must be the language of the provision on which Gore relies to show his right to raise this contest: that the previously certified result in Bush's favor was produced by "rejection of a number of legal votes sufficient to change or place in doubt the result of the election." Fla. Stat. § 102.168(3)(c) (2000). None of the state court's interpretations is unreasonable to the point of displacing the legislative enactment quoted. As I will note below, other interpretations were of course possible, and some might have been better than those adopted by the Florida court's majority; the two dissents from the majority opinion of that court and various briefs submitted to us set out alternatives. But the majority view is in each instance within the bounds of reasonable interpretation, and the law as declared is consistent with Article II.

1. The statute does not define a "legal vote," the rejection of which may affect the election. The State Supreme Court was therefore required to define it, and in doing that the court looked to another election statute, § 101.5614(5), dealing with damaged or defective ballots, which contains a provision that no vote shall be disregarded "if there is a clear indication of the intent of the voter as determined by a canvassing board." The court read that objective of looking to the voter's intent as indicating that the legislature probably meant "legal vote" to mean a vote recorded on a ballot indicating what the voter intended. *Gore v. Harris* (Dec. 8, 2000) [pages 71–73]. It is perfectly true that the majority might have chosen a different reading. See, *e.g.,* Brief for Respondent Harris et al. 10 (defining "legal votes" as "votes properly executed in accordance with the instructions provided to all registered voters in advance of the election and in the polling places"). But even so, there is no constitutional violation in following the majority view; Article II is unconcerned with mere disagreements about interpretive merits.

2. The Florida court next interpreted "rejection" to determine what act in the counting process may be attacked in a contest. Again, the statute does not define the term. The court majority read the word to mean simply a failure to count [pages 73–74]. That reading is certainly within the bounds of common sense, given the objective to give effect to a voter's intent if that can be determined. A different reading, of course, is possible. The majority might have concluded that "rejection" should refer to machine malfunction, or that a ballot should not be treated as "rejected" in the absence of wrongdoing by election officials, lest contests be so easy to

claim that every election will end up in one. Cf. *id.,* at [pages 85–86] (Wells, C. J., dissenting). There is, however, nothing nonjudicial in the Florida majority's more hospitable reading.

3. The same is true about the court majority's understanding of the phrase "votes sufficient to change or place in doubt" the result of the election in Florida. The court held that if the uncounted ballots were so numerous that it was reasonably possible that they contained enough "legal" votes to swing the election, this contest would be authorized by the statute.[1] While the majority might have thought (as the trial judge did) that a probability, not a possibility, should be necessary to justify a contest, that reading is not required by the statute's text, which says nothing about probability. Whatever people of good will and good sense may argue about the merits of the Florida court's reading, there is no warrant for saying that it transcends the limits of reasonable statutory interpretation to the point of supplanting the statute enacted by the "legislature" within the meaning of Article II.

In sum, the interpretations by the Florida court raise no substantial question under Article II. That court engaged in permissible construction in determining that Gore had instituted a contest authorized by the state statute, and it proceeded to direct the trial judge to deal with that contest in the exercise of the discretionary powers generously conferred by Fla. Stat. § 102.168(8) (2000), to "fashion such orders as he or she deems necessary to ensure that each allegation in the complaint is investigated, examined, or checked, to prevent or correct any alleged wrong, and to provide any relief appropriate under such circumstances." As Justice Ginsburg has persuasively explained in her own dissenting opinion, our customary respect for state interpretations of state law counsels against rejection of the Florida court's determinations in this case.

C

It is only on the third issue before us that there is a meritorious argument for relief, as this Court's *per curiam* opinion recognizes. It is an issue that might well have been dealt with adequately by the Florida courts if the state proceedings had not been interrupted, and if not disposed of at the state

---

1. When the Florida court ruled, the totals for Bush and Gore were then less than 1,000 votes apart. One dissent pegged the number of uncounted votes in question at 170,000. *Gore v. Harris,* [page 96] (opinion of Harding, J.). Gore's counsel represented to us that the relevant figure is approximately 60,000, Tr. of Oral Arg. 62, the number of ballots in which no vote for President was recorded by the machines.

level it could have been considered by the Congress in any electoral vote dispute. But because the course of state proceedings has been interrupted, time is short, and the issue is before us, I think it sensible for the Court to address it.

Petitioners have raised an equal protection claim (or, alternatively, a due process claim, see generally *Logan v. Zimmerman Brush Co.*, 455 U.S. 422 (1982)), in the charge that unjustifiably disparate standards are applied in different electoral jurisdictions to otherwise identical facts. It is true that the Equal Protection Clause does not forbid the use of a variety of voting mechanisms within a jurisdiction, even though different mechanisms will have different levels of effectiveness in recording voters' intentions; local variety can be justified by concerns about cost, the potential value of in-novation, and so on. But evidence in the record here suggests that a dif-ferent order of disparity obtains under rules for determining a voter's in-tent that have been applied (and could continue to be applied) to identical types of ballots used in identical brands of machines and exhibiting iden-tical physical characteristics (such as "hanging" or "dimpled" chads). See, *e.g.*, Tr., at 238–242 (Dec. 2–3, 2000) (testimony of Palm Beach County Canvassing Board Chairman Judge Charles Burton describing varying stan-dards applied to imperfectly punched ballots in Palm Beach County dur-ing precertification manual recount); *id.*, at 497–500 (similarly describing varying standards applied in Miami-Dade County); Tr. of Hearing 8–10 (Dec. 8, 2000) (soliciting from county canvassing boards proposed proto-cols for determining voters' intent but declining to provide a precise, uni-form standard). I can conceive of no legitimate state interest served by these differing treatments of the expressions of voters' fundamental rights. The differences appear wholly arbitrary.

In deciding what to do about this, we should take account of the fact that electoral votes are due to be cast in six days. I would therefore remand the case to the courts of Florida with instructions to establish uniform stan-dards for evaluating the several types of ballots that have prompted differ-ing treatments, to be applied within and among counties when passing on such identical ballots in any further recounting (or successive recounting) that the courts might order.

Unlike the majority, I see no warrant for this Court to assume that Florida could not possibly comply with this requirement before the date set for the meeting of electors, December 18. Although one of the dissenting justices of the State Supreme Court estimated that disparate standards po-tentially affected 170,000 votes, *Gore v. Harris, supra,* [page 96], the number at issue is significantly smaller. The 170,000 figure apparently represents all uncounted votes, both undervotes (those for which no Presidential choice was recorded by a machine) and overvotes (those rejected because of votes for more than one candidate). Tr. of Oral Arg. 61–62. But as Justice Breyer has pointed out, no showing has been made of legal overvotes uncounted, and counsel for Gore made an uncontradicted representation to the Court that the statewide total of undervotes is about 60,000. *Id.*, at 62. To recount these manually would be a tall order, but before this Court stayed the effort to do that the courts of Florida were ready to do their best to get that job done. There is no justification for denying the State the opportunity to try to count all disputed ballots now.

I respectfully dissent.

JUSTICE GINSBURG, with whom JUSTICE STEVENS joins,
and with whom JUSTICE SOUTER and JUSTICE BREYER
join as to Part I, dissenting

I

The Chief Justice acknowledges that provisions of Florida's Election Code "may well admit of more than one interpretation." *Ante*, at [page 110] (concurring opinion). But instead of respecting the state high court's province to say what the State's Election Code means, The Chief Justice maintains that Florida's Supreme Court has veered so far from the ordinary practice of judicial review that what it did cannot properly be called judging. My colleagues have offered a reasonable construction of Florida's law. Their construction coincides with the view of one of Florida's seven Supreme Court justices. *Gore v. Harris* (Fla. 2000) [pages 83–87] (Wells, C. J., dissenting); *Palm Beach County Canvassing Bd. v. Harris,* (Fla., Dec. 11, 2000) (on remand) (confirming, 6-1, the construction of Florida law advanced in *Gore*). I might join The Chief Justice were it my commission to interpret Florida law. But disagreement with the Florida court's interpretation of its own State's law does not warrant the conclusion that the justices of that court have legislated. There is no cause here to believe that the members of Florida's high court have done less than "their mortal best to discharge their oath of office," *Sumner v. Mata,* 449 U.S. 539, 549 (1981), and no cause to upset their reasoned interpretation of Florida law.

This Court more than occasionally affirms statutory, and even constitutional, interpretations with which it disagrees. For example, when reviewing challenges to administrative agencies' interpretations of laws they implement, we defer to the agencies unless their interpretation violates "the unambiguously expressed intent of Congress." *Chevron U.S.A. Inc. v. Natural Resources Defense Council, Inc.,* 467 U.S. 837, 843 (1984). We do so in the face of the declaration in Article I of the United States Constitution that "All legislative Powers herein granted shall be vested in a Congress of the United States." Surely the Constitution does not call upon us to pay more respect to a federal administrative agency's construction of federal law than to a state high court's interpretation of its own state's law. And not uncommonly, we let stand state-court interpretations of federal law with which we might disagree. Notably, in the habeas context, the Court adheres to the view that "there is 'no intrinsic reason why the fact that a man is a federal judge should make him more competent, or conscientious, or learned with respect to [federal law] than his neighbor in the state courthouse.'" *Stone v. Powell,* 428 U.S. 465, 494 (1976) (quoting Bator, Finality in Criminal Law and Federal Habeas Corpus For State Prisoners, 76 Harv. L. Rev. 441, 509 (1963)); see *O'Dell v. Netherland,* 521 U.S. 151, 156 (1997) ("The Teague doctrine validates reasonable, good-faith interpretations of existing precedents made by state courts even though they are shown to be contrary to later decisions.") (citing *Butler v. McKellar,* 494 U.S. 407, 414 (1990)); O'Connor, Trends in the Relationship Between the Federal and State Courts from the Perspective of a State Court Judge, 22 Wm. & Mary L. Rev. 801, 813 (1981) ("There is no reason to assume that state court judges cannot and will not provide a 'hospitable forum' in litigating federal constitutional questions.").

No doubt there are cases in which the proper application of federal law may hinge on interpretations of state law. Unavoidably, this Court must sometimes examine state law in order to protect federal rights. But we have dealt with such cases ever mindful of the full measure of respect we owe to interpretations of state law by a State's highest court. In the Contract Clause case, *General Motors Corp. v. Romein,* 503 U.S. 181 (1992), for example, we said that although "ultimately we are bound to decide for ourselves whether a contract was made," the Court "accords respectful consideration and great weight to the views of the State's highest court." *Id.,* at 187 (citation omitted). And in *Central Union Telephone Co. v. Edwardsville,* 269 U.S. 190 (1925), we upheld the Illinois Supreme Court's interpretation of a state waiver rule, even though that interpretation resulted in the forfeiture of federal constitutional rights. Refusing to supplant Illinois law with a federal definition of waiver, we explained that the state court's declaration "should bind us unless so unfair or unreasonable in its application to those asserting a federal right as to obstruct it." *Id.*, at 195.[1]

In deferring to state courts on matters of state law, we appropriately recognize that this Court acts as an "'outsider' lacking the common exposure to local law which comes from sitting in the jurisdiction." *Lehman Brothers v. Schein,* 416 U.S. 386, 391 (1974). That recognition has sometimes prompted us to resolve doubts about the meaning of state law by certifying issues to a State's highest court, even when federal rights are at stake. Cf. *Arizonans for Official English v. Arizona,* 520 U.S. 43 (1997) ("Warnings against premature adjudication of constitutional questions bear heightened attention when a federal court is asked to invalidate a State's law, for the federal tribunal risks friction-generating error when it endeavors to construe a novel state Act not yet reviewed by the State's highest court."). Notwithstanding our authority to decide issues of state law underlying federal claims, we have used the certification devise to afford state high courts an opportunity to inform us on matters of their own State's law because such restraint "helps build a cooperative judicial federalism." *Lehman Brothers,* 416 U.S. at 391.

Just last Term, in *Fiore v. White,* 528 U.S. 23 (1999), we took advantage of Pennsylvania's certification procedure. In that case, a state prisoner brought a federal habeas action claiming that the State had failed to prove an essential element of his charged offense in violation of the Due Process Clause. 528 U.S. at 25–26. Instead of resolving the state-law question on which the federal claim depended, we certified the question to the Pennsylvania Supreme Court for that court to "help determine the proper state-law pred-

---

1. See also *Lucas v. South Carolina Coastal Council,* 505 U.S. 1003, 1032, n. 18 (1992) (South Carolina could defend a regulatory taking "if an objectively reasonable application of relevant precedents [by its courts] would exclude . . . beneficial uses in the circumstances in which the land is presently found"); *Bishop v. Wood,* 426 U.S. 341, 344–345 (1976) (deciding whether North Carolina had created a property interest cognizable under the Due Process Clause by reference to state law as interpreted by the North Carolina Supreme Court). Similarly, in *Gurley v. Rhoden,* 421 U.S. 200 (1975), a gasoline retailer claimed that due process entitled him to deduct a state gasoline excise tax in computing the amount of his sales subject to a state sales tax, on the grounds that the legal incidence of the excise tax fell on his customers and that he acted merely as a collector of the tax. The Mississippi Supreme Court held that the legal incidence of the excise tax fell on petitioner. Observing that "a State's highest court is the final judicial arbiter of the meaning of state statutes," we said that "when a state court has made its own definitive determination as to the operating incidence, . . . we give this finding great weight in determining the natural effect of a statute, and if it is consistent with the statute's reasonable interpretation it will be deemed conclusive." *Id.,* at 208.

icate for our determination of the federal constitutional questions raised."
Id., at 29; *id.,* at 28 (asking the Pennsylvania Supreme Court whether its recent interpretation of the statute under which Fiore was convicted "was always the statute's meaning, even at the time of Fiore's trial"). The Chief Justice 's willingness to reverse the Florida Supreme Court's interpretation of
Florida law in this case is at least in tension with our reluctance in *Fiore* even
to interpret Pennsylvania law before seeking instruction from the Pennsylvania Supreme Court. I would have thought the "cautious approach" we
counsel when federal courts address matters of state law, *Arizonans,* 520 U.S.
at 77, and our commitment to "building cooperative judicial federalism,"
Lehman Brothers, 416 U.S. at 391, demanded greater restraint.

Rarely has this Court rejected outright an interpretation of state law by
a state high court. *Fairfax's Devisee v. Hunter's Lessee,* 7 Cranch 603 (1813),
NAACP v. Alabama ex rel. Patterson, 357 U.S. 449 (1958), and *Bouie v. City
of Columbia,* 378 U.S. 347 (1964), cited by The Chief Justice, are three
such rare instances. See *ante,* at [page 110] and n. 1. But those cases are
embedded in historical contexts hardly comparable to the situation here.
Fairfax's Devisee, which held that the Virginia Court of Appeals had misconstrued its own forfeiture laws to deprive a British subject of lands secured to him by federal treaties, occurred amidst vociferous States' rights
attacks on the Marshall Court. G. Gunther & K. Sullivan, Constitutional
Law 61–62 (13th ed. 1997). The Virginia court refused to obey this
Court's *Fairfax's Devisee* mandate to enter judgment for the British subject's
successor in interest. That refusal led to the Court's pathmarking decision
in *Martin v. Hunter's Lessee,* 1 Wheat. 304 (1816). *Patterson,* a case decided
three months after *Cooper v. Aaron,* 358 U.S. 1 (1958), in the face of Southern resistance to the civil rights movement, held that the Alabama Supreme
Court had irregularly applied its own procedural rules to deny review of a
contempt order against the NAACP arising from its refusal to disclose
membership lists. We said that "our jurisdiction is not defeated if the non-
federal ground relied on by the state court is without any fair or substantial support." 357 U.S. at 455. *Bouie,* stemming from a lunch counter "sit-
in" at the height of the civil rights movement, held that the South Carolina
Supreme Court's construction of its trespass laws—criminalizing conduct
not covered by the text of an otherwise clear statute—was "unforeseeable"
and thus violated due process when applied retroactively to the petitioners. 378 U.S. at 350, 354.

The Chief Justice's casual citation of these cases might lead one to believe they are part of a larger collection of cases in which we said that the

Constitution impelled us to train a skeptical eye on a state court's portrayal of state law. But one would be hard pressed, I think, to find additional cases that fit the mold. As Justice Breyer convincingly explains, see [pages 136–38] (dissenting opinion), this case involves nothing close to the kind of recalcitrance by a state high court that warrants extraordinary action by this Court. The Florida Supreme Court concluded that counting every legal vote was the overriding concern of the Florida Legislature when it enacted the State's Election Code. The court surely should not be bracketed with state high courts of the Jim Crow South.

The Chief Justice says that Article II, by providing that state legislatures shall direct the manner of appointing electors, authorizes federal superintendence over the relationship between state courts and state legislatures, and licenses a departure from the usual deference we give to state court interpretations of state law. *Ante,* at [page 112] ("To attach definitive weight to the pronouncement of a state court, when the very question at issue is whether the court has actually departed from the statutory meaning, would be to abdicate our responsibility to enforce the explicit requirements of Article II."). The Framers of our Constitution, however, understood that in a republican government, the judiciary would construe the legislature's enactments. See U.S. Const., Art. III; The Federalist No. 78 (A. Hamilton). In light of the constitutional guarantee to States of a "Republican Form of Government," U.S. Const., Art. IV, § 4, Article II can hardly be read to invite this Court to disrupt a State's republican regime. Yet The Chief Justice today would reach out to do just that. By holding that Article II requires our revision of a state court's construction of state laws in order to protect one organ of the State from another, The Chief Justice contradicts the basic principle that a State may organize itself as it sees fit. See, *e.g., Gregory v. Ashcroft,* 501 U.S. 452, 460 (1991) ("Through the structure of its government, and the character of those who exercise government authority, a State defines itself as a sovereign."); *Highland Farms Dairy, Inc. v. Agnew,* 300 U.S. 608, 612 (1937) ("How power shall be distributed by a state among its governmental organs is commonly, if not always, a question for the state itself.").[2] Article II does not call for the scrutiny undertaken by this Court.

2. Even in the rare case in which a State's "manner" of making and construing laws might implicate a structural constraint, Congress, not this Court, is likely the proper governmental entity to enforce that constraint. See U.S. Const., amend. XII; 3 U.S.C. §§ 1–15; cf. *Ohio ex rel. Davis v. Hildebrant,* 241 U.S. 565, 569 (1916) (treating as a nonjusticiable political question whether use of a referendum to override a congressional districting plan enacted by the state legislature violates Art. I, § 4); *Luther v. Borden,* 7 How. 1, 42 (1949).

The extraordinary setting of this case has obscured the ordinary principle that dictates its proper resolution: Federal courts defer to state high courts' interpretations of their state's own law. This principle reflects the core of federalism, on which all agree. "The Framers split the atom of sovereignty. It was the genius of their idea that our citizens would have two political capacities, one state and one federal, each protected from incursion by the other." *Saenz v. Roe,* 526 U.S. 489, 504, n. 17 (1999) (citing *U.S. Term Limits, Inc. v. Thornton,* 514 U.S. 779, 838 (1995) (Kennedy, J., concurring)). The Chief Justice's solicitude for the Florida Legislature comes at the expense of the more fundamental solicitude we owe to the legislature's sovereign. U.S. Const., Art. II, § 1, cl. 2 ("Each *State* shall appoint, in such Manner as the Legislature *thereof* may direct," the electors for President and Vice President) (emphasis added); *ante,* at [page 117] (Stevens , J., dissenting).[3] Were the other members of this Court as mindful as they generally are of our system of dual sovereignty, they would affirm the judgment of the Florida Supreme Court.

II

I agree with Justice Stevens that petitioners have not presented a substantial equal protection claim. Ideally, perfection would be the appropriate standard for judging the recount. But we live in an imperfect world, one in which thousands of votes have not been counted. I cannot agree that the recount adopted by the Florida court, flawed as it may be, would yield a result any less fair or precise than the certification that preceded that recount. See, *e.g., McDonald v. Board of Election Comm'rs of Chicago,* 394 U.S. 802, 807 (1969) (even in the context of the right to vote, the state is permitted to reform "'one step at a time'") (quoting *Williamson v. Lee Optical of Oklahoma, Inc.,* 348 U.S. 483, 489 (1955)).

Even if there were an equal protection violation, I would agree with Justice Stevens, Justice Souter, and Justice Breyer that the Court's concern about "the December 12 deadline," *ante,* at [page 108], is misplaced. Time is short in part because of the Court's entry of a stay on December 9, several hours after an able circuit judge in Leon County had begun to super-

3."[B]ecause the Framers recognized that state power and identity were essential parts of the federal balance, see The Federalist No. 39, the Constitution is solicitous of the prerogatives of the States, even in an otherwise sovereign federal province. The Constitution . . . grants States certain powers over the times, places, and manner of federal elections (subject to congressional revision), Art. I, § 4, cl. 1 . . . , and allows States to appoint electors for the President, Art. II, § 1, cl. 2." *U.S. Term Limits, Inc. v. Thornton,* 514 U.S. 779, 841–842 (1995) (Kennedy, J., concurring).

intend the recount process. More fundamentally, the Court's reluctance to let the recount go forward—despite its suggestion that "[t]he search for intent can be confined by specific rules designed to ensure uniform treatment," *ante*, at [page 105]—ultimately turns on its own judgment about the practical realities of implementing a recount, not the judgment of those much closer to the process.

Equally important, as Justice Breyer explains, *post*, at [page 140 (dissenting opinion), the December 12 "deadline" for bringing Florida's electoral votes into 3 U.S.C. § 5's safe harbor lacks the significance the Court assigns it. Were that date to pass, Florida would still be entitled to deliver electoral votes Congress *must* count unless both Houses find that the votes "had not been . . . regularly given." 3 U.S.C. § 15. The statute identifies other significant dates. See, *e.g.,* § 7 (specifying December 18 as the date electors "shall meet and give their votes"); § 12 (specifying "the fourth Wednesday in December"—this year, December 27—as the date on which Congress, if it has not received a State's electoral votes, shall request the state secretary of state to send a certified return immediately). But none of these dates has ultimate significance in light of Congress' detailed provisions for determining, on "the sixth day of January," the validity of electoral votes. § 15.

The Court assumes that time will not permit "orderly judicial review of any disputed matters that might arise." *Ante*, at [page 107]. But no one has doubted the good faith and diligence with which Florida election officials, attorneys for all sides of this controversy, and the courts of law have performed their duties. Notably, the Florida Supreme Court has produced two substantial opinions within 29 hours of oral argument. In sum, the Court's conclusion that a constitutionally adequate recount is impractical is a prophecy the Court's own judgment will not allow to be tested. Such an untested prophecy should not decide the Presidency of the United States.

I dissent.

JUSTICE BREYER, with whom JUSTICE STEVENS and
JUSTICE GINSBURG join except as to Part I-A-1, and with whom
JUSTICE SOUTER joins as to Part I, dissenting.

The Court was wrong to take this case. It was wrong to grant a stay. It should now vacate that stay and permit the Florida Supreme Court to decide whether the recount should resume.

I

The political implications of this case for the country are momentous. But the federal legal questions presented, with one exception, are insubstantial.

A

1

The majority raises three Equal Protection problems with the Florida Supreme Court's recount order: first, the failure to include overvotes in the manual recount; second, the fact that all ballots, rather than simply the undervotes, were recounted in some, but not all, counties; and third, the absence of a uniform, specific standard to guide the recounts. As far as the first issue is concerned, petitioners presented no evidence, to this Court or to any Florida court, that a manual recount of overvotes would identify additional legal votes. The same is true of the second, and, in addition, the majority's reasoning would seem to invalidate any state provision for a manual recount of individual counties in a statewide election.

The majority's third concern does implicate principles of fundamental fairness. The majority concludes that the Equal Protection Clause requires that a manual recount be governed not only by the uniform general standard of the "clear intent of the voter," but also by uniform subsidiary standards (for example, a uniform determination whether indented, but not perforated, "undervotes" should count). The opinion points out that the Florida Supreme Court ordered the inclusion of Broward County's undercounted "legal votes" even though those votes included ballots that were not perforated but simply "dimpled," while newly recounted ballots from other counties will likely include only votes determined to be "legal" on the basis of a stricter standard. In light of our previous remand, the Florida Supreme Court may have been reluctant to adopt a more specific standard than that provided for by the legislature for fear of exceeding its authority under Article II. However, since the use of different standards could favor one or the other of the candidates, since time was, and is, too short to permit the lower courts to iron out significant differences through ordinary judicial review, and since the relevant distinction was embodied in the order of the State's highest court, I agree that, in these very special circumstances, basic principles of fairness may well have counseled the adoption of a uniform standard to address the problem. In light of the majority's disposition, I need not decide whether, or the extent to which, as a remedial matter, the Constitution would place limits upon the content of the uniform standard.

2

Nonetheless, there is no justification for the majority's remedy, which is simply to reverse the lower court and halt the recount entirely. An appropriate remedy would be, instead, to remand this case with instructions that, even at this late date, would permit the Florida Supreme Court to require recounting *all* undercounted votes in Florida, including those from Broward, Volusia, Palm Beach, and Miami-Dade Counties, whether or not previously recounted prior to the end of the protest period, and to do so in accordance with a single-uniform substandard. The majority justifies stopping the recount entirely on the ground that there is no more time. In particular, the majority relies on the lack of time for the Secretary to review and approve equipment needed to separate undervotes. But the majority reaches this conclusion in the absence of any record evidence that the recount could not have been completed in the time allowed by the Florida Supreme Court. The majority finds facts outside of the record on matters that state courts are in a far better position to address. Of course, it is too late for any such recount to take place by December 12, the date by which election disputes must be decided if a State is to take advantage of the safe harbor provisions of 3 U.S.C. § 5. Whether there is time to conduct a recount prior to December 18, when the electors are scheduled to meet, is a matter for the state courts to determine. And whether, under Florida law, Florida could or could not take further action is obviously a matter for Florida courts, not this Court, to decide. See *ante*, at [page 108] (*per curiam*).

By halting the manual recount, and thus ensuring that the uncounted legal votes will not be counted under any standard, this Court crafts a remedy out of proportion to the asserted harm. And that remedy harms the very fairness interests the Court is attempting to protect. The manual recount would itself redress a problem of unequal treatment of ballots. As Justice Stevens points out, see *ante*, at [page 119 and n. 4 (Stevens, J., dissenting opinion), the ballots of voters in counties that use punch-card systems are more likely to be disqualified than those in counties using optical-scanning systems. According to recent news reports, variations in the undervote rate are even more pronounced. See Fessenden, No-Vote Rates Higher in Punch Card Count, N. Y. Times, Dec. 1, 2000, p. A29 (reporting that 0.3% of ballots cast in 30 Florida counties using optical-scanning systems registered no Presidential vote, in comparison to 1.53% in the 15 counties using Votomatic punch card ballots). Thus, in a system that allows counties to use different types of voting systems, voters already arrive at the polls with an unequal chance that their votes will be counted. I do not see how the fact that this results from counties' selection of different voting machines rather than a court order makes the outcome any more fair. Nor do I understand why the Florida Supreme Court's recount order, which helps to redress this inequity, must be entirely prohibited based on a deficiency that could easily be remedied.

B

The remainder of petitioners' claims, which are the focus of the Chief Justice's concurrence, raise no significant federal questions. I cannot agree that the Chief Justice's unusual review of state law in this case, see *ante*, at [pages 129–31] (Ginsburg, J., dissenting opinion), is justified by reference either to Art. II, § 1, or to 3 U.S.C. § 5. Moreover, even were such review proper, the conclusion that the Florida Supreme Court's decision contravenes federal law is untenable.

While conceding that, in most cases, "comity and respect for federalism compel us to defer to the decisions of state courts on issues of state law," the concurrence relies on some combination of Art. II, § 1, and 3 U.S.C. § 5 to justify the majority's conclusion that this case is one of the few in which we may lay that fundamental principle aside. *Ante*, at page 109 (Opinion of Rehnquist, C. J.) The concurrence's primary foundation for this conclusion rests on an appeal to plain text: Art. II, § 1's grant of the power to appoint Presidential electors to the State "Legislature." *Ibid*. But neither the text of Article II itself nor the only case the concurrence cites that interprets Article II, *McPherson v. Blacker*, 146 U.S. 1 (1892), leads to the conclusion that Article II grants unlimited power to the legislature, devoid of any state constitutional limitations, to select the manner of appointing electors. See *id.*, at 41 (specifically referring to state constitutional provision in upholding state law regarding selection of electors). Nor, as Justice Stevens points out, have we interpreted the Federal constitutional provision most analogous to Art. II, § 1–Art. I, § 4—in the strained manner put forth in the concurrence. *Ante*, at pages 127–28 and n. 1 (dissenting opinion).

The concurrence's treatment of § 5 as "inform[ing]" its interpretation of Article II, § 1, cl. 2, *ante*, at [page 110] (Rehnquist, C. J., concurring), is no more convincing. The Chief Justice contends that our opinion in *Bush v. Palm Beach County Canvassing Bd.*, *ante*, [pages 46–52] (*per curiam*) (*Bush I*), in which we stated that "a legislative wish to take advantage of [§ 5] would counsel against" a construction of Florida law that Congress might deem to be a change in law, *id.*, [page 52], now means that this Court "must ensure that post-election state court actions do not frustrate the legislative desire to attain the 'safe harbor' provided by § 5." *Ante*, at [page 110]. However, § 5 is part of the rules that govern Congress' recognition of slates of electors. Nowhere in *Bush I* did we establish that this Court had the authority to enforce § 5. Nor did we suggest that the permissive "counsel against" could be transformed into the mandatory "must ensure." And nowhere did we intimate, as the concurrence does here, that a state court decision that threatens the safe harbor provision of § 5 does so in violation of Article II. The concurrence's logic turns the presumption that legislatures would wish to take advantage of § 5's "safe harbor" provision into a mandate that trumps other statutory provisions and overrides the intent that the legislature did express.

But, in any event, the concurrence, having conducted its review, now reaches the wrong conclusion. It says that "the Florida Supreme Court's interpretation of the Florida election laws impermissibly distorted them beyond what a fair reading required, in violation of Article II." *Ante*, at [page 111] (Rehnquist, C. J, concurring). But what precisely is the distortion? Apparently, it has three elements. First, the Florida court, in its earlier opinion, changed the election certification date from November 14 to November 26. Second, the Florida court ordered a manual recount of "undercounted" ballots that could not have been fully completed by the December 12 "safe harbor" deadline. Third, the Florida court, in the opinion now under review, failed to give adequate deference to the determinations of canvassing boards and the Secretary.

To characterize the first element as a "distortion," however, requires the concurrence to second-guess the way in which the state court resolved a plain conflict in the language of different statutes. Compare Fla. Stat. § 102.166 (2001) (foreseeing manual recounts during the protest period) with § 102.111 (setting what is arguably too short a deadline for manual recounts to be conducted); compare § 102.112(1) (stating that the Secretary "may" ignore late returns) with § 102.111(1) (stating that the Secretary "shall" ignore late returns). In any event, that issue no longer has any practical importance and cannot justify the reversal of the different Florida court decision before us now.

To characterize the second element as a "distortion" requires the concurrence to overlook the fact that the inability of the Florida courts to conduct the recount on time is, in significant part, a problem of the Court's own making. The Florida Supreme Court thought that the recount could be completed on time, and, within hours, the Florida Circuit Court was moving in an orderly fashion to meet the deadline. This Court improvidently entered a stay. As a result, we will never know whether the recount could have been completed.

Nor can one characterize the third element as "impermissible distorting" once one understands that there are two sides to the opinion's argument that the Florida Supreme Court "virtually eliminated the Secretary's discretion." *Ante,* at [page 114] (Rehnquist, C. J, concurring). The Florida statute in question was amended in 1999 to provide that the "grounds for contesting an election" include the "rejection of a number of legal votes sufficient to . . . place in doubt the result of the election." Fla. Stat. §§ 102.168(3), (3)(c) (2000). And the parties have argued about the proper meaning of the statute's term "legal vote." The Secretary has claimed that a "legal vote" is a vote "properly executed in accordance with the instructions provided to all registered voters." Brief for Respondent Harris et al. 10. On that interpretation, punchcard ballots for which the machines cannot register a vote are not "legal" votes. *Id.,* at 14. The Florida Supreme Court did not accept her definition. But it had a reason. Its reason was that a different provision of Florida election laws (a provision that addresses damaged or defective ballots) says that no vote shall be disregarded "if there is a clear indication of the intent of the voter as determined by the canvassing board" (adding that ballots should not be counted "if it is impossible to determine the elector's choice"). Fla. Stat. § 101.5614(5) (2000). Given this statutory language, certain roughly analogous judicial precedent, *e.g., Darby v. State ex rel. McCollough,* 75 So. 411 (Fla. 1917) (*per curiam*), and somewhat similar determinations by courts throughout the Nation, see cases cited *infra,* at [page 138], the Florida Supreme Court concluded that the term "legal vote" means a vote recorded on a ballot that clearly reflects what the voter intended. *Gore v. Harris* (2000) [page 72]. That conclusion differs from the conclusion of the Secretary. But nothing in Florida law requires the Florida Supreme Court to accept as determinative the Secretary's view on such a matter. Nor can one say that the Court's ultimate determination is so unreasonable as to amount to a constitutionally "impermissible distort[ion]" of Florida law.

The Florida Supreme Court, applying this definition, decided, on the basis of the record, that respondents had shown that the ballots undercounted by the voting machines contained enough "legal votes" to place "the results" of the election "in doubt." Since only a few hundred votes separated the candidates, and since the "undercounted" ballots numbered tens of thousands, it is difficult to see how anyone could find this conclusion unreasonable—however strict the standard used to measure the voter's "clear intent." Nor did this conclusion "strip" canvassing boards of their discretion. The boards retain their traditional discretionary authority during the protest period. And during the contest period, as the court stated, "the Canvassing Board's actions [during the protest period] may constitute evidence that a ballot does or does not qualify as a legal vote." *Id.* at [page 77. Whether a local county canvassing board's discretionary judgment during the protest period not to conduct a manual recount will be set aside during a contest period depends upon whether a candidate provides additional evidence that the rejected votes contain enough "legal votes" to place the outcome of the race in doubt. To limit the local canvassing board's discretion in this way is not to eliminate that discretion. At the least, one could reasonably so believe.

The statute goes on to provide the Florida circuit judge with authority to "fashion such orders as he or she deems necessary to ensure that each allegation . . . is *investigated, examined, or checked,* . . . and to provide any relief appropriate." Fla. Stat. § 102.168(8) (2000) (emphasis added). The Florida Supreme Court did just that. One might reasonably disagree with the Florida Supreme Court's interpretation of these, or other, words in the statute. But I do not see how one could call its plain language interpretation of a 1999 statutory change so misguided as no longer to qualify as judicial interpretation or as a usurpation of the authority of the State legislature. Indeed, other state courts have interpreted roughly similar state statutes in similar ways. See, *e.g., In re Election of U.S. Representative for Second Congressional Dist.,* 231 Conn. 602, 621, 653 A.2d 79, 90–91 (1994) ("Whatever the process used to vote and to count votes, differences in technology should not furnish a basis for disregarding the bedrock principle that the purpose of the voting process is to ascertain the intent of the voters"); *Brown v. Carr,* 130 W. Va. 455, 460, 43 S.E.2d 401, 404–405 (1947) ("Whether a ballot shall be counted . . . depends on the intent of the voter. . . . Courts decry any resort to technical rules in reaching a conclusion as to the intent of the voter").

I repeat, where is the "impermissible" distortion?

II

Despite the reminder that this case involves "an election for the President of the United States," *ante,* at [page 109] (Rehnquist, C. J., concurring), no preeminent legal concern, or practical concern related to legal questions, required this Court to hear this case, let alone to issue a stay that stopped

Florida's recount process in its tracks. With one exception, petitioners' claims do not ask us to vindicate a constitutional provision designed to protect a basic human right. See, *e.g., Brown v. Board of Education,* 347 U.S. 483 (1954). Petitioners invoke fundamental fairness, namely, the need for procedural fairness, including finality. But with the one "equal protection" exception, they rely upon law that focuses, not upon that basic need, but upon the constitutional allocation of power. Respondents invoke a competing fundamental consideration—the need to determine the voter's true intent. But they look to state law, not to federal constitutional law, to protect that interest. Neither side claims electoral fraud, dishonesty, or the like. And the more fundamental equal protection claim might have been left to the state court to resolve if and when it was discovered to have mattered. It could still be resolved through a remand conditioned upon issuance of a uniform standard; it does not require reversing the Florida Supreme Court.

Of course, the selection of the President is of fundamental national importance. But that importance is political, not legal. And this Court should resist the temptation unnecessarily to resolve tangential legal disputes, where doing so threatens to determine the outcome of the election.

The Constitution and federal statutes themselves make clear that restraint is appropriate. They set forth a road map of how to resolve disputes about electors, even after an election as close as this one. That road map foresees resolution of electoral disputes by *state* courts. See 3 U.S.C. § 5 (providing that, where a "State shall have provided, by laws enacted prior to [election day], for its final determination of any controversy or contest concerning the appointment of . . . electors . . . by *judicial* or other methods," the subsequently chosen electors enter a safe harbor free from congressional challenge). But it nowhere provides for involvement by the United States Supreme Court.

To the contrary, the Twelfth Amendment commits to Congress the authority and responsibility to count electoral votes. A federal statute, the Electoral Count Act, enacted after the close 1876 Hayes-Tilden Presidential election, specifies that, after States have tried to resolve disputes (through "judicial" or other means), Congress is the body primarily authorized to resolve remaining disputes. See Electoral Count Act of 1887, 24 Stat. 373, 3 U.S.C. §§ 5, 6, and 15.

The legislative history of the Act makes clear its intent to commit the power to resolve such disputes to Congress, rather than the courts:

"The two Houses are, by the Constitution, authorized to make the count of electoral votes. They can only count legal votes, and in doing so must determine, from the best evidence to be had, what are legal votes .... The power to determine rests with the two Houses, and there is no other constitutional tribunal." H. Rep. No. 1638, 49th Cong., 1st Sess., 2 (1886) (report submitted by Rep. Caldwell, Select Committee on the Election of President and Vice-President).

The Member of Congress who introduced the Act added:

"The power to judge of the legality of the votes is a necessary consequent of the power to count. The existence of this power is of absolute necessity to the preservation of the Government. The interests of all the States in their relations to each other in the Federal Union demand that the ultimate tribunal to decide upon the election of President should be a constituent body, in which the States in their federal relationships and the people in their sovereign capacity should be represented." 18 Cong. Rec. 30 (1886).

"Under the Constitution who else could decide? Who is nearer to the State in determining a question of vital importance to the whole union of States than the constituent body upon whom the Constitution has devolved the duty to count the vote?" *Id.*, at 31.

The Act goes on to set out rules for the congressional determination of disputes about those votes. If, for example, a state submits a single slate of electors, Congress must count those votes unless both Houses agree that the votes "have not been . . . regularly given." 3 U.S.C. § 15. If, as occurred in 1876, one or more states submits two sets of electors, then Congress must determine whether a slate has entered the safe harbor of § 5, in which case its votes will have "conclusive" effect. *Ibid.* If, as also occurred in 1876, there is controversy about "which of two or more of such State authorities . . . is the lawful tribunal" authorized to appoint electors, then each House shall determine separately which votes are "supported by the decision of such State so authorized by its law." *Ibid.* If the two Houses of Congress agree, the votes they have approved will be counted. If they disagree, then "the votes of the electors whose appointment shall have been certified by the executive of the State, under the seal thereof, shall be counted." *Ibid.*

Given this detailed, comprehensive scheme for counting electoral votes, there is no reason to believe that federal law either foresees or requires resolution of such a political issue by this Court. Nor, for that matter, is there any reason to that think the Constitution's Framers would have reached a different conclusion. Madison, at least, believed that allowing the judiciary to choose the presidential electors "was out of the question." Madison, July 25, 1787 (reprinted in 5 Elliot's Debates on the Federal Constitution 363 (2d ed. 1876)).

The decision by both the Constitution's Framers and the 1886 Congress to minimize this Court's role in resolving close federal presidential elections is as wise as it is clear. However awkward or difficult it may be for Congress to resolve difficult electoral disputes, Congress, being a political body, expresses the people's will far more accurately than does an unelected Court. And the people's will is what elections are about.

Moreover, Congress was fully aware of the danger that would arise should it ask judges, unarmed with appropriate legal standards, to resolve a hotly contested Presidential election contest. Just after the 1876 Presidential election, Florida, South Carolina, and Louisiana each sent two slates of electors to Washington. Without these States, Tilden, the Democrat, had 184 electoral votes, one short of the number required to win the Presidency. With those States, Hayes, his Republican opponent, would have had 185. In order to choose between the two slates of electors, Congress decided to appoint an electoral commission composed of five Senators, five Representatives, and five Supreme Court Justices. Initially the Commission was to be evenly divided between Republicans and Democrats, with Justice David Davis, an Independent, to possess the decisive vote. However, when at the last minute the Illinois Legislature elected Justice Davis to the United States Senate, the final position on the Commission was filled by Supreme Court Justice Joseph P. Bradley.

The Commission divided along partisan lines, and the responsibility to cast the deciding vote fell to Justice Bradley. He decided to accept the votes by the Republican electors, and thereby awarded the Presidency to Hayes. Justice Bradley immediately became the subject of vociferous attacks. Bradley was accused of accepting bribes, of being captured by railroad interests, and of an eleventh-hour change in position after a night in which his house "was surrounded by the carriages" of Republican partisans and railroad officials. C. Woodward, Reunion and Reaction 159–160 (1966). Many years later, Professor Bickel concluded that Bradley was honest and impartial. He thought that "'the great question' for Bradley was, in fact, whether Congress was entitled to go behind election returns or had to accept them as certified by state authorities," an "issue of principle." The Least Dangerous Branch 185 (1962). Nonetheless, Bickel points out, the legal question upon which Justice Bradley's decision turned was not very important in the contemporaneous political context. He says that "in the circumstances the issue of principle was trivial, it was overwhelmed by all that hung in the balance, and it should not have been decisive." *Ibid.* For present purposes, the relevance of this history lies in the fact that the participation in the work of the electoral commission by five Justices, including Justice Bradley, did not lend that process legitimacy. Nor did it assure the public that the process had worked fairly, guided by the law. Rather, it simply embroiled Members of the Court in partisan conflict, thereby undermining respect for the judicial process. And the Congress that later enacted the Electoral Count Act knew it.

This history may help to explain why I think it not only legally wrong, but also most unfortunate, for the Court simply to have terminated the Florida recount. Those who caution judicial restraint in resolving political disputes have described the quintessential case for that restraint as a case marked, among other things, by the "strangeness of the issue," its "intractability to principled resolution," its "sheer momentousness, . . . which tends to unbalance judicial judgment," and "the inner vulnerability, the self-doubt of an institution which is electorally irresponsible and has no earth to draw strength from." Bickel, *supra*, at 184. Those characteristics mark this case.

At the same time, as I have said, the Court is not acting to vindicate a fundamental constitutional principle, such as the need to protect a basic human liberty. No other strong reason to act is present. Congressional statutes tend to obviate the need. And, above all, in this highly politicized matter, the appearance of a split decision runs the risk of undermining the public's confidence in the Court itself. That confidence is a public treasure. It has been built slowly over many years, some of which were marked by a Civil War and the tragedy of segregation. It is a vitally necessary ingredient of any successful effort to protect basic liberty and, indeed, the rule of law itself. We run no risk of returning to the days when a President (responding to this Court's efforts to protect the Cherokee Indians) might have said, "John Marshall has made his decision; now let him enforce it!" Loth, Chief Justice John Marshall and The Growth of the American Republic 365 (1948). But we do risk a self-inflicted wound—a wound that may harm not just the Court, but the Nation.

I fear that in order to bring this agonizingly long election process to a definitive conclusion, we have not adequately attended to that necessary "check upon our own exercise of power," "our own sense of self-restraint." *United States v. Butler,* 297 U.S. 1, 79 (1936) (Stone, J., dissenting). Justice

Brandeis once said of the Court, "The most important thing we do is not doing." Bickel, *supra*, at 71. What it does today, the Court should have left undone. I would repair the damage done as best we now can, by permitting the Florida recount to continue under uniform standards.

    I respectfully dissent.

Supreme Court of Florida

No. SC00-2431

Albert Gore, Jr., and Joseph I. Lieberman, Appellants, *v.*
Katherine Harris, as Secretary, ETC., ET AL., Appellees.

ORDER ON REMAND

December 14, 2000

This case is before the Court on remand from the United States Supreme
Court. See *Bush v. Gore,* No. 00-949 (U.S. Dec. 12, 2000) [page 108]. The
per curiam opinion of the Supreme Court majority specified that in order
for a manual recount to continue:

> It would require not only the adoption (after opportunity for argu-
> ment) of adequate statewide standards for determining what is a le-
> gal vote, and practicable procedures to implement them, but also or-
> derly judicial review of any disputed matters that might arise. In
> addition, the Secretary of State has advised that the recount of only
> a portion of the ballots requires that the vote tabulation equipment
> be used to screen out undervotes, a function for which the machines
> were not designed. If a recount of overvotes were also required, per-
> haps even a second screening would be necessary. Use of the equip-
> ment for this purpose, and any new software developed for it, would
> have to be evaluated for accuracy by the Secretary of State, as re-
> quired by Fla. Stat. § 101.015 (2000).

Id. at [pages 107–08]. The Supreme Court majority ultimately concluded
that:

> Because it is evident that any recount seeking to meet the December
> 12 date will be unconstitutional for the reasons we have discussed,
> we reverse the judgement of the Supreme Court of Florida ordering
> a recount to proceed.

Id. at [page 108].

On the date of the subject election, the Florida Election Code did not
provide the element necessary for a resolution of the disputed issues, based

on the constitutional parameters expressed by the United States Supreme Court. Accordingly, relief cannot be granted, and this case is dismissed. Opinion may follow.

No motion for rehearing will be allowed.

CHIEF JUSTICE WELLS and JUSTICES SHAW, HARDING, ANSTEAD, PARIENTE, LEWIS, and QUINCE concur.

[OPINION]
December 22, 2000

PER CURIAM

This case is before the Court on remand from the United States Supreme Court. See *Bush v. Gore*, No. 00-949 (U.S. Decided Dec. 12, 2000) [page 108].[1] In our previous opinion, we ordered the Circuit Court of Leon County to tabulate by hand 9000 contested Dade County ballots. See *Gore v. Harris* (Fla. Decided Dec. 8, 2000) [page 80]. This Court further held that relief would require manual recounts in all Florida counties where undervotes existed which had not previously been subject to manual tabulation. *See id.* at [pages 80–81]. The standard we directed be employed in the manual recount was the standard established by the Legislature in the Florida Election Code, i. e., that a vote shall be counted as a "legal" vote if there is a "clear indication of the intent of the voter." *See id.* at [page 81] (citing section 101.5614(5), Florida Statutes (2000)). The "intent of the voter" standard adopted by the Legislature was the standard in place as of November 7, 2000, and a more expansive ruling would have raised an issue as to whether this Court would be substantially rewriting the Code after the election, in violation of article II, section 1, clause 2 of the United States Constitution and 3 U.S.C. § 5 (1994).

The per curiam opinion of the Supreme Court held that the Florida statutory standard for the manual examination of ballots violates equal protection rights. See *Bush*, [pages 104–05]. Although the Supreme Court found the legislatively prescribed standard to be unobjectionable as an abstract proposition and starting principle, it noted "[t]he problem inheres in the absence of specific standards to ensure its equal application." *Id.* [at page 104] The Supreme Court specified that in order for a manual recount to continue:

1. This opinion follows our dismissal of this cause by order of December 14, 2000.

It would require not only the adoption (after opportunity for argument) of adequate statewide standards for determining what is a legal vote, and practicable procedures to implement them, but also orderly judicial review of any disputed matters that might arise. In addition, the Secretary of State has advised that the recount of only a portion of the ballots requires that the vote tabulation equipment be used to screen out undervotes, a function for which the machines were not designed. If a recount of overvotes were also required, perhaps even a second screening would be necessary. Use of equipment for this purpose, and any new software developed for it, would have to be evaluated for accuracy by the Secretary of State, as required by Fla. Stat. § 101.015 (2000).

Id. at [pages 107–08]. The Supreme Court ultimately mandated that any manual recount be concluded by December 12, 2000, as provided in 3 U.S.C. § 5. See *id.* at [page 108]. In light of the time of the release of the Supreme Court opinion, these tasks and this deadline could not possibly be met. Moreover, upon reflection, we conclude that the development of a specific, uniform standard necessary to ensure equal application and to secure the fundamental right to vote throughout the State of Florida should be left to the body we believe best equipped to study and address it, the Legislature.

Accordingly, pursuant to the direction of the United States Supreme Court, we hold appellants can be afforded no relief.

It is so ordered.

Justices SHAW, ANSTEAD, PARIENTE, LEWIS, and QUINCE concur.

CHIEF JUSTICE WELLS concurs in result only with an opinion.

JUSTICE SHAW concurs with an opinion.

JUSTICE HARDING concurs in result only.

JUSTICE PARIENTE concurs with an opinion.

No motion for rehearing will be allowed.

CHIEF JUSTICE WELLS concurring in result only. I concur only in the result which this Court decided in its order on remand in this case, which was that no relief could be granted and the case be dismissed.

JUSTICE SHAW concurring. This case has torn the nation and the judiciary. It is quintessentially divisive and confounding. The problem, I believe, lies not in the partisan nature of the issues but rather in the deeply rooted, and conflicting, legal principles that are involved.

A. THE GENERAL WELFARE

A fundamental principle underlying all legal proceedings is the search for the truth. Once the truth is uncovered, we assume that a remedy can be fashioned. The present case posed a simple question: Who won the presidential election in Florida? The answer, in the eyes of many, also was simple: The truth lies in the vaults and storage rooms throughout the state where the untabulated ballots of thousands of Floridians are sequestered.

A second deeply rooted principle is the right of suffrage. The right to vote, and to have each vote counted, is a preeminent civil right[2] and has been won at great cost. It was not too far in our nation's past that throngs of citizens marched in the streets to protest the suppression of this right and risked being beaten with nightsticks and set upon with tear gas, firehoses, and dogs. Some were jailed. A few—men, women, and children—were killed. The suppression of this right is now anathema to the nation. The right to vote, and to have each vote counted, goes to the very heart of this case.[3]

Both the search for the truth and the right to vote are of paramount importance, but they are circumscribed by a higher, overarching concern—the general welfare of our democracy. The general welfare is informed by our law.[4] The law infuses the fabric of our society and breathes life into all our legal principles. Inherent in the law are the basic concepts of fairness, reliability, and predictability; and the constitutional safeguards of due process and equal protection were designed to promote these interests. Although the pursuit of the truth and the preservation of the right to vote are worthy goals, they cannot be achieved in a manner that contravenes these principles.

2. See, e. g., Yick Wo v. Hopkins, 118 U.S. 356, 370 (1886) ("[The right of suffrage] is regarded as a fundamental political right, because preservative of all rights.").

3. See generally Reynolds v. Sims, 377 U.S. 533, 561–62 (1964) ("The right of suffrage is a fundamental matter in a free and democratic society. Especially since the right to exercise the franchise in a free and unimpaired manner is preservative of other basic civil and political rights, any alleged infringement of the right of citizens to vote must be carefully and meticulously scrutinized.").

4. The concern for the general welfare of our democracy is implicit in the United States Constitution, which provides in part:

> We the People of the United States, in Order to form a more perfect Union, establish Justice, insure domestic Tranquility, provide for the common defence, promote the general Welfare, and secure the Blessings of Liberty to ourselves and our Posterity, do ordain and establish this Constitution for the United States of America.

U.S. Const. pmbl.

B. THE RECOUNT DILEMMA

A unanimous Florida Supreme Court in *Palm Beach County Canvassing Board v. Harris*, (Fla. Nov. 21, 2000) [pages 24–47], applied traditional rules of statutory construction to resolve several conflicts and ambiguities in the Florida Election Code ("Code"). The Court concluded that countywide manual recounts had been improperly cut off in the "protest" phase[5] by an advisory statement issued by the Florida Secretary of State, and we ordered that the counties must be given a commensurate window of opportunity in which to complete the manual recounts and submit supplemental returns. The United States Supreme Court vacated the judgment,[6] but this Court on remand reaffirmed our prior holding.[7]

In *Gore v. Harris* (Fla. Dec. 8, 2000) [pages 58–81] , a majority of the Florida Supreme Court authorized a manual recount of untabulated ballots in the "contest" phase.[8] To comport with due process and equal protection concerns, the Court ordered that the recount be conducted statewide and that the results be adjudicated by a single judge. I dissented because I felt that the recount, as formulated, lacked sufficient guidelines and could not be completed promptly and fairly. The United States Supreme Court on the first day of the recount, *i. e.,* December 9, stayed the recount and at 10 p.m., December 12, ruled that additional guidelines were required. The Court further held that December 12 was a mandatory deadline under the Florida Election Code and that any recount extending beyond that date was violative of Florida law, thus foreclosing the possibility of a recount.[9]

---

5. *See* § 102.166, Fla. Stat. (2000).
6. See *Bush v. Palm Beach County Canvassing Bd.,* (Dec. 4, 2000) [page 51]
7. *See Palm Beach County Canvassing Bd. v. Harris* (Fla. Dec. 11, 2000)
8. *See* § 102.168, Fla. Stat. (2000).
9. The United States Supreme Court ruled as follows:

   Because it is evident that any recount seeking to meet the December 12 date will be unconstitutional for the reasons we have discussed, we reverse the judgment of the Supreme Court of Florida ordering a recount to proceed.

   . . . Because the Florida Supreme Court has said that the Florida Legislature intended to obtain the safe-harbor benefits of 3 U.S.C. § 5, Justice Breyer's proposed remedy—remanding to the Florida Supreme Court for its ordering of a constitutionally proper contest until December 18—contemplates action in violation of the Florida election code, and hence could not be part of an "appropriate" order authorized by Fla. Stat. § 102.168(8) (2000).

Bush v. Gore, No. 00-949 (U.S. Dec. 12, 2000) [page 108].

First, in my opinion, December 12 was not a "drop-dead" date under Florida law. In fact, I question whether any date prior to January 6 is a drop-dead date under the Florida election scheme.[10] December 12 was simply a *permissive* "safe-harbor" date to which the states could aspire.[11] It certainly was not a mandatory contest deadline under the plain language of the Florida Election Code (i. e., it is not mentioned there) or this Court's prior rulings.[12] Second, regardless of the safe-harbor date, I am not convinced that additional safeguards could have been formulated that would have satisfied the United States Supreme Court. Given the tenor of the opinion in *Bush v. Gore*, 2000 U.S. No. 00-949 (U.S. Dec. 12, 2000), I do not believe that the Florida Supreme Court could have crafted a remedy under these circumstances that would have met the due process, equal protection, and other concerns of the United States Supreme Court.[13]

10. Title III, section 15, United States Code, provides that regardless of prior dates, Florida is entitled to deliver its electoral votes to Congress prior to January 6 at which time Congress must count those votes unless Congress determines that the votes "have [not] been regularly given." [*Eds.* quotation of 3 U.S.C. § 15 omitted]

11. Title III, section 5, United States Code, provides that where a dispute concerning the appointment of electors is settled at least six days prior to the date set for the meeting of electors (i. e., at least six days prior to December 18, 2000), the state's decision concerning the settlement is conclusive. [*Eds.*: quotation of 3 U.S.C. § 5 omitted]

12. Contrary to the ruling of the United States Supreme Court in *Bush v. Gore,* No. 00-949 (U.S. Dec. 12, 2000), our prior opinions discussed Title III vis-à-vis the Florida Secretary of State's authority to reject late returns arising from a pre-certification protest action, not vis-a-vis a court's obligation to stop a recount in a post-certification *contest* action. *See Palm Beach County Canvassing Bd. v. Harris,* 2000 (Fla. Nov. 21, 2000), and *Palm Beach County Canvassing Bd. v. Harris* (Fla. Dec. 11, 2000). To mix these two actions is to confuse apples and oranges.

13. The United States Supreme Court summarized the constitutional requirements for a recount:

> [I]t is obvious that the recount cannot be conducted in compliance with the requirements of equal protection and due process without substantial additional work. It would require not only the adoption (after opportunity for argument) of adequate statewide standards for determining what is a legal vote, and practicable procedures to implement them, but also orderly judicial review of any disputed matters that might arise.

Bush v. Gore, No. 00-949 (U.S. Dec. 12, 2000) [page 107]. The Court then adopted the position of the Florida Secretary of State concerning untabulated ballots:

> In addition, the Secretary of State has advised that the recount of only a portion of the ballots requires that the vote tabulation equipment be used to screen out undervotes, a function for which the machines were not designed. If a recount of overvotes were also required, perhaps even a second screening would be necessary.

C. HUMAN FAILINGS

Admittedly, the present scenario is surreal: All the king's horses and all the king's men could not get a few thousand ballots counted. The explanation, however, is timeless. We are a nation of men and women and, although we aspire to lofty principles, our methods at times are imperfect.

First, although the untabulated Florida ballots may hold the truth to the presidential election, we still—to this day—cannot agree on how to count those ballots fairly and accurately. In fact, we cannot even agree on if they should be counted. Second, although the right to vote is paramount, we routinely installed outdated and defective voting systems and tabulating equipment at our polls prior to the present election. And finally, although the rule of law is supreme, the key legal text in this case— i. e., the Florida Election Code—is fraught with contradictions and ambiguities, and the key legal ruling— i. e., the United States Supreme Court's final decision in *Bush v. Gore* (U.S. Dec. 12, 2000)—was denigrated and rejected by nearly half the members of that Court.

D. CONCLUSION

I commend the public officials, employees, and volunteers of this state— each election supervisor, judge, court clerk, board member, and all the others—who worked tirelessly in a star-crossed effort to count every vote. I commend the people of our state and nation who looked faithfully to the courts to interpret and apply the law. I also commend Vice President Gore for persevering in the labor of Sisyphus; each time he attempted to comply with the Code, he was forced to begin anew. And I commend President-elect Bush for remaining stalwart in the face of charges of suppressing the truth (i. e., of obstructing the counting of ballots) and disenfranchising the voters of this state. And finally, I especially commend the other justices of this Court, each of whom approached this case with a sworn resolve to be objective, honorable, and fair.

Our nation has been through an ordeal, but we have learned from the experience. At this point, I know one thing for certain: The basic principles of our democracy are intact.

Bush, [page 107]. And finally, the Court construed Florida law to give the Secretary a decisive evaluative role:

> Use of the equipment for this purpose, and any new software developed for it, would have to be evaluated for accuracy by the Secretary of State, as required by Fla. Stat. § 101.015 (2000).

Bush, [pages 107–08].

JUSTICE PARIENTE concurring.

I concur fully with the majority opinion. However, I write separately to discuss several concerns with Florida's present Election Code and the use of different voting systems in place in Florida's sixty-seven counties, particularly in light of the United States Supreme Court decision in *Bush v. Gore* (U.S. Dec. 12, 2000). Just as the lessons learned from the last major presidential election dispute—the election of 1876—prompted substantial reform, so my vision is that the valuable lessons we have learned from the 2000 presidential election will strengthen and reinvigorate our democracy.[14]

Whatever the reason, we now know that not every vote intended to be cast for a candidate in this November 7, 2000, presidential election in Florida was tabulated and counted as a vote. Further, although manual recounts were completed in several counties,[15] in other counties the ballots for which the machine did not register a vote—the "undervotes"—were never examined manually to ensure that all legal votes were counted. What should concern all of us is not whether the uncounted votes were for President-Elect Bush or for Vice President Gore, but that thousands of voters in Florida did not have their vote included in this State's presidential election.

It is essential to our great democracy that all citizens have confidence in the integrity and reliability of the electoral process. As the Florida House

---

14. In modern times, we have never experienced a post-election court dispute in the election for the President of the United States. The time limits Congress enacted for resolving contests in Presidential elections were established in a far different time, when our country looked far different—and was far less populous than today. Indeed, Congress enacted the safe harbor provision, 3 U.S.C. section 5, and other election-related dates, in 1887, as a result of the Hayes-Tilden post-election dispute. See *Bush v. Gore,* No. 00-949 (U.S. Dec. 12, 2000) [page 139] (Breyer, J., dissenting). The significance of these time limits is not entirely clear. *See id.* at [page 132] (Ginsburg, J., dissenting) (explaining that "the December 12 'deadline' for bringing Florida's electoral votes into 3 U.S.C. § 5's safe harbor lacks the significance the Court assigns it. . . . None of these dates has ultimate significance in light of Congress' detailed provisions for determining on 'the sixth day of January,' 'the validity of electoral votes. § 15"). Accordingly, although we have become a society accustomed to immediate results—communications delivered via fax with rapid speed and news stories broadcast over the Internet as they occur—perhaps the time has come for Congress to explore whether, in the rare case of a post-election presidential controversy, a thirty-five day time limit for a final resolution of a presidential contest is realistic or reasonable.

15. Full hand counts were done at the request of the Florida Democratic Executive Committee ("Committee") in Volusia, Broward, and Palm Beach Counties. See *Palm Beach County Canvassing Board v. Harris,* Nos. SC00-2346, SC00-2348, SC00-2349, [slip op. at 3] (Fla. Dec. 11, 2000)].

of Representatives Committee on Election Reform 1997 Interim Project on Election Contests and Recounts expressly declared:

> Recounts are an integral part of the election process. *For one's vote, when cast, to be translated into a true message, that vote must be accurately counted, and if necessary, recounted.* The moment an individual's vote becomes subject to error in the vote tabulation process, the easier it is for that vote to be diluted.

Id. at 15 (emphasis supplied) (footnotes omitted). As we have stated most forcefully, this Court remains committed to the principle that:

> the real parties in interest here, not in the legal sense but in realistic terms, are the voters. They are possessed of the ultimate interest and it is they whom we must give primary consideration. The contestants have direct interests certainly, but the office they seek is one of high public service and of utmost importance to the people, thus subordinating their interests to that of the people. *Ours is a government of, by and for the people. Our federal and state constitutions guarantee the right of the people to take an active part in the process of that government, which for most of our citizens means participation via the election process. The right to vote is the right to participate; it is also the right to speak, but more importantly the right to be heard.* We must tread carefully on that right or we risk the unnecessary and unjustified muting of the public voice. By refusing to recognize an otherwise valid exercise of the right of a citizen to vote for the sake of sacred, unyielding adherence to statutory scripture, we would in effect nullify that right.

Boardman v. Esteva, 323 So. 2d 259, 262–63 (Fla. 1975) (emphasis supplied).[16] With these principles in mind, I turn to a review of some of the

16. John Greenleaf Whittier's nineteenth-century poem, "The Poor Voter on Election Day," more eloquently echoes the importance of this fundamental right to vote as the great equalizer between all citizens:
> To-day, of all the weary year,
> A king of men am I.
> To-day, alike are great and small,
> The nameless and the known;
> My palace is the people's hall,
> The ballot-box my throne!
> The rich is level with the poor,
> The weak is strong to-day;
> And sleekest broadcloth counts no more
> Than homespun frock of gray.

provisions of the Election Code and the voting systems in place at the time of the November 7, 2000, presidential election.

Statewide manual recounts: According to the official figures reported on November 8, 2000, the day after the election, out of almost six million votes cast in Florida, the difference between the vote totals for the two candidates was a margin of only 1784 votes—0.0299% of the total Florida vote. See *Siegel v. Lepore,* No. 00-15981 (11th Cir. Dec. 6, 2000). Because the margin of victory was less than "one-half of a percent . . . of the votes cast," pursuant to Florida's Election Code, an automatic machine recount was conducted in each county in this State.[17] § 102.141(4), Fla. Stat. (2000). However, the Florida Election Code did not provide for an automatic procedure to allow for the option of one candidate to request a statewide manual recount according to uniform, "objective" standards.[18] Thus, one of the issues that should be considered in any future study of Florida's Election Code is whether such a procedure should have been in place.

Instead of a procedure for requesting a statewide manual recount, the statutes in place as of November 7, 2000, provided that a candidate had the option pursuant to section 102.166(4), Florida Statutes (2000), to request a manual recount from an individual county canvassing board. Based upon the express language in section 102.166, however, the individual county canvassing board is vested with discretion to conduct the initial manual re-

---

To-day let pomp and vain pretence
My stubborn right abide;
I set a plain man's common sense
Against the pedant's pride.
The wide world has not wealth to buy
The power in my right hand!

17. Although there were assertions made that the votes were counted and recounted, apparently in some counties the votes were not even subjected to a second machine count—only the machines were checked. See Phil Long & Dan deVise, *Not All Florida Counties Obeyed Order To Do Recount,* Miami Herald, December 15, 2000. Further, the automatic machine recount in Nassau County actually showed fewer overall votes than the initial machine count. *See Gore,* [page 59]. The fact that the two machine counties showed differing vote totals should raise concerns about the reliability of machine counts in close elections. This disparity shows yet one more reason why "our society has not yet gone so far as to place blind faith in machines." *Palm Beach Canvassing Board,* [slip op. at 15] (Fla., Dec. 11, 2000)].

18. At oral argument on November 20, 2000, "we inquired as to whether the presidential candidates were interested in our consideration of a reopening of the opportunity to request manual recounts in all counties. neither candidate requested such an opportunity." *Palm Beach Canvassing Bd.,* [slip op. at 30], n. 21 (Fla. Dec. 11, 2000).

count of at least three precincts.[19] Once the initial sampling shows an "error in the vote tabulation which could affect the outcome of the election," the county canvassing board is required to exercise one of three options, with the third option being a manual recount of all ballots. § 102.166(5)(a)–(c), Fla. Stat. (2000). In counting the ballots manually, the statute provides that if the "counting team is unable to determine a voter's intent in casting a ballot, that ballot shall be presented to the county canvassing board for it to determine the voter's intent." § 102.166(7)(b), Fla. Stat. (2000).

Although in a local or countywide election the discretion of whether to conduct a manual recount may be properly vested in an individual canvassing board, the discretionary nature of the decision raises concerns of uniformity and completeness in a statewide election. In a case where a manual recount is sought in several counties based on the identical assertion, as occurred in this presidential election, there are additional constitutional concerns raised if a manual recount is conducted and completed in some but not all the counties where the recount is requested.[20]

This concern is demonstrated dramatically in this past election. On November 9, 2000, Vice President Gore requested manual recounts in four counties—Miami-Dade, Broward, Palm Beach and Volusia. *See Gore v. Harris,* [page 74] n. 16 (Fla. Dec. 8, 2000), *rev'd and remanded, Bush v. Gore,* No. 00-949, (U.S. Dec. 12, 2000). The reasons for this request included the extraordinary closeness of the statewide margin, as well as concern as to whether the vote totals reliably reflected the true will of the Florida voters. Of the four counties in which Vice President Gore requested a full manual recount, only the Miami-Dade Canvassing Board did not

19. The current statute does not set forth any criteria to guide the determination of when the decision to conduct a preliminary manual recount is appropriate. See § 102.166(4)(c), Fla. Stat. (2000) ("The county canvassing board may authorize a manual recount.").

20. If manual recounts are requested by a candidate in several counties, and one board conducts a full manual recount and another board does not, then, as the Attorney General noted in his November 14, 2000, opinion letter to the Honorable Charles E. Burton, Chair, Palm Beach County Canvassing Board [pages 14–18], an unconstitutional two-tiered system may have been created. [*Eds.:* quotation omitted] It should be noted that the Attorney General's opinion did not address constitutional concerns of manual recounts not being conducted in all counties, but rather specifically addressed constitutional implications if one county canvassing board refused to conduct a manual recount requested by a candidate while other county canvassing boards agreed to conduct a manual recount.

complete a manual recount. The Miami-Dade Board's failure to complete the recount was attributed to a variety of factors but in the end the Board suspended the full recount, stating as its reason that it determined that it could not meet this Court's certification deadline. See *Gore v. Harris* [page 76], n. 17; *see also Miami-Dade County Democratic Party v. Miami-Dade County Canvassing Board,* No. 3 D00-3318 (Fla. 3d DCA, Nov. 22, 2000).[21] This Court ultimately held that the Miami-Dade Canvassing Board had no discretion to stop its full manual recount once it had started. See *Gore v. Harris,* [page 75]. Nonetheless, the end result was that some voters in Miami-Dade County whose votes were not recorded by machine never had their votes counted in this election.[22] It would thus seem appropriate that any revised statutory scheme should include more specific standards to govern the exercise of county canvassing boards' discretionary authority in a statewide election.

Further, questions have been raised about the unequal treatment of voters in counties where recounts were not requested. Because section 102.166(4) provides that only a political party or a candidate may request a manual recount under section 102.166(4), there are additional issues regarding the potential for unequal treatment of voters in those counties in which a manual recount is neither requested by the candidate nor conducted by the canvassing board. Because of our concerns that if some of the undervotes were to be counted in an election contest, all of the undervotes should be counted, we held in *Gore v. Harris* [page 81] that in fashioning relief under section 102.168(8), a manual recount should be conducted in all Florida counties where there was an undervote and where no

21. Miami-Dade did not commence the full manual recount until days after Broward and Palm Beach Counties commenced their manual recounts. In fact, the Miami-Dade Canvassing Board had initially decided not to conduct a full manual recount after receiving the results obtained from the sample recount of three precincts. *See Gore* at [page 74].

22. When the Miami-Dade Canvassing Board stopped the recount, approximately 20% of the votes had been manually recounted countywide, resulting in 168 net votes for Gore. However, at least 9000 undervotes were never counted. See *Gore v. Harris,* [pages 74–75]. Further, Palm Beach County did not finish its recount until after 5 p. m. on November 26, 2000, and the Secretary did not include the amended results in the statewide certification. See *id.* at [pages 76–77]. There have been those that have argued that any manual recount under the Election Code must be completed within seven days of the election. However, as we have seen, that is simply not a realistic time period and operates to the detriment of voters in the more populous counties. This problem, in itself, could raise implications of disparate treatment based solely on the voter's county of residence.

manual recount had been conducted.[23] Our paramount interest was that the "election should be determined by a careful examination of the votes of Florida's citizens" so that the "outcome of elections be determined by the will of the voters," which "forms the foundation of the election code enacted by the Florida Legislature and has been consistently applied by this Court in resolving elections disputes." *Id.* at [page 67]. Thus, any comprehensive review of the Election Code should address both the scope of the manual recount statute, section 102.166, to allow for statewide manual recounts, and the scope of the contest statute, section 102.168, to fashion appropriate relief on a statewide basis.

In addition, the United States Supreme Court's decision in *Bush v. Gore* has also called into question the constitutionality of any statutory scheme that does not have more specific standards for evaluating votes when conducting manual recounts than the one currently codified by Florida law, which is whether the intent of the voter can be ascertained.[24] *Bush v. Gore,* [pages 104–06] However, before the 2000 presidential election, neither the Legislature nor the Secretary of State had prescribed more explicit criteria to govern the determination of the voter's intent.[25]Although each county canvassing board may be properly vested with discretion to make this determination for a countywide race, the potential for differing substandards utilized by boards in different counties raises questions of unequal treatment among similarly situated voters in statewide races.[26] See *id.* at [pages

23. I remain confident that if the recount had continued in a timely manner, any obvious disparity in counting votes would have been reviewed by Judge Terry Lewis whose initial order on December 8, 2000, demonstrated an orderly and objective approach to the recount procedures.

24. See *Bush,* [page 118], n. 2 (Stevens, J. dissenting), in which Justice Stevens noted that the "Florida statutory standard is consistent with the practice of the majority of States, which apply either an "intent of the voter" standard or an "impossible to determine the elector's choice" standard in ballot recounts. *Id.*

25. Neither candidate raised the constitutionality of Florida's election laws as an issue on appeal to this Court. See *Palm Beach County Canvassing Board v. Harris,* [slip op. at 8], n. 7 (Fla. Dec. 11, 2000). Instead, President-Elect Bush chose to bring a separate challenge to the constitutionality of section 102.166 in federal court. See *Siegel v. LePore,* 120 F. Supp. 2d 1041 (S. D. Fla.) (denying a request for a preliminary injunction to stop the recount), *aff'd,* No. 00-15981 (11th Cir. Dec. 6, 2000).

26. For example, although much of the focus has been on the potential disparity in counting votes in punchcard counties, it appears the potential for disparity could exist in counties utilizing optical scanning machines when one county adopts a per se rule and another employs a totality of the circumstances approach to evaluate voter intent. *See* Jeff Kunerth, Scott Maxwell & Maya Bell, *Voter Never Had Chance,* Orlando Sentinel, December 17, 2000 (explaining that in Lake County, the canvassing board decided against

105–106.] This in turn requires an evaluation of whether there is a need for more specific standards, particularly in statewide elections, to be in place to ensure uniformity in the assessment of votes and in the determination of voters' intent when dealing with similar voting systems.[27]

The Failure to Count Undervotes: Throughout this litigation, both the Secretary of State and President-Elect Bush asserted that the manual recount statute, section 102.166, was never intended to apply to allow for the counting of undervotes.[28] Florida's Election Code currently provides for a manual recount where there is an "error in the vote tabulation which could affect the outcome of the election." § 102.166(5). Utilizing traditional methods of statutory construction, we concluded in our decision in *Palm Beach County Canvassing Board v. Harris,* [slip op. at 13–15], that "an error in vote tabulation" triggering a manual recount included the failure of a properly functioning machine to discern the choices of the voters as revealed by the ballots.

Further, in *Gore v. Harris,* we construed the term "legal vote" as used in the contest statute, section 102.168(3)(c), to be one where an examination of the ballot reveals a "clear indication of the intent of the voter." *Gore v. Harris,* at [pages 72–73]. In defining "legal vote," we looked to the Florida Election Code and once again applied traditional methods of statutory construction as amplified by our prior case law.[29] We found that both the statutes and this Court's jurisprudence have consistently paid homage to

---

counting votes of residents who filled in the circle next to a candidate's name but who also wrote in the same name on the ballot; whereas in Orange County, canvassing officials counted such votes, stating that intent was clear). If a manual recount would have been undertaken in any county using a per se rule, there could be a real potential that legal votes would not have been counted. This potential demonstrates the pitfalls of any per se rule, even while this past election raised concerns about the application of a totality of the circumstances approach to determine voters' intent when employed on a county-to-county basis.

27. The statutory scheme that stresses local autonomy results from the present administration of all elections in Florida, which includes statewide and local controls. Although the Secretary of State is the chief election officer of the state, see section 97.102(1), Florida Statutes (2000), the actual conduct of elections occurs in Florida counties with the county canvassing boards in each county responsible for counting the votes given each county. See §§ 102.131(1), § 102.141(2), Fla. Stat. (2000).

28. Initially, their position in this Court had been that any attack on the problems with punchcard ballots and the increased percentage of undervotes should not be raised under the protest provisions of section 102.166(4), but in the contest provisions of section 102.168. *But see Gore v. Harris,* [page 61, n. 7] (noting parties' change of position that section 102.168 does not apply to a presidential election).

29. *See, e. g., State ex rel. Carpenter v. Barber,* 144 Fla. 159, 163–64, 198 So. 49, 50–51 (1940); *Wiggins v. State ex rel. Drane,* 106 Fla. 793, 795–97, 144 So. 62, 63 (1932).

the principle that "every citizen's vote be counted whenever possible, whether in an election for a local commissioner or an election for President of the United States." *Id.* [at 63].

The position, however, has been espoused—most specifically by the Secretary of State in an advisory opinion issued after the November 7, 2000, election—that the manual recount statute does not provide for the counting of undervotes.[30] Further, the Secretary of State has taken the position that a "legal vote" is only one where the vote is "properly executed in accordance with the instructions provided to all registered voters in advance of the election and in the polling places." *Bush v. Gore,* at [page 123] (Stevens, J., [*Eds.*: Souter, J.] dissenting) (citing Brief of Respondent Harris et al. at p. 10).

In other words, according to the positions taken by the Secretary of State in this litigation, if a voter does not completely dislodge the chad or mark the optical scan card in strict accordance with the instructions, resulting in the machine not registering a vote, that vote should not constitute a "legal vote." Under the Secretary's interpretation of the manual recount statute and narrow definition of "legal vote," there would never be an opportunity to resort to a manual method of counting the undervotes under either the protest or contest provisions of Florida's Election Code. The implication of these dual positions would be that voters who cast votes that were incapable of being read by the machine would not be counted through a manual recount either pursuant to section 102.166 or section 102.168—even if upon a manual review the voter's intent was clearly ascertainable.[31] In short, these votes would not be counted at all.

There are obviously important implications that flow from the Secretary of State's position that will affect elections long after this one. The Department of State is charged, among other responsibilities, with adopting rules to achieve and maintain the maximum degree of correctness, impartiality, and efficiency of the procedures of voting, including write-in voting, and of counting, tabulating, and recording votes by voting systems used in this state.[32] However, before the November 7, 2000, election, this State had a patchwork of different voting systems and ballots selected on a coun-

30. See Division of Elections Advisory Opinion, DE 00-13, November 13, 2000 [pages 12–14]

31. In fact, the Texas statute, as well as the statutes in many other states, clearly anticipates that in a manual recount all punchcard ballots would be reviewed even where the chad is not completely detached, with the overarching concern being the "clearly ascertainable intent of the voter." [*Eds.*: quotation (of Tex. Elec. Code Ann. § 127.130) omitted]

32. Further, pursuant to section 101.015(2), "each odd-numbered year the Department of State shall review the rules governing standards and certification of voting sys-

tywide basis and necessarily approved by the Secretary of State. If the Secretary's restrictive view of "legal votes" and manual recounts is ultimately adopted through amendments to the Election Code, there are potential constitutional implications, especially if the different voting systems continue to remain in operation. Simply put, the failure to allow for a manual recount would have a disparate effect on those counties that employed punchcard systems.[33]

As noted by the trial court in this case, Miami-Dade and Palm Beach Counties have been "aware . . . for many years" of the problems with "voter error, and/or, less than total accuracy, in regard to the punchcard voting devices utilized. *Gore v. Harris*, at [page 55]. As the United States Supreme Court noted in *Gore v. Bush*, at [page 103], "[t]his case has shown that punch card balloting machines can produce an unfortunate number of ballots which are not punched in a clean, complete way by the voter." For a variety of reasons ranging from the voter's failure to precisely follow directions to difficulties with the machine itself, punchcard systems have a higher percentage of ballots that the machine does not register as a vote as compared to the optical scanner system. Therefore, if the safeguard of a manual recount is not available to protect the integrity and reliability of the electoral process or if a "legal vote" is narrowly defined, voters in punchcard counties would be treated unequally as compared to voters in counties that utilize more reliable voting machinery, such as optical scanning technology.[34] Until there is modernization and uniformity of voting systems that will minimize the likelihood of a vote not being recorded and

---

tems to determine the adequacy and effectiveness of such rules in assuring that elections are fair and impartial."

33. As Justice Stevens points out, carried to its logical conclusion "Florida's decision to leave to each county the determination of what balloting system to employ—*despite enormous differences in accuracy*—might run afoul of equal protection." *Bush*, [page 119] (Stevens, J., dissenting) (emphasis supplied). Justice Stevens notes that "the percentage of nonvotes in counties using a punch-card system was 3.92%; in contrast, the rate of error under the more modern optical-scan system was only 1.43%. Put in other terms, for every 10,000 votes cast, punch-card systems result in 250 more nonvotes than optical-scan systems." *Id.* at [page 119], n. 4 (citations omitted). In fact, in the 1996 presidential election, in Brevard County and Volusia County, votes tallied on punch cards showed twenty-six of every 1000 voters failed to cast a valid presidential vote. In 2000, after both counties switched to optical scanning, the proportion fell to fewer than two of every 1000 presidential votes in Brevard County and three of every 1000 in Volusia County. See Peter Whoriskey & Joseph Tanfani, *Punch Card Problems Were Ignored for Years*, Miami Herald, December 17, 2000.

34. As reported, prior studies have shown various problems with the punchcard sys-

until punchcard systems are retired from use, statewide disparity in voting systems could operate to disenfranchise a number of otherwise eligible voters based upon their county of residency.[35]This disparity, based only on one's county of residence, might have constitutional implications.[36]

Conclusion: The realities of this past election have indeed "demonstrated the vulnerability of what we believe to be a bedrock principle of democracy: that every vote counts." *Gore v. Harris,* at [page 79, n. 20]. I thus applaud Governor Jeb Bush's creation of a Task Force that will study the state's elections process and recommend improvements to "ensure the fairness of our system" and to fully modernize our voting and counting mechanisms.[37] As we enter the twenty-first century, we must strive to ensure that our Election Code and system of voting operates so that in all future elections, each

---

tem and the fact that it has a higher failure rate than more modern systems. In fact, a 1988 National Bureau of Standards report recommended their elimination. See Peter Whoriskey & Joseph Tanfani, *Punch Card Problems Were Ignored for Years,* Miami Herald, December 17, 2000; Brooks Jackson, *Punch-Card Ballots Notorious for Inaccuracies,* http://www. cnn. com/2000/ALLPOLITICS/stories/1115/ jackson. punchcards/index. html; see also Rafeal Lorente, '96 *Analysis: Minority Votes for President More Likely* to *Go Uncounted,* Sun Sentinel, December 7, 2000 (explaining that in 1996, twenty-six out of every 1000 votes cast using the punchcard system were disqualified, versus only seventeen of every 1000 votes using the optical scanning system); Scott Maxwell, *Palm Beach Has Had Trouble Before,* Orlando Sentinel, December 5, 2000 (explaining that Palm Beach County's elections supervisor reported in 1996 that faulty voting machines led to an unusually high number of ballots for which there was no vote for President).

35. It does appear that a significant part of the problems have resulted from the outmoded voting systems in place in many counties in this State and nationwide. This is in contrast with what appears to be the use in other countries of more modern, uniform and efficient methods of making sure that every vote is counted. See Mary McGrory, *Just Fine Without a Chad,* Washington Post, December 10, 2000, at B1 (describing the voting systems in Mexico, Canada and India); Stephen Buckley, *Brazilians' Pride Grows in Electronic Voting System,* Washington Post, December 2, 2000, at A18 (explaining Brazil's electronic voting system, which includes the use of a machine that looks like a miniature ATM).

36. See *Moore v. Ogilvie,* 394 U.S. 814 (1969) (invalidating a county-based procedure that diluted the influence of citizens in larger counties in the nominating process).

37. See *Jeb Bush Appoints Task Force to Recommend Improvements in the Way Florida Votes,* CNN.com (Dec. 14, 2000), http://www. cnn. com/2000/ALLPOLITICS/stories/12/ 14/fla. elections/. As Governor Jeb Bush recently stated: "Real electoral reform is not only updating our technology and clarifying our standards. It also means reaffirming our commitment to making sure every citizen has faith and confidence in our electoral system— even when the margin of victory in a race is very close." Mary Ellen Klas, *Panel to Ensure Vote Debacle Won't Recur,* The Palm Beach Post (Dec. 15, 2000), http://www. gopbi. com/partners/pbpost/epaper/editions/ today/news_ 3. html.

eligible voter both has the opportunity to cast a vote and that every vote intended to be cast for a candidate will be counted.[38]

38. Although much of the discussion herein has been focused upon problems with the present election code and the actual voting systems, it is clear that the subject of election and voting reform will be far broader. Issues ranging from the difficulty with the actual form of the ballot in certain counties to concerns with the practices surrounding the casting of absentee ballots, and even concerns over whether voters were denied access to the polls, have opened our collective eyes to see that meaningful and comprehensive reform in many areas may be required.

Commentary

NOVEMBER 7–21, 2000

N O V E M B E R	5	6	**7**	**8**	**9**	**10**	**11**	
	12	**13**	**14**	**15**	**16**	**17**	**18**	
	19	**20**	**21**	22	23	24	25	
	26	27	28	29	30	1	2	
	3	4	5	6	7	8	9	D E C E M B E R
	10	11	12	13	14	15	16	
	17	18	19	20	21	22	23	
	24	25	26	27	28	29	30	

E.J. DIONNE JR.

Scrap This System

The Washington Post

Our political system blew up on Tuesday. No matter who takes office as president next January, the legitimacy of his election will be in doubt. A nation that is split into almost perfectly symmetrical political halves will spend four years preparing for the struggle of 2004 in which each will seek to avenge the wrong done it by a flawed system.

What's wrong here is not simply that the ever-so-narrow winner of the popular vote, Al Gore, might be denied election by a George W. Bush who would capture the electoral college on the basis of a handful of votes in Florida.

It now also appears that Democrats will be able to ascribe Bush's margin of victory in Florida—if there turns out to be a margin of victory—to the flawed configuration of a punch-card ballot in Palm Beach County. The ballot was so badly set up, Democrats argue with plausibility, that perhaps 3,000 voters who thought they were casting a ballot for Gore actually voted for Pat Buchanan.

As Rep. Robert Wexler, a Florida Democrat, pointed out, his party's complaints about the ballot flowed in long before the polls closed, and Buchanan's vote in the liberal Democratic county was far out of line with the thin support he won in surrounding areas.

The fate of the nation should not hang on an arcane local electoral dispute. Both parties can at least agree that this is no way to pick a president.

Take the problem first from the Republicans' perspective. When it was thought in the week before the election that Al Gore might win the electoral vote but lose the popular vote, Democrats were quick to say that both Gore and Bush played by the same rules and should abide by them.

Knowing those rules, Bush and Gore chased each other in and out of the same battleground states. They sought whatever narrow advantage might secure them all the electoral votes under a winner-take-all system that applies in every state except Maine and Nebraska.

Washington Post, late ed., November 9, 2000, p. A29. © 2000, The Washington Post Writers Group. Reprinted with permission.

If the system had been built on popular votes rather than the electoral college, each would have pursued a different strategy. Each would have spent more time churning up enthusiasm within his political base. Gore would have spent more time campaigning in New York and California, Bush in Texas and the deep South.

So if Bush ekes out the narrowest of margins in Florida and thus the electoral college, Republicans will have every reason to be infuriated by any Democratic claim that his election lacks legitimacy. Information retrieval systems will make it easy for Republicans to find Democrats who, just days before, spoke of the glorious traditions embodied in our system of indirect presidential elections.

But especially in light of the questions now being raised by that weird Palm Beach ballot, how can any self-respecting Democratic partisan just sit by and let Bush take the White House and with it leadership of an all-Republican government in Washington? Republican control of the White House and both houses of Congress can't possibly be seen as reflecting the will of an electorate that spoke in moderate tones on issues.

The exit polls made abundantly clear that a large and critical portion of Bush's support came from voters who are closer to Gore on the issues but had personal doubts about the vice president and also President Clinton. If Bush takes office, you can count on his being seen by Democrats as an Accidental President leading an Accidental Congressional Majority.

What is to be done? This electoral college system must be scrapped. The truth is that electors are not a deliberative group like representatives or senators. They are the product of a system created in less democratic times by Founders who wanted to temper the popular will. The same spirit meant that until the second decade of the 20th century, senators were elected by state legislatures, not the people. We amended the Constitution in 1913 because we decided the people should rule in the Senate. We ought to follow that logic in presidential elections.

But that is for later. The imperative now is that both Gore and Bush understand that they hold in their hands the legitimacy of the government itself. Before the lawyers and partisans raise charges and countercharges, Gore and Bush need to sit down together and agree on how they'll work out this dispute, much as the country created an electoral commission to resolve the even more hotly disputed 1876 election.

The fact is that the prize both men seek is now tainted—through no fault of their own. Each must now be seen as understanding why his opponents are so angry and dispirited. They must reunite the country, because no one else can. ▌

DAVID TELL AND WILLIAM KRISTOL

Gore's Spoiled Ballot

The Weekly Standard

The presidential election of 2000 is the impeachment drama of 1998–99 all over again. And Al Gore is Bill Clinton. Only Gore's behavior is worse—worse because Clinton's misdeeds were of a gravity about which people might at least plausibly disagree. What Gore has done is directly challenge something explicitly articulated in the Constitution and therefore indisputable—and indisputably central to our system of government: the mechanism by which we have selected our chief executives for more than 200 years. This is rather a big deal, is it not?

No good can come of the massive confusion Gore's designated lieutenants have deliberately sown, in his name and at his behest, since Election Day last week. They have publicized unsubstantiated—indeed, altogether baseless—accusations of illegality against the popular-vote canvass conducted in Palm Beach County, Florida. They have loudly insisted that this purported illegality will be corrected only when Gore is finally awarded Florida's 25 decisive electoral votes—*whether or not* it can ever be shown that his name was checked on a plurality of valid ballots originally cast in that state. Worst, perhaps, they have done violence to civic understanding in America by repeatedly suggesting that because Gore appears to have won a plurality of the nationwide popular vote, he somehow *deserves* Florida's electoral votes—and thus the presidency.

It is a scandal that any major-party presidential candidate should ever authorize such a claim to be made on his behalf. As a matter of constitutional law, the nationwide popular vote is an entirely irrelevant consideration here. No man has ever campaigned for the nationwide popular vote, and no man has ever been elected president because he's won it. Like it or not, the Electoral College is *everything*. Intimating otherwise, and in the same breath circulating fictions about polling-place irregularities, the Gore camp has done its best to ensure that should George W. Bush eventually be elected president, some faint whiff of illegitimacy will hang over his administration. It will be unfair and corrosive. We hope that doesn't happen.

Weekly Standard, November 20, 2000, pp. 9–10 (on sale November 13). Reprinted with permission.

But if it does, it will still be better than either of the two alternatives Team Gore prefers. It remains possible that Gore's campaign will yet succeed by more or less legal and ordinary means—that the ongoing review of Florida's Election Day ballot will ultimately secure him the votes he needs to overtake Bush. In which case it will be proper and necessary for Gore to be inaugurated come January. Trouble is, our president will then be a man who has in the meantime proved himself wholly unconscious of, even hostile to, the most fundamental obligations of his office. The same will be true in the unlikely event that Gore captures the White House by the bizarrely extralegal means he and his lawyers are now proposing to the Florida courts: that Palm Beach County's November 7 ballot be invalidated and replaced by a full-scale, do-over election in that lone jurisdiction. In which case Gore will have become president by instigating a *genuine* crisis of governmental legitimacy from which the country—for reasons we will come back to—might have difficulty recovering.

No one should be surprised by what's already transpired, really. Not long ago, after all, Bill Clinton made systematic assault on essential elements of our democracy's republican character. That the president must consistently accept and respond to questions about his conduct; that his subordinates must never become a personal palace guard; that he must always obey the law—all these traditional doctrines of constitutional formalism Clinton defied. Democratic partisans, nearly the whole of the party, sustained him in this defiance. They thereby signaled their rejection of constitutional formalism—its organization of government around impartially administered rules and procedures—in favor of a politics devoted first and foremost to the business of winning this week's fight.

Then these same Democrats nominated one of their own, Clinton's unflaggingly loyal vice president, to succeed him. And now Al Gore has made war, for the convenience of his ambition, on *the* rule and *the* procedure around which the nation's entire public life quadrennially revolves: the election of the president.

We should all of us clearly understand the precise nature of this war. In late October, when suspicions emerged that the Democratic ticket might triumph on Election Day without a popular plurality, Gore spokesmen were quick to broadcast a preemptive demand that no one dare question the legitimacy of such a result. And they were right to do so. Hours after the polls closed last Tuesday, however, when it seemed clear that Gore and his running mate had won the popular vote—but might actually *lose* the Electoral College by a hair in Florida—Democratic campaign representatives and associated party leaders wasted no time at all executing a total *volte face* of spin.

By 4:00 a.m. on Wednesday, Gore talkers had begun ritually asserting that of "first" importance was the fact that Gore had won the popular vote—and that this fact was somehow inextricably related to the "will of the people" the election was meant to express. By Wednesday afternoon, Senate minority leader Tom Daschle had declined to promise that his Democratic caucus would accept the "legitimacy" of a Bush presidency. Democratic National Committee chairman Joe Andrew had announced that George W. Bush was absent from the election's "big picture"—that Gore alone had "earned and won the support of the American people." In New York, Hillary Rodham Clinton had wished aloud that Gore should be given all the votes she knew people "intended for him to have."

And in Nashville, Gore himself had popped briefly into view to share his concern that developments he left unspecified had called into question "the fundamental fairness of the process as a whole." And incidentally, he offered, "Joe Lieberman and I have won the popular vote."

Then Gore retreated, Bill Clinton–style, into silence. And soon enough his lawyers were litigating, David Kendall–style, all those purported "illegalities" in Palm Beach County. And his fund-raisers, Terry McAuliffe–style, were ponying up the cash the lawyers would need to litigate some more. And Jesse Jackson, Jesse Jackson–style, was in Florida collecting—but not revealing—evidence that Gore-supporting minority voters had been subjected to "intimidation" at polling stations across the state. And the usual know-nothing celebrities and cynical law professors were taking out another full-page ad in the *New York Times,* this one decrying the fact that while Al Gore had been elected president by "a clear constitutional majority of the popular vote and the Electoral College" (whatever that is), that result had so far been "nullified" in a manner that threatens "our entire political process." Maybe we should have "new elections in Palm Beach County," this Emergency Committee of Concerned Citizens suggested.

During the Lewinsky scandal, the last time a leading political figure so spectacularly violated some taboo, the nation listened in passive astonishment as the malefactor's allies constructed a similarly ridiculous set of excuses for him—and launched heedless attacks on anyone or anything that might stand in the way of his victory. The nation listened and listened and listened. Until the arguments seemed no longer bogus but comfortably familiar. And we lost all collective capacity for effective resistance.

This time, this year, as the order and integrity of a presidential election hangs in the balance, it is important that Americans stay focused and alert to the end. It is important that they know and remember two things in particular.

First, it is a *lie* that Palm Beach's presidential ballot last week was "patently illegal," as Gore partisans charge. True, as you have no doubt heard, Florida election law requires standard paper ballots to list candidates in a specified order, with the check box to the right of each name. True, too, Palm Beach observed neither of these strictures.

But that is because Palm Beach County employs machine-readable ballot cards, to which the rules for paper ballots do not apply. A separate provision of the Florida Code governs the use of such cards. The arrangement of their printed text is supposed to conform to that of paper ballots, but only "as far as practicable." And the placement of their check boxes need not conform to paper ballot requirements at all: The boxes may appear "in front of or in back of the names of the candidates."

Palm Beach's ballot was approved by representatives of both major parties in advance of the election. It was then published in the newspaper and distributed to the voters by mail. And it was used successfully, without complaint or incident, by upwards of 95 percent of those voters on Election Day. Yes, it does seem likely that some number of Palm Beach voters were confused by the ballot and failed to cast the votes for Al Gore they had intended. There may even have been enough of them to give Gore a statewide plurality—had they cast valid ballots.

But they didn't. And as a narrow legal matter, there really isn't much more to say than that. Two thousand confused voters cannot render invalid several hundred thousand ballots cast by Palm Beach voters who managed to follow the rules. And nothing in Florida statute or precedent says otherwise. The Palm Beach ballot was legal.

And yet, say Gore's men, the confused Palm Beachers *wanted* to vote for Gore, which means that Florida as a whole wanted to vote for Gore, which means that Gore really should have won the state's electoral votes and really should be declared our president-elect. The "will of the people," as reflected in the nationwide popular vote, must be effected, or last week's entire election was a fraud.

Ah. Here's the second and broader point Americans must remember as they listen to this complaint in the coming days. It is not true, as Gore campaign chairman Bill Daley has contended, that our national elections are designed to ensure that "the candidate who the voters preferred becomes our president." Our national elections instead are designed to ensure that the candidate the voters *voted for* becomes our president. And it is only from such votes, filtered through the Electoral College, that any meaningful "will of the people" can be determined. Any effort to impute such a national will from some other source and use the imputation to delegitimize an election whose results seem vaguely inconsistent is an effort to overthrow the constitutional system and replace it with banana republic–level chaos. In the United States, we do not conduct mulligan ballots whenever some losing candidate's supporters claim they were somehow prevented from getting it right the first time.

If, when Florida concludes its recount, it turns out Al Gore won Florida on Election Day, he should be president. If Bush proves the winner, the same should be true. No other outcome is acceptable. And none should be tolerated. ∎

AKHIL REED AMAR

The Electoral College, Unfair from Day One

The New York Times

As we await results from the Florida recount, two things should be clear. First, if George W. Bush, having apparently lost the popular vote, does indeed win at least 270 electoral votes when the Electoral College meets, he is the lawful winner, who played by the Constitution's rules and won.

Second, we must realize that the Electoral College is a hopelessly outdated system and that we must abolish it. Direct election would resonate far better with the American value of one person, one vote. Indeed, the college was designed at the founding of the country to help one group—white Southern males—and this year, it has apparently done just that.

In 1787, as the Constitution was being drafted in Philadelphia, James Wilson of Pennsylvania proposed direct election of the president. But James Madison of Virginia worried that such a system would hurt the South, which would have been outnumbered by the North in a direct election system. The creation of the Electoral College got around that: it was part of the deal that Southern states, in computing their share of electoral votes, could count slaves (albeit with a two-fifths discount), who of course were given none of the privileges of citizenship. Virginia emerged as the big win-

Originally published in *The New York Times,* late ed., November 9, 2000, p. A23. Akhil Reed Amar is a law professor at Yale University.

ner, with more than a quarter of the electors needed to elect a president. A free state like Pennsylvania got fewer electoral votes even though it had approximately the same free population.

The Constitution's pro-Southern bias quickly became obvious. For 32 of the Constitution's first 36 years, a white slaveholding Virginian occupied the presidency. Thomas Jefferson, for example, won the election of 1800 against John Adams from Massachusetts in a race where the slavery skew of the Electoral College was the decisive margin of victory.

The system's gender bias was also obvious. In a direct presidential election, any state that chose to enfranchise its women would have automatically doubled its clout. Under the Electoral College, however, a state had no special incentive to expand suffrage—each got a fixed number of electoral votes, regardless of how many citizens were allowed to vote.

Now fast-forward to Election Night 2000. Al Gore appears to have received the most popular votes nationwide but may well lose the contest for electoral votes. Once again, the system has tilted toward white Southern males. Exit polls indicate that Mr. Bush won big among this group and that Mr. Gore won decisively among blacks and women.

The Electoral College began as an unfair system, and remains so. So why keep it?

Advocates of the system sloganeer about "federalism," meaning that presidential candidates are forced to take into account individual state interests and regional variations in their national campaigns.

But in the current system, candidates don't appeal so much to state interests (what are those, anyway?) as to demographic groups (elderly voters, soccer moms) within states. And direct popular elections would still encourage candidates to take into account regional differences, like those between voters in the Midwest and the East. After all, one cannot win a national majority without getting lots of votes in lots of places.

Direct election could give state governments some incentives to increase voter turnout, because the more voters a state turned out, the bigger its role in national elections and the bigger its overall share in the national tally. Presidential candidates would begin to pay more attention to the needs of individual states that had higher turnouts.

The nation's founders sought to harness governmental competition and rivalry in healthy ways, using checks and balances within the federal government and preserving roles for state governments. Direct presidential elections would be true to their best concepts—democracy and healthy competition—rather than to their worst compromises. ∎

THE EDITORS

A Gore Coup d'Etat?

The Wall Street Journal

The cliff-hanging Florida results won't be final until the absentee-ballot deadline of November 17, but yesterday Gore campaign head William Daley told a news conference that no amount of recounting would do. Only one outcome would be acceptable: "If the will of the people is to prevail, Al Gore should be awarded a victory in Florida and be our next President." And if the election results don't do that, the Gore campaign will try to find a judge to do it instead. In your ordinary banana republic, this would be recognized as a Gore coup d'etat.

When the day began yesterday, we set to work writing an editorial for these columns that in fact was going to express some sympathy for what appears to have happened to some confused voters in Palm Beach County, and suggesting that we really do need a better-run electoral process not only in Florida but across the land. This is still a valid point, but was overwhelmed when Bill Daley and other Gore campaign officials announced that the Democrats intended to go to the mattress to cling to political power.

Mr. Daley said the Vice President wasn't going to settle for the recount result, suggesting of course they knew it would go against them and so some pretext needed to be found fast to prevent the election from ending. "Let the legal system run its course," Mr. Daley said. "We will be working with voters from Florida in support of legal actions to demand some redress." He added, "We believe with so much at stake, steps should be taken to make sure that the people's choice becomes our President."

Shortly after this, guess what happened? The Democratic Palm Beach plaintiffs seeking "redress" suddenly withdrew their suit from federal court. Why? Because they wanted to shop around for a favorable judge. They had happened to draw federal district Judge Kenneth Ryskamp, whose nomination to the appeals court years back had been defeated in the Senate by Joe Biden. The Palm Beach plaintiffs then announced they would file in state court.

Obviously they are judge-shopping, reducing this noble enterprise on behalf of the people's choice to the level of backwater justice. Not only Judge Ryskamp, but any reasonably neutral judge would likely dismiss the case outright.

At no point has the Gore campaign suggested that voter fraud has cost them votes. Were that the case, we would be in wholehearted support of their complaint. Voter fraud is one of this country's most corrosive, unaddressed problems. Instead, Warren Christopher, a former Secretary of State, yesterday cited "serious and substantial irregularities." Their argument is that the irregularities deprived citizens of Constitutional rights, so undo the whole election.

Yes, voting irregularities do significant damage to elections in America. No serious person involved in politics would doubt that incompetent, flawed or antique voting procedures all over this country disenfranchise some voters in every national election—for the House, the Senate and the Presidency.

None of these concerns, however, is sufficient cause for allowing competing squads of political lawyers to force the people of this country into an unprecedented political crisis, which is precisely what the Gore campaign has shown itself willing to do.

By turning over the Presidential election to the lawyers, the Democrats guarantee that the Republicans would respond in kind, seeking similar irregularities, as are commonly found in South Florida, or anywhere else people voted in the U.S. last Tuesday. The constant harping on the poor souls confused by the Palm Beach butterfly ballot makes for good TV visuals and stirring speeches about the "denial of justice." But no one should pretend this is going to fly through the courts without a substantial counteroffensive by the GOP's own lawyers.

And in any event, there is the prospect of recounts elsewhere. In Wisconsin and Iowa, where Mr. Gore's margin of victory was several thousand votes, automatic triggers may set off recounts. Moreover, the national vote isn't over. Votes are still being completed in many states, with a million absentee votes from California alone. It is not beyond imagining that when this process is done, the current result will be different, or even reversed.

Poor Florida. It is being put under a national microscope to determine the credibility of its voting system. No surprise, what we're seeing is that the results aren't always particularly edifying. There is no basis in law, however, to believe that demanding that a vote be restaged because of "irregularities" in Florida's election system, or any other state's for that matter, is going to survive in court. Were that true, there'd have been hundreds of restaged votes in this country.

Mr. Gore, Mr. Daley and all the Democratic lawyers know this. Their case about irregularities and confusion is merely a pretext for finding some friendly jurist who will overrule the voters in an excruciatingly close contest. This is a destructive course of action for the Republic and the Constitution. Also, by the way, for a Democratic Party already tainted by eight years of its own irregularities, that is to say, by a habit of trashing the rule of law in the pursuit of political advantage. ▌

THE EDITORS

A Time to Act Presidential

The Washington Post

If they are worthy of being president, the goal of both Al Gore and George W. Bush at this stage ought to be more than just winning. That's not the beginning of a sermon but an appeal to mutual self-interest. Not just for the country's sake but for their own, they ought to be seeking a resolution that will be perceived by as many people as possible as fair—one in which the winner, instead of looking as if he snatched the office, and possibly going down in history that way, will be able to govern more or less normally.

They and the people doing battle for them in Florida plainly are not headed in that direction now. They're engaged in a high-stakes tactical duel with a heavy overlay on each side of overblown public relations. The presidency ought not come down to that kind of shabby maneuvering: which man's tacticians or lawyers were able to strike the last or shrewdest blow.

If the candidates were so inclined, their teams could shape a compromise even now. The Bush people are opposed to the further counting of ballots by hand. They went into federal court yesterday to stop it, and were rightly rebuffed; now they are appealing. Florida's Republican secretary of state, meanwhile, also moved to stop the counting, ordering the state's counties to have their results in by this afternoon, well before all hand recounts could be completed. She claimed she had no choice under state law, but others instantly disputed that. A judge was expected to rule this morning.

Washington Post, final ed., November 14, 2000, p. A42. ©The Washington Post.

The hand counts are important because the machines used for counting miss a fair number of votes—enough conceivably to make a difference in an election as close as this. If the hole beside a candidate's name is only partly punched out, the machine may not record a vote that can be caught by the human eye. There may be many such votes; the Bush people want to ignore them. That isn't right. The Gore people, on the other hand, have petitioned to count them only in four counties that Mr. Gore carried. Such a selective hand count isn't right either.

In our view, the candidates ought to agree to a full hand count throughout the state, or in as many counties as seem salient to either side. One would win; both would agree in advance to embrace the outcome as legitimate. The Bush campaign argues that the hand count is too subject to bias. But Florida law envisions such counts for a reason; and our sense is that the people entrusted with the responsibility will by and large rise to it, as citizens generally do in such contexts. What's vital is that the hand count not be skewed by being confined to one side's strongholds.

Our guess is that the country would accept such a compromise, or some variation, and think the better by far of the candidates for having risen above the scrap. Faced with a joint request from both candidates, the secretary of state would likely find a way to let it happen. One week after Election Day, it seems to us that only the candidates can take the steps on which both their reputations will ultimately depend, and we hope they do. ▮

GRIFFIN BELL

Counting the Vote: Stop This Litigation

The Wall Street Journal

Both George W. Bush and Al Gore should forswear lawsuits over the election vote, and they should call upon their supporters to do the same. Each candidate should wait for the election officials in the close states to announce the final vote totals and then accept those results with grace and dignity.

Wall Street Journal, November 14, 2000, p. A26. Reprinted from *The Wall Street Journal* © 2000 Dow Jones & Company, Inc. All rights reserved. Griffin Bell was a judge on the U.S. Court of Appeals for the Fifth Circuit from 1961 to 1976, and U.S. attorney general from 1977 to 1979, under President Jimmy Carter. He represented President George Bush in the Iran-Contra investigation.

Instead, we have seen lawsuits in state court brought by Democratic voters, followed by a federal court suit filed as a defensive measure by Mr. Bush. Yesterday a federal judge refused the Bush campaign's request to stop manual recounting in four counties. Now, Mr. Gore is seeking an injunction to postpone today's deadline for certifying Florida's votes—a deadline issued by Florida's secretary of state, and clearly established by the state legislature in a statute that would appear to allow no discretion.

None of this should be acceptable to responsible citizens. The selection of the next president should rest with state election officials and, ultimately, with the Electoral College—not with the courts, and certainly not in a broadcast media circus.

I was the Georgia campaign manager for John Kennedy in 1960, and so I recall that election well. While Kennedy carried Georgia with 62% of the vote, the election was close in other states, especially Illinois and Texas. A difference of less than 9,000 votes in Illinois, and less than 50,000 votes in Texas, would have given Vice President Nixon a narrow majority of the electoral college, and he would have become president.

Many of Nixon's advisors urged him to contest the results in Illinois and Texas. His finest hour was when he decided, against their advice, to accept the results as reported. In this instance, Nixon set an example that both Mr. Bush and Mr. Gore should follow.

I do not deny that the federal courts have jurisdiction to vindicate rights under the U.S. Constitution in the context of elections for federal office—that has been settled since 1962, when the Supreme Court first adopted the principle of one person, one vote in *Baker* v. *Carr*. And the Florida courts, of course, have jurisdiction over their own state's elections. The important question, however, is not whether the courts, federal or state, have jurisdiction; instead, it is whether Mr. Bush or Mr. Gore should permit the selection of our next president to be decided by the courts.

Courts, as institutions, are not suited to resolve the election of a president. The election of a president requires speed, finality and certainty. Courts are slow, and different courts often reach inconsistent conclusions.

There are mechanisms to resolve inconsistent results, but those mechanisms take time. Having multiple judges compete to determine the outcome of the election will undermine the legitimacy of both the courts and the election. Also, my experience has been that parties to lawsuits become more inflexible and committed to their respective positions with each passing day they spend in court. They have more and more trouble distinguishing the important from the trivial.

If these lawsuits go forward, especially if accompanied by an O.J. Simpson-like media circus, we will sink in a quagmire of litigation. There will be delays, inconsistent decisions by different courts, and appeals.

The results may not be clear either by mid-December, when the electors are to meet in their states and vote; or by early January, when Vice President Gore, as president of the Senate, opens the sealed lists of the electors' votes; or even by Jan. 20, when the new president must take office. As the lawsuits move ahead, the parties will become less attentive to the core concern, which is the good of the country. Mr. Bush and Mr. Gore have an obligation to put a stop to the litigation.

The vice president's advisors have stressed repeatedly that he appears to have won the popular vote, albeit by a margin only of about 200,000 votes out of more than 100 million votes cast. They seem to imply that if the vice president indeed has a majority of the popular vote then that majority somehow justifies involving the courts. Yet, just as Theodore White said of Kennedy's victory in 1960, the "margin of popular vote is so thin as to be, in all reality, nonexistent."

The reality here is that both Mr. Bush and Mr. Gore have broad support in the country, but neither has a clear majority of the popular vote. The popular vote cannot justify a resort to the courts.

The Electoral College determines which candidate will be president, and both campaigns directed their efforts and resources to winning an Electoral College majority. That one campaign may have received a thin majority of the national popular vote in state-by-state election contests is constitutionally irrelevant. The repeated emphasis by the vice president's advisers on the popular vote seems to suggest that they do not accept the Electoral College. This is a very dangerous suggestion.

The constitutional convention in 1787 took 60 votes on the method of electing the president; several times, the Framers voted in favor of having Congress select the president, which would have weakened the office greatly, and against direct popular election.

The Electoral College was not some ill-considered tag-along in the Constitution; instead, it is an integral part of the Great Compromise that included giving each state, regardless of population, two senators. That compromise enabled the formation of the Union. We have amended the process for electing the president several times, and there have been proposals in the Senate to do away with the Electoral College, but we have always retained the essential fabric of the college—wisely, in my view.

The broadcast media need to understand that our election system is changing in ways that may delay the final result for days. Oregon, for ex-

ample, now conducts its elections by mail. Increasing numbers of voters vote
by absentee ballot. We do not elect the president, or any other official, by
exit polls; they are elected by ballots.

Messrs. Bush and Gore now have an opportunity to be more than politicians. They have an opportunity to be statesmen, and they should seize it.
Like Nixon in 1960, they should disagree with their advisers. They should
announce their intent to accept the vote totals determined by the responsible state election officials and to abstain from litigation. They should forswear the courts. ▊

JANE MAYER

Dept. of Close Calls: George W.'s Cousin

The New Yorker

"Jebbie'll be calling me like eight thousand times a day," John Ellis said. It
was the morning after the morning after Election Night, and Ellis, the forty-
seven-year-old first cousin of Jeb and George W. Bush, who heads up the
Fox News Channel election-decision team, was padding through his big
house in Irvington, New York, in gym socks, khakis, and a baggy navy
sweatshirt. He looked exhausted but cautiously exhilarated, despite one
cousin's shrinking Florida lead and the other's incessant phone calls. "I'm
not worried," Ellis said. "Not yet, anyway."

He hadn't always felt so confident about his cousin's prospects. Ellis said
that at the start of the election season he considered the race "unlosable" for
Vice-President Al Gore. "I kept wondering," he said, "why, during the debates, Gore didn't just turn to Bush and ask, 'What, exactly, is it about peace
and prosperity that you don't like?'" And in 1998 Ellis was quoted as saying that George W. at the age of forty was "on the road to nowhere." Now,
however, Ellis believes that his cousin will be the next President. And he
doesn't think that the Democrats will risk pushing for a revote in West Palm
Beach. Any attempt to do so, he warned, could lead to the electoral version
of mutually assured destruction. "I just can't imagine that they want to go
there," he said, a bit ominously.

Ellis, whose mother, Nancy Ellis, is the sister of former President George Bush, had spent Election Night perched in front of a bank of computer monitors in Fox's midtown headquarters. It was his responsibility to tell the network's anchors when they could safely project the outcome in each state. He also stayed in constant touch with his cousins in Austin, relaying early vote counts as they showed up on his screens.

As the afternoon wore on, things weren't looking good for George W. Bush. At about 6 P.M., after two waves of exit polls, Fox News's chairman, Roger Ailes, called Ellis into his office for a private briefing. "What's your gut say?" Ailes asked him. Silently, Ellis slid an index finger across his throat.

Soon afterward, Ellis received a telephone call from the Bush brothers. "They were, like, 'How we doin'?'" Ellis recalled. "I had to tell them it didn't look good." The brothers were gloomy. "I think the reality is that George thought he'd win it, and not in a nail-biter," Ellis said. In the next hour, it got worse. "We had a South that was not delivering Bush his margin," Ellis said. "Dominoes usually fall only one way on Election Night, and so at one point I looked at the others in the newsroom and said, 'We're building a Gore electoral victory.'"

Like any other newsman, Ellis wanted to get the story first, even if it spelled doom for his own family's campaign. By 7:52 P.M., Fox had joined the other networks in predicting that Gore would win Florida. Jeb called Ellis and asked, in an edgy voice, "Are you sure?" Ellis told him, "We're looking at a screen full of Gore."

But then Ellis's computer, displaying data from the Voter News Service, started countermanding the Gore win. "The computer goes into this status called REV"—shorthand for reversal. Before long, Florida was leaning heavily toward Bush. At 2 A.M., Ellis called his cousins and told them, "Our projection shows that it is statistically impossible for Gore to win Florida." They were elated. "Their mood was up, big time," Ellis recalled. "It was just the three of us guys handing the phone back and forth—me with the numbers, one of them a governor, and the other the President-elect. Now, *that* was cool."

Brit Hume, the Fox News anchor, went on the air and declared Bush the next President. "Everyone followed us," Ellis said. An hour later, Ellis got another message on his computer: the V.N.S. numbers, apparently, were wrong. Ellis called his cousins again. "You gotta be kidding me," George W. Bush said. And for the second time that night "we had to pull it back," Ellis said sadly. "And that, my dear, is where we sit." ∎

E.J. DIONNE JR.

Suddenly, Bush Likes the Lawyers

The Washington Post

Let's be clear about a few things in this difficult election. It's not Al Gore's fault, and it's not George W. Bush's fault, that this election is so close. The voters did that, and they had every right to.

A close election magnifies the inevitable flaws in any voting system. When a few ballots can make so much difference, errors that are acceptable in normal times are much harder to justify. The legitimacy of the system will not be undermined by the exposure of its flaws. It will be undermined if those flaws aren't dealt with openly, and in a way that's widely seen as fair.

And let's also be clear about this: No one has won this election yet. The Bush campaign's presumptuous claim to the presidency was based on a mistaken call by the television networks, and a lead so thin it wouldn't be used as the basis for calling a congressional race.

The weekend decision of Bush consigliere James Baker to file a lawsuit to block hand recounts of the Florida vote can only suggest that the Bush forces believe their man would lose if the votes in Democratic counties were recorded accurately. The same James Baker warned against lawsuits and "unduly attempting to prolong the country's national presidential election."

If Baker cared about not prolonging the election, he'd let the recount go forward quickly while we wait for Florida's overseas ballots, which aren't due until Friday. If Baker cared about accuracy, he'd push for recounts in Republican areas that might help his man. Baker clearly fears that if Bush's margin were overturned even temporarily, the effort to railroad Gore out of the race would collapse.

A federal judge denied Baker's motion on the recount Monday afternoon, but the Republicans weren't out of maneuvers. Even before the judge ruled, Republican Secretary of State Katherine Harris announced that she would not certify any county's returns reported in after 5 p.m. today—three days before the overseas ballots are due. But most of the hand counts aren't likely to be finished by the deadline. Even if Harris's ruling is overturned in court,

Washington Post, final ed., November 14, 2000, p. A43. © 2000, The Washington Post Writers Group. Reprinted with permission.

Democrats will highlight the spectacle of a Bush ally preventing a recount that might help Gore.

The multiple inconsistencies of the Republican effort are obvious. Republicans are for states' rights and against judicial activism, right? But here is Bush asking a federal judge to override a local process.

The Bush spin before Baker's move was very anti-lawyer. Haley Barbour, the buoyant Republican lobbyist, put it plainly: "The Democrats are trying to take the election of the president out of the election process, which is controlled by voters, and put it in the court process, which is controlled by lawyers." That statement is now inoperative. If stopping the recount requires lawyers, bring 'em in.

Yes, the Gore side made a bad mistake when Bill Daley, the campaign manager, came out last Thursday threatening lawsuits and suggesting that any count that didn't show Gore ahead would be illegitimate. Gore sources say Daley knows he erred. Elite opinion in Washington hates the idea of delaying the election result. Uncharacteristically, Daley played against elite opinion.

There's a strong case now for Gore saying publicly that if he gets the recount he wants, he'll drop all other legal action, even against that stupidly designed Palm Beach County ballot. This would leave Gore in a strong political position, whether he won or lost.

But let no one pretend that the problems with that Palm Beach ballot are trivial. Consider a report by the *Palm Beach Post* about two predominantly African American precincts in Riviera Beach. In Precinct 66, the vote was 1,203 for Gore, 25 for Bush and 256 ballots were thrown out. In Precinct 59, it was 1,206 for Gore, 21 for Bush and 250 ballots discarded. If the invalidated ballots were intended for Gore in roughly the same proportion as the counted ballots, these two precincts alone might give Gore a statewide lead.

There is no good solution to this problem. Having a new election in a single county raises a slew of difficulties. But the fact that the problem exists should make the Bush campaign all the more wary of denying Gore a fair chance to get the rest of his vote counted.

When Rutherford B. Hayes was elected president in 1876 on the basis of disputed ballots (Florida was involved in that one too), he came to be ridiculed as "His Fraudulency." By doing all they can to block a fair count in Florida, the Bush legal militants are claiming that title for George W. He's being ill-served. It's not fair to him, or the country, that he might have to govern after such a tainted victory. ∎

DAVID TELL
for the editors

The Gore Coup

The Weekly Standard

"Well, we just have to win, then."—*Bill Clinton, concluding that candor about Monica Lewinsky might destroy his presidency.*

"I'm not like George Bush. If he wins or loses, life goes on. I'll do anything to win."—*Al Gore, explaining this year's campaign.*

As we go to press, state circuit court judge Terry P. Lewis has decided that Florida and the nation need not sit still while the Democratic party attempts to manufacture an Al Gore presidency from after-the-fact "recounts" of ambiguous or altogether invalid Election Day ballots. But the state supreme court has enjoined Lewis's ruling pending an appeal scheduled for Monday, November 20.

We're sure of this much: Should Judge Lewis eventually be upheld, all who cherish the integrity of American law will be entitled to celebrate. And yet, even then . . . how close we will have come to having the central processes of our democracy upended by the fanatic ambition of a single demagogue. And what glaring weaknesses in our politics will have been revealed by the astonishing extent of the Gore assault. So, yes, celebrate if things end honorably. But also remember this:

Al Gore's attempted coup has exactly tracked the trajectory of the Monica Lewinsky episode, his mentor's own triumph over ancient taboos of American public life. And an all-too-familiar scandal narcosis has already set in across the country, for Gore has pursued his goal with a speed and cynical genius that Bill Clinton never dreamed of. Once again, the overarching grossness of the thing has been obscured in a succession of televised "developments," each dominated by the guilty party's super-litigator frontmen, who insist that ultimate justice must turn on microscopic obscurities of the statute books. What constitutes an "error in the vote tabulation" under Title IX, Chapter 102.166(5) of the Florida code? May a "county canvassing board"

Weekly Standard, November 27, 2000, pp. 9–10 (on sale November 20). Reprinted with permission.

consider a "pregnant chad" on an "undercounted ballot" the binding expression of a "voter's intent"? And if such questions are properly answered, does it not become obvious that our boy is defending the Constitution?

With hardly a peep of disunity, the regular army of Democratic brahmins and activists and "intellectuals" has once again heard this bell and begun barking whatever daily dishonesties are approved by the central office. Which has once again guaranteed that only Republicans will be left to mumble back the countervailing truth. Which has once again persuaded the mainstream media to cover the spectacle as they would any other essentially "partisan" dispute: with only passing attention to its genuine origins, and an idiot's agnosticism about what conclusion is to be preferred. Which agnosticism has now been broadcast everywhere, so that you can practically feel it in the air. What not long ago would have been completely unthinkable—the outcome of a presidential election formally reversed to conform to the losing side's conception of "popular will"—is beginning to seem already thunk.

As indeed in some sense it has already been thunk. Two years ago, a sitting American president decided he would "just have to win," despite the fact that all signs pointed to his complicity in an impressive series of felonies. He did wind up winning, of course. It is really no surprise, then, the precedent for such ugly triumph firmly established, that Bill Clinton's understudy would conclude that he himself can and should "do anything to win" the White House. The only surprise is that we would find Gore still reaching for "anything to win" even after it is clear he's lost—and that he would make the grab without suffering universal condemnation.

By mid-afternoon on Election Day, word had reached Nashville of exit polls showing an extraordinarily close race, nationwide and particularly in Florida. Nashville had also become aware of anecdotal reports that a handful of voters in Palm Beach were complaining about the design of their local punch-card ballot. Gore's men knew nothing more than that. But it was enough. Before the polls closed in Florida, phone banks were calling registered Democrats in Palm Beach to warn that "you may have voted for the wrong candidate for president." And twelve hours later, at 5 a.m.—only after it emerged that Florida would in fact be decisive in the Electoral College, and that the state had been lost by fewer than 1,800 votes—Al Gore authorized his senior aides to squeeze profit from the Palm Beach frenzy they had preemptively whipped up. At an emergency meeting in his campaign headquarters, senior Democratic strategists resolved that recounts of the Florida vote would be demanded—on the basis of "ballot irregularity" allegations they could not (and still can't) substantiate.

Gore lawyers have since argued two things: first, that Palm Beach's punch cards were "illegal," and the county must therefore conduct its entire election over again; second, that Election Night computer tabulations in several other Florida counties might have missed some crucial number of votes—which suspicion, they claimed, was legally sufficient to justify a hand inspection of every ballot cast in those jurisdictions. Of course, Palm Beach's punch cards were not illegal, as we explained last week. And nothing in Florida law, honestly construed, otherwise contemplates what Team Gore has generally proposed: that an apparently defeated candidate be permitted to direct an explicitly partisan, extra-innings treasure hunt through the spoiled or incomplete ballots of voters he guesses meant to support him. For bravely sticking to her guns on this point, Florida secretary of state Katherine Harris has now been systematically smeared by flunkies of the vice president. They are wrong and Harris is right, but what should that matter? As Gore's campaign chairman, Bill Daley, has lately announced, mere "technicalities"—like the law—should no longer determine our presidential elections.

They should be determined instead, apparently, by naked thievery. Ask yourself: Why has public opinion not angrily rebelled against Gore's transparently self-interested call for hand recounts in Florida? Because Bush's margin of victory there—not counting absentee ballots from overseas—remained a paper-thin 300 votes late last week, and most folks think it common sense that we make sure we've got it nailed before such a puny number elects our president. Okay, but how is it that Bush's popular vote advantage ever got so small in the first place, when authoritative Election Night tallies had given him a lead nearly six times as large? Well, you say, Florida's mandatory next-day recount of its ballots—conducted impartially, by machine—corrected for various simple errors and glitches, and quickly produced more reliable figures. Which by purest chance broke 80 percent in Al Gore's direction.

No. Virtually impossible. And it is among the most amazing aspects of this most amazing historical event that so little attention has so far been paid to the impossibility.

There are 67 counties in Florida. The mandatory recount in one of them, Pinellas, suggested innocent human error on Election Night; ballot officials had mistakenly fed one set of punch cards through the computer twice, and had never processed another set at all. Amended returns from Pinellas produced a net gain of 343 votes for Gore. Mandatory recounts in 63 other Florida counties shifted things this way and that, each of them negligibly and at random, as statistical probability would have indicated. Together, these 63 counties gave Gore an additional net gain of fewer than 200 votes. And we have thus cleanly accounted for roughly a third of the lead Bush lost immediately following the election.

The other two thirds came entirely from three remaining counties. And the situation in each of them fairly stinks of impropriety or outright corruption.

A recount in Volusia County lopped nearly 100 votes off the gap between Bush and Gore. Officials there explain that they suddenly discovered 320 ballots they'd missed the first time. Which would be fine, perhaps. Except that last Thursday, state attorney general Bob Butterworth, who happens to be Gore's Florida campaign chairman, phoned Volusia's elections board and "requested" they perform a second recount, by hand. They agreed. And by the time they were done, 264 previously counted absentee ballots had . . . disappeared. And Al Gore, voilà, had gained a new chunk of votes (not yet certified, thank heavens, by Katherine Harris). Very fishy.

Fishier still is Gadsden County, where last Wednesday the canvassing board met privately, in violation of state law, and examined more than 2,000 ballots that had been rejected by voting machines because they each were marked for more than one presidential candidate. Gadsden, one canvassing board member admits, then "reconstructed" certain of these ballots—again, in violation of state law—and accorded 170 of them to Gore.

And fishiest of all is Palm Beach County, now notorious for the standardless, on-again-off-again manual recount sought by its grotesquely partisan canvassing board. It should be notorious for something else. On Election Day, Palm Beach voters cast only about 7 percent of the state's presidential ballots. But the putatively "neutral" machine recount Palm Beach conducted 24 hours later all by itself produced fully 45 percent of Gore's subsequent climb toward a Florida plurality: a net shift of 682 votes. How could this be? No other county experienced results anything close to these. Much larger Broward County, for example, ran its ballots through the machines a second time and changed just a single vote—in Bush's favor.

In our bones, we're pretty sure what happened here. In the middle of the night on November 8, Democratic ultraloyalists like the people who run elections in Volusia, Gadsden, and Palm Beach counties watched a fevered Bill Daley announce that things were still close in Florida—and that his party's campaign would "continue" until the rectification of unspecified "irregularities" in that state made Al Gore president. The ultraloyalists read this hint for what it was. And next, they set about, fast as lightning, before anyone was watching, doing "anything to win."

We're pretty sure, too, on whose instructions Daley issued his hint. Every Florida machination, after all, has been engineered by Al Gore personally. "He's making every decision," his aides now brag. "This is totally him."

In our next issue, we hope to be commenting on the news that one court or another has finally called a halt to the Al Gore coup of election year 2000. The news will please us. But still we will wonder: How on earth did such a man, leading such a crowd of knaves, in such a disreputable and anti-constitutional effort, ever come within a million miles of the American presidency? ▮

THOMAS L. FRIEDMAN

Can Gore Ever Win?

The New York Times

While it all may sound like just partisan noise coming out of Florida these days, there's actually a big difference between how Al Gore and George W. Bush have been behaving.

Mr. Gore has behaved as if this were the closest election in our modern history, and therefore every vote should be counted, recounted and hand counted, and should George W. Bush win Mr. Gore would have no problem declaring him the legitimate president. But one has to ask Mr. Bush: Is there any condition under which you would now accept Al Gore as the legitimate winner?

I don't think so. Mr. Bush has behaved as if this were not a close election at all, as if he had won by a landslide, and therefore the notion that every last vote be hand-counted to determine the winner is only an effort to steal the election from him—the already obvious winner. And therefore, in Mr. Bush's view, under no condition can Al Gore ever be deemed the legitimate next president. By opposing any hand counts with a scorched-earth media blitz, Mr. Bush has left himself no room to be a gracious loser. He has left no scenario in which to say: "I lost fairly. Now let's all rally behind Al Gore."

Mr. Bush needs to remember that he lost the popular vote in the country and he was ahead in Florida by only 300 votes out of six million before the absentees were counted. The fact is, this election was too close to call,

Originally published in *The New York Times*, late ed., November 21, 2000, p. A25.

and therefore conducting a hand count is both legal and legitimate, especially when it's being done under the same rules that apply in Texas.

Mr. Gore made a fair proposal to hand-count every ballot in Florida, but Mr. Bush rejected that. Now that a more limited hand count is going forward, the Bush team is making wild, unsubstantiated allegations that the hand counters are engaged in fraud. No doubt there will be disputes, and mistakes, but there is no proof of systematic fraud. Where Mr. Gore is vulnerable is on which hand counts to count. Texas law allows for "dimpled" but unperforated ballots to be counted, and some Florida counties are doing that. But Mr. Gore needs to think hard about whether he wants to win on dimples.

Either way, though, the Bush team will smear him. It is out to create an impression in the public's mind that if Mr. Gore wins by a hand count then by definition he stole the election.

That is wrong, and so was Mr. Bush's spokeswoman, Karen Hughes, when she basically accused Mr. Gore of conspiring to have the absentee ballots of U.S. military personnel not counted, implying that this made him unfit to be commander in chief. Democrats and Republicans both know that many absentee ballots are always thrown out. Absentee balloting historically has been rife with fraud, so there are a lot of technical requirements—including that a ballot be postmarked by Election Day. And in this case the decision to follow the strict Florida absentee balloting rules, as opposed to the looser Federal ones, was set by the Republican secretary of state, Katherine Harris. I believe absentee ballots from soldiers should also be hand-counted to divine whether the absence of a postmark can be excused. But to allege fraud in this regard is utterly reckless.

Our armed forces, the courts, the federal government—these are the nonpartisan institutions we need to hold our country together once there is a partisan outcome to this election. It was out of line for Ms. Hughes to imply that our armed forces are pro-Republican and that the Democrats were trying to prevent them from voting. Ms. Hughes might as well have called Mr. Gore a traitor. It would be like Mr. Gore accusing Mr. Bush of bigoted motives because he resisted recounts in counties with heavy black and Jewish populations. You just don't talk that way about the man who might be our next president.

Mr. Bush needs to remember that there is a difference between what you can say about your opponent during the campaign and what you can say about him after the election is over, with the outcome too close to call, and with each side legitimately seeking to ensure that every vote is properly tabulated. Smearing your opponent during the campaign is politics as usual; smearing him during the recount after a vote too close to call is a threat to our institutions and the next presidency. ▮

RICHARD LOWRY

Why the Restraint?

The National Review

Sunday by 5 P.M.? Why not Sunday by 4 P.M.? Or Sunday by 6 P.M.? Or Saturday? Or even Monday? Why not make Katherine Harris accept the hand counts wearing a red dress? Or while patting her head and rubbing her belly at the same time? Or while wearing Groucho Marx glasses and a party hat? Why not flat-out mandate that dimple chads count *twice* to compensate the near-disenfranchisement of these voters in keeping with the court's "broad equitable power"? Why not make Al Gore and George W. Bush meet, as the vice president suggests? Why not mandate that the "tone" of discourse be raised, as the vice president suggests? Why not just dispense with "hyper-technicalities" altogether and make Al Gore the next president of the United States? And why not go all the way and "reconcile the constitutional scheme" of Florida by eliminating the legislative and executive branches, thus laying bare what we are now experiencing—the naked power of an arbitrary and capricious judiciary. ▮

National Review Online, November 21, 2000. Reprinted with permission.

Commentary
NOVEMBER 22–DECEMBER 9, 2000

5	6	7	8	9	10	11
12	13	14	15	16	17	18
19	20	21	**22**	**23**	**24**	**25**
26	**27**	**28**	**29**	**30**	**1**	**2**
3	**4**	**5**	**6**	**7**	**8**	**9**
10	11	12	13	14	15	16
17	18	19	20	21	22	23
24	25	26	27	28	29	30

NOVEMBER · DECEMBER

ALAN BRINKLEY AND MICHAEL McCONNELL

What Now?

Slate

Slate asked Alan Brinkley and Michael McConnell to keep a running commentary on the presidential endgame. [The following is their exchange from November 22.]

From Michael McConnell

Dear Alan,

The Florida Supreme Court's decision was far worse than I had expected. From its denunciation of "hyper-technical reliance upon statutory provisions" to its fabrication of new statutory deadlines, out of whole cloth, the court showed contempt for the authority of the legislature to set the rules for the conduct of elections, which is explicitly vested in them by Article II of the U.S. Constitution.

All this was in the name of ascertaining "the will of the people." According to the court, the statutory deadline for reporting is "unnecessary" and "unreasonable." (Since none of the litigants challenged the constitutionality of the deadline, however, the court's opinion of the statutory scheme should have been irrelevant.) In fact, the court's decision will make it far more difficult to determine "the will of the people" in time for Florida's votes to be counted.

Under the statute (as I explained yesterday), counties have seven days after the election to certify their results. That certification triggers a 10-day period during which any voter may lodge a protest about the results. In combination, these provisions establish a 17-day period for counts and recounts, including manual recounts. If, at the end of that period, the manual recounts indicate that Gore has won the election, voters can use that as the basis for a protest. In other words, Secretary of State Harris should have been permitted to certify the results as of last Saturday, which is her clear statutory

Slate, November 22, 2000. Reprinted with permission of the authors. Alan Brinkley is Allan Nevins Professor of History at Columbia University. Michael McConnell is the Presidential Professor of Law at the University of Utah.

duty, but this would not have been final. The final result comes only after protests have been made and adjudicated.

The Florida Supreme Court scrapped the statutory deadlines and imposed new ones of its own creation. The effect was to delay certification by eight days, thus subtracting 18 days from the time available to resolve disputes about the manual recount. Under the court's ruling, the counties have until Nov. 26 or 27 to certify their results. Voters will then have 10 days during which to lodge protests. That means that protests can be filed as late as Dec. 6 or 7. That leaves only five or six days before the Florida electors must be certified on Dec. 12, which everyone agrees is the drop-dead date.

Consider what must be accomplished in that six-day period. There are literally thousands of ballots in Broward and Palm Beach counties (Miami-Dade County dropped its manual recount moments ago) that have been set aside because the voter's intent is unclear. Most of these are dimpled ballots. Once these ballots have been decided, one way or the other, the losing side will undoubtedly challenge those decisions in court (as is their right). In addition, over 1,000 absentee ballots have been excluded on grounds that even Democratic leaders now admit were improper. And there are increasing numbers of allegations from Republican observers of ballot-counting improprieties.

It will take time to resolve these issues. Thanks to the Florida Supreme Court, there will not be enough time. I hate to be paranoid or alarmist, but since the initial decisions will be made by boards of canvassers dominated by Democrats, the clock will run out precisely at the point when Republicans are challenging judgment calls that were made by political bodies loaded against them. At that point, the choice will be between disregarding Republican protests (or treating them summarily) and sacrificing Florida's representation in the Electoral College. Which course do you think the Florida Supreme Court will choose? Is that any way to get a "full, fair, and accurate count"?

From Alan Brinkley

Dear Michael,

Could this story get any stranger or more complicated? Life goes on for us non-combatants, and I'm in holiday mode already, so I will be brief today.

If anyone thought the Florida Supreme Court would bring closure or conciliation to this imbroglio, think again. "INSANITY" was the headline in the reliably partisan *New York Post* today, and that only slightly overstates the furious reaction of the Bush campaign last night and this morning. So furious, in fact, that they may well have intimidated the Dade County election board (which was, as you'll recall, somewhat reluctant to start a recount in the first place) into calling their recount off this morning—a huge blow indeed to Gore.

I think the court's decision was legally sound, although perhaps more assertive than is currently the fashion in American jurisprudence. The election law that the Republicans are defending as if it were the Bill of Rights is, in fact, ambiguous and contradictory—and clearly never envisioned, as one could have, a situation like this. It seems fair to me to allow legally sanctioned recounts to continue and to ensure that the results be counted.

The "dimpled chad" issue is another matter. There is, of course, no universally agreed-upon standard for judging the intent of voters on punch-card ballots. (And if nothing else good comes out of this mess, let us hope that it persuades counties across the nation never again to use punch-card voting.) "Dimpled chads" may well be a perfectly fair way to judge such intent. But having rejected that standard earlier in the counting, it seems to me politically unwise, to say the least, to change the standard simply because the original standard wasn't producing enough Gore votes. That does seem calculating and unfair to me, even as a Democrat and a Gore supporter.

But what is legally justified, or fair in some abstract sense, is more or less irrelevant now. Because there is only one standard by which either side judges any event in this drama now: What is most likely to help them win. And why should we be surprised? A close election like this—a "dead heat," as Jim Baker called it—is always incredibly contested. Look at Gorton-Cantwell in Washington state, where they're still counting and likely soon recounting; or Holt-Zimmer in New Jersey; or the upper East Side state Senate race here in New York; or countless other close races over the last decades, which dragged on and on, increasingly acrimoniously, through the courts and through the press. These circumstances are probably inevitable, exaggerated this time only by the stakes.

Is there a way out? Certainly not through one side or another throwing in the towel, as Republicans like to believe Nixon did in 1960. (In fact, Nixon did not—as David Greenberg made clear in *Slate* and the *Los Angeles Times;* he contested the election in state after state until the day before the electors met. The image of magnanimous concession in 1960 is a complete myth.)

Probably our best hope for a non-catastrophic resolution is for the recounts simply not to produce a Gore majority, which the Miami-Dade action today certainly makes more likely. That would not be a happy solution for Democrats. But the alternative—given the Republican ferocity on this issue (a ferocity the Democrats would almost certainly match if they were in the same situation)—is a long fight through the courts, through the state legislature, and ultimately through the Congress, which in the end Gore would very likely lose in any case.

Had the court followed Michael's advice—certify the vote as it is, and then let the Democrats contest—the situation would probably now be marginally more civil, but only for a little while.

In the end, I suppose, we have to concede that there is no way to get a true picture of how Florida voted. The initial, recounted returns, which the GOP wants to certify, are certainly not entirely accurate. But the results of a hand recount in a few counties would not be accurate either. Most people probably would now admit that Gore would have carried Florida fairly clearly were it not for the flawed Palm Beach ballot, but there is nothing to be done about that now. So whatever the result, we are going to have to choose our next president on nothing more than a guess about how Florida really voted. ■

GEORGE F. WILL

This Willful Court

The Washington Post

"The accumulation of all powers legislative, executive and judiciary in the same hands . . . may justly be pronounced the very definition of tyranny."—*James Madison, Federalist 47*

Al Gore's assault on the rule of law, crowned with success by Florida's lawless Supreme Court, has become a crisis of the American regime. See above.

In asking that court do what Gore wanted, attorney David Boies on Nov. 20 uttered a notable understatement: "I believe that there is going to have to be a lot of judgment applied by the court." Consider the radicalism—it far exceeds routine judicial activism—of what the court did with its "judgment."

Barry Richard, a George W. Bush lawyer, accurately told the court that Gore was asking it to read a statute, which says returns "must" be filed by a date and time certain, as though it says returns may be filed by a date and time certain. And, Richard said, Gore was asking the court to read a statute that says Florida's secretary of state "may" accept late returns as though it says she "must" accept late returns. So, Richard said, in order to rule for Gore the court must "disregard the well-established and long-standing doctrines" regarding the "clearly erroneous" standard, and regarding "implied repeal."

The "clearly erroneous" standard is this: For a higher court to overturn the ruling of a lower court, it must find the lower court clearly erroneous. In this case, it must find that the trial court had no reasonable basis for ruling that Florida's secretary of state did not abuse her discretion when she acted as though the statute reads the way it actually does, rather than the opposite way that Gore wants it to be read. Furthermore, when a court reads a statute as having a meaning directly contrary to its clear language, the court implicitly repeals the statute.

So the court, in a trifecta of willfulness, traduced all three branches of government. It says it acted out of respect for "the will of the people." But not the people's will as expressed by the people's elected representatives in the legislature that wrote the election laws. And not the people's will as expressed in the election of the secretary of state to enforce the laws.

During oral arguments on Nov. 20, a justice, foreshadowing what would happen the evening of Nov. 21, mused, "Are we just going to reach up from some inspiration and put it down on paper?" On the evening of Nov. 21, addressing the question of "under what circumstances may a board authorize a countywide manual recount," the court plucked from thin air a Sunday, or maybe Monday deadline for such recounts. On the morning of Nov. 22, Miami-Dade authorities, deciding they could not do a countywide recount by then, announced that they will recount only a particularly promising (for Gore) portion of the ballots. Controlling legal authority? None.

In Federalist 81, Alexander Hamilton said the "supposed" danger of judicial "encroachments on the legislative authority" is a "phantom." In Federalist 78, he pronounced the judicial branch the "least dangerous" to political rights because it neither wields "the sword" nor controls "the purse," and hence " can take no active resolution whatever. It may truly be said to have neither force nor will, but merely judgment; and must ultimately depend upon the aid of the executive arm even for the efficacy of its judgments."

No, a lawless court, using the force of its willfulness to impose its judgment, also depends on the deference of both political branches. Will Florida's legislature defer to the Supreme Court's usurpation of legislative powers in the service of Gore's attempted usurpation of the presidency?

By legislating—by airily rewriting Florida's election law and applying it retroactively to this election—the court has thrown down a gauntlet to the state's legislature. Responding in the climate of cynicism and trickery Gore has created, legislators could decide that deference now would betoken decadence; they could exercise their legal right to select Florida's presidential electors. If in the third week after the election Gore at last managed, by getting selected ballots judged by frequently adjusted standards, to manufacture enough votes to take the lead, his electors would be no more legitimate than any others created by raw assertions of power.

Addressing the court on Nov. 20, Boies, speaking for Gore, used the language of contemporary liberalism's relish for judicial imperialism. Nine times Boies urged the court to wield its "power." In doing just that, the court has refuted Hamilton's sanguine assurance (in Federalist 81) that although "misconstructions and contraventions of the will of the legislature may now and then happen," they can never "affect the order of the political system." We are a sadder but wiser nation now. ▌

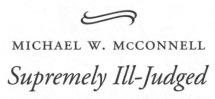

MICHAEL W. MCCONNELL

Supremely Ill-Judged

The Wall Street Journal

One sentence of the Florida Supreme Court's decision on hand recounts tells it all: "The will of the people, not a hyper-technical reliance upon statutory provisions, should be our guiding principle."

That is like saying, of a disputed umpire call in the World Series: "Athletic superiority, not a hyper-technical reliance upon the rules of baseball, should be our guiding principle." In our system, the will of the people is manifested through procedures specified in advance. When those rules are changed in mid-stream, something has gone terribly wrong.

Wall Street Journal, November 24, 2000, p. A16. Reprinted from *The Wall Street Journal* © 2000 Dow Jones & Company, Inc. All rights reserved. Michael McConnell is the Presidential Professor of Law at the University of Utah College of Law.

Article II of the U.S. Constitution provides: "Each State shall appoint, in such Manner as the Legislature thereof may direct, a Number of Electors . . ." The Florida legislature has enacted a detailed election code, including an unambiguous deadline of seven days after the election for counties to report their results. No party to the litigation has argued that this statutory scheme is unconstitutional under either the federal or the state constitution.

If any counties fail to report on time, one section of the law states that "all missing counties shall be ignored," and another that "such returns may be ignored." As the Florida Supreme Court pointed out on Tuesday night, these provisions are inconsistent. But the court purported to reconcile the "shall" with the "may" by holding that late returns may not be ignored. It did this because it believed that enforcement of the statutory deadline would be "a drastic measure," and that to "disenfranchise electors" on account of the statutory deadline would be "unreasonable" and "unnecessary."

But since the legislature made the rules, and no one claimed they were unconstitutional, the court's opinion about their wisdom or necessity should have been irrelevant. Presumably, the rules could work to one side's advantage in one election and the other side's advantage in another election. Can you imagine the screams from the Gore campaign if votes cast in favor of George W. Bush had been counted after a statutory deadline?

In any event, the deadline is far from "unnecessary." Under Florida law, all voters have 10 days after the initial certification of election results to contest it. (In my opinion, perhaps contrary to the Republicans' arguments, the manual recounts can proceed and, if they are validated and demonstrate a change in the result, could be the basis for such a contest. Despite their high potential for arbitrariness and even fraud, manual recounts, like deadlines, are a feature of the Florida law.) Those contests will take time to adjudicate.

Thousands of ballots have already been put aside in Broward and Palm Beach counties because the voter's intent is not clearly ascertainable. Fortunately, Miami-Dade is now out of the picture. But the suspect ballots in the two other counties may well determine the election.

Some of the questionable ballots have "dimples" in the spots for more than one presidential candidate, yet Democrats say they should be counted for Al Gore. Some of the ballots have clear votes (no dimples, no hanging chads) for every other office on the ballot, but a dimple in the presidential vote. Such a voter obviously knows how to cast a vote. The failure to perforate the ballot in the presidential vote most likely means the voters decided, at the last moment, that they didn't like any of the candidates. Yet Democrats say these votes should be counted for Mr. Gore.

Indeed, while there may be individual cases where a dimple "clearly reflects the voter's intent" (in the language of the Florida Supreme Court), such as where the entire ballot is filled with dimples, in most cases there is an insoluble ambiguity. No one knows whether the voter intended to cast a vote, or changed his mind. Presumably, that is why the canvassing boards initially decided not to count them. Yet Gore lawyers have gone to court to demand that all dimpled ballots be counted.

The absentee ballot issue is also yet to be resolved. Over a thousand absentee ballots—many of them from military voters—have been excluded, despite being properly signed and dated, because foreign post offices failed to postmark them, or the postmark was smudged, or postmarks are not available. Even Sen. Joe Lieberman and Florida Attorney General Robert Butterworth have conceded that this is unacceptable. But nothing has been done. Will it require yet another lawsuit to ensure that "the voter's intent" counts, even when it likely favors Mr. Bush?

Moreover, if Republican allegations have any substance, there will be charges and countercharges of fraud and mishandling of ballots. With 2-1 Democratic majorities on the county canvassing boards (and the sole Republican having resigned in one of the counties), there is every reason to suspect that many of the disputed ballot decisions will reflect unintentional bias, at best. To achieve a "full, fair, and accurate count" (in Mr. Gore's language) there must be ample opportunity for GOP observers to get a fair hearing.

Resolving these thousands of disputes will not be a speedy process. That is why the Florida statutory scheme, so casually dismissed by the court, made sense. Under that scheme, counties have seven days to certify an initial result. Voters then have 10 days to file protests. That gives a total of 17 days for counts and recounts, and leaves about a three-week period for full consideration of contests.

The Florida Supreme Court, by fiat, has reduced the time for review of these difficult questions by at least eight days. Now, contests can be initiated as late as Dec. 6, 10 days after the court's arbitrary deadline. Electors must be chosen by Dec. 12. That leaves less than a week for the real issues of this election to be adjudicated. It is hard to see how that can be done, at least with any pretense of fairness.

At this point—and thanks in no small part to the Florida Supreme Court's decision to supersede the statute—there are two possible scenarios, neither of them happy. In one scenario, the Democrats succeed in treating virtually all the dimpled ballots as valid votes, despite their inherent ambiguity. If that occurs, it will be evident to the American people that the re-

sults of the Florida count did not reflect "the will of the people," but only
the inexorable process of finding more Gore votes, no matter what.

In the second scenario, each disputed ballot will receive due attention.
The dimple will be evaluated in light of "the totality of the circumstances,"
and ultimate decisions will be made by the county boards of canvassers, with
appeals to the courts. That will take time, almost certainly longer than the
six days the court's decision allows. Under this scenario, the process will not
be complete by Dec. 12.

Under either scenario, the Florida legislature will be tempted to interfere,
to ensure that the Florida vote tally is conducted in accordance with the law.
Since the legislature is a political body, with a Republican majority, such a
step will be enormously controversial. It should only be a last step, to be en-
tertained only if the alternative is either manifest error or inability to choose
electors. It would have been far better for the Florida Supreme Court to resist the temptation to rewrite the state's laws, and to leave in place a system
that—however imperfect—could have reached a result that fair-minded
Americans could view as legitimate. ∎

JONATHAN RAUCH

Hands Off: Why Florida Election
Law Isn't So Crazy After All

The New Republic

Last week, after she tried to slam the door on hand recounts in three Democratic counties, Florida Secretary of State Katherine Harris received
enough abuse to sink the USS *Cole*. The Florida Supreme Court's subsequent ruling overturning her efforts only reinforced the view that Harris is
a partisan hack. Maybe so. But that doesn't necessarily mean she's wrong
or the court is right. There is, in fact, a strong, substantive argument for
slamming the door on manual recounts—even if some voters' fingers get
mashed.

New Republic, December 4, 2000, pp. 24–26 (on sale November 27). Reprinted with
permission. Jonathan Rauch is a senior writer for the *National Journal* and a writer-in-res-
idence at the Brookings Institution.

It's true that many jurisdictions (including George W. Bush's Texas) provide for manual recounts in contested elections. But what's appropriate for state and local elections is not necessarily appropriate for a presidential election that could be tipped by a handful of counties in a single state. If it takes a long time to seat a governor, attorney general, or member of Congress whose claim to victory is tenuous, that is unfortunate, but it will not weaken the presidency, embarrass America abroad, or erode the legitimacy of the country's only national election. The presidency is different. Post-election wrangling, including protracted recounts, should be avoided, even at great cost. And manual recounts are especially dangerous—for two reasons.

First, hand recounts under conditions of extreme partisanship and stress almost inevitably raise suspicion. Machines err, and they may well be more error-prone than people. But machines don't carry party membership cards. They may bungle elections, but they don't steal them (at least not as far as we know; see "Rage Against the Machine," by Ronnie Dugger, [*New Republic*, December 4, 2000] page 22). Reporters watching through windows and party observers standing over tabulators' shoulders will never, and probably should never, obviate the fear that recounts in jurisdictions controlled by Democrats (or Republicans) will tend to favor Democrats (or Republicans).

Second, and more fundamental: In one crucial respect, the first vote count is the best. It is the only count that is truly double-blind. That is, neither the voters nor the vote counters can more than guess at the effects of their decisions on the overall outcome.

This is no longer the case, of course, after the initial vote count. Partisans on both sides then know exactly how many additional votes it would take to tilt the election to their candidate. And this knowledge inevitably raises questions about every decision made regarding the subsequent recount efforts. In Florida, Democratic demands for selective recounts in Democratic-leaning counties are troublesome enough, smacking as they do of cherry-picking. If the selective recounts are performed manually, the problem is compounded. When partisan election officials know for a fact that a few votes could change the outcome, they can't help but be tempted to tilt their recounts accordingly. And, even if they resist the temptation, who will believe them? The counters simply know too much about the votes' importance to seem above suspicion.

Consider Broward County, a Democratic stronghold. Democratic canvassing-board officials there justified their manual recount on the grounds that it might affect the election and that a test recount had turned up a few additional votes for Gore. Broward's canvassing board, unlike Palm Beach

County's, possessed no compelling external evidence that anything was wrong with the original machine tally: no Election Day complaints from voters, no unusually large number of ballots thrown out. The board went ahead anyway, on a party-line vote.

The Broward Democrats insisted they just wanted accuracy, and I'm sure they believed themselves. What corrupted them was not their intentions but their knowledge. Because they knew in advance that their recount would favor Gore and might win him the election, their procedure, however well-intentioned, was indistinguishable, even in principle, from vote-rigging: recounting with the specific purpose of changing the outcome.

There's a case for banning manual recounts in presidential elections, but that's probably not politically feasible—anyway, no one thought to do it in Florida. An imperfect but still effective solution, however, might limit the damage. For instance, a state could set a time limit. The state could presume that the first count is the best and demand that, absent widespread fraud or machine breakdown or intervening acts of God, any subsequent recounts must be finished by some early date certain. What date? Well, a month after Election Day seems unreasonably long; a day seems unreasonably short. How about a week? That sounds as reasonable—or unreasonable—as any other deadline, and it is essentially what Florida law, as interpreted by Harris, would have done. True, a one-week drop-dead date arbitrarily limits the same manual recounts that it authorizes. But that is precisely its advantage. It sets a tight limit on backward-looking recounts, and does so *before* the election—that is, before anyone knows what sort of deadline helps or hurts any particular candidate.

In its decision, the Florida Supreme Court took the opposite tack: It adjusted the deadline to fit the recount, instead of the other way around. It effectively accepted the rationale offered last week by Palm Beach County, which asked Harris for more time on the grounds that "clearly the results of the manual recount could affect the outcome of this very close presidential election if the manual recounts in the other precincts also vary in this degree from the machine counts." That, however, is precisely the rationale for *not* permitting recounts after preset deadlines. After all, some ballots are always ambiguous, and those ambiguous ballots only matter when they might "affect the outcome of [a] very close presidential election"—something that can be known only after the fact. If the rule is going to be that election-tipping ballots get counted by hand after the rest of the returns are in, then the whole principle of the double-blind election goes out the window.

Preserving that principle—that is, preventing selective recounts by partisan officials who know more than they should—is not about electing one candidate or another. It is not even mainly about finishing elections quickly. It is about preserving the blindfolded integrity of the electoral process and ensuring that, to the greatest extent possible, no votes receive special treatment (or are counted in light of special information, which amounts to the same thing). If those aren't worthy principles, I've never seen any.

Unfortunately, "Let's get this over with" was about the closest the Bush people came to a principled argument. That didn't sound particularly compelling against Gore's characteristically pious (and characteristically sly) demand that "every vote [be] counted fairly and accurately." Instead of arguing for their policy on its merits, the Bush campaign, along with Harris, argued on the law. The public thus had little reason to doubt that, as *The New York Times* editorialized in a news story, Harris's effort "seemed a clear tactical move to freeze the election results in Mr. Bush's favor."

Right from the start of the campaign, Bush adopted thoughtful and principled policies that he had trouble explaining in thoughtful and principled terms. In Florida, his campaign is ending as it began. ∎

THOMAS E. MANN

Gore Owes It to Nation to Fight On

The Boston Globe

Sunday's certification of the results of the presidential election in Florida have prompted a near acceptance speech by Governor George W. Bush and a chorus of calls for Vice President Al Gore to finally acknowledge the inevitable, forgo any further legal appeals, and concede the election now.

Gore should do no such thing. Quite apart from his own obvious self-interest in the outcome, Gore owes it to the country, to the American constitutional system, and to the next president of the United States, whomever he may be, to pursue in a timely fashion all remedies permitted by Florida law to achieve as full and accurate vote count as possible.

Boston Globe, 3d ed., November 28, 2000, p. A15. Reprinted with permission. Thomas E. Mann is the W. Averell Harriman Senior Fellow at the Brookings Institution.

A week or so ago I thought otherwise. Once the manual recount was completed and the revised vote tabulated, I thought Gore should accept the outcome.

While he may continue to believe, with justification, that a plurality of
Florida voters intended to and believed that they voted for him, unintentional failures in ballot design and instructions to voters that produced
spoiled ballots could not reasonably be undone after the election. His only
recourse, I believed, was to request a hand recount of the unusually large
number of undervotes and live with the results of that effort.

But three events have intervened to render that course of action inappropriate. First, the decision of the Miami-Dade canvassing board, in the
face of a tight deadline and an intimidating political demonstration, to suspend the manual recount and to throw away the ballots already counted for
Gore, makes a mockery of the Florida Supreme Court's eloquent statement
about the paramount importance of the right of voters to be heard. The convenience and comfort of local officials should not trump the right of citizens to have their vote counted. So the manual recount remains incomplete.

Second, on the appeal of the Bush campaign, the U.S. Supreme Court
has agreed to consider whether the decision of the Florida Supreme Court
is unconstitutional or inconsistent with federal law. Given the highly con-
tentious nature of the presidential vote count, it is critical that the highest
court in the land now be heard. A premature concession by Gore would render the case before the Court moot.

Third, and most important, a careful and deliberative resolution of the
Florida vote count is essential to dilute the venom that has been injected
into the country's political bloodstream.

In 30 years of watching Congress and the presidency, I have never en-
countered rhetoric as vituperative and destructive of the constitutional order as has emanated from established figures in the Republican Party and
their partisan allies.

"Coup d'etat." "Stealing elections." It makes the impeachment battle look
like child's play.

The assumption behind this verbal fusillade is that there is only one legitimate outcome—the election of George W. Bush as president—and the
means by which the count is resolved are to be judged solely in terms of the
outcome produced. Yet that is precisely the reverse of our constitutional design. Due process is paramount. No individual or party is entitled to public office, whatever the projection of the networks on election night. Courts
are to be judged by the nature and quality of their decisions, not reflexively
dismissed as bastions of partisan hacks.

The time has come to end the permanent campaign, to push the public relations specialists and ideological activists to the sidelines and pursue a reasonable conclusion to a very difficult situation. A satisfactory resolution will require widespread acceptance that the election resulted in a dead heat, inevitable errors in vote counting make it impossible to determine who "really won," and both Bush and Gore have reasonable grounds for believing themselves the victor. The least damaging and ultimately most acceptable way of resolving the impasse is to achieve as accurate and fair a count of the Florida vote as possible in a manner provided for by statute and sanctioned by the courts. As impatient as we all naturally are, we can afford to take another week or two to allow the legal process to play out.

American democracy depends critically on the acceptance of political opposition. Two hundred years ago our nascent democracy earned its spurs by accommodating the first peaceful transfer of power after a long and bitter presidential election battle in the House of Representatives. There can be no more appropriate celebration of the bicentennial of the Election of 1800 than a judicious, respectful, and legitimate resolution of the presidential election of 2000. A President Bush or President Gore, and our constitutional democracy more generally, will be stronger for it. ∎

CHARLES KRAUTHAMMER

Our Imperial Judiciary: We Need to Bring a Gavel Down on Arrogant Judges Like Florida's Supremes

Time

Constitutional crisis in Florida. Oh, the hand wringing at the prospect of the Florida legislature challenging the state supreme court's decision in *Gore* vs. *Bush*. Constitutional crisis? Why not? It's about time we had one.

It might finally allow a cathartic resolution of the debilitating constitutional problem we have been suffering under for 40 years: arrogant, activist

Time, December 4, 2000, p. 46 (on sale November 27). Reprinted with permission.

courts trampling the prerogatives of elected legislatures and elected governments in deciding how we are to live. Christmas creches snatched from public displays under the baroque, three-pronged "Lemon test"; Miranda rules
plucked out of thin air; the right to abortion suddenly located in the
"penumbra" of the Constitution.

I happen to like Miranda. I happen to support legalized abortion. But many
citizens don't. And they rightly feel aggrieved that these momentous decisions
were made by unelected grandees in black robes. (The U.S. is the only West-
ern country to have legalized abortion without the consent of its legislature.)

Americans have suffered their disenfranchisement largely because of a
traditional, habitual respect for the U.S. Supreme Court. They have no such
instinctive respect for the Florida Supreme Court, which until yesterday they
had never heard of. Its attempt to throw a presidential election by inventing
post facto election law is surely a bridge too far. It begins with the justices
setting themselves up as defenders of the "will of the people" against what
they contemptuously call "hypertechnical reliance upon statutory provisions," or what other people call "adherence to the law."

Hypertechnical? The law's single technicality was that ballots be counted
by 5 p.m., Nov. 14. This was hardly a law riddled with minutiae. It had a
simple, clear standard. The court's real problem is not technicality but legality, what it disdainfully terms "sacred, unyielding adherence to statutory
scripture." Courts, it seems, write scripture; legislatures write talking points.

The justices then denounce Florida secretary of state Katherine Harris
for "imposing an arbitrary seven-day deadline." They then proceed, without irony, to impose their own arbitrary five-day deadline. (Hers, unlike
theirs, was not arbitrary but statutory.)

They accuse her of attempting to "summarily disenfranchise innocent
electors" by adhering to the deadline. Really? Then what about the court's
own deadline of Nov. 26? It caused Miami-Dade officials to shut down their
recount completely. According to its own logic, the court has disenfranchised thousands of Miami-Dade voters. But the whole disenfranchisement
charge is absurd in any case. The plain fact is that any deadline must necessarily "disenfranchise" voters—or it would not be a deadline, i.e., a date
after which otherwise legal ballots must be ignored. We must nonetheless
have deadlines, or no election would ever end.

Moreover, the court repeatedly defined its role as tribune of the unspo-
ken plaintiffs, citizens whose votes have gone un(re)counted. Why then did
it not order a recount of all the counties of Florida? If refusing to reconsider
spoiled ballots disenfranchises voters of Palm Beach, how could the court

tolerate residents of 64 other counties having their dimpled ballots languish forever in un-hand-counted obscurity?

This central contradiction alone—elevating recounts in Democratic counties to high principle while ignoring recounts in the rest of the state—renders the court's ruling a travesty. A welcome travesty, however. Because this time the lawless lawmaking was made in the full glare of publicity and with such obvious partisanship. (All seven judges are Democratic appointees; the selection to the court of five of them was strongly influenced by Dexter Douglass, a Gore lawyer who addressed the court during the dramatic oral argument.) And because its very outrageousness—rewriting the rules of a presidential election after the election—dramatizes the extent of judicial usurpation as has nothing since *Roe* v. *Wade*.

Hence the search for remedies: the Florida legislature threatening to reassert its prerogative to make law, either by reaffirming the original language of the election law that the court grossly misconstrued, or by simply appointing their own presidential electors; Congress contemplating exercising its own authority to recognize electors, should the Florida delegation turn out to have been manufactured by a court.

This would indeed be a constitutional crisis, but one brought on by the courts themselves, and one we have long needed to confront.

The issue is judicial supremacy. We acquiesce to it for one very good reason. The reason is not theoretical (it being hard to understand why the one unelected branch should be supreme over the other two) but practical. We all need a place where the buck stops. When Nixon and Congress were at odds over the White House tapes, the supremacy of the Supreme Court enabled a final resolution of the issue.

Fine. But for the judiciary to earn—and sustain—that pre-eminence, it needs to exercise restraint. After all, it has no power of its own. Unlike the legislature, it can raise no revenues. Unlike the executive, it commands no police forces. Its power rests entirely on people's belief in its legitimate authority. But that belief can—and should—be forfeited when courts do what the Florida Supreme Court has done: wantonly usurp their two coequal branches, denying both the plain language of a law and the plain authority of the official elected to administer that law.

Such a court deserves to be challenged. Yes, that will create a crisis. But crisis is preferable to supine acquiescence. Should the Florida court be put in its place—overridden and thus shorn of its emperor's new clothes—we will have at last begun to rectify the constitutional imbalance created by the imperial judiciary. This is not a constitutional crisis. This is a constitutional opportunity. ∎

WILLIAM KRISTOL

Crowning the Imperial Judiciary

The New York Times

So four decades of judicial activism, at both the state and federal levels, mostly unchallenged by the other branches of government, culminates in this: Judges may now select the next president of the United States.

Almost no one seems to think this odd. Al Gore wants the election resolved by the Florida courts and told us that "respect for the rulings of our independent judiciary is an essential building block of the American Republic."

The Bush campaign, even while asking the Florida courts to stay out of the electoral process, continues its appeal to the United States Supreme Court. Tom Daschle, the Senate minority leader, says on television, matter-of-factly, that "what's relevant is what's going to happen in the course of the next several days in the courts" and that "this will be largely resolved in the courts."

Commentators, liberal and conservative, have both largely agreed with the politicians. In their view, only the courts, especially the United States Supreme Court, have the political legitimacy to resolve the struggle over the presidency.

They are wrong. Now is the time to rethink decades of judicial activism, which has undermined the rule of law and enfeebled self-government. After all, the people of Florida voted on Nov. 7. An automatic recount took place, as mandated by state law. The appropriate official, Katherine Harris, the secretary of state, was ready to certify the winner, as provided by statute, on Nov. 14, pending only the receipt of the overseas absentee ballots. A Florida circuit court judge supported the secretary of state in her intention to follow the law.

Then the Florida Supreme Court stepped in. First it blocked the secretary of state's planned certification. Then the court seized upon an ambiguity in Florida law as to whether the secretary of state had to enforce the deadline or could waive it, and ruled that she had no choice but to waive it. The court then established its own set of election procedures. The Bush campaign appealed to the United States Supreme Court, which to the surprise of many observers, granted a hearing to consider the state court's actions.

Originally published in *The New York Times,* late ed., November 28, 2000, p. A29.

Why did the nation's highest court take the case? Perhaps to save the reputation and authority of the judiciary in general against foolish over-reaching by the justices' Florida cousins, and against the rebuke that seemed to be in the offing from the State Legislature.

The United States Supreme Court may act to check the pretensions of the Florida court. But it may not. The Florida Legislature has to be ready to assert its own constitutional prerogative against the Florida courts' intervention in the electoral process. The United States Constitution provides that presidential electors may be appointed in such manner as the state legislatures may direct.

On or before Dec. 12, the Florida legislature may have to choose to ratify the slate of electors certified by the secretary of state against the wishes of the Florida Supreme Court. That decision would then have to be upheld by the United States Congress. This would be a constitutional crisis, to be sure—but forcing such a "crisis" is preferable to supine yielding to an imperial judiciary.

Three weeks ago, at 4 a.m. the morning after Election Day, William Daley, the Gore campaign chairman, stepped to the microphones. He did not say, as he should have, that the campaign was over but a recount was available under Florida law and of course we should all await the results of that recount. Instead he proclaimed, "Our campaign continues."

What he meant was: Let our litigation begin.

Now Mr. Daley has disappeared and David Boies has become the de facto Gore campaign chairman. It is bad enough when litigation replaces legislation as a way to make decisions in the public arena, as in the tobacco lawsuits. Worse still is the trial-lawyerization of our electoral politics. But it follows from the politicizing of the courts.

As governor, George W. Bush made tort reform a priority. As president, he can build on this by seeking reform of the legal system. He can propose federal tort reform, appoint judges who are more likely to respect the proper judicial role and use his bully pulpit to advance a more strict interpretation of the Constitution and the separation of powers.

Mr. Bush has run as an apostle of compassionate conservatism. But the present crisis suggests that a revival of constitutional conservatism is the more urgent and more important task. ∎

MICHAEL KINSLEY

Deadlines and Dishonesty

The Washington Post

The Bush argument for denying Al Gore a fair recount has long since been distilled to a few hard, shiny deceits: We've had plenty of recounts; you don't change the rules in the middle of the game; and so on. Sunday night brought a new one: The Florida results have been certified. Like it or lump it, the game's over. Gore's refusal to give up is bad sportsmanship. In fact, it's downright unpatriotic.

"Now the Gore campaign lawyers want to shift from recounts to contesting the election outcome," sneered James Baker Sunday evening. His client, George W. Bush, said a few minutes later: "Until Florida's votes were certified, the vice president was working to represent the interests of those who supported him." But now? "Now that they're certified, we enter a different phase. If the vice president chooses to go forward, he is filing a contest to the outcome of the election. And that is not the best route for America."

In this hoarse dispute, I've almost given up trying to convince people of things that seem obvious to me. What difference does it make how many recounts you've already done, if they all leave out the same group of ballots? Blah blah blah. But this claim that certification should close the issue is so staggeringly dishonest that I'm going to make one more attempt.

Here goes. The right to "contest" an election result after certification was central to every legal argument the Bush side made to get them to their Sunday evening triumph. It was the very reason Secretary of State Katherine Harris said she needed to enforce a strict deadline for certification. It was the reason she gave why Gore would not be unfairly harmed by certification on her schedule. Her briefs criticized Gore for raising issues before certification instead of waiting until afterward, where they belonged. Briefs for George W. Bush endorsed these arguments. Leaving enough time to contest certification was the very reason the Florida Supreme Court gave for setting the Sunday evening deadline!

Harris to the Florida Supreme Court: "The Legislature had good reason to set strict time limits for the certification of election. . . . Importantly, the

Washington Post, final ed., November 29, 2000, p, A39. Reprinted with permission. Michael Kinsley is editor of *Slate*.

time for filing an election contest commences upon certification. . . . To delay certification affects the ability to have an election contest heard and possibly appealed and to implement whatever remedy the court might fashion. Each day that certifications are not made and the right to contest is not triggered, the likelihood of a court's ability to effectively deal with a legitimate election failure is adversely affected."

It gets even better. The brief asserts that Gore is "confused" in saying that all the "facts and circumstances" should be known before certification. "This is illogical because such facts and circumstances are usually discovered and raised in a contest action that cannot begin until after the election is certified."

Bush to the Florida Supreme Court: "Florida law provides for contests to be filed after the fact. . . . The contest mechanism provides an adequate and therefore exclusive avenue for relief if Petitioners are correct that the Secretary of State was legally bound to accept late-filed returns."

The Florida Supreme Court ruling: "Accordingly, in order to allow maximum time for contests . . . , amended certifications must be filed with the Election Canvassing Commission by 5 p.m. on Sunday, November 26, 2000 and the Secretary of State . . . shall accept any such amended certifications" up to the same magic moment.

The Harris brief to the U.S. Supreme Court: "The Legislature imposed a deadline for certification because of the short time frame within which to begin and conclude an election contest."

The Bush brief to the U.S. Supreme Court: "That statute [the Florida election law] clearly anticipates that results will be certified in a timely fashion, in order for the results to be contested in court."

The U.S. Supreme Court: Yet to be heard from.

So before the certification, they argued that Gore had no right to bring up his complaints—or even to establish the "facts and circumstances" of what went on—because all that should wait until after certification. Leaving enough time for him to do this was the very reason certification was so pressing. And the Supreme Court agreed, which is why it laid down the Sunday 5 p.m. deadline that Katherine Harris enforced with such cynical exactitude.

Although certification was delayed, many votes were never counted—or were counted and discarded—to meet the deadline: a deadline allegedly imposed for Gore's benefit. And several reasonable issues have never had their day in court. Yet now Gore is being told he should be ashamed of asserting the right of which Bush and Harris were so solicitous, lo, these many days ago.

When a reporter touched on all this in the brief Q&A after James Baker's statement Sunday evening, Baker denied that he meant to suggest that Gore's decision to contest the certification was so much as "inappropriate." Baker said, "I didn't say it was inappropriate, and I didn't say it was not provided for in the statutes of Florida. I did say that it was an extraordinarily unusual approach. . . ."

Q: "Could I follow up?"

Baker: "And what I did say was that we've had count after count after recount. . . ." Blah blah blah.

Of course he and the Bush sound-bite brigade are implying or outright saying that Gore's decision not to give up is a lot worse than "inappropriate." How does he—how do they—do it with a straight face? The answer must be: the same way you get to Carnegie Hall. ▊

RAMESH PONNURU

The Judicial-Activist State: It's Not Just Florida

The National Review

Few court rulings have been denounced as swiftly or as harshly as the Florida supreme court's decision on the night of November 21. At issue was a state statute establishing that within seven days of an election, the results are to be certified. In order to give three Florida counties time to complete their hand recounts of the presidential ballots, the court threw out the seven-day deadline and replaced it with a new one of its own devising. The decision helped Al Gore, and Republicans—outraged—believed that it was designed to do so. The next day, George W. Bush said, "We believe the justices have used the bench to change Florida's election laws and usurp the authority of Florida's election officials." The day after that, George F. Will wrote a ferocious column—all of his columns on Gore's postelection campaign have been wonderfully ferocious—about the decision. The Florida court's "radicalism," he wrote, went far beyond "routine judicial activism." These criticisms were correct: The Florida court did exceed its lawful powers, with astonishing inventiveness, in a case where the political

National Review, December 18, 2000, pp. 20–24 (on sale November 30). Reprinted with permission.

stakes could hardly be higher. But the court's many defenders had a good point, too, when they said that the justices had not departed from widely accepted legal norms. The difference between their activism and the everyday activism of the courts is one of degree only. Yes, the decision is a scandal. But so is the legal culture of which it is a piece. If the decision has any salutary effect, it will be to draw attention to that culture's pathologies.

Consider the Florida court's arrogance. It overturned choices made by all three branches of Florida's government: by the state legislature, which wrote the certification deadline into law; by the governor, who signed the law, and the secretary of state, who tried to enforce it; and by the circuit-court judge who had approved the secretary of state's effort to enforce it. Remarkable. But is it any more remarkable than a U.S. Supreme Court that, this year, nullified laws passed in 31 states, usually with large margins, to prohibit partial-birth abortion? that, last year, in a case on grade-school "sexual harassment," changed the rules governing every public school in the country? The Florida court claims to be defending "the will of the people" by overruling laws passed by the men and women those people elected. The Supreme Court claimed a similar oracular role for itself in its 1992 *Casey* decision on abortion. The Florida court reasoned that two state laws were in conflict. One provision said that returns filed after the deadline "shall be ignored," while another said that returns filed after that date "may be ignored." Gore's team argued that the fact that the secretary of state may ignore late returns does not mean she must ignore them; indeed, she must not ignore them. The Florida justices followed Gore's lawyers through the looking glass. They did so notwithstanding the traditional rule that statutes should be interpreted so as to avoid conflicting with each other. The U.S. Supreme Court has performed similar sleights of hand. For a few years, it insisted that the Constitution prohibits the death penalty, which the document specifically contemplates. Federal courts are willing to overturn traditional doctrines of interpretation that get in their way, too. Under those doctrines, the courts would have waited to see whether the bans on partial-birth abortion were being applied in an unconstitutional manner; instead, they generally issued an injunction preventing the laws from ever taking effect and then threw them out entirely. And they did so by interpreting the statutes in the most prejudicial way possible.

One of the Florida justices, Harry Lee Anstead, asked during oral argument whether a deadline for recounts would be tougher on large counties, which need more time. Joseph Klock, representing the secretary of state, reminded him that "the fact of the matter is, the Florida legislature has all of this in front of it." Anstead came back, "How do we know that they considered this specific issue?" He thus entirely missed Klock's point, which was that he was raising considerations that should properly be raised in the legislature. The judge was making legislative determinations.

As do the federal courts. They strike down laws based on their authoritative knowledge of the effects of public prayer on the psyches of graduating highschool seniors. They issue detailed regulations (e.g., it's okay to have a creche on public property if Santa Claus is featured too) and apply them retrospectively.

Republicans complained that the Florida supreme court effectively threw out sections of the state's election law even though it had not shown that law to violate either the state's, or the country's, constitution. Again, the federal courts have acted similarly. In *Dickerson*, the U.S. Supreme Court this June threw out a federal law on evidentiary standards for confessions. The justices carefully refrained from saying their decision was required by the Constitution, since that would have been difficult to say with straight faces. Instead, they said that the decision had "constitutional underpinnings." Critics of the Florida decision have remarked on its gratuitous swipes at Katherine Harris, Florida's secretary of state. The justices accused her of trying "to summarily disenfranchise innocent electors," which "is unreasonable, unnecessary, and violates longstanding law." According to the critics, the justices were joining a nasty Democratic campaign against Harris.

This, too, isn't as unusual as it sounds. The Supreme Court often strikes down laws it deems "irrational." It struck down an initiative passed by the voters of Colorado on the grounds that it was motivated by "animus" toward homosexuals. These are essentially insults to state legislators and voters. As Robert E. Nagel writes in Judicial Power and American Character, "to a remarkable extent our courts have become places where the name-calling and exaggeration that mark the lower depths of our political debate are given a more acceptable, authoritative form."

The Florida justices suffered some embarrassment when it turned out that their decision had mischaracterized an Illinois case about the interpretation of chads. They had accepted Gore's lawyers' false claims about that case. Surely the Supreme Court in Washington would never fall for such a ruse? Wrong. In *Roe* v. *Wade*, seven justices relied on a proabortion academic's claim that abortion was not illegal in British common law—a claim that has subsequently been shown to be false. There's a reason I've mentioned the Supreme Court's abortion decisions so often. The Florida decision is a product of an antidemocratic legal culture thoroughly formed by those decisions. *Roe* was the least defensible and most ridiculed of the high court's misadventures, and the task of protecting it has required immense intellectual and legal contortions. Legal academics have expended vast stores of energy devising ever more strained justifications for the *Roe* holding. They have purported to find abortion rights in the Ninth Amendment's reference to "unenumerated rights," the First Amendment's guarantee of religious freedom, even the Thirteenth Amendment's abolition of involuntary servitude. No doubt some enterprising academic is even now at work proving that a right to abortion is entailed by the Constitution's prohibition on letters of marque and reprisal. The result is a legal culture—including the legal academy, the judges it favors, and the most influential reporters who write about them—that celebrates freewheeling judicial activism as statesmanship. The Court's corruption has trickled down to lower courts, just as it did a century ago, when state courts took their cue from it to block economic regulations. In today's legal culture, judges moved by their own views of what constitutes "fairness" do not hesitate to cast aside the rules that impede it. Statutes of limitation in product-liability cases can be ignored, for instance, if they would prevent "justice" for victimized consumers. Recount deadlines can be abandoned if they get in the way of a "fair count." And the biggest procedural rule of all—that laws are to be passed by the legislature—will often lead to outcomes that judges find unjust.

The courts, of course, continue to claim that they interpret the law rather than make it up. They go as far as they must to reach their desired results, and no farther. Once they leave the Constitution behind, however, their restraint becomes as unprincipled as their activism. Thus the Florida court offhandedly suggests—in a footnote!—that it might have extended the deadline for requesting recounts, too. In the sentence to which the footnote is attached, the justices piously affirm their "reluctance to rewrite the Florida election code." ("Reluctance" is not quite refusal.)

In the past, people who have suggested that the courts were behaving lawlessly and usurping power were dismissed, even by many conservatives, as alarmist. Four years ago, the conservative journal *First Things* published a symposium on the subject entitled "The End of Democracy?" That symposium was bitterly criticized, and for many reasons. Prominent among the criticisms was that its title was intemperate. Fr. Richard John Neuhaus, the journal's editor, was said to be irresponsible in suggesting that judicial usurpation was changing the character of the American regime and undermining its legitimacy. A lot of the commentary since the Florida court made its decision has echoed that earlier controversy. Bush is being chastised for trying to "delegitimize" the court. He is being urged to respect "the rule of law." And what is the rule of law? Gore's campaign chairman, William Daley, explained that it was not a collection of "technicalities." (The rule of law is not a law of rules.) The rule of law turns out to be whatever judges decide to do. They read the will of the people, or the Constitution, the way Democratic canvassers divine the intent supposedly expressed by a disputed ballot.

If Gore somehow wins, judges acting beyond their authority will have effectively picked the next president. But a Bush win would hardly be a resounding defeat for judicial usurpation. Many Republicans want him to win in the Supreme Court, not the Florida legislature. Why? Because, as *Wall Street Journal* editor Robert L. Bartley pointed out, "the Supreme Court is the one body with the prestige to lend legitimacy to any decision." He's probably right.

Maybe Fr. Neuhaus deserves an apology. ▌

RONALD DWORKIN

The Phantom Poll Booth

The New York Review of Books

As I write, the extraordinary 2000 presidential election remains undecided, because it remains uncertain which candidate will receive Florida's twenty-five electoral votes. By the time this issue is published, the overseas ballots, the legal battles over manual recounts, or both, may finally have given Gore the presidency, or he may have conceded the presidency to Bush. Or the election may still be undecided, because recounts are demanded in other states, or because lawsuits challenging the Florida electoral process, some of which have already been filed, are still pending. In any case, however, the election has raised a great number of new and perplexing legal and political issues, and it is important to confront these, for the future, whether or not the presidency still hinges on how they are decided.

New York Review of Books, December 21, 2000, pp. 96–98 (on sale November 30). Reprinted with permission of the author. This article was written on November 15, 2000. Ronald Dworkin is Professor of Law and Philosophy at New York University and Quayne Professor of Jurisprudence at University College, London.

Legitimacy is the issue. When an election is so close, and there are serious grounds for suspicion of inaccuracy in the count, how can officials decide who won in a way that the public should and would see as legitimate? It appears that Gore won the popular vote—according to the most recent reports, he received more votes across the country than Bush did. That fact has in itself no legal significance, or course, but neither does it have much moral significance. Which eligible voters actually voted—in fact approximately only 52 percent of them did—and for whom depended on a host of arbitrary factors or accidents. If the election had been held a day later or earlier, if the weather had been better in one place or worse in another, or if any number of other decisions or chance facts had been different, the popular vote would also have been different, and perhaps different enough to change who "won" it. There is much to be said against the Electoral College system—it gives individual voters in small states consistently more impact in presidential elections than those in large states, for example—but the fact that it permits the winner of the popular vote in a very close election to lose in the Electoral College is not one of them.

It *is* of central importance to the issue of legitimacy, however, whether more Florida voters actually intended to vote for Gore than for Bush, so that, if the Electoral College process had worked as it should, Gore would have won the state's electoral votes and the presidency. The system did not work because the ballot in Palm Beach County was confusing, and many voters—perhaps more than twenty thousand—who intended to vote for Gore actually voted for Pat Buchanan or voted for two candidates and therefore found their ballots ignored. Nor would the system have worked if Gore finally wins because there was a manual recount only in heavily Democratic counties rather than in the whole state. Katherine Harris, the Florida secretary of state and co-chairman of the Bush campaign in Florida, has declared that no manual recounts submitted after November 14 will be counted. It is unclear as I write whether her ruling will be overturned, and, if it is, which counties will be recounted. Even a full manual recount in the entire state would not solve the central problem, moreover: if Gore still lost, the confusion in Palm Beach County would still raise doubts about the legitimacy of Bush's presidency.

Some commentators urge that we simply accept the damaged result, because uncertainty and delay is against the public interest. But we have, in any case, a president and an administration until January, and though it is undoubtedly desirable to know who the new president will be as soon as possible, it would not be catastrophic for the nation and world to wait for a few weeks longer—it has been waiting months already—for the answer. Any harm that might come from a short period of delay and uncertainty must be balanced, moreover, against the harm, likely to be both more serious and much longer lasting, of inaugurating a president while a cloud of suspicion hangs over his election. Even if the public were apprehensive about the delay—many polls suggest that it is not[1]—and willing to accept the risk of an inaccurate result in exchange for a quick settlement, that sentiment would be unlikely to hold when the president makes bitterly controversial decisions—about, for example, the nomination of Supreme Court justices—and people are invited to remember that his election was dubious. Rushing the process to an untrustworthy conclusion seems the riskier course.

It is wrong, in any case, to consider the question of legitimacy solely or even largely as a matter of the public's interest because individual rights—the right of each citizen not to be disenfranchised—are at stake. We would not decide whether some ordinance that limited the free speech of particular citizens was constitutional by asking whether the public wanted them to speak or whether the country would be better off if they did not, and we should not use that test to decide whether the basic rights of the voters of Palm Beach County were compromised. True, voters do not have a right to an electoral system that will guarantee perfect accuracy in a large national election: no such system exists. But they do have a right that whatever system has been established by law be respected, and there is a very strong argument that the now infamous "butterfly" ballot was not only confusing but inconsistent with Florida law.

The Florida code requires that the names of the two major-party presidential candidates be listed first on the ballot, with minority-party candidates below, and that the space for marking or punching a vote for a particular candidate be uniformly to the right of that candidate's name.

The Palm Beach County ballot listed candidates not in one column as other counties did, but in two columns, placing Bush/Cheney in the highest box in the left column, Gore/Lieberman in the box below, and Buchanan/Foster at the top of the right column slightly above the opposite Gore box, and it placed voting holes not to the right of each candidate, but between the two columns. There were therefore two holes to the right of Gore's box, and the first of these was actually Buchanan's. An arrow in the Gore/Lieberman box pointed to the third hole, but many voters later said that they assumed that the second hole was Gore's, as it should legally have been. Others said that they thought that there were two holes next to the Gore/Lieberman box because it was necessary to vote for each of those candidates separately, and others that they were uncertain where the arrow pointed and so punched out both of the holes next to the Gore box in order to make sure that they voted for him. All ballots with two holes punched—over 19,000 of them—were thrown out altogether. Statistical models show that both the Buchanan vote and the number of excluded double-punched ballots was much higher than the demography of the county or the results in comparable counties would have predicted.[2]

What is the appropriate remedy when it is discovered that a completed election was in some important respect illegal? A new election would be expensive and cause delay, and would be unlikely in any case to produce the same result as a legal ballot would have produced on election day. In Palm Beach County, for example, many of those who voted for Ralph Nader on November 7 might well vote for Gore in a rerun. Scholars have suggested a variety of other solutions: that Florida's Supreme Court order it to send no electors to the Electoral College, for example, or that it divide Florida's electoral votes thirteen for Bush and twelve for Gore. But it would be unprecedented for a court to make any such radical change in a state's electoral procedures, and each of these solutions could be attacked as arbitrary and political. (Either would automatically make Gore president.)

Many lawyers have therefore argued that there should be no remedy at all: some innocent violations of complex elections laws are inevitable in any national election, they say, such mistakes are sufficiently random so as not to benefit any one party or group or region in the long run, and trying to correct them would involve awkward procedures that would inevitably make our electoral process more clumsy and litigious. If a new election were ordered in Palm Beach County, they warn, then every presidential election for decades would be followed by lawsuits demanding repeat elections in different counties across the nation.

That argument seems decisive against allowing new elections in marginal cases, or when nothing important turns on how the county in which the error is alleged has voted. But it would be wrong to declare, as a flat rule, that no remedy is ever available for demonstrable and grave illegality in the electoral process, no matter how clear the mistake or how evident that it changed the final national result, because that would value the right to vote too cheaply. We do not need so absolute a disclaimer of judicial power to ensure that future elections are not routinely decided in court, and no court, as far as I am aware, has suggested it. The Florida Supreme Court recently insisted, for example, that Florida courts have "authority to void an election" when "reasonable doubt exists as to whether a certified election expressed the will of the voters . . . even in the absence of fraud or intentional wrongdoing."[3] Courts in Florida and in other jurisdictions have orderd new elections when the mistake was not as serious or the results so grave as in the Palm Beach County case.[4]

So we should consider what standard for ordering a new election would recognize the crucial importance of the right to vote but nevertheless rarely encourage politicians to seek such an order. Such a standard might provide, for example, that an election will not be voided for a non-fraudulent mistake unless the following four conditions are clearly demonstrated: (1) that the electoral process violated legal requirements; (2) that the violation more likely than not created a result significantly different from what those who voted collectively intended; (3) that based on available evidence, including evidence about vote totals and challenges in other states, the overall result of the election—in this case, the national election of a president—would have been different had that violation not occurred; and (4) that a new election could be designed so that the result could be expected to be closer to what the voters originally collectively intended. The burden of proof with respect to each element would be on the party seeking the order. This standard does respect the high importance of the right to vote: it allows a new election when there is a substantial chance that the violation of that right defeated the result that the disenfranchised voters hoped to help realize. But it is not likely to encourage much litigation in the future. It is, after all, forty years since the last occasion when it was even suggested that a legal challenge might change a presidential election.[5]

We do not know whether this standard would permit a new election if applied to the Palm Beach County case: the facts have not yet been examined in any court, and may never be.[6] But it is important that we continue to study and debate, even after the 2000 presidential election is finally over, how our electoral process can be improved in the light of what that election revealed, and focusing on the appropriate conditions for a local rerun should be part of that discussion. Allowing important electoral safeguards to be fashioned, tested, and enforced in court is not, as many have claimed, a corruption of our democracy. On the contrary, it is an affirmation of our democracy's strength; even when elections are breathtakingly close, we settle them on the basis of examined principle and not in the streets.

Notes

1. See "Americans Patiently Awaiting Election Outcome," *The New York Times,* November 14, 2000, p. A1.

2. For a sample analysis, see the article posted on the Web at madison.hss.cmu.edu.

3. *Beckstrom* v. *Volusia County Canvassing Board,* 707 So. 2d 720 (1998).

4. See, for example, *Craig* v. *Wallace,* 2 Fla. L. Weekly Supp. 517a (1994), *Ury* v. *Santee,* 303 F. Supp. 119 (N.D. Ill. 1969), *Akizaki* v.*Fong,* 461 P. 2d 221 (Hawk. 1969), and *Adkins* v. *Huckabay,* 755 So. 206 (La. 2000).

5. Republicans charged illegality in the vote count in Illinois and Texas in the 1960 election, and switching the electoral votes of those two states would have changed the result. Some commentators hail Nixon's decision not to challenge as an act of patriotism, though others say he feared discovery of Republican as well as Democratic fraud in Illinois.

6. Would the result of a new election in that county be closer to original intentions than the recorded first vote was? Professor Laurence Tribe of Harvard suggested in *The New York Times* of November 12 that any new election be limited to those who voted in the first one, and that the votes for Bush and Nader should be held at their initial totals, so that only the votes for Gore and Buchanan could change.

It would also help to limit a possible Gore vote to his original total plus the number of initial Buchanan and double-punched ballots. That would not in fact prevent Nader voters from switching to Gore, perhaps making his total larger than it would have been the first time but for the confusion, but it would reduce the impact of any such switches. ∎

E.J. DIONNE JR.

Florida Fatigue

The Washington Post

You are growing weary of reading about the Florida recount. I am growing weary of writing about it. Gov. George W. Bush's campaign is counting on our shared weariness to hand him the presidency.

Bush's spin doctors figure we'll eventually lose interest in what Bush is trying to do in Florida, which is to bury ballots so no one will ever have a look at them.

The burden is supposed to be on Vice President Al Gore. Why, so many ask, is he prolonging this process? But the burden should be on Bush. He could get us to a resolution easily. The simple way to resolve this problem is for him to agree that we need to take a look at those 10,700 ballots cast in Miami-Dade County on which no vote for president was registered.

Washington Post, December 1, 2000, p. A35. © 2000, The Washington Post Writers Group. Reprinted with permission.

The Bush people say there are no presidential votes on those ballots. But if they're so sure of that, why are they going to such lengths to prevent the public from seeing what is on them?

The reason is obvious. The Bush campaign fears that if these ballots—or, as should have happened, all the ballots—are thus counted in Florida, Bush might lose. That's why the Bush people are going to court after court after court using lawyer after lawyer after lawyer to keep those ballots out of the light of day. Speed is good when it comes to pushing Gore out of the race. Speed is bad when it comes to counting votes.

Listen to Bush's lawyer, Barry Richard: "The fact that this case involves the presidential election is not sufficient reason for us to suspend basic due process or the fundamental rules of procedure designed to provide the contestants with a fair opportunity to be heard and the court with a reasonable opportunity to have the evidence presented."

Read that over a couple times and wonder whether the Bush side is really on the level.

The same Bush lawyers and spinners who argue that Gore should forget about his fundamental rights to due process so we can get the election over with say that when it comes to counting ballots: No, hold on, slow this thing down, let's take a lot of time. Let's take so much time that no American ever sees those contested ballots. Get the country so bored and frustrated that we all give up and let Bush become president. The Bush campaign is giving cynicism a bad name.

Please permit me a personal comment: I'm surprised at how angry I am over this controversy. Normally, I don't find it too difficult to understand the views of those with whom I disagree. Even in this case, I understand perfectly well why Republican rank-and-filers think Gore should drop out, and I accept that there are fair arguments on both sides of the issue of counting those "dimpled" chads.

What's enraging is the effort by the leadership of the Bush campaign to obfuscate and cover up what it's really doing: trying to stop the public from seeing ballots that, if counted, might reverse the election. This is profoundly irresponsible, and it's wrong. If those ballots are ever examined after Bush becomes president and they show he lost, what will the country do then? How will that affect Bush's ability to govern?

Given all the electoral snafus in Florida, it's not surprising that even Bush's rank-and-file supporters around the country have doubts about whether most Florida voters intended to support him when they arrived at the polls on Nov. 7. According to a *New York Times*/CBS News Poll, nearly a third of

Bush's voters said they don't know whom Floridians intended to vote for, and 10 percent of Bush's own backers said the state's voters probably favored Gore.

Given such doubts, isn't it better to have as many facts out in public as possible—notably the contents of those disputed ballots? Once it's known if there are potential votes on the ballots, the campaigns can battle openly over what standard should be used to count them.

We Americans regularly advise emerging democracies to be as open and transparent as possible in the way they reach an election result. Are we to be the only democracy in the world that refuses to follow our own advice?

You have to hope that the U.S. Supreme Court and the Florida Supreme Court bear that in mind as they ponder the direction in which they choose to nudge this process.

But above all, you wish George W. Bush himself would want to win this election not by burying ballots but by letting every American see them and find out what they say. It would be a fine way to establish himself as a uniter, not a divider. ▊

JOHN YOO

A Legislature's Duty

The Wall Street Journal

"Without the intervention of the State Legislatures, the President of the United States cannot be elected at all," explained James Madison in Federalist Paper No. 45. "They must in all cases have a great share in his appointment, and will perhaps in most cases of themselves determine it."

This week we will learn if the Florida legislature possesses the courage to live up to Madison's expectations. In an unprecedented special session, lawmakers will consider whether to end the election crisis by directly appointing the state's 25 presidential electors. They will undergo a hailstorm of criticism from the Gore campaign, the media, and liberal academics, who will argue that such intervention would bypass the democratic process.

Florida's legislators have a constitutional duty to ensure their state appoints electors. Article II, Section 1 of the Constitution says that "each State shall appoint, in such Manner as the Legislature thereof may direct, a number of Electors." Despite the Florida Supreme Court's free-wheeling approach to statutory interpretation, the Constitution's use of the word "shall" requires the legislature to ensure participation in the Electoral College.

The U.S. Supreme Court has upheld the exclusive right of state legislatures to appoint electors. In *McPherson* v. *Blackmer*, in 1892, the Court declared that "the appointment of these electors is thus placed absolutely and wholly with the legislatures of the several states." No other branch of state government can interfere with the power and duty of the legislature to fulfill the Constitution's command. As the court said, "this power is conferred upon the legislatures of the States by the Constitution of the United States and cannot be taken from them or modified by their State constitutions."

In an ordinary election, legislative intervention would be unnecessary. As in other states, the Florida Legislature has delegated its power to choose electors to popular elections, and these elections usually have produced a decisive winner. The problem is that the vote in Florida was so close—a 597-vote margin for George W. Bush, out of six million cast—that it has convinced Al Gore to serially litigate the results in the state courts. This plethora of lawsuits has so prolonged Florida's electoral process that it threatens to deprive Florida of any electoral votes at all.

Democrats claim that Florida Secretary of State Katherine Harris's certification of Mr. Bush's victory last week guarantees that Florida has its electoral votes. Unfortunately, they ignore two deadlines imposed by federal law. In Title 3 of the U.S. Code, Congress explains how it will exercise its constitutional duty to count the electoral votes. One section promises that Congress will treat as "conclusive" a state's electoral votes so long as the state has resolved any challenges to the election by Dec. 12. Another explains that Congress has established Dec. 18 as the date the Electoral College must meet in each state and send its votes to Washington.

Mr. Gore's refusal to drop his victory-through-litigation strategy raises the very real possibility that Florida will fail to meet both the Dec. 12 and Dec. 18 deadlines. If the legal challenges to Mr. Bush's victory do not reach a final conclusion in eight days, Congress might be entitled to reject Florida's electoral votes—disenfranchising all of Florida's six million voters—regardless of the Bush certification. If the litigation is not completed within two weeks, Florida may have no electoral votes to render. Or suppose that between Dec. 12 and Dec. 18 the Florida courts find that Mr. Gore should prevail. Florida then might send forward two slates of electors, triggering rules that could allow Congress to reject both sets—again disenfranchising all Florida citizens.

While Mr. Gore no doubt wants to bring the litigation to a swift conclusion, our judicial system is not built for speed—it is built for fairness. And fairness means that both sides must have the opportunity to present their case, to question the evidence, and to appeal errors to higher courts. This takes time. Only now is the first of the election lawsuits under consideration by U.S. Supreme Court, and this after vastly accelerated schedules. Imagine how long it will take the many lawsuits filed just last week to reach a similar point. Our commitment to due process almost ensures that Florida will fail to meet Congress's deadlines.

Congress seems to have anticipated that at times the legislature would have to intervene to ensure a state selected its electors on time. Title 3 of the U.S. Code authorizes the state legislature to appoint electors "whenever any State has held an election for purposes of choosing electors, and has failed to make a choice" by Dec. 12. Democrats amazingly claim that Florida has already made that choice (Mr. Bush's certification) even as they attempt to overturn that decision. But while Floridians have voted, they have not been allowed to conclusively choose their electors. In fact, the Gore litigation strategy is designed precisely to prevent that. Even so, in oral argument Friday before the U.S. Supreme Court, Mr. Gore's counsel confessed that he was unsure about the Florida Legislature's right to intervene.

Even without Title 3, the Florida legislature would still have the constitutional authority to choose electors. Contrary to Democratic rhetoric, the people have no right to vote for president or even the Electoral College; that power is only delegated to them by the grace of the legislature. In appointing the electors itself, the legislature would be directly taking up its constitutional functions again. We should not forget that the legislature itself is elected by the people of Florida; in a close race—a virtual statistical tie—it makes sense to defer to the most popularly responsible branch of the state government.

As the court made clear in McPherson, the Constitution holds that "whatever provisions may be made by statute, or by the state constitution, to choose electors by the people, there is no doubt of the right of the legislature to resume the power at any time, for it can neither be taken away or abdicated." There is perhaps no better justification for such legislative action than a breakdown in the system of voting due to litigation and judicially required recounts.

To forestall the likelihood that Mr. Gore's lawsuits will drive Florida into electoral purgatory, the state legislature must prepare to choose presidential electors regardless of the outcome of the litigation. Not only would the legislators be doing Florida a service, they would be fulfilling their constitutional duty and helping to bring the electoral crisis to a timely conclusion, should the U.S. Supreme Court and the Florida courts fail to do so this week. ▌

PETER M. SHANE

Rein in the Legislature

The Washington Post

As the various courts of Florida and the United States government do their jobs—including the orderly resolution of the Florida presidential election—the state's legislators stand poised to push the nation toward constitutional crisis. Let's hope they desist.

The right to vote is protected by the 14th Amendment, whether that right is viewed as a form of constitutionally protected liberty or as an intangible property right created by state law. In either case, a legislature may not deprive supporters of any candidate of the legal consequence of their votes without due process. In this instance, a legislative determination to award Florida's electors to either of the two major candidates would violate due process in three ways.

First, as argued by Gov. George W. Bush's brief in the U.S. Supreme Court (albeit in an unpersuasive context): "[C]onstitutional principles of due process and fundamental fairness preclude the states from adopting 'a post-election departure from previous practice' and applying that post-election rule retroactively to determine the outcome of an election."

Nothing in Florida's law made the Nov. 7 election merely advisory to the state legislature. To change the rules now would be a gross insult to fundamental fairness.

Washington Post, final ed., December 1, 2000, p. A35. Reprinted with permission of the author. Peter Shane is visiting professor of law and public policy at the H. John Heinz III School of Public Policy and Management at Carnegie Mellon University.

Second, in purporting to adjudicate the actual outcome of the Nov. 7 election, the Florida legislature would be seizing judicial authority in violation of due process. It was just such state legislative usurpation of judicial power during the 1780s that motivated the Philadelphia drafters to provide the nation an independent federal judiciary and oust Congress from adjudication except with regard to impeachment and judging the qualifications and conduct of its own members. Now that the 14th Amendment imposes due process obligations upon the states, state legislatures should be deemed to have the same limits on them.

Finally, the legislature would be depriving Floridians of the right to participate directly in the selection of Florida's electors.

As originally drafted in 1787, the Constitution gave state legislatures plenary authority to provide for the appointment of electors in any manner at all, including direct legislative selection. Although arguments were made from the first for the right of the people to participate in the choice of electors, it was conventionally understood before the Civil War that legislatures could appoint electors directly if they so chose. As it happens, between 1832 and 1860, only South Carolina employed legislative selection. Legislatures chose state electoral slates only twice after the Civil War, in Florida in 1868 and in Colorado in 1876.

Today, democratic principles should lead us to interpret the due process clause as protecting the people's right to participate directly in the selection of presidential electors. That participation has become, in the words of Justice John Marshall Harlan, one of the nation's "basic values implicit in the concept of ordered liberty."

Since the ratification of the 14th Amendment, we have added 13 other amendments to the U.S. Constitution. Six were specifically intended to further our constitutional commitment to democracy: extending the vote to persons of all races, providing for the direct election of senators, extending the franchise to women, permitting District of Columbia voters to choose electors, eliminating poll taxes and lowering the voting age to 18. It is unthinkable, against this history of constitutional development, that a state legislature would still be deemed authorized to usurp the people's role in choosing presidential electors.

One could go further. The 14th Amendment also provides: "No State shall make or enforce any law which shall abridge the privileges or immunities of citizens of the United States." The court has never defined "privileges or immunities" comprehensively, but it has invoked the clause as a basis for invalidating inconsistent state legislation as recently as 1999.

In 1872 the Supreme Court wrote that at least some "privileges and immunities" would be those that "owe their existence to the Federal government, its National character, its Constitution, or its laws."

It is frequently said that, on Election Day, Americans do not hold a national election for president but rather 51 elections in the states and in the District of Columbia for presidential electors. But it is clear by now that what presidential elections have become is a vehicle—perhaps the single most important vehicle—for Americans to exercise their rights of political association and expression across state lines.

This has so long been the case that it is hardly fanciful to imagine a U.S. Supreme Court decision in the year 2000 declaring that the "privileges and immunities" protected by the 14th Amendment include the rights of Floridians and non-Floridians to associate for the political support of a presidential candidate on a national basis. And if I am right about this, then a decision by the Florida legislature to interject itself in the current controversy would violate not only the rights of Floridians but also the rights of voters in every state who are entitled to depend on each state's fidelity to its popular vote in appointing presidential electors.

Once ballots are cast on Election Day, discerning the winner may require the rule of law to work its course in cases of controversy. Our agents for guiding that task, however, are the courts. The Florida legislature has only one immediate duty—to defer. ▌

JOHN MINTZ AND DAN KEATING

Florida Ballot Spoilage Likelier for Blacks: Voting Machines, Confusion Cited

The Washington Post

Heavily Democratic and African American neighborhoods in Florida lost many more presidential votes than other areas because of outmoded voting machines and rampant confusion about ballots, a precinct-by-precinct analysis by the *Washington Post* shows.

Washington Post, final ed., December 3, 2000, p. A1. ©2000, The Washington Post. Reprinted with permission. Thomas B. Edsall contributed to this report.

As many as one in three ballots in black sections of Jacksonville, for example, did not count in the presidential contest. That was four times as many as in white precincts elsewhere in mostly Republican Duval County.

According to the *Post* analysis, in Miami-Dade County precincts where fewer than 30 percent of the voters are black, about 3 percent of ballots did not register a vote for president. In precincts where more than 70 percent of the voters are African American, it was nearly 10 percent.

Such patterns have helped fuel questions in the black community about whether the vote was fair on Election Day. A number of African American leaders say faulty ballot machines and long lines at polling places sowed confusion among many black voters and ended up nullifying many of their votes.

Aides to Texas Gov. George W. Bush say the kinds of errors Florida voters made are typical of elections across the nation. Vice President Gore, by contrast, has placed allegations concerning disqualified black votes at the center of his appeal to hold recounts in Miami-Dade County, and he is making his case with rhetoric reminiscent of civil rights struggles. Democrats say the errors suggest a manual recount of ballots would show that Gore won Florida.

A computer analysis of election returns suggests there were anomalies in the Florida vote, particularly in African American areas. The more black and Democratic a precinct, the more likely it was to suffer high rates of invalidated votes.

Some 40 percent of the state's black voters were new voters, and election experts say they were the most vulnerable to confusion about oddly designed ballots. Moreover, a higher percentage of blacks than whites live in counties with voting machines more prone to not registering a vote. And similarly, African American voters are somewhat more likely to live in areas where poll workers do not immediately check ballots for errors—so blacks were less likely than whites to get a chance to correct their ballots if they messed them up.

"We keep talking about 'every vote counts,' and, boy, I feel like mine doesn't count," said Lon Fanniel, 40, a retired Marine captain from Jacksonville. He fears that confusion over the ballot led him to accidentally leave two marks for president, invalidating his vote for Gore.

Florida was one of the nation's most viciously fought battleground states, with both parties pouring in millions of dollars during the final days to get their core supporters to the polls.

It turns out that one reason for the high rate of invalidated votes this election was the NAACP's massive get-out-the-vote effort in Florida, which brought many inexperienced or first-time voters to the polls. Black turnout in Florida set records—893,000 African Americans cast ballots on Nov. 7, a 65 percent jump over 1996.

At times—especially when polling places were crowded and voters felt rushed to mark their votes—it appears large numbers of these new or infrequent voters were confounded by technical problems in the ballot. Florida listed an unusually high 10 presidential tickets, which contributed to confusing ballot designs in some counties.

A prime example is Duval, a north Florida county that hosts thousands of naval aviators. A ballot that perplexingly spread presidential names over two pages led to many accidental double votes, which are automatically voided. Although Bush carried the county 58 percent to 41 percent, the spoiled ballots were concentrated in African American sections of downtown Jacksonville.

In the most heavily white precincts, about 1 in 14 ballots were thrown out, but in largely black precincts more than 1 in 5 ballots were spoiled—and in some black precincts it was almost one-third. (By comparison, in the District of Columbia, fewer than 1 in 50 ballots were not counted as votes for president.)

There are several reasons why a voting machine would not record a vote. A voter may have intentionally abstained. Or the voter could have tried to vote but messed up the ballot—either by mistakenly voting for two candidates, which automatically disqualifies a ballot and is called an "overvote," or by failing to mark the ballot cleanly (which, along with the ballots deliberately left unmarked, is known as an "undervote").

Gore wants the undervotes recounted, and because so many of them took place in pro-Gore precincts, his advisers are confident they could overturn Bush's lead if a court permitted such a recount.

Bush allies say most undervotes were intentional. "We believe that in most if not virtually all so-called undervotes, individuals didn't intend to vote for president," said Bush spokesman Ray Sullivan.

He also said Bush did not ask for a statewide hand recount because recounts are "flawed and inaccurate," as he said was shown in manual recounts in Broward and Palm Beach counties that showed Gore picking up votes.

Republicans note that Florida's rate of failed ballots is lower than four other states among 35 states for which the GOP has examined data—Idaho, Illinois, Georgia and Wyoming. In those states, the spoiled ballots represent a small fraction of the winning margin for president, but in Florida the 180,000 invalid ballots were 335 times Bush's margin.

The GOP says recounts are not needed because voting mistakes occur everywhere. Voting expert Curtis Gans said about 2.5 million voters across the nation cast presidential ballots that didn't register as votes. Given these large numbers outside Florida, and what he believes are the inequities in all types of ballot recounting, Gans said "it's an irrelevant exercise" to recount votes in Florida.

The Bush campaign's Sullivan added that some of the Florida counties with high rates of invalidated ballots—he cited Hamilton, Hendry and Lafayette—were won by Bush. But Democrats point out those counties are sparsely populated and had a total of only 1,310 votes thrown out. The three counties Gore asked be recounted—Palm Beach, Broward and Miami-Dade—had 72,000 invalidated ballots.

Senior GOP strategists say privately that a key reason the Bush campaign did not ask for a statewide recount was it feared that Gore would pick up more votes than Bush, because of the high rate of ballot spoilage in black precincts.

"The NAACP did a tremendous job of turnout in Florida," one Republican strategist said. "But in a way they overachieved, and got people out who couldn't follow instructions."

The irony is that in Duval, the sample ballot designed by the Republican election supervisor explicitly instructed people to "vote all pages" on the ballot—which led thousands of people to invalidate their ballots because the list of presidential candidates was spread over two pages. The rule of thumb in election administration is that candidates for a single office should be listed in one column on one page to avoid confusion.

A case in point: Sharon Lewis of Jacksonville, who brought her 18-year-old son Ernest to their polling place. The high school senior had just registered to vote. But she was mortified when he, upon leaving the booth, told her proudly, "I voted on every page." She said they complained to the poll workers but "they said there's nothing we could do about it."

"He had that 'I Voted' sticker on his shirt—the only kid at his school who voted," she said. "But his vote didn't count."

"I'm proud of the turnout we had in Florida," said Anita Davis, the NAACP's state president. But she added, "I'm very concerned that so many of our votes were being disenfranchised. . . . In a lot of Florida counties, these [black] votes have been thrown out for years, and we had no idea about it."

The NAACP has filed formal allegations with the Justice Department saying some blacks were discouraged from voting by unfair demands for identification or long lines. But a Justice Department official said so far investigators have not found enough evidence to justify a full-fledged investigation.

"I fought for the right to have a good vote," said Fanniel, the retired Marine captain who fought in the Persian Gulf War. "I feel like that was taken away from me."

Election experts say inexperienced voters are the most likely to be confused when a ballot contains more than about six names for one office. Beyond that, confoundment rises exponentially with each name added to the ballot. Florida's ballots listed 10 presidential candidates—which tied for the most with four states.

Black Floridians also were more likely to face unforgiving voting equipment. About 26 percent of black voters live in counties that verify ballots as valid in precincts as soon as they're cast—so poll workers can immediately tell voters they disqualified ballots, and voters have a second chance to vote a valid ballot. By comparison, 34 percent of white voters live in these areas. That means white voters are more likely to have their votes counted than blacks—a point made by Gore.

"These cheap and unreliable machines are much more likely to be found in areas of low-income people and minorities and seniors," Gore said in an interview on CBS last week.

Voters whose ballots were checked right away were using cutting-edge optical scanners, which read pen marks. The other voters were using either optical scanners that don't check ballots instantly, or punch-card machines in which voters punch out "chads," tiny cardboard rectangles, to make a selection.

In the 23 counties that check a ballot as soon as the voter completes it—all using optical scan gear—fewer than 1 percent of ballots did not register a choice for president, said Ion Sanchez, Leon County election supervisor. By contrast, in the 26 punch-card counties, none of which perform the instant check, about 4 percent failed to register a presidential selection, Sanchez said.

"The only difference is the technology," said Sanchez. "That's the dirty little secret about election machines."

"Poor people are more likely to invalidate ballots" because of difficulty mastering punch-card systems, said Herb Asher, an Ohio State University balloting expert who studied the issue in 1978, when Ohio first used the machines. Voters in prosperous suburbs invalidated their ballots 2 percent of the time, he said, while voters in Dayton's poor areas did so by up to 20 percent.

For decades, 2 percent of ballots cast nationally have traditionally not recorded a presidential vote. But in Florida this year, it was 2.9 percent. In 21 of Florida's 67 counties, the ratio of disqualified votes to total votes cast was more than 6 percent. Those with the largest numbers of both disqualified and double votes were largely Democratic and black areas. Double votes are not reviewed in hand recounts, because there is no way to discern a voter's intent.

Gadsden County, a largely poor black rural area, had a 12 percent spoilage rate, mostly because presidential candidates were listed in two columns—and the great majority were overvotes.

Almost 2,000 voters nullified their ballots by double-voting on a ballot that listed the first eight presidential candidates in one column, and a second column listing Constitution Party or Workers World Party candidates, in what could be mistaken for a second election.

Denny Hutchinson, Gadsden's election administrator, blamed voters, not the ballot. "Some of our high rate of presidential overvotes was attributable to so many names on that ballot," he said. "Some people voted for every candidate. . . . People didn't prepare themselves to come to the polls."

But Rep. Alcee L. Hastings, a black Florida Democrat, said Bush's claim that almost all undervotes were intentional is "pure hogwash."

"We've designed a voting system not understandable to many voters," Hastings said, "and it takes fair-minded people to design one ensuring every vote counts."

NOEMIE EMERY

First Principles in Florida: Conservatives Believe in Rules, Liberals Want to Be "Fair"

The Weekly Standard

Al Gore and Joe Lieberman *know* they won Florida. Can they prove this? Of course not. So how can they know this? They just *know*. They know, because more people *wanted* to vote for them, even if somehow they didn't. And how do they know this? Because of some ballots that were double-

Weekly Standard, December 11, 2000, pp. 24–25 (on sale December 4). Reprinted with permission. Noemie Emery is a frequent contributor to the *Weekly Standard*.

punched and other ballots that weren't punched at all. Did these ballots tell them what their voters wanted? Of course not. Then how do they know what these people intended? They *know*. And because they do, they are free to do whatever is required to fulfill these "intentions." Republicans meanwhile are apoplectic at these bouts of mind reading, at the moving deadlines which somehow aren't deadlines, at the elusive non-standards, at the dimples that do, or don't, count.

Is the apoplexy irrational? Is this all just a scorched-earth power struggle in Florida, with both sides arguing whatever is convenient and looks likely to produce victory? No. It turns out that our two parties are deeply divided about first principles, oddly enough. Al Gore and George W. Bush have ended up fighting to vindicate the deepest beliefs of their respective parties. Democrats believe in intentions and feelings—and to hell with the facts and the evidence. Republicans believe in the rules.

This critical difference runs wide and deep. And it pops up in all sorts of issues that divide the two parties. The Democrats are the party of the dimpled chad, from which one tries to intuit an unknown voter's intention. And they are also the party that has given us the theory of hate crimes, in which prosecutions turn not on the usual rules of evidence but on what the criminal *meant* by his crime. The interpretation of "intent" is the crucial thing, and Democrats are not lacking in confidence that such interpretations are fairly simple. A party-line vote on a ballot that seems to show no vote for president? The voter must have felt weak; and, oh yes, that looks like a dent in the chad. A cross-racial crime? One must assume it is racist; there is no such thing as color-blind savagery. In the hate-crime context, one is punished not just for what one does, but for what one is thinking while doing it. In the context of voting, the evidence of the ballot matters less than the canvasser's guess as to what was intended. Subjective intent trumps objective reality.

Democrats are the party of malleable standards, in the interests of what they think of as just. Republicans are the party of bright lines and hard and fast rules, in the interests of what they think of as just. Democrats are the party that ratcheted down the physical-fitness standards of the armed forces, so that the women would look just as qualified, and then pretended that nothing had changed. They are the party that ratcheted down academic standards in the name of fairness, instead of doing the harder work of helping students meet the original standards. They are the party that is trying to codify what is ethereal, seeking legal remedies for things that cannot be measured.

The parties' opposing ideas of how justice is to be achieved show up in their purest form with the issue of race. Democrats want courts and well-intended politicians to intervene to engineer outcomes they think are fair, through quotas and preferences and set-asides. Republicans want to create a set of rules that apply equally to everyone, and let the chips fall where they may. Republicans believe in specific remedies for proven examples of prejudice, but think prejudice can no longer simply be assumed. When Republicans see unequal results, they do not automatically conclude that these are due to injustice. Democrats reason than an outcome they disapprove of must be an injustice that calls for a remedy, judicial or otherwise.

Conservatives know that life is unfair, that some people start life under terrible burdens, and that a country that prides itself on equal opportunity should take special steps to correct this. They think a decent society in the name of fairness will do all sorts of things to help the disadvantaged—from scholarships to outreach and mentoring programs—but that the *law* must be neutral. They want to help people meet rigorous standards, but insist that the standards be rigorous. They do not believe laws should be calibrated to account for individual instances of unfairness, as there is no legal system conceivable that can begin to account for all the myriad forms of unfairness life metes out. Yet the liberals do keep on trying. In 1997, the Clinton Justice Department created guidelines to preserve racial set-asides in government contracts. Government agencies were tasked with determining "the level of minority contracting that would exist in a given industry absent the effects of discrimination." Who is capable of such feats of imagination? Precisely the same kind of official who is able to stare at the crease on a Florida ballot and understand, absent the effects of the Votomatic machine, what the voter had in mind.

Democrats claim to *know* they lost Florida because the "uncounted" ballots in several precincts deprived them of thousands of votes. The Bush people, however, have claims of their own. They "know" that the TV networks' premature prediction of a Gore victory in Florida, which gave the sense of a Gore landslide, depressed Republican turnout in the Panhandle, where the polls were still open. They "know" that it cost them untold hundreds of thousands of votes in the critical midwestern battlegrounds, some of them lost by a very small margin, and in the West, where it was then 5 o'clock.

But, of course, they don't really know any of these things. None of it is provable. The networks' early call of Florida for Gore, which was later rescinded, probably depressed the Bush vote in Florida and hurt him elsewhere. But the later call for Bush of Florida, and of the whole country, which was also rescinded, gave Bush the aura of legitimacy which he has still not relinquished and cast Gore as the whiny sore loser. Both calls were unfair, but they made a rough balance, which is the sort of result conservatives are prepared to live with. The final vote on Election Day, after all, was made up of millions of small contingencies and glitches that weighed back and forth on each side of the ledger—bad ballots, lost ballots, lazy voters, dopey voters, mistakes, and misfortune. There is no way to remove error from human endeavor. Life is chaotic, which is why we need rules to channel it, to give order to happenstance, and keep things from reeling out of control.

This is why we have and need rules for elections, which are standard and neutral and fixed ahead of time. Elections happen on *one* day, not 12, and not 90. Polls are open during specified hours, and if you are late, it's unfortunate. You get to vote once, not over and over. All votes are counted by one standard, not some once and some four times, with selected votes being subject to interpretation. All voters are equal, and all ballots are equal, or else there is chaos. When *rules* are chaotic—when deadlines are stretched and at last become meaningless, when votes are read differently, when standards have vanished—then chaos is everywhere. Chaos is everywhere in Florida now, and Republicans have an aversion to this that is not simply partisan.

The Republicans who trooped down to observe the recounting and bang drums for George W. are of course partisan, and of course they are boosting their candidate. But beyond this, they are boosting system and order and law. This is what accounts for their exceptional unity, and the intensity that they bring to this case. The mundane political divisions among them are the same as ever: They are pro-life and pro-choice and profoundly ambivalent; they pushed impeachment, or were uneasy about it; they are libertarians, or proponents of national greatness; they like Teddy Roosevelt or they like Calvin Coolidge; but in the end they are pro-law and pro-rules and pro-order. Social conservatives like John Engler and Frank Keating, social moderates like Kay Bailey Hutchison, social liberals like George Pataki and Christie Todd Whitman are all bug-eyed with horror at the creative accounting, the on-the-fly changing of standards, the malleable nature of fact. *This* is the litmus test that truly unites them. They are the party of law and objective reality, against the party of intent and feeling.

What the Democrats may not have sensed until recently is that chaos cannot be just partly released. Once they try to bend laws, they cannot have just a few bent for their benefit without having others bent back against them. They can't have their lawyers drag things out and obstruct things without having others try to obstruct their desires. They can't first play for time, and then demand that things be done in a hurry. And they can't pick at one dangling thread of an error without having the whole larger fabric unravel, casting everything, even their own special claims and assertions, into confusion and doubt. Caught now in the uncontrolled mess they created, the Democrats might ponder what could happen should the Gore ethic be vindicated. Do they really want elections that are infinitely reviewable, subject to challenge on every slight glitch, every hurt feeling, every bright sense of outrage? Do they think life can be fair without law? ▍

THOMAS OLIPHANT

Gov. Bush's Cynical End-Around in the Florida Legislature

The Boston Globe

Alas, poor Katherine Harris; seems her Tallahassee and Austin masters in the Bush campaign only needed her for a meaningless photo opportunity.

Proving that he wants to be president in the worst way, George W. Bush is presiding over an operation in which last week's cause, last week's climactic moment, is this week's inconvenient minor memory.

Surely you recall the carefully staged TV moments when Florida's Bush campaign co-chair, solemnly cloaked in the powers of the public office she corrupted for that political purpose, used her authority as secretary of state to "certify" the Texas governor's then-extant vote totals for president, supposedly cementing the state's 25 electors. The candidate himself even emerged from seclusion to declare on national television ("Titanic" viewers excepted) that he had won and would begin his transition.

As if these photo opportunities needed a sequel, it was then arranged for his brother, the governor of Florida, to sign something called a certificate of "ascertainment" (who thinks up these terms?) that absolutely, positively had to get up here overnight so the "fact" of this nailing of the state's electoral votes could be federally recorded. It was.

Boston Globe, 3d ed., December 3, 2000, p. D8. Copyright 2000 by Globe Newspaper Co. (MA). Reproduced with permission of Globe Newspaper Co. (MA).

The show was good for a short spike in the quickie polls, decent television, and allegedly sufficient for the "finality" the Bushies say they crave.

Now it turns out it was all a hoax.

If the Bush campaign is to be believed this week, last week's show resolved nothing. Now, "finality" is said to require that the state Legislature step in and elect Bush's electors, regardless of what the state's courts decide in their judging of the contests to Harris's certification that are being pursued under state law. Indeed, the effort now underway may even proceed regardless of any decision reached by the U.S. Supreme Court.

This is no rogue operation by crazed right-wingers. This comes straight from the top. It was the ultimate Bushie, James Baker, who gave it the official wink and nod the night the Florida Supreme Court found Harris's original moves to stop recounts to fly in the face of law.

That signal galvanized the troops. What began as a seemingly off-the-wall suggestion by the new Republican speaker of the very Republican lower house, Tom Feeney, quickly became a deadly earnest gambit involving the GOP-dominated Senate and its presiding boss, John McKay. And more important, the key strategist after flimsy camouflage was stripped away turned out to be Governor Jeb Bush himself, who coordinated details with the Bush managers in Texas and the lawyers in Florida.

The cover story for this farce of a special legislative session that looms later this week is that naming the Bush electors is simply a form of insurance that Florida will in fact be represented in the Electoral College on Dec. 18 should disputes over certification threaten to leave the electors out of the process.

The cover story is false, as witness the statements last week by Harris as she certified, and by Jeb Bush as he signed the fancy certificate. As things stand this instant, George W. Bush already has 25 pledged electors, ready for the trek to Tallahassee to cast their votes.

The truth is that Harris's photo opportunity was designed to obscure the fact that certification can be challenged under state law and that trial judges and, ultimately, the state Supreme Court decide these contests. They can reject them or they can support them and order remedies (like their own recounts of disputed ballots) that could change the previously certified result, the official tally showing who got more votes.

And that's the real reason for his special session. As John Yoo, a Cal-Berkeley law professor, former clerk for Clarence Thomas, and one of the conservative legal types summoned by the Republicans to give them scholarly cover for their power grab, told the legislators last week: "In a sense, it doesn't matter what the state constitution or state law says."

What counts, he and others maintained, is that the Legislature has the power to ram Bush's electors through and should use it, regardless of what the final, official vote count is and regardless of a state legal process that might produce 25 Al Gore electors.

I'm happy to leave the legal arguments to lawyers. But what counts right now is that Bush is prepared to do what Gore is not. Cynicism may teach that all ethics in politics is situational, but Gore will fold his tent if that is the import of Florida and U.S. Supreme Court decisions.

Bush is the one prepared by formal strategy to go around them. He is also the only one prepared to grab the presidency after finishing second in the popular vote, second in the electoral vote outside Florida, and even after finishing an official second in Florida. What a uniter! ▌

BOB HERBERT

Keep Them Out!

The New York Times

The tactics have changed, but the goal remains depressingly the same: Keep the coloreds, the blacks, the African-Americans—whatever they're called in the particular instance—keep them out of the voting booths.

Do not let them vote! If you can find a way to stop them, stop them.

So here we go again, this time in Florida.

It turns out that the state of Florida is using a private company with close ties to the Republican Party to help "cleanse" the state's voter registration rolls. Would it surprise anyone anywhere to learn that the cleansing process somehow managed to improperly prevent large numbers of African-American voters from voting in the presidential election?

Gregory Palast, a reporter with the online magazine *Salon,* has done a number of articles on this. He noted that the company, ChoicePoint, and its subsidiary, Database Technologies Inc. (DBT), came up with a "scrub list" of 173,000 names. These were the names of people registered to vote in Florida who, according to ChoicePoint, could be knocked off the rolls for one reason or another.

Originally published in *The New York Times,* late ed., December 7, 2000, p. A39.

There was good reason for Florida to be concerned about the integrity of its voter registration rolls. In 1997 the mayor of Miami was removed from office because widespread fraud had occurred in the election. The following year a law was passed requiring counties in Florida to purge the rolls of duplicate registrations, the names of deceased persons and felons.

So far, so good. The problems developed when the state turned to ChoicePoint, which compiles and sells vast amounts of frequently shaky information about individuals. (ChoicePoint, which acquired DBT last May, was fired by the state of Pennsylvania for breaching the confidentiality of driving records.) With this private outfit in the picture it soon became clear that top Republican officials would be trying to reap a partisan political advantage from a law designed to correct an egregious wrong. And that partisan advantage would be realized in large part by trampling on the voting rights of minorities.

Over the spring and summer ChoicePoint was forced to acknowledge that 8,000 voters it had listed as felons had in fact been guilty only of misdemeanors, which would not have affected their right to vote. What is maddening is that when such an erroneous list of names gets into the hands of county election officials, as this one did, it is very difficult—often impossible—to find out what's correct and what's not correct.

That snickering you hear is from Republican operatives who know that these kinds of foul-ups, because they are based on criminal records, will disproportionately affect minority voters.

ChoicePoint eventually came up with a "corrected" list of 173,000 names of people it targeted as ineligible because they were deceased, or were registered more than once, or had been convicted of a felony.

But it was a lousy list, riddled with mistakes. And in an interview with me yesterday, Marty Fagan, a ChoicePoint vice president, said there had never been any expectation that the list would be particularly accurate. Remember now, we're talking about a list that would be used to strip Americans of the precious right to vote.

Mr. Fagan said the list focused on people who "might" have been deceased, or might have been listed twice, or "possible felons." He said it was "important to know" that the information needed to be "verified" by county election officials.

That was interesting, because ChoicePoint came up with 58,000 people—people registered to vote—who would fall into the category he calls "possible felons." How in the world were county election officials supposed to check out each and every one and find out if they were felons or not?

They couldn't. They didn't.

The horror stories about perfectly innocent black voters being turned away from the polls because they had been targeted as convicted felons started coming in early on the morning of Nov. 7, Election Day. And they're still coming in.

Blacks turned out to vote in record numbers in Florida this year, but huge numbers were systematically turned away for one specious reason after another.

The tactics have changed, but the goal remains the same. ▌

HAROLD MEYERSON

W. Stands for Wrongful

LA Weekly

Al Gore has had a crummy week, but popular sovereignty in America has had a catastrophic one. In Tallahassee, Judge N. Sanders Sauls ruled that a lagging campaign could not contest the outcome of an election by having a court inspect uncounted ballots. At the U.S. Supreme Court, Justice Antonin Scalia asserted during Friday's oral arguments that "There is no right of suffrage in presidential elections under Article II" of the Constitution— that is, state legislatures have given their citizens the right to vote in presidential elections, and can take it away if the spirit moves them. And though the court carefully avoided a political firestorm by remanding the recount decision to the Florida Supremes for reconsideration, Scalia's insistence on the non-existence of the public's right to vote for president was reflected in his court's decision.

Two contradictory lessons, then, are emerging from November's presidential election. One, in view of the excruciating closeness of the contest, is that every vote counts. The other, propounded by conservative jurists at play in the fields of 18th-century law and values, is that it's not even the case that any vote counts. Or at least, that there's no constitutional right to vote for president.

LA Weekly, December 8, 2000, p. 20. Reprinted with permission.

It's not news, of course, that the Supreme Court's one-person, one-vote standard applies to reapportionments but not to the selection of presidents. The inequities of the Electoral College are a constant of American electoral life; it's only when we get a squeaker of an election that they matter. In this election, since W. won a disproportionate number of the smallest states, they mattered a great deal: Among the 18 states (including the District of Columbia) with three, four or five electoral votes, W. prevailed by a 42-to-26 margin over Gore. That is, the Electoral College, which awards every state two votes at the outset for its U.S. senators, padded W.'s total. Take that senatorial two out of each state's vote in the total electoral tally, and Gore wins the Electoral College—even with W. taking Florida—by a 225-211 margin. It's this small-state padding that explains the difference between the Electoral College vote, which will go to W. by a 271-267 margin if he carries Florida, and the popular vote, which Gore leads by about 337,000—three-tenths of 1 percent of the total vote.

But we knew this was a ticking time bomb. Political scientists and Democratic operatives have been writing for years that in an extremely close election, the Republican presidential candidate could prevail even though losing the popular vote because of this electoral affinity for small states. What we didn't know until this week—what, to my knowledge at least, nobody was writing about at all — was that the very right to vote for president is still entirely a creation of state legislatures, that it is not, fundamentally, our own.

There are many ways to give the weight of law to an anti-democratic bias, of course, and Judge N. Sanders Sauls found one on Monday that was likely less constitutionally grounded than Scalia's. Sauls rejected the vice president's petition to count untallied ballots, and to look again at some dubiously tallied ones, in a ruling of such vehemence that Gore could count himself lucky he didn't actually draw jail time.

The key to Sauls' decision was his finding that if he ordered a re-counting, "There is no credible statistical evidence and no other competent substantial evidence to establish by a preponderance a reasonable probability that the results of the statewide election in the state of Florida would be different" from the result that Katherine Harris certified. Sauls had already made sure this would be the case, first by refusing to inspect the 9,000 ballots from Dade County that the Gore attorneys argued could turn the election around, and second by forbidding David Boies from cross-examining a pro-W. statistician on what those ballots would show if they reflected the already counted ballots in Dade County. In short, Sauls ruled that Gore had failed to demonstrate that which he had refused to allow Gore to demonstrate.

But Sauls' was the kind of routine contempt for scrupulous elections that over the past month has become all but synonymous with Floridian democracy in action. Antonin Scalia's case against popular rule, on the other hand, was a genuine bolt from the blue. Certainly, no attorney for W. had argued that the Florida Supremes had erred in assuming a constitutional bias toward suffrage in presidential elections. With the Gore folks constantly intoning, "Let every vote count," it hardly seemed politic for W.'s guys to respond, "Actually, there's no right to vote for president." That kind of argument, repeated often enough, might just dim the luster of W.'s appeal for votes during the next presidential campaign.

Antonin Scalia, of course, doesn't face voters, and his entire career seems bent on giving new life to every obscure anti-democratic statute that others have happily let slumber. The mistake of the Florida Supremes, he asserted, was their apparent belief in a popular franchise independent of the legislature. "There's a right of suffrage in voting for the legislature," he told Gore attorney Lawrence Tribe during Friday's arguments, "but Article II makes it very clear that the legislature can, itself, appoint the electors."

This case was made at greater length last week during the hearing that Florida's Republican Legislature convened to see if it could indeed appoint its own slate of electors just in case a court-ordered recount ended in the intolerable anomaly of a Gore majority. Boalt Hall law professor John Yoo, a former clerk for Clarence Thomas, argued that the legislators would be remiss if they didn't prepare themselves to appoint a slate. Writing this week in the friendly confines of the *Wall Street Journal* editorial page, Yoo elaborated his argument that the very notion of popular sovereignty is a partisan plot. "Contrary to Democratic rhetoric," he asserted, "the people have no right to vote for president or even the Electoral College; that power is only delegated to them by the grace of the legislature. In appointing the electors itself, the legislature would be directly taking up its constitutional functions again." Like Scalia, Yoo cites what is apparently the Supreme Court's only previous decision on this point—in 1892, for *McPherson* vs. *Blacker*, which leaves the choice of presidential electors unambiguously in the hands of the legislatures.

In sum, the now month-long democratic dysfunction in Florida is likely to result not only in W.'s presidency, but in the reassertion of one of the most elitist and anti-democratic features of our governmental structure, justly and understandably repressed for many decades. No wonder W. is in hiding: He's taking power by virtue of votes not counted, because of the Electoral College's bias against one-person, one-vote, and now on the wings of a ringing assault on popular rule.

We Americans have a hit-and-miss record of enlarging our democracy. Lincoln took Jefferson's assertion of human equality and expanded it so that slavery came to be seen as inconsistent with the nation's defining principles. Another hundred years had to pass before all citizens were assured of their right to vote (though we've learned from Florida in the past couple weeks that even that right is inconsistently applied).

Many of our original structures of government plod along unaltered to this day, though they are rooted in assumptions and biases that have been not only rejected, but in many instances forgotten. In 1892, when the court affirmed the power of the legislatures to choose electors, it was still the case that those legislatures elected United States senators. Not until the 17th Amendment to the Constitution in 1913 was that right given directly to the people. As for the Electoral College, it is a direct outgrowth of slavery. Had the constitution mandated a popular vote for president back in 1787, the North— with a far larger population of white males than the South—would have seen its presidential candidates routinely prevail. By apportioning electors in accord with a state's population, however—that is, by counting bodies, not voters—the predominantly Southern drafters of the constitution enabled slave states to dominate presidential elections.

Today, conservatives like Scalia and Yoo cheerfully defend the rights of legislatures over people, but prudently decline to invoke the demophobic and aristocratic beliefs that led to the establishment of these rights. Conservatives like George Will defend the Electoral College but omit any glowing references to slavery when they make their case. No account of W.'s rise, however, should rely on such a sanitized version of history. If he prevails, the first president of the 21st century will owe his office to the institutional legacies of the most repugnant biases of the 18th. The past, as Faulkner reminded us, isn't dead—and when it comes to selecting our presidents, apparently it isn't even past. ▮

E.J. DIONNE JR.

Double Standard

The Washington Post

You know you're confronting a double standard when the argument you're hearing reminds you of the schoolyard phrase: Heads I win, tails you lose. Let's examine the double standards that have been put in place to block Al Gore from becoming president.

For days now, the common wisdom, even among Democrats, has held that if Gore loses his case in the Florida Supreme Court, he should concede to George W. Bush and be "gracious."

It's not an unreasonable view, especially because many of the Florida justices tried hard during oral arguments yesterday to give Gore his due. Justices such as Harry Lee Anstead were forceful in questioning the strange decision of Circuit Court Judge N. Sanders Sauls to issue a sweeping ruling against Gore without looking at the core evidence in the case, the disputed ballots.

Since we're all lawyers now, let's stipulate that Gore should drop out if this court rules against him. Shouldn't the same expectation apply to George W. Bush? If the court orders recounts that show Gore won Florida, shouldn't Bush also be "gracious" and concede?

But no one expects that to happen. Already the Republican-dominated Florida legislature has moved to name Bush electors who would contest Gore electors chosen by the people.

There was a revealing moment in the courtroom yesterday when Joseph Klock, who otherwise did an excellent job as an attorney for Secretary of State Katherine Harris, underscored that the legislature would have no compunction about taking the choice of presidential electors away from the people.

For now, he said, "the legislature has allowed the people to make that choice." Note that word allowed, which makes the legislature the parent and the voters a bunch of children. If the lawmakers don't like what the people did, they can disallow the people.

Washington Post, final ed., December 8, 2000, p. A41. © 2000, The Washington Post Writers Group. Reprinted with permission.

And Bush, who got slapped back by the 11th U.S. Circuit Court of Appeals on Wednesday in his effort to stop all hand recounts, can also be counted on to appeal any ruling by the Florida Supreme Court to the U.S. Supreme Court.

So Gore has to drop out quickly, but Bush can keep fighting. *Heads Bush wins, tails Gore loses.*

Or take those cases on illegally processed absentee ballots in Seminole and Martin counties. The facts are clear: Republican officials doctored applications to make sure that some 2,000 absentee ballots in Seminole County and a smaller number in Martin County got sent out. No one disputes that what the Republicans did was against the law.

Yet any effort to throw out the illegal ballots—which could give the election to Gore—will be condemned for denying citizens who themselves broke no law their legitimate right to vote. Fair enough, except that no such solicitude is shown toward voters who lost their ballots because of well-documented problems with Florida's voting equipment.

Think about the arguments being made here. When Broward County ballot counters were examining legally cast ballots, Republicans charged that counting any dimpled chads for Gore constituted some corrupt, outrageous violation. Yet Republicans who claim to be strict constructionist, throw-the-book-at-'em, law-and-order types suddenly go squishy and say the problems with the Seminole and Martin ballots are only "technicalities."

Can you imagine the vituperation that would issue from Rush Limbaugh or James A. Baker III if these were Democratic ballots in Democratic counties? Pity Todd Schmick, the political director of the Florida Republican Party. On the stand Wednesday night in the Martin County trial, he looked uncomfortable in confirming that the elections supervisor "was going to correct the problem internally in Martin County." In other words, the fix was in.

Thus, the new Bush slogan is: Illegally obtained ballots, yes. Dimpled chads, no. *Heads Bush wins, tails Gore loses.*

Here's what the double standard asks of Gore. He must: (1) ignore any illegally cast Bush votes; (2) never get to examine ballots in Miami-Dade that have already been shown to contain votes for him; (3) accept the exclusion of 215 ballots cast in Palm Beach that, by a strict standard the Bush campaign praised, were recounted in Gore's favor; (4) forget about elderly or African American voters disenfranchised by equipment that made it hard for their votes to be registered. Oh, yes, and then Gore must concede graciously.

And here is what the double standard asks of Bush: absolutely nothing.

As I write, we await decisions from the Florida Supreme Court and the two absentee ballot cases. If the courts go against Gore, the pressure on him to quit will be enormous.

As for Bush, he's above the courts, above the vote counts, above inconvenient questions about whether he really won the election. If the courts rule against Bush, he'll just keep going until January. Will anyone say a word? *Heads Bush wins, tails Gore loses.* ▌

COLBERT I. KING

Ghosts in Florida

The Washington Post

The ghosts of Campaign 2000 in the form of Florida's controversial presidential vote will trail the next president into the White House. If it is George W. Bush, his first year will be haunted by a decision reached this week in Washington. If it is Al Gore, he can sit back and watch the fun.

After several daily meetings with FBI and Civil Rights Division staff to review intelligence concerning alleged voting irregularities, senior Justice Department officials concluded that there were sufficient grounds to send federal lawyers to Florida last Monday. The decision was a long time coming.

Since Election Day, civil rights groups have demanded that the Justice Department probe numerous complaints of improprieties, minority vote dilution and violation of federal civil rights laws in Florida voting precincts. This week, the federal government finally agreed to act—with too little and too late, critics say. Maybe not.

The introduction of Justice Department lawyers certainly won't change the election results or alter court decisions reached yesterday. But the current information gathering effort may get converted into a formal Justice Department investigation. If that happens, the civil rights probe could reach out and touch Florida Bush backers in a way that street protests, demonstrations and heated cyberspace traffic never could.

By Jan. 20, the judicial jousting and Florida's Supreme Court justices will be a memory. Not so the charges of African American voters being denied the right to vote due to discrimination, intimidation and fraud. There's no such thing as the clock's running out on the fight against racism.

If the Justice Department finds that voters of color were disenfranchised and left unprotected by the Florida state government—that U.S. laws indeed were broken—the issue will be alive and squarely in the lap of the next administration. And the problem will come with a twist that is sure to make a Bush White House squirm.

Simply put, a George W. Bush appointed attorney general could not be entrusted to investigate and prosecute illegal voter suppression activities in the state that gave Bush the presidency and in which his brother Jeb is governor. A civil rights probe in Florida, on the other hand, would be no problem for a president Gore.

Faced with a formal Justice Department investigation, the Bush administration would have no choice but to seek the appointment of a special counsel to conduct an independent inquiry into possible federal violations in Florida. Only an impartial outsider, not beholden to Bush or his attorney general, can be expected to serve the interest of justice. Nothing short of an independent team of lawyers and investigators interviewing witnesses and probing the nooks and crannies of the likes of Volusia, Broward and Miami-Dade counties, will reassure the public that politics and special preference won't rule the day in a Bush White House.

Investigating voting irregularities in Florida will not be a game of trivial pursuit. Some troubling allegations have already surfaced, such as:

—The names of law-abiding voters, disproportionately African American, wrongly removed from the rolls or identified for purging.

—Registered African American voters banished from the polls because their names couldn't be found on voter registration lists.

—Voting sites in African American precincts switched without timely notice or any notification at all.

—African American voters harassed and intimidated near the polling places.

—Ballot boxes in African American precincts not collected, predominantly minority polls understaffed, language assistance sought but denied, old and unreliable voting machinery.

And the list of alleged irregularities does not include the disproportionate number of ballots in predominantly minority precincts that were thrown out.

For those of you tempted to dismiss these complaints as the predictable whining of blacks who find themselves on the losing side, I say not so fast. Experience, old and new, has been a great teacher.

I commend to you the observations of Hugh Price, president of the National Urban League, on National Public Radio's "Talk of the Nation" show. Price backs calls for the Justice Department to get into the Florida situation in a strong way. He told listeners: "I'm reminded of what happened in the case of racial profiling in New Jersey when the first response to the allegation was, 'We don't do this,' a staunch denial. "Then we discovered there were some correlations between race and who was being stopped, but there was still a lot of denial. . . . And then it turned out that it was happenstance. And now that the *New York Times* has dug into and received mounds of paper they have found that it was an outright, point-blank, in-your-face conspiracy on the part of the New Jersey troopers to stop people of color."

All the media attention today is on Florida courts, the presidential contenders and the potential winning candidate's thrill of victory. Come next year, the limelight shifts to Washington—and maybe to another scene—an all-too familiar tale about the uphill struggle of a people who tried in vain to live out the American Dream on Election Day. ▮

Commentary

DECEMBER 10–13, 2000

NOVEMBER						
5	6	7	8	9	10	11
12	13	14	15	16	17	18
19	20	21	22	23	24	25
26	27	28	29	30	1	2
3	4	5	6	7	8	9
10	**11**	**12**	**13**	14	15	16
17	18	19	20	21	22	23
24	25	26	27	28	29	30

WILLIAM KRISTOL

A President by Judicial Fiat

The Weekly Standard

As a result of Friday's Florida Supreme Court decision, Al Gore may be sworn in as president on January 20. If he is, he will receive our best wishes upon assuming the burdens of office. We will support his policies when we think they are right for the country. We will pay proper respect to the office of the presidency. We will hope (some will pray) that Al Gore's presidency proves a success, and that it leaves the United States of America a stronger and better nation.

But some of us will not believe that Al Gore has acceded to the presidency legitimately. The action of the Florida court is not constitutionally defensible. We will therefore continue to insist that he gained office through an act of judicial usurpation. We will not "move on." Indeed, some of us will work for the next four years to correct this affront to our constitutional order. This does not mean simply, indeed it does not mean primarily, defeating Al Gore in 2004. It means defeating the understanding of the rule of law, the role of the courts, and the meaning of the Constitution embodied by this decision.

It would of course be better if this decision were reversed in the next few days. The U.S. Supreme Court may save us from its Florida brethren. If it does not, the Florida legislature, and then the U.S. Congress, may act under the Constitution and under federal law to vindicate the Constitution and the rule of law.

But the U.S. Supreme Court may fail to act, and there will then be enormous pressure from friends of the judiciary to yield to the Florida court. The assault from the law schools, the media, and all enlightened quarters on the state legislature, if it moves to act, will be massive. If our elected officials find it in them to stand up to such an assault, it will be a healthy moment for the country.

Forty-two years ago, the U.S. Supreme Court claimed in *Cooper* v. *Aaron* that "the federal judiciary is supreme in the exposition of the law of the Constitution." This is not so — nor is a state judiciary supreme in the exposition

Weekly Standard, December 18, 2000, p. 9 (on sale December 11). Reprinted with permission.

of a state constitution—though we have acted as if it were for two generations. While the judicial branch has the obligation to interpret laws in light
of the Constitution, the other branches have an equal obligation to act consistently with the Constitution; and no branch is superior to any other. In
practice, the role of the Supreme Court (or of state supreme courts) tends to
give them, on any given issue, the last word. But the last word on any particular case cannot be the last word forever.

As always, Lincoln put it best, in his first inaugural:

> I do not forget the position assumed by some, that constitutional
> questions are to be decided by the Supreme Court; nor do I deny that
> such decisions must be binding in any case, upon the parties to a suit,
> as to the object of that suit, while they are also entitled to very high
> respect and consideration in all parallel cases, by all other departments
> of the government. And while it is obviously possible that such deci-
> sion may be erroneous in any given case, still the evil effect following
> it, being limited to that particular case, with the chance that it may
> be over-ruled, and never become a precedent for other cases, can bet-
> ter be borne than could the evils of a different practice. At the same
> time the candid citizen must confess that if the policy of the govern-
> ment, upon vital questions, affecting the whole people, is to be irrev-
> ocably fixed by decisions of the Supreme Court, the instant they are
> made, in ordinary litigation between parties, in personal actions, the
> people will have ceased to be their own rulers, having, to that extent,
> practically resigned their government into the hands of that eminent
> tribunal.

Perhaps the Florida state legislature and the U.S. Congress will now rise to
the occasion. But perhaps not. If not, we will have a presidency achieved by
litigation and judicial fiat. The best that can be hoped for under such circumstances is that this illegitimately gained presidency will give rise to a determination on the part of the people to resume the burden and the privileges
of self-government. Two generations of judicial usurpation is enough. ∎

ROBERT N. HOCHMAN

Our Robed Masters: What the Court Did Was a Power Grab, Pure and Simple

The Weekly Standard

Before this election, if you had read the Florida election code, you might have thought it entirely reasonable, if unremarkable. It seems to divide the responsibility of counting votes among different governmental bodies. You might have thought that the county canvassing boards had the primary responsibility. That power appeared to be restrained somewhat by the secretary of state's authority to enforce a deadline for submitting results. Most important, the quintessentially political act of counting votes and certifying election results seemed to be in the hands of politically responsible officers. To be sure, you would have noticed that the Florida courts have the power to ensure that all these political officers follow the law in performing their vote-counting duties. But that would not have seemed a very prominent feature of the law.

Wrong, or so the Florida Supreme Court has just told us. In ruling in Al Gore's favor on Friday, the Florida Supreme Court has announced that Florida's election code makes a bare majority of the Florida Supreme Court the most authoritative election officers in the state. All of a sudden, Florida's election code is entirely unreasonable and quite remarkable. That's a fairly good sign that the court got it wrong.

Let us be clear about what the court has done. It has ordered a statewide manual recount of all "undervotes" not previously manually recounted, simply because the election was close. No election officer broke the law. No election officer abused his discretion. Al Gore showed that there were 9,000 "undervotes" that had not been manually recounted, and that he trails by only a few hundred votes. This, we are told, proves that election officials rejected "a number of legal votes sufficient to place in doubt the result of the election."

Weekly Standard, December 18, 2000, pp. 14–15 (on sale December 11). Reprinted with permission. Robert Hochman, a former Supreme Court clerk, practices law in Chicago.

It's not as if these 9,000 ballots had been ignored. They were counted twice by machine and, having failed to register a vote, were treated by the canvassing board as not containing a vote for president. The court not only fails to respect this determination by duly authorized election officials, it effectively presumes it was wrong.

But the reader should rest assured that the court is not simply substituting its judgment for that of state election officials. Indeed, it turns out that the court thinks that state election officials can authoritatively determine whether ballots contain a vote for president. They just have to make that determination in the way the court (and Al Gore) want them to: by manual recount. The court simply gave Al Gore the vote gains from the too-late Palm Beach manual recount (215) and from the Dade partial manual recount (168). If anyone thought we were getting a statewide review of ballots under a reasonable and uniform standard, consider that Broward County's infamous dimple-crazy manual recount gets to stand, under this court's order, without court review. Counting by hand, then, is both necessary and entirely sufficient (no matter the standard employed) for preferential treatment under this court's rule.

The court's opinion rests solely on the view that the Florida legislature has expressed a preference for manual recounts. That is demonstrably false. First, it seems like ages ago, but we can all remember back to November 8, when we learned that Florida law provides for a mandatory recount when the first count shows a margin of victory of less than 0.5 percent. That recount, however, is by machine. Florida law expressly provides for a manual recount only in the protest provision. And in that statute, a county canvassing board is never required to do a manual recount. The only place the Florida Supreme Court can find a preference for manual recounts is in its own (and Al Gore's) head.

The court's naked preference for manual recounts has led it to do precisely what the Dade County canvassing board decided not to do: manually recount its ballots. The court emphasizes that the contest provision, which it reads to authorize its recount, is distinct from the protest provision, which permits the county canvassing board to manually recount. That's true, but it reveals a stunning sense of judicial imperialism: It is the court that has the final say not just on the lawfulness of how votes were counted (a traditionally judicial function), but also on the manner in which votes are to be counted (a traditionally political function).

The sudden ascent of the Florida courts to the role of vote-counters may come as a shock to those who have followed this controversy over the past month. Didn't this court champion the role of the county canvassing boards in counting ballots in its Thanksgiving-spoiling opinion? The canvassing boards were so important then that the court magically transformed November 14 into November 26. Now we learn that the county boards were really just court aides, doing the court's work, until the court decided it could formally start giving marching orders to all of Florida's election officials.

Like field generals, the four members of the court's majority will now watch as its minions scramble to carry out its orders. Like grand statesmen, they will listen as many praise their zealous pursuit of the "will of the people." Generals and statesmen, perhaps. But let no one pretend that they have acted as judges. ▮

E.J. DIONNE JR.

Let the Voters Decide

The Washington Post

The story is told of the bank robber who is caught red-handed by a policeman. As the officer watches the man stuff money into his sack, the thief brazenly denies he's robbing the bank and then asks: "Who do you believe, me or your own eyes?"

In ruling in favor of the hand-recounts across Florida that began and then abruptly stopped yesterday, the Florida Supreme Court majority wisely and bravely decided that the one way to make sure neither side steals this election is to say: Let's look at all these unexamined ballots with our own eyes so we can know—really know—who won.

And that is why the nation will greatly regret the decision of the five U.S. Supreme Court justices who voted yesterday afternoon to force a halt to the Florida hand counts. The court had every right to review the Florida Supreme Court action. But given Tuesday's deadline on getting to a result, the court's decision to stop all counting until it hears the case tomorrow will forever be seen as blatant political interference on the side of George W. Bush—and, yes, the heavy-handed use of federal power against a state court that was trying to ensure an honest election.

Washington Post, final ed., December 10, 2000, p. B7. © 2000, The Washington Post Writers Group. Reprinted with permission.

In words that will ring through our history, Justice John Paul Stevens spoke for the four Supreme Court dissenters and millions of Americans in declaring: "Preventing the recount from being completed will inevitably cast a cloud on the legitimacy of the election." As Stevens argued, counting "every legally cast vote cannot constitute irreparable harm." But shutting down the count, he said, could.

Could it be that the Supreme Court majority feared that if the counting went forward and showed that Al Gore had won the election, the court would then have put itself in the position of overturning the will of the people? The fact that this question even occurs shows the danger of the court's decision.

Consider the alternative view, the central argument of the Florida Supreme Court. "This election," it wrote, "should be determined by a careful examination of the votes of Florida's citizens, and not by strategies extraneous to the voting process." In other words, not judges, not Supreme Court justices, not legislators but voters should decide who won Florida's 25 electoral votes.

All this could have been resolved long ago—and without the Supreme Court besmirching itself in a political fight—if the Bush campaign had simply accepted Al Gore's suggestion of a statewide recount. The Bush campaign's furious efforts to block recounts make it ever more difficult to escape the conclusion that the Bush side and the Gore side actually agree that a fair recount would show Gore won Florida.

It's obvious that both Gore and Bush want to win this election. But at the heart of this dispute is a deeper argument, and it's the argument over which the U.S. Supreme Court is now so sharply divided. It's between one camp that makes extensive use of the word "constitutional" and another that talks a great deal about "democracy."

The constitutionalists see any effort by the Florida Supreme Court to get the votes recounted fairly as a form of judicial activism to be rejected. Bush, they'll argue, has every right to block further counts—and would have had the right to ignore them even had they shown Gore winning Florida. The constitutional solution, they say, is for the Florida legislature to name electors and for Congress accept them. Or, in the case of the U.S. Supreme Court majority, to stop counting altogether.

The democracy side says the Florida court in this case represents not itself and not judicial activism but the rights of thousands of individual voters who may have been disenfranchised by machine errors. At stake, said Justice Stevens in yesterday's dissent, is "the basic principle, inherent in our Constitution and our democracy, that every legal vote should be counted."

This side notes further that while the Constitution vests responsibilities for choosing electors in state legislatures, those legislatures have, for well over a century, transferred that responsibility to the voters—to the people. Why? Because, as the liberal writer Harold Meyerson pointed out in an article last week in the *LA Weekly*, we are a much more democratic nation now than we were 200 years ago.

At the time the Founders wrote the Constitution, they imagined that all electors might be chosen by legislatures. There were many restrictions on the right to vote. Over the years, while retaining the Founders' framework, we have steadily extended the right to vote to people without property and then to African Americans and women. Popular election of those who would select our president was part of this democratic advance.

To step back from the idea that voters should name electors—and thus to step back from the idea of a fair count of Florida's votes—is to retreat into a less democratic world, to a time when the people's will was thought to need buffering by those, including state legislators, who claimed to know better.

There have always been two ways to settle this dispute. The most sensible and democratic way is to recount the ballots and let the voters decide Florida and the election. The alternative way is to block those counts on supposedly constitutional grounds, or, as has been suggested, to have the Florida legislature just step in and name electors. Down the recount path lies clarity and democratic legitimacy. Down the other path lies a retreat from democracy, and chaos.

Unless one of the five justices who stopped the recounts yesterday has the prudence to switch sides in the final decision, we will face the spectacle of a narrow conservative majority on the Supreme Court allying itself with a political campaign to stop the people from knowing how the voters of Florida really cast their ballots. That cannot be good for the court, or for our country. ▌

MICHAEL GREVE

The Equal-Protection Card:
The Worst Grounds May Be the Best

The National Review

Predicting the outcome of a Supreme Court case on the basis of oral arguments has never been more hazardous than in *Bush* v. *Gore*—or more tempting. Here goes, then: The justices' questions in today's proceeding suggest that the Court may follow its worst instincts and decide the case on equal-protection grounds, rather than the crisp and clear language of Article II of the Constitution or federal statutory law.

Article II Section 1 of the Constitution invests the states' legislatures, not their courts, with the plenary power to appoint presidential electors. Today's arguments produced an agreement of sorts concerning the application of that language to the Florida supreme court's escapades. Responding to Justice Anthony Kennedy's questioning, Gore attorney David Boies opined that the Florida legislature could not have legislated the post-election procedures and remedies that the Florida supreme court enacted in its decisions. That, Mr. Boies said, would constitute new law and thus contravene the applicable federal statute (Section 5 of Volume 3 of the United States Code), which provides that the electors' appointments must proceed under "laws enacted prior to" Election Day. The judicial enactment of the same procedures, in contrast, is mere routine "interpretation."

Justice Kennedy reacted with predictable incredulity. Whereupon Mr. Boies conceded that if SCOFLA's decision and opinion are a mere "sham" and totally unreasonable, they might constitute new law after all. Mr. Bush's position—forcefully argued by Theodore Olson—is that the Florida court's rulings are a sham and, moreover, acts of defiance both of the Florida legislature's plenary Article II authority and the United States Supreme Court's order to vacate SCOFLA's first ruling.

National Review Online, December 11, 2000. Reprinted with permission. Michael Greve is the John G. Searle Scholar at the American Enterprise Institute and director of AEI's Federalism Project.

The Supreme Court, however, may decline to decide the squarely presented sham/Article II question. A decision and opinion along those lines would certainly come out 5:4. It would have to delve into matters of state law (how else tell a sham from routine interpretation?) and, moreover, characterize the Florida justices as tyrants. While five justices are probably prepared to do these things, respect for state law, coupled with a general affection for free-floating lawmaking in the guise of legal interpretation, may make the centrist justices—and Justice Kennedy in particular—look for alternative paths.

The most obvious alternative is equal-protection analysis—more precisely, the fact that the vote counts mandated by the Florida supreme court would follow no intelligible, fair procedure. Mr. Boies averred that varying standards to determine the voters "intent" would pose no equal-protection problem even if the applied standards differed from county to county, or table to table within each county. That position irritated not only the five conservative justices but also Justices Ginsburg, Breyer, and Souter. Mr. Boies did not help himself by suggesting, in response to Chief Justice Rehnquist's query about the time pressures, that maybe the recount need not be conducted in all counties—just the ones that could get around to it.

In contrast to the hard-and-fast Article II issue, then, a finding that the Florida supreme court's order violates equal protection (and perhaps due process) might attract a sixth or seventh vote. Liberal Justices might view an expansive equal protection argument as a means of salvaging something of value from the case. The federalism scruples that may make the centrist Justices squirm in addressing the Article II question do not apply to equal protection: Whacking the states with the all-purpose 14th Amendment club is what the Supreme Court does for a living.

The remedy that would flow from an equal-protection ruling is anybody's guess. (Who would formulate a recount standard that does pass muster—the Florida supreme court, or the secretary of state? The judge in Leon County?) Whatever standard anybody designs, is there any way of precluding yet another round of appeals? In light of the time pressures, the most likely practical consequence of an equal-protection ruling is that the election is over. Bush won.

Bush's equal-protection argument is powerful and, at some level, unanswerable. (Mr. Boies certainly did not answer it.) Still, a ruling on these grounds would be the worst possible way of reaching a desirable outcome. If there is any merit to the Florida supreme court's rulings, it has been to bring the country face to face with the dire consequences of judicial imperialism. It is bad enough, though perhaps unavoidable, that judicial imperialism should be dealt a setback by the imperial Supreme Court rather than the Florida legislature or the United States Congress. It would be worse if the means of curbing judicial overreach should be the Court's favored interventionist tool: Such a ruling would in some sense validate, rather than redress, judicial arrogance.

Mr. Olson valiantly, and rightly, resisted Justice Ginsburg's suggestion that an equal-protection ruling in Bush's favor would render the Article II issue academic. Even he, however, will take an equal-protection victory—and fight the battle over judicial imperialism another day. So should the rest of us. ∎

PAMELA S. KARLAN

The Court Casts Its Vote

The New York Times

Who wins the presidential election often alters the Supreme Court, both by determining who appoints new justices and by subtly influencing the court's decisions. But when should the Supreme Court alter who wins an election? That is the question posed by the court's decision this weekend to halt Florida's recount of the ballots.

The last two times the Supreme Court intervened so decisively in the political process were in the mid-1960s, when it announced the requirement of one person, one vote and when the court upheld the Voting Rights Act's re-enfranchisement of black Americans. The concerns that justified those dramatic and rare interventions explain why the current incursion into the political thicket is so ill-advised.

The one person, one vote principle enunciated in 1964 required the reapportionment of virtually every state's legislature and most states' congressional districts. The representatives of grotesquely underpopulated districts would never give up power willingly. The state courts were often powerless to act because the malapportionments were written into state constitutions. Congress itself was malapportioned and not interested in reform. If the Supreme Court did not act, no one else would. The political arteries had

Originally published in *The New York Times*, late ed., December 11, 2000, p. A31. Pamela S. Karlan is a professor at Stanford Law School.

hardened. The political process could not cure itself. A judicial bypass was necessary.

It was also necessary in the case of black disenfranchisement. The court needed to step in to guarantee the ability of black voters to vote in places that had barred them from registering, unfairly tossed out their ballots or organized the election system to dilute their voting strength.

The Supreme Court's incursion into the Florida case is entirely different. There was no reason to jump in immediately. Whatever else we might say about Florida, its political system has not been frozen into inaction. The state's judges, elected by Florida citizens, have been sorting out difficult election law questions. The state's legislature has been wrestling with how to ensure that the state's voice will be heard in the Electoral College. It, too, may be acting prematurely. But its jumping the gun is preferable to the Supreme Court's doing so—after all, it remains accountable to the voters. And Congress has been gearing up to fulfill its responsibilities under the Constitution and federal law to ensure an orderly determination of who should be the 43rd president.

Self-government may be messy, time-consuming and partisan. But in the Florida recount case, the political actors are vigorous and functioning.

Unless the five justices who voted for the stay reverse course, they are risking much of the court's reputation as a protector of voting rights, since the court's action makes it less likely that every lawful vote will be counted.

They also risk further undermining the legitimacy of this already clouded election. Florida's freedom of information act will make the disputed ballots available for public inspection. The ballots may eventually be examined by the press and civic groups. So one day we may know who got the most votes in Florida. If the Supreme Court's short-circuiting of the recount means that we discover that the wrong man sits in the Oval Office, five justices will have dealt democracy and the court itself a serious blow.

Gov. George W. Bush's lead has shrunk steadily—from about 1,700 on election night to perhaps less than 100 when the Supreme Court stepped in to stop the counting. If Governor Bush is to win, ultimately, by one vote, fine. But let that one vote be cast by a Floridian, and not by a justice of the United States Supreme Court. ▌

RANDY E. BARNETT

Left Tells Right: "Heads I Win, Tails You Lose"

The Wall Street Journal

I have long been amused by those modern liberals and leftists who try to instruct conservatives as to what "true" conservatism requires of them—particularly when conservatives get uppity and actually gain control of some institution of governance. Conservatism, say the scolds, requires that one accept and "conserve" the welfare/regulatory state that "progressives" have been building for 60 years.

We are now experiencing a judicial version of this phenomenon: judicial activists and nationalists instructing conservatives and federalists about the meaning of judicial restraint and federalism. Typically the words "activism" and "restraint" lack content and I prefer to avoid them. But here "judicial activism" refers to courts that are willing to overstep the bounds of either the Constitution, or unquestionably constitutional statutes, to impose their will on the other branches of government and on the people themselves.

That this is what the Florida Supreme Court did in its 4-3 ruling last week has been pointed out by others, including the chief justice of that court. Still, it is useful to recall that the whole mess began way back on Nov. 17 when the Florida Supreme Court issued the following stay: "In order to maintain the status quo, the Court, on its own motion, enjoins the Respondent, Secretary of State and Respondent, the Elections Canvassing Commission from certifying the results of the November 7, 2000, presidential election, until further order of this Court." Had they restrained themselves back then, Al Gore would already have conceded the election and David Boies would be looking for another Microsoft to sue.

Everything we have experienced since Nov. 14 stems from that supremely activist intervention into the recount process, but it was not until this past Saturday that the charges of judicial partisanship began to fly furiously. Not

Wall Street Journal, December 12, 2000, p. A26. Reprinted from *The Wall Street Journal* © 2000 Dow Jones & Company, Inc. All rights reserved. Randy Barnett is a professor at Boston University School of Law.

at the Four Horseman of the Florida Supreme Court mind you, but at the Party of Five "conservatives" on the U.S. Supreme Court who took away the keys to the punch-card counters by issuing a stay of their own to "preserve the status quo" in Florida. Then came the cry, as if in unison: How dare these conservatives interfere with states' rights? How dare they act by a bare majority? Aren't they the ones always preaching about federalism and judicial restraint? Well, this reveals the conservative justices for the hypocrites they have always been!

As one who believes in a judiciary that actively polices the lines between the powers of government and the rights retained by the people, as well as between the powers of the national government and those of the states, and between the powers of one branch and those of another, I find this argument amusing. For it amounts to a "heads I win, tails you lose" theory of judging. Conservative justices confronted with activist legislatures must roll over in the name of restraint, thus creating a convenient one-way ratchet of constantly expanding government and the erosion of any separation of powers or federalism.

And now we learn that, in the name of federalism and judicial restraint, conservative and federalist justices must "defer" to a state supreme court that showed no deference whatever to the legislature which set election deadlines and procedures, to the Florida secretary of state—a constitutional officer—who attempted to adhere to those deadlines, to the circuit court judge who ruled that the secretary of state had acted within her statutory discretion, to the circuit court judge who ruled that the canvassing boards had not abused their discretion, and to the U.S. Supreme Court itself, which had unanimously urged the Florida Supreme Court to retreat to a neutral corner.

Where were the panel discussions on judicial deference and restraint then? No, back then we were instructed that it was shockingly bad form for James Baker III or anyone else to question the integrity of a supreme court.

Well, the rules of decorum have switched again. Now, and only now, we are urged that judges must exercise "restraint." Or at least we are urged that conservative judges must exercise the restraint they say they believe in. It is a convenient argument indeed. A kind of intellectual jujitsu that tries to turn an opponent's own thrusts against him. Activist judges are acting true to their principles when they escape the bounds of the law, while conservative justices are hypocrites if they abandon their principles of "restraint" to bring wayward courts back to earth. Heads, activist justices win; tails, conservative justices lose.

The counter to this maneuver is the simple proposition that conservatives of both the political and judicial variety sometimes forget: It is a judge's role to actively adhere to the Constitution and protect the rights of the people. If this means "actively" striking down legislation or lower court rulings that violate the clear mandates of the Constitution or that exceed the proper powers of a legislature or government official, then that is what we have judges for. Restraint means staying within the boundaries of the Constitution and of constitutional laws. Restraint in the face of those who exceed those boundaries is simply an abdication of judicial authority.

If the U.S. Supreme Court was correct to find that the Florida Supreme Court had likely overstepped the bounds of Article II of the 14th Amendment, or of federal law, it was no violation of "judicial restraint" to stop the Florida vote count marathon. And it will be no violation of restraint to reverse the rule of the Florida judges and to restore the rule of law. Conservatives would be wise to remember this in the future whenever when they find themselves urging judicial restraint in the face of other types of usurpations by judges, by legislatures or by law enforcement. ∎

RONALD BROWNSTEIN

In Blocking Vote Count, High Court Shows Which Team It's Rooting For

The Los Angeles Times

Perhaps it's too much to expect intellectual consistency from anyone involved in this war for the White House. But the five-member conservative majority on the U.S. Supreme Court may have set a new standard for swallowing its previous convictions when it intervened, perhaps decisively, for fellow Republican George W. Bush on Saturday.

Under Chief Justice William H. Rehnquist, the five-member majority on this court has been defined by its defense of states' rights against federal intrusions. It struck down a federal law banning guns near schools as an unacceptable infringement on state prerogatives. On similar grounds, it struck

Los Angeles Times, December 11, 2000, p. A5. Reprinted with permission.

down a federal law allowing rape victims and battered spouses to sue their assailants in federal court. It said Washington could not compel local sheriffs to conduct background checks on handgun purchasers. And it has said states cannot be sued in either state or federal court for violating federal laws. As one court scholar has written: "The five justices . . . harken back to pre-Civil War Jeffersonian notions exalting state sovereignty."

Yet on Saturday, those same five conservative justices, all appointed by Republican presidents, outvoted the four most moderate and liberal justices (two appointed by Republicans, two by Democrats) to block a decision by Florida's highest court interpreting state law on a matter—the administration of elections—historically left to the states.

Most striking in the U.S. Supreme Court's stunning ruling was its decision to stop the hand counts that had resumed Saturday morning—and its openly political logic for doing so.

On television, in the hours before the Supreme Court abruptly pulled the plug, the nation saw a recount process that, while plagued by confusion in some counties, was generally unfolding with order and dispatch. The eight Leon County circuit judges recounting 9,000 disputed ballots from Miami-Dade County were prepared to finish their work by Saturday night, and had established a process sufficiently rigorous for assessing "voter intent" that even a Bush spokesperson praised it on CNN. In populous Hillsborough County, just as the Supreme Court ruled, officials had efficiently finished sorting the ballots on which machines had failed to record a presidential preference and were prepared to begin counting several hours ahead of schedule.

In both parties, the assumption was this statewide review of ballots unread by the machine would favor Al Gore. But Bush was doing better than expected in some places, suggesting that the process was not guaranteed to provide Gore enough votes to overcome the Republican's slender lead. What the process did seem guaranteed to provide was the fullest picture the country has yet received of how Florida voted last month.

Which apparently was exactly what the five-member Supreme Court majority feared. In his concurring opinion, Justice Antonin Scalia was unusually blunt about one critical reason for blocking the recount: the fear that if Gore took the lead as the new votes were counted, the legitimacy of Bush's presidency would be endangered even if the Supreme Court subsequently invalidated those results.

"The counting of votes that are of questionable legality does in my view threaten irreparable harm to Bush, and to the country, by casting a cloud upon what he claims to be the legitimacy of his election," Scalia wrote. "Count first, and rule upon legality afterward, is not a recipe for producing election results that have the public acceptance democratic stability requires."

As a matter of political logic, that seems inverted. As the four dissenting justices pointedly wrote: "Preventing the recount from being completed will inevitably cast a cloud on the legitimacy of the election."

But the more disturbing possibility is that Scalia and his allies were worried less about Bush's legitimacy than their own. Surely the Supreme Court is within its rights to carefully question the aggressive—and also sharply divided—decision from the Florida Supreme Court on Friday authorizing the recounts. And nothing would have prevented the high court from erasing the results of those recounts, with a stroke of the pen, if they decided that the Florida Supreme Court—all of whose members were appointed by Democratic governors—somehow had violated the federal statute barring the revision of election laws after election day.

But the decision to preemptively block the counting leaves open the troubling possibility that the five-member majority on the U.S. Supreme Court wanted to avoid a situation where overturning the state court also meant nullifying a popular vote count that, for the first time, put Gore ahead in Florida. It appears the majority may have tried to reduce its own short-term political exposure—even at the price of increasing the long-term uncertainty about who really won Florida.

As it stands, the decision to stop counting has provided Bush an enormous tactical advantage—perhaps doing "irreparable harm" to Gore in the process. Even if the U.S. Supreme Court ultimately reverses course and upholds the Florida court decision, the delay in counting ballots greatly increases the odds that the Republican-controlled state Legislature will intervene for Bush.

With oral arguments not scheduled in the U.S. Supreme Court case until today, it seems impossible that the court could rule quickly enough to allow the counting to be completed by Tuesday—the day on which federal law says a state's electoral college slate must be chosen if it is to be immune to congressional challenge. And the failure to meet that deadline would provide the Legislature justification to directly appoint its own slate of electors for Bush this week. Such a move would guarantee another round of court and congressional challenges—leaving Gore in an uncertain position even if the Supreme Court eventually reauthorizes the recount and that puts him ahead.

The last time America faced a similar dilemma—the contested 1876 presidential election between Republican Rutherford B. Hayes and Democrat Samuel J. Tilden—five Supreme Court justices were drafted onto the committee Congress established to resolve the impasse. The justices proved indistinguishable from the members of Congress, voting with their own party on every issue. "The fact is the justices acted as partisans," says historian Eric Foner.

Many things have changed since 1876, but apparently not the tendency of even U.S. Supreme Court justices to side with the home team when the stakes are this high. ▌

NICHOLAS CONFESSORE

Florida's Silver Lining: For Gore and the Democrats, Losing Ugly Beats Losing Nicely

The American Prospect

Within a day or two, the U.S. Supreme Court may reverse last Friday's decision by the Florida Supreme Court and thereby effectively end Al Gore's chances of becoming president in January. It would be deeply hypocritical—and wrong, moreover—were Democrats to question the legitimacy of the Supreme Court's decision, however objectionable it is and regardless of the lines along which it is delivered. But as Gore prepares himself and his party for that possibility, it is crucial to point out that, up until that point, he has executed precisely the kind of endgame that the situation demanded. Even had he known from the beginning that he would lose in the end, Gore was right to wage the fight—right to file his lawsuits, right to appeal and re-appeal, right to muster his party and his constituents, right to ignore the polls, and right to ignore those who urged him to pack it in for the good of the nation.

The first thing Gore's stubbornness accomplished was to bring out the absolute worst in an otherwise annoyingly temperate George W. Bush camp.

Within days of the first, automatic recount, the Bush camp was getting more truly negative press than it had, really, at any point during the campaign— first due to blatant hypocrisy (attacking the Democrats for threatening legal contests, before filing the first in a long series of such contests), and then for resorting to the kind of distasteful right-wingery the Bushies had long eschewed. The most prominent was Bush consigliere James Baker, whose bitter attack on the Florida Supreme Court's first ruling was widely criticized, correctly, as an unjustified assault on judicial integrity. But let's not forget Karen Hughes, whose suggestion that Gore was unpatriotic was wonderfully reminiscent of the redbaiting of yore. Together, Hughes and Baker managed to overshadow Gore's own inconsistencies—particularly his challenging of overseas absentee ballots on technical grounds even as he argued, publicly, for the fullest possible recount.

But that was just the beginning. Once Bush's immediate surrogates lashed out, they lost whatever rein they had on the more overtly partisan Republican activists and officials. The conservative intelligentsia were the quickest to go nuclear: *The Weekly Standard* and George Will both accused Gore of waging a coup; *The National Review* shrieked that Gore was stealing the election; and the typically hysterical Peggy Noonan called for a nationwide uprising (a peaceful one, natch). Right behind them came House Whip Tom DeLay and his latter-day Newties, who collectively constitute the most effective public relations tool in the Democratic arsenal. Within days, Republican activists flown in from around the country—with various Hill staffers at the helm, according to press reports—had organized a full-scale riot outside the offices of the Miami-Dade County elections board, a move which, while it may have intimidated the board into stopping their hand recount, was a colossal public relations blunder. Not satisfied with such disruption, DeLay then began talking about having the House of Representatives reject any slate of pro-Gore Florida electors that came down the pike.

All this was so extreme, so over-the-top, that it had the unintended consequence of shoring up Gore's support among his own party, where, at that point, he needed it most. Within days, House Minority Leader Dick Gephardt and Senate Minority Leader Thomas Daschle had organized a conference call with Al Gore, promising him publicly that they were "supportive of going ahead with this contest." Members of Congress like Virginia's James P. Moran and Indiana's Tim Roemer, never very vocal Gore supporters, rallied to the vice president's side. Even Bob Kerrey—perhaps the most outspokenly anti-Clinton, anti-Gore Democrat in Congress—flew down to Florida to help out.

It's been obvious from the beginning, of course, that the consequences of the recount fight would resonate long past Inauguration Day. What matters is how. And from the looks of things, the long-range effects will benefit the Democratic Party.

Bush's main advantage through this whole election has been his aura of moderation and his distinctly unrevolutionary tones, achieved largely through the remarkable discipline of Republican conservatives. By contrast, the Democrats' main disadvantage has been their relative disunity, especially the substantial body of conservative and moderate congressional Democrats who would, in the face of a clean Gore defeat, be willing to play ball with a Bush Administration.

But the result of the 2000 election—the Republican sweep contrasted against clear signs that the public favors the core Democratic agenda—seem to have changed that dynamic. Obviously no one likes to be cheated, and the Republican shenanigans of the past month have aroused more unifying anger among Democrats than anything since impeachment. But the sneering triumphalism of Republicans like DeLay and Texas Senator Phil Gramm—who both seem to think that this election heralds the end of the beginning of the Reagan Revolution, rather than vice versa—seems to have reminded certain Democrats of why, in the end, they are Democrats, complicating Bush's presumptive strategy of co-optation. It's one thing to play ball when your party controls one or two branches of government; it's quite another when the other party controls *all* branches of the government and mistakes the narrowest of victories for the broadest of public mandates. The more DeLay and Gramm crow, the worse it is for Bush, and the better it is for the Democrats.

This kind of partisan autocatalysis can't go on forever, of course. If the Supreme Court rules against Gore, it may finally be to his advantage—as it was not before—to pack it in. All good things, as the saying goes, come to an end. And for the Democrats, the Florida recount fight as been a *very* good thing. ∎

JESSE L. JACKSON AND JOHN J. SWEENEY

Let the Count Continue

The Washington Post

Today the Supreme Court may be poised to find that some or all aspects of a manual recount in Florida violate the equal protection clause of the 14th Amendment to the U.S. Constitution.

It's too soon to say that a majority of the justices is bent on keeping all the votes from being counted. But it's not too soon to note the disturbing irony of the Bush campaign and Justice Antonin Scalia pointing to the equal protection clause as the reason not to count tens of thousands of ballots disproportionately cast by African Americans in Florida. The hand count ordered by the Florida Supreme Court was, in fact, the only small remedy for the massive violation of the promise of equal protection that happened in Florida on Election Day.

Can anyone deny that hundreds of thousands of Florida voters have already been denied the equal protection of the laws? Wasn't that what happened when voters in predominantly minority communities had to vote using antiquated machines that weren't properly maintained? When they were given misleading ballots with faulty instructions? When they had to brave police checkpoints to get to their polling stations? When polling stations were moved in the middle of the night? When minority voters' registration applications weren't processed and when longtime voters had their names illegally removed from the voting rolls?

And don't forget—while the state of Florida's election authorities did everything they could to place obstacles in the way of African American and other minority voters, other election officials in Florida were conspiring with the Republican Party to make sure that no matter what mistakes white Republican voters made on their absentee ballot applications, those voters would still get a ballot.

There were dozens of gross injustices in the Florida election. The huge number of undervoted ballots, concentrated in minority precincts across

Washington Post, final ed., December 12, 2000, p. A47. Reprinted with permission. The Reverend Jesse Jackson is president and founder of the Rainbow/PUSH Coalition. John Sweeney is president of the AFL-CIO.

Florida, was the only one for which there appeared to be a partial remedy—and that remedy was the recount ordered by the Florida Supreme Court on Friday. For all the rest—the police blockades and the midnight moves of polling places, the discriminatory purges—there is going to be no remedy.

Now it appears, from the words of Justice Scalia, that the only meaning of the equal protection clause is that there must be no remedy at all for those who have been discriminated against.

The final irony is that the equal protection clause was added to the Constitution of the United States after the Civil War for the express purpose of protecting African Americans against the efforts of state officials in Florida and other states of the South to deny emancipated slaves the equal protection of the laws. Now we are poised to have those fine, noble words become the excuse used not only to thwart the will of the people of the United States as to who should be president but to ensure that the efforts of state officials to disenfranchise the descendants of slaves will succeed.

There are lots of reasons for the Supreme Court to let the count continue—deference to the Florida courts' interpretation of Florida law and the sanctity of the right to vote and have that vote counted among them. But if it comes down for the justices to the 14th Amendment and the promise of equal protection, one can only hope for the sake of the country that they consider how not counting all the votes mirrors too closely the habits of heart and mind that brought us slavery and segregation—the original sins of our nation that the equal protection clause sought to repair. ▮

LARRY D. KRAMER

No Surprise. It's an Activist Court

The New York Times

The Supreme Court has reached out aggressively to solve the nation's election problem, inserting itself into a major political controversy. News commentators and legal experts seemed surprised when the court stepped into this thicket. They shouldn't have been.

Originally published in *The New York Times*, late ed., December 12, 2000, p. A33. Larry Kramer is a professor of law at New York University.

The Rehnquist Court has been using law to reshape politics for at least a decade. We keep hearing that it consists of "strict constructionists" who (as George W. Bush put it during the debates) oppose "liberal judicial activism." That's because conservative judicial activism is the order of the day. The Warren Court was retiring compared to the present one.

Warren Court activism was largely confined to questions of individual rights, mainly racial equality and the treatment of criminal defendants. The Rehnquist Court has been just as active in this domain. To list a few examples, it has disowned affirmative action, finding no difference between Jim Crow and laws designed to help disadvantaged minorities. It has overturned decades of jurisprudence that protected religious minorities from laws that intruded on their rituals. And it has all but eliminated the right to federal review of state criminal cases.

Individual rights are important, but they actually affect only a small portion of what government does. The real guts of our democracy lie in the system's structure and the way powers are allocated. And here the Warren Court was extremely deferential to other branches of government. Not so the Rehnquist Court, which has abandoned restraint in this area as well.

The court cast aside nearly 70 years of precedent in the area of federalism, holding that Congress cannot use its powers under the Commerce Clause or the 14th Amendment to regulate matters that touch on state interests, unless the court approves. It has declared, among other things, that Congress could not address violence against women, could not impose liability on state governments for age discrimination, could not hold states accountable for violating copyright laws and more.

But perhaps the most audacious instance of judicial activism is the way the court has extended the doctrine of judicial review itself. It was the Warren Court that first clearly established, in connection with school desegregation, that the Supreme Court has the final word about the meaning of the Constitution. Still, that court usually (though not always) gave great weight to the interpretations of other political actors. But the Rehnquist Court has no such inclination. Thus the court struck down the Religious Freedom Restoration Act because it was unwilling to give Congress the authority to provide greater protection to religious minorities than the court itself would give.

Many have viewed the court's actions as aimed at protecting states by limiting the federal government. But the Florida case shows that state governments get no more deference than other branches of government when they run afoul of the court's views of what the law ought to be. Judicial prerogative, it seems, not states' rights, has been at the heart of the Rehnquist Court's docket.

The court's confidence in its own supremacy may have propelled it to try to settle this presidential crisis. And if the court succeeds, the nation may well breathe a sigh of relief, grateful that someone brought this mess to a close. But the court's credibility will surely suffer. And if that diminishes a confidence that has begun to veer toward arrogance, this may not be such a bad thing. ▌

GEORGE F. WILL

Judicial Activism on Trial

The Washington Post

There was poetic justice—the prosaic sort is being deliberated by the Supreme Court as this is written Tuesday afternoon—in Monday's oral argument. The court was dragged into a new centrality in American politics by liberals' successful 1987 fight against the confirmation of Robert Bork. And Monday, Justice Anthony Kennedy, who occupies the seat for which Bork was nominated, asked the question which properly should have signaled checkmate against Al Gore's protracted search for a way to get a court to make him president.

The gravamen of Kennedy's question to Gore's lawyer, David Boies, was this: Suppose that, after the Nov. 7 election, Florida's legislature had made by statute the changes—new deadlines for recounting and certifying votes, selective re-counts, and so on—that Florida's Supreme Court made by fiat. Would that have violated the federal law that requires presidential elections to be conducted under rules in place prior to Election Day?

Boies, somewhat flummoxed, began his answer, "I think that it would be unusual. I haven't really thought about that question." Boies's admission that he had never thought about the large question of political philosophy involved in the Florida turmoil was altogether believable.

Given the spirit of contemporary liberalism, and given the culture of the trial lawyers' profession, in which the spirit of judicially driven liberalism is distilled to its essence, it indeed probably has never occurred to Boies that, in a republic, legislatures might have policy-making powers equal to, let alone superior to, those of courts. Recovering his equilibrium, Boies replied to Kennedy that, yes, it would be contrary to the federal law for Florida's legislature to have done what Florida's highest court did because that "would be a legislative enactment, as opposed to a judicial interpretation of an existing law."

Note well: Boies said it would have violated that federal "prior to Election Day" law if Florida's legislature had *created precisely the same post-election facts that Florida's court created.* This sad and awful month will be partly redeemed if it brings to a rolling boil a new chapter in America's political argument, a chapter concerning government by courts.

Until now, the central question in that argument has been: How much government do we want? For some while—at least since the New Deal—the basic answer has been clear: Lots of it. But now that question about the *quantity* of government should be supplanted at the center of political discourse by this question: What should be the principal *source* of government—the judiciary or the political branches?

This question, and the exchange between Kennedy and Boies, is, of course, also pertinent to the Constitution's Article II stipulation that "each state shall appoint" presidential electors "in such manner as the *legislature* thereof may direct" (emphasis added). Regarding this, Gore's lawyers argue, in effect, that the word "legislature" in Article II should be read as "the legislature, as its statutes are filtered through improvising state judges." Which brings us to an exchange between Boies and Justice Sandra Day O'Connor, who, like Kennedy, is often a swing vote on a court that last term produced 19 decisions by 5 to 4 margins.

When Boies, in a colloquy with Justice Antonin Scalia, said the U.S. Supreme Court has generally shown "deference to state supreme court decisions," O'Connor pounced. Citing Article II's presumption of the plenary power of state legislatures regarding presidential elections, she asked Boies this: Must not a state court, in interpreting a legislative act, "give special deference to the legislature's choices insofar as a presidential election is concerned?"

Boies again said that what Florida's Supreme Court did was "within the normal ambit of judicial interpretation" of the legislature's handiwork." But the problem with American governance today is what has become normal in the name of judicial interpretation. O'Connor replied:

"I'm sorry. You are responding as though there were no special burden [for state courts] to show some deference to legislative choices in this one context. Not when courts review laws generally, for general elections, but in the context of selection of presidential electors, isn't there a big red flag up there, 'Watch out'?"

But to Boies, his client the vice president and other advocates of liberalism by judicial fiat, the idea of deference to the political branches of government is like a red flag to a bull. What began in Florida as an argument about who will be the next president has become something much larger and more lasting—an argument about the proper sources of government in this republic. ▌

Commentary

DECEMBER 14, 2000 ...

N O V E M B E R	5	6	7	8	9	10	11	
	12	13	14	15	16	17	18	
	19	20	21	22	23	24	25	
	26	27	28	29	30	1	2	
	3	4	5	6	7	8	9	D E C E M B E R
	10	11	12	13	**14**	**15**	**16**	
	17	**18**	**19**	**20**	**21**	**22**	**23**	
	24	**25**	**26**	**27**	**28**	**29**	**30**	

FRANK CERABINO

A Place Forever Changed by Indecision 2000

The Palm Beach Post

In the end, this will be our story.

The gods who dole out notoriety and fame usually don't stop at our door, except for the occasional hurricane or Kennedy family mishap.

But this election has changed all that. Not only has it rewritten a nation's history. But it has rewritten ours as well.

Palm Beach County used to be a quiet backwater on the American continent, a place where refugees from Caribbean-island poverty and brutal North American winters sought shelter.

It was the land of proud grandparents and polo ponies, of lazy winter vacations, and the inexorable strain of suburbia pushing deeper into Florida's watery heart.

It was a place noted for both its number of golf courses and Viagra prescriptions, a comfortable place to both live and face whatever may come.

But it was never really the hub of a wheel that turned a nation.

Not until Nov. 7.

New York got the Subway Series. Miami got Elian. And Palm Beach County got this crazy presidential election, a dubious honor, at best.

What a surprise.

Sure, we could have listened to the political prognosticators.

For weeks before the election, we'd heard predictions that Florida would decide whether George W. Bush or Al Gore would be the next president, and that the Democrats hinged their chances in Florida on the turnout in Palm Beach and Broward counties.

But nobody predicted this. Nobody predicted that Election Day would turn into Election Month, and that the future of the country would be meted out in a hurricane bunker at the grubby intersection of Southern Boulevard and Military Trail in suburban West Palm Beach.

Baffling center of a baffling state.

Palm Beach Post, final ed., December 14, 2000, p. A25. Copyright 2000 The Palm Beach Post.

For once, America would stop seeing us for our palm trees, and start seeing us as the land of dimpled chads, butterfly ballots, and accidental Pat Buchanan voters.

The word "confused" would be the adjectival pilot fish we'd have to carry on our backs, as much a part of us now as the venerable early-bird special. And while we're at it, replace that image of a limousine cruising down Worth Avenue with a Ryder truck full of ballots heading up Florida's spine.

The world would come to know us as the baffling center of a baffling state, helplessly unprepared to overcome the dual limitations of our old technology and casual citizenship, which was expressed in tens of thousands of undecipherable votes.

We were the heels, the electoral Bill Buckners, who let the easy grounder go between our legs, turning a routine task into a disaster.

And we were the victims, victims of an alignment of events and election night surprises that pushed us into the spotlight when it mattered most. Other Florida counties would pop up with issues and irregularities of their own. But no other place in America seemed to sustain the drama of the election more than here.

Nowhere else were ballots counted longer, and in the end, no place seemed to count more for the candidate's election hopes than Palm Beach County.

We provided the nation with the visuals: from the pack of angry condo women griping on MSNBC, to Jesse Jackson's street march up Flagler Drive. From county canvassing board Chairman Charles Burton squinting up at a ballot card, to the infamous butterfly ballot, which has been reincarnated into everything from restaurant menus to full-page computer advertisements to jewelry.

And so the closest election in our history was like a coin standing on its edge, waiting for our gentle breezes to blow one way or another. And so we blew it.

It was a horrible position to be in, and no one among us had it worse than Theresa LePore, the Palm Beach County elections supervisor.

If you're looking for a compelling—and arguably, heroic—character in the "As the Election Turns" soap opera, it would be LePore.

The woman who came to be called Madame Butterfly never sought to trick or confuse the Democrats voting in her county. She had been working in the elections office since she was in high school, and after 28 years, she had come to be known as kind, quiet, and fair.

And yet, as the rubble settled on election night, her unintentionally confusing ballot design provided the most tangible "what if" across America.

What if all those tearful people hadn't voted for Buchanan in error? What if that confusion hadn't lead to some of the 19,000 ballots that were invalidated by double punches?

How could a Democrat like LePore bring this on the Democrats? Palm Beach County, assumed to be the Democrats' stronghold, had become its nightmare.

And this is where LePore's character became even more complex. Her job wasn't over on Election Day. She couldn't go on vacation and hide until the furor died down. She is one of the three members of the county canvassing board. That meant that she and Burton and County Commissioner Carol Roberts would eventually get to do a hand count of the county's ballots.

It would also mean she would have a chance to undo what was being called "the butterfly factor" in the election.

She had every reason to want to find more Gore votes during that recount. Converting questionable ballots into Gore votes would have quieted the "re-vote" protests going on outside her office.

Yet, LePore didn't do that. The all-Democrat canvassing board would ultimately disappoint Democrat partisans again, by converting relatively few questionable ballots to real votes.

In reviewing the ballots that were unreadable by the tabulation machine, the board converted only 8 percent of them into votes—far less than the 25 percent conversion rate the board in Broward County had found.

Why was Palm Beach County's all-Democrat board—and especially LePore—so conservative in its assessment on these ballots?

While Democrat partisans wonder whether Burton and LePore were really Republicans in disguise, a more noble—and ultimately uplifting explanation—is possible.

A fair shake for Bush.

George W. Bush had talked during the campaign about trusting people. And yet, his lawyers did everything they could to take the ballots out of the hands of the canvassing boards, fearing that Democrats would not give them a fair shake.

But that's what Bush got from Palm Beach County. A fair shake. From Democrats. And so, in the midst of our ridicule, there's something enobling to consider—and possibly even a lesson for a new president.

In a dispute where even U.S. Supreme Court justices had become predictable by party affiliation, there was one place where things didn't shake out according to the script.

The Democrats got thumped in Palm Beach County, not by Republicans, but by members of their own party.

A misdemeanor court judge and an elections supervisor in one of Florida's 67 counties didn't play their assumed roles. Burton and LePore may have hell to pay from their party.

But during a time when so many others just paid lip service to the idea of fairness, it might be here, in Palm Beach County, that something truly winning happened.

And that's why in the end, this will be our story. ∎

RICHARD A. EPSTEIN

Constitutional Crash Landing: No One Said It Would Be Pretty

The National Review

No one said that the end—for it is the end—of the interminable electoral dispute between Al Gore and George Bush would be pretty. And like everything else in this sorry affair, it turns out to have been ugly.

Pundits everywhere had hoped that this case could end with a unified showing in the United States Supreme Court so as to preserve its legitimacy and to promote that of the winner of the election, now George Bush. Instead we got a literal potpourri of decisions that can only confuse an electorate that has grown weary of this political circus, and only dismay academics who wished in a sense for something better.

As a political matter, the proper response should not be criticism of the arguments contained in the various opinions, but relief that the entire matter has come to its inglorious end. But this law professor has no special read of the pulse of nation, so he will revert to type and give an instant analysis of the legal arguments made in the case.

Up first is the five-vote conservative majority that brought the entire proceedings to an end by invoking the proposition that the erratic conduct of the recount, without any discernible guidance from the Florida supreme court, counted as a violation of the equal protection clause of the United

National Review Online, December 13, 2000. Reprinted with permission. Richard Epstein is a professor at the University of Chicago School of Law.

States Constitution. In one sense this result is odd, to say the least, because it is hard to identify which individuals were prejudiced by the errors, and which were not.

This is not a case like the equal-protection voting rights cases that led to the "one man, one vote" disputes of the 1960s. There it was clear that folks in rural counties had far greater clout in the state legislators because their small districts had equal power with the larger districts carved out for urban voters. The argument there was, quite simply, if it takes 10,000 votes to elect a legislator in the rural areas and 100,000 votes to elect a legislator in the urban areas, then the dilution of the urban votes leads to a systematic distortion of the electoral process that places excessive political power in the hands of a small minority. No political solution is possible because the ill-constituted legislature has no incentive to reform itself. Our situation is quite different because here the individuals who did not punch through the chads did not need reapportionment to participate in the election. They just had to read the instructions contained on their ballots.

At various points, the five-member majority also hinted that these erratic procedures could count also as a violation of due-process guarantees. But once again they engaged in elliptical constitutional interpretation. The due-process clause provides that no state shall deprive any person of life, liberty or property, without due process of law. The vote therefore has to be regarded as a form of liberty or property, which is a nice interpretive question of its own. But even if it is, the case founders on the same problem as before in that it is not possible to find any systematic deprivation of that right by the state. No person was excluded from the polls. None had his ballot rejected for improper reasons. The voter who does not punch through only has himself to blame. The arbitrariness of the recount procedure is not easily tied to some violation of an individual right.

The case in my view goes a lot better as a structural case, one which holds that the odd interpretations of Florida law by the Florida supreme court were so far off the mark that they counted as judicial legislation. Once that is established, then the constitutional violation is easier to make out. Electors are to be chosen in the manner designated by the state legislature, and not by a Jerry-built procedure created by a state supreme court that make things up on the fly.

Justice Ginsburg in her dissent strongly disputed the charge that the Florida court engaged in lawless acts of judicial legislation. She noted that although she might agree with their interpretation, they fell within some established zone of reasonableness. In making that analysis, she confined her attention solely to the issues in dispute in the second Florida court opinion: what counts as a "legal ballot," what is meant by "rejection." In her view, the Florida court was within reason when it said that "the rejection of a legal vote" means a failure to count dimples that express a voter's intention, even though it looks from the statute far more plausible to assume that it meant what was said: the refusal to allow people eligible to vote to cast their ballots.

But it is not just that last element in the case that provokes consternation with the performance of the four-member majority in Florida. Rather, the entire process suggests that the Florida court really did go off the rails in ways that lend a lot of strength to the concurrence written by Chief Justice Rehnquist, which Justice Scalia confirmed.

In a nutshell the difficulties began with the question of who controls the recount process. Here the right answer is that, for the first week, control rests in the canvassing boards. But what counts as a recount? It was at this point that the case first went off the rails. The right interpretation of that conception is that one looks at the ballots by hand to see if they were correctly read by the machine. By that standard light has to shine through the ballot so that the dimples are out as a matter of law. That said, it becomes easy to complete the recount in time, and the outcome does not change from Bush to Gore. But once the Gore people started to pressure the local canvassing officials to broaden the purpose of the recount, then we were off to the races. Now it takes a long time to decide whether dimples count, and if so which ones.

The arbitrariness of the process thus became built-in at the ground floor.

The secretary of state, Katherine Harris tried to use her discretion to stop this exercise, but was rebuffed by the Florida supreme court which extended the recount process and authorized a use of some expansive standard of what counts as a legal vote. But it did not say what that standard was. One oddity of the equal protection argument is that the Florida supreme court could have pulled off its electoral coup if it had said, flat out, that "all dimples count"—for now there is a uniform standard throughout Florida that skirts the equal-protection problem, even if it represents a radical shift in the rules of the game after the race has been won. When its maneuvers got slapped down the first time in the Supreme Court, the case then went into the contest phase (that is, the legal proceedings after the certification). It was here that it became evident, at least to this observer, that the four-member majority of the Florida supreme court overstepped its boundaries.

A contest is a trial at which sides have to present evidence in accordance with law. But what the Florida supreme court ordered was a continuation of the recount under the guise of a contest resolution. In so doing it, it refused to give the Bush forces any chance to challenge the broad definition of a vote that was used in Broward County and, to a lesser extent, in Palm Beach County.

It is impossible to say that we have a trial from scratch and then to turn around and to hold without any hearing at all that one side's case need never be heard. Worse still, the Florida majority then ordered recounts everywhere else. There was no hint of recognition that the contest phase of an election dispute requires more than a recount: the folks who collect this information have to become fact witnesses, subject to cross-examination and the like. By putting the issue in this fashion, the Florida supreme court, in effect, confused protests with contests, and eliminated the contest phase altogether.

And by appointing Judge Terry Lewis to oversee what was in essence the continuation of the recount, it in effect usurped the function of the secretary of state and short-circuited its own contest rules. That strikes me as a pretty substantial deviation from the legal norm. The Article II arguments look therefore stronger than the equal protection arguments. If they are correct, the proper remedy was not to continue the stay, which allows this case to end in a kind of judicial limbo. It should have been to certify the second machine count, ensuring that the entire Florida procedure received the decent burial it deserved. ∎

E.J. DIONNE JR.

So Much for States' Rights

The Washington Post

A narrow ideological majority on the U.S. Supreme Court has made George W. Bush our next president. A decent patriotism requires all of us to hope—and those of us so inclined to pray—that Bush's four years in office will be successful for our country.

But a robust patriotism demands that we never forget how he achieved office, in order to make sure that this terrible venture away from the territory of democracy never happens again. And a genuine patriotism does not

Washington Post, final ed., December 14, 2000, p. A35. © 2000, The Washington Post Writers Group. Reprinted with permission.

require anyone to accept the logic of five Supreme Court justices who clearly contorted their own principles and created new law to achieve this result.

The most troublesome aspect here is not that the five most conservative appointees on the court ruled in favor of the Republican presidential candidate. It is that the same five chose to intrude in Florida's election process having always claimed to be champions of the rights of states and foes of "judicial activism" and "judicial overreach."

It is nearly grotesque that the majority opinion invoked the equal protection doctrine to stop a recount whose very purpose was to move more closely toward equal protection of all those voters—many of them poor and members of minority groups—who may have lost their ballots because of unreliable voting equipment.

It is amazing, as well, that the court showed an admirable concern for the need to count "overvotes" (ballots on which more than one candidate was chosen) as well as "undervotes"—and then offered absolutely no remedy for either. Because the Florida court didn't fix all of the problems, the Supreme Court majority chose to block its efforts to fix any of the problems.

"Ideally, perfection would be the appropriate standard for judging the recount," Justice Ruth Bader Ginsburg wrote in her brilliantly stinging dissent. "But we live in an imperfect world, one in which thousands of votes have not been counted. I cannot agree that the recount adopted by the Florida court, flawed as it may be, would yield a result any less fair or precise than the certification that preceded that recount."

By the logic of the majority, the entire election in Florida could have been thrown out, since the certified result already includes a mix of counting methods. But that wouldn't have helped Bush.

And suddenly, there is this touching bit of judicial restraint: "Our consideration is limited to the present circumstances, for the problem of equal protection in election processes generally presents many complexities." No kidding. But not so many as to stop the Supreme Court majority from doing the one thing that will prevent our knowing in a timely way who really won Florida.

Justices David Souter and Stephen Breyer shared the majority's concern for equal protection, but they dissented sharply when it came to stopping the count. They held what seemed on this day to be an exotic principle: The high court couldn't condemn a lower court and then offer it no opportunity to right a perceived wrong.

"There is no justification for denying the state the opportunity to try to count all disputed ballots now," wrote Justice Souter. Justice Breyer called the majority's bluff by pointing out how sweeping, interventionist and activist its ruling really was, when he wrote that "the majority's reasoning would seem to invalidate any state provision for a manual recount of individual counties in a statewide election." So much for states' rights.

And just to make sure its decision left the bitterest possible taste in the mouths of those who disagreed with it, the majority that had abruptly stopped the recounting of ballots on Saturday afternoon on the theory that Al Gore would suffer no "irreparable harm" proved the opposite. Oops, said the majority, sorry, that Dec. 12 deadline Gore's lawyers were worried about is upon us. It's too late to have a recount that "comports with minimal constitutional standards."

Bush, with lots of help from the nation's highest court, was allowed to run out the clock in what is not supposed to be a mere game. This court majority has handed Bush the presidency in a way that can only make an excruciating job even more difficult.

The great conservative writer Robert A. Nisbet wrote long ago about the difference between "power" and "authority." Power, he said, is "based upon force." Authority is "based ultimately upon the consent of those under it." In a democracy, we recognize the authority even of leaders with whom we disagree because we accept the legitimacy of the process that got them there. Bush now has power. He will have to earn authority. ∎

MICHAEL W. MCCONNELL

A Muddled Ruling

The Wall Street Journal

The U.S. Supreme Court defied predictions of a partisan split. Seven justices joined in a decision holding that the manual recount, as ordered by the Supreme Court of Florida, would be unconstitutional. That achievement is a tribute to the institution. Special credit goes to Justices Stephen Breyer and David Souter, who must have felt ideological tugs to decide in Al Gore's favor. They join an honor roll of liberal Democratic judges in

Wall Street Journal, December 14, 2000, p. A26. Reprinted from *The Wall Street Journal* © 2000 Dow Jones & Company, Inc. All rights reserved. Michael McConnell is the Presidential Professor of Law at the University of Utah College of Law.

Florida who put the law ahead of what must have been a strong partisan temptation.

On the radio, I have heard this decision described as "sharply split." But it was not. To be sure, the justices divided on the issue of remedy, but on the central question of whether to affirm or reverse the Florida Supreme Court, they were close to unanimous.

That 7-2 decision rested on a simple premise: If there is going to be a manual recount, it should be conducted properly. It is not permissible for some counters to treat unperforated ballots as votes, and others as nonvotes. Nor is there any apparent reason to count undervotes but not overvotes. And the Florida court's decision to certify dubious results from Broward County and the most heavily Democratic precincts of Miami-Dade, without any judicial scrutiny, had no legitimate justification. Any of these errors might be of sufficient magnitude, in so close an election, to swing the result. It is no surprise that seven justices of the Supreme Court would hold that a recount under these conditions is unlawful.

To be sure, there are good arguments that there should not have been a manual recount at all. The Florida Supreme Court's ruling involved substantial alteration of the voting scheme as set forth in the Florida election code. Only "legal votes" may be counted, and the most straightforward definition of a "legal vote" is one that was in compliance with the clear voting instructions.

Moreover, the Florida statutes entrust the primary responsibility for vote counting to county boards, subject to the supervision of the secretary of state, with judicial review to ensure that they have not abused their discretion. For the state supreme court to transfer this authority to the courts was a significant change.

Finally, the Florida law clearly states that if a manual recount is ordered, it must include "all ballots." This is an important safeguard against cherry picking. Yet the Florida court ordered a manual recount only of the undervotes.

Ordinarily, these would be issues of state law, on which the state courts are the final authority. But Article II, Section 1 of the U.S. Constitution, which provides that electors must be chosen in the manner directed by the state legislature, requires federal review to ensure that the state courts have followed the mandates of the state legislature, instead of their own preferences on election procedures. This issue is a federal question in the unique circumstance of the choice of electors. George W. Bush's lawyers made a powerful case that the Florida ruling violated that standard.

But only three justices—William Rehnquist, Antonin Scalia, and Clarence Thomas—were ultimately persuaded by the Article II argument. The majority rested entirely on the theory that the recount, as ordered by the Florida court, would violate the equal protection of the laws by failing to provide a uniform standard for vote counting, by counting some over-votes and not others, and by failing to recount the challenged results in Broward and Miami-Dade. That rationale was sufficiently uncontroversial to command widespread assent among the justices—even those presumably favorable to Mr. Gore.

It was far from clear, however, what the high court could do, at this late date, to correct these problems. The Florida Supreme Court placed the U.S. Supreme Court in a very difficult position by ordering a recount, without constitutionally adequate safeguards, at the latest possible date. Conducting a recount under proper standards would take time. Certainly, a recount would prevent the state from meeting Tuesday's deadline for "safe harbor" treatment under federal law. Indeed, it appears all but impossible that the court could have completed a proper recount by the constitutional deadline of Dec. 18, when the electors meet and vote.

Some of the dissenting justices blamed this delay on the Supreme Court's grant of a stay. But that is unfair. Even if there had been no stay, the recount would have to start afresh, and under proper standards. The stay had nothing to do with it. The real cause of the delay was a series of decisions by the Florida Supreme Court. The first was its Nov. 21 decision to reduce the contest period by eight days to permit more recounting prior to certification. The second was its failure to initiate the statewide recount weeks ago, when there was still time to do so on an orderly basis.

The third was its decision, last Friday, to proceed without constitutionally adequate standards. Mr. Gore deserves some of the responsibility for these decisions, since in each case he got what his lawyers had asked for in court.

The question of remedy is the troubling aspect of the decision. The five justices in the majority held that, since there is no time to complete a proper recount by Dec. 12, all recounting must end. Justices Breyer and Souter argued that the real deadline is Dec. 18, and that the court should remand for the Florida court to decide whether to try to accomplish a recount by that time.

As a matter of federal law, Justices Breyer and Souter have the better argument. The Dec. 12 "deadline" is only a deadline for receiving "safe harbor" protection for the state's electors. A state is free to forego that benefit if it chooses. The majority opinion responded that the Florida court itself had treated Dec. 12 as the operative date for concluding the vote count. That's true. Indeed, in its first decision, the Florida court calculated the time allowable for recounting votes by counting backward from Dec. 12. Nonetheless, the decision is one for the state to make. It would have been the better course, as a federal court, to remand.

It would also have been the better course politically. Such a disposition would have maintained the 7-2 majority for the entire holding, which the American public would find vastly more reassuring. To be sure, it is probably impossible to conduct a proper recount by Monday, but by cutting off the possibility, the court encouraged critics to blame the court majority—rather than the passage of time—for the outcome.

Worst of all, this combination—approving a manual recount under proper standards, but forbidding the state to conduct a recount because of time constraints—deprives Mr. Bush of the clarity of victory that he must surely desire.

If the court had held that no manual recount was permitted, as the three conservatives suggested, the dispute would be over. The decision would have been controversial, but it would have provided closure. If there had been a recount under proper standards, many objective observers predicted that Mr. Bush would have been confirmed the winner, maybe even by a wider margin. Mr. Gore's best hopes for victory lay in getting votes recounted only in the most Democratic counties by Democrat-dominated boards subject to variable standards.

In a fair recount, Mr. Bush would most likely have emerged the winner, with enhanced public confidence in the results. As it is, the election ends by the clock. Many of the vice president's supporters will continue to believe—probably to their graves—that their man would have won if only they had been given more time.

The court did not have the resolution to declare that no recount was necessary, or the patience to declare that a proper recount should proceed. That means, unfortunately, that Mr. Bush will take office under conditions of continued uncertainty. I do not think that part of the decision did him, or the nation, a favor. ▌

ERIC FONER

Partisanship Rules

The Nation

The Supreme Court decision effectively handing the presidency to George W. Bush reveals the intensely partisan nature of the Court's current majority. The Court, to be sure, has always been political, but rarely as blatantly as today. Nor are there many precedents for Justices trampling on their own previous convictions to reach a predetermined conclusion.

Chief Justice Roger Taney enlisted the aid of President-elect James Buchanan in persuading Northern Justices to join the pro-slavery majority in *Dred Scott.* Franklin Roosevelt conferred regularly with Justice Louis Brandeis, and Justice Abe Fortas served as a trusted political adviser of Lyndon Johnson. But never has there been a public statement as partisan as Antonin Scalia's when first suspending the recounts that the Court needed to insure "public acceptance" of a Bush presidency.

If there is a silver lining, it is that the last month suggests an agenda for democratic reform. First, the Electoral College should be abolished. The product of an entirely different political era, when the electorate excluded women, nonwhites and propertyless males, the Electoral College was created by a generation fearful of democracy. Its aim was to place the choice of President in the hands of each state's most prominent men, not the voters. It unfairly enhances the power of the least populous states and can produce the current spectacle of a candidate receiving a majority of the votes but losing the election. At the very least, electors should be chosen in proportion to the popular vote in each state.

Second, the Florida fiasco should lead to the reform of voting procedures. As with schools, roads and public services, the wealthiest districts have the best system of voting. The machines used in poor black precincts of Florida, the *Miami Herald* demonstrated, are so flawed that they are guaranteed to produce a larger number of spoiled or uncounted ballots than in affluent suburban areas.

The Nation, January 1, 2001, pp. 6–7 (on sale December 14, 2000). Reprinted with permission from the January 1, 2001 issue of *The Nation.* Eric Foner is DeWitt Clinton Professor of History at Columbia University.

One can only view with deep cynicism the Court majority's invocation of "equal protection" in rejecting a recount. Added to the Constitution in the Fourteenth Amendment after the Civil War, this language was intended to protect former slaves from discriminatory state actions and to establish the principle that citizens' rights are uniform throughout the nation. The current Court's concept of equal protection has essentially boiled down to supporting white plaintiffs who claim to be disadvantaged by affirmative action.

Nonetheless, by extending the issue of equal protection to the casting and counting of votes, the Court has opened the door to challenging our highly inequitable system of voting. Claims of unequal treatment by voters in poorer districts are not likely to receive a sympathetic hearing from the current majority. But *Bush* v. *Gore* may galvanize demands for genuine equality of participation in the democratic process that legislatures and a future Court may view sympathetically.

Equally difficult to accept at face value is the majority's disdain for the principle of federalism these very Justices have trumpeted for the past several years. Like the South before the Civil War, which believed in states' rights but demanded a fugitive-slave law that overrode the North's judicial and police machinery, today's majority seems to view constitutional principles as remarkably malleable when powerful interests are at stake.

The next time this Court turns down an appeal by a death-row inmate on the grounds that federalism requires it to respect local judicial procedures, the condemned plaintiff may well wonder why his claims do not merit the same consideration as those of the Republican candidate for President. ∎

MARY MCGRORY

Supreme Travesty of Justice

The Washington Post

The Supreme Court's decision to elect George W. Bush is a travesty. The best that can be said about it is that it might be marginally better for them to have the last word than for the panting Florida Legislature or the possessed House of Representatives.

Washington Post, final ed., December 14, 2000, p. A3. Taken from the "Mary McGrory" column by Mary McGrory. ©2000 Dist. by Universal Press Syndicate. Reprinted with permission. All rights reserved.

The majority opinion is all trees, a catalogue of technical and legal problems that makes it impossible for the voters of Florida to decide who won. The minority concentrated on the forest, the universal suffrage that is the bedrock of democracy. The majority hardly makes a pretense of seeking fairness or living up to the motto inscribed over its facade, "Equal Justice Under Law." It reinforces the widespread opinion that holds that Vice President Gore won Florida, or why else would the Bush forces have spent the last five weeks doing everything short of burning the ballots to stop a recount?

The majority, led by Justice Antonin Scalia, who might as well have been wearing a Bush button on his robes, did acknowledge, in a subordinate clause, that yes, the Constitution seems designed to "leave the selection of the President to the people through their legislatures"; all they did was to assume an "an unsought responsibility."

That is not so. They became involved on Nov. 24 through their own folly. They received the Bush complaint that the Florida Supreme Court had imperiled the Republic by ordering the recount of some 60,000 "undercounted" ballots. The U.S. Supremes stopped the recount, and instructed the Floridians to "clarify" their decision.

The Florida Supreme Court had confused their betters on the high bench by claiming that the right to vote is the supreme and sacred right for every citizen of a democracy. Scalia had taken satisfaction in reminding the country that the Constitution does not guarantee the right to vote for president, but only the chance to choose the state legislators who will pick the members of the electoral college.

Once they got into it, the justices realized they really didn't have the "federal question" that would justify their meddling. But the majority fell right into the Bush strategy of delaying until the new deadline was almost upon them. Then, in their late-night decision, they groaned, "Oh, dear, where did the time go?"

The court had institutional reasons to jump in. They could look good where everyone else had failed. But there were individual motivations, well known, which should have warned them away from politicking: Chief Justice William H. Rehnquist would retire if he could be sure of a Republican successor. Justice Scalia would like to become chief justice.

At Monday's hearings, Justice Sandra Day O'Connor, who often follows Scalia, complained that the Florida Supreme Court had dissed the real Supremes by failing to answer a question that had been put to them when the case was sent back for "clarification." It was pretty clear from the opinion, a belated reply from Tallahassee, that the Florida bench had followed its own statutes, which make a big deal about having everybody vote and every vote counted. Justice O'Connor sounded petulant: "It just seemed to . . . assume that all those changes in deadlines were just fine, and they'd go ahead and adhere to them."

At Monday's hearing, the divided court resumed its search for the elusive "federal question." Finally, the "equal protection" clause loomed up in the murk. Due to the bizarre quality of Florida's election supervision, ballots with dimpled chads were counted in some counties and were not in others. It seemed a promising line of questioning except it could open matters up to a national recount.

It was left to Justice John Paul Stevens, a native of Chicago, a city that, more than most, cherishes political reality, to sort out the casualties of a decision that tells Americans they have a situation they can do nothing about. Usually, "can't" is a fighting word. We went west, went to the moon. Can't count in time? Has Scalia ever seen a town on the Mississippi that when the river rises slings sandbags around the clock?

The decision, says Mario Cuomo, who was once offered a place on the court, was "a calamity." It's also an insult.

But Rehnquist, Anthony M. Kennedy, O'Connor, Scalia and his silent shadow, Clarence Thomas, would feel easier with another Bush picking their colleagues.

Stevens gave a stinging summary: "Although we may never know with complete certainty the identify of the winner of this year's presidential election, the identity of the loser is perfectly clear. It is the nation's confidence in the judge as an impartial guardian of the rule of law." ▮

LINDA GREENHOUSE

Another Kind of Bitter Split

The New York Times

The Supreme Court justices who drove off into the night on Tuesday left behind more than a split decision that ended a disputed presidential election.

Originally published in *The New York Times*, December 15, 2000.

They also left behind an institution that many students of the court said appeared diminished, if not actually tarnished, by its extraordinary foray into presidential politics.

They point to the contradiction between the majority's action in this case and those justices' usual insistence on deference to the states. The members of the majority appeared at pains to refute any suggestion that the court had intervened unduly by stopping the Florida recount on Saturday or by ruling Tuesday that it could not resume. It was "our unsought responsibility to resolve the federal and constitutional issues" in the case, the majority said in its unsigned opinion.

And Justice Clarence Thomas, a member of the 5-to-4 majority, told a group of high school students at the court today that "I have yet to hear any discussion, in nine years, of partisan politics" among the justices.

"I plead with you that, whatever you do, don't try to apply the rules of the political world to this institution; they do not apply," Justice Thomas said, adding, "The last political act we engage in is confirmation."

Be that as it may, the events of the last few days were jarring even for people who pride themselves on being realists rather than romantics about how the court works.

One federal judge, a Republican appointee who was a Supreme Court law clerk decades ago, said today that he had long since become accustomed to watching the justices "making it up as they go along." That aspect of the majority opinion, which he called analytically weak and untethered to precedent, did not particularly bother him, he said.

"But the very peculiar aspect" of the case, the judge said, was "why they made it up."

He added, "It just seemed so politically partisan."

Another federal judge, a Democrat with many close Republican ties, wondered openly in conversation today about what steps the Supreme Court could take to "rehabilitate itself."

The way the court structured and then released its opinion, just before 10 o'clock at night, added to the sense of unease. The justices gave no hint of a reason for the unprecedented late-night release—whether to avoid pushing Florida over the midnight "safe harbor" deadline for immunizing its electors from Congressional challenge, or perhaps out of fear that the explosive and highly divisive decision might leak overnight if the court waited until morning to announce it. No matter. It resulted in an hour or more of frantic confusion that the court did nothing to prevent or alleviate.

While the sight of network correspondents fumbling in the dark on the court plaza to make sense of the decision was deeply unsettling to viewers who urgently wanted to know whether the 2000 election was over, the fault this time was much more the court's than television's. The 65-page document omitted the usual headnote, the synopsis that accompanies opinions and identifies which justices voted on which side.

Furthermore, the opinion was labeled "per curiam," meaning "by the court," a label used by courts almost exclusively for unanimous opinions so uncontroversial as to not be worth the trouble of a formal opinion-writing process. There was no indication of what the vote actually was. The names of Justices Sandra Day O'Connor and Anthony M. Kennedy, one or both of whom was likely the author, did not appear anywhere on the document.

Unlike the Florida Supreme Court, whose spokesman, Craig Waters, became almost a cult figure for his uninflected but informative announcements of the court's opinions in the election cases, the United States Supreme Court does not authorize its public information staff to make public statements or give any guidance about the decisions.

Since the justices themselves skipped the usual oral announcement of a decision, which takes place in public session in the courtroom and includes the opinion's author summarizing its main points, there was no interpretive guide at all for the correspondents who had to dash off to their waiting cameras. The crux of the per curiam opinion, the conclusion that there was no time to conduct any further counting of the votes in Florida, came deep inside and was highlighted neither at the beginning nor at the end.

Among the most baffling aspects of the opinion was its simultaneous creation of a new equal protection right not to have ballots counted according to different standards and its disclaimer that this new constitutional principle would ever apply in another case. "Our consideration is limited to the present circumstances, for the problem of equal protection in election processes generally presents many complexities," the court said.

Joseph Goldstein, a Yale Law School professor who died this year, wrote in his book *The Intelligible Constitution* that the members of the court "have an obligation to maintain the Constitution, in opinions of the court and also in concurring and dissenting opinions, as something intelligible—something We the People of the United States can understand."

Mr. Goldstein wrote: "That the Constitution be intelligible and accessible to We the People of the United States is requisite to a government by consent."

The justices will not meet again until Jan. 5, the date for their next scheduled conference to review new and pending cases. The passions and pain revealed in Tuesday's opinions will undoubtedly have cooled by then; these are justices who are accustomed to both bitter division—often by the same 5-to-4 alignment—and to moving on to the next case.

But there is something different about *Bush* v. *Gore* that raises the question about whether moving on will be quite so easy. This was something more than a dispute rooted in judicial philosophy. In fact, as Prof. Suzanna Sherry of Vanderbilt Law School said today, had members of the majority been true to their judicial philosophy, the opinion would have come out differently.

"In the past, the 5-to-4 decisions have been jurisprudentially predictable," Professor Sherry said in an interview. "Some justices are for more federalism, some for less; some for more activism, some for less. Those are not political decisions. By and large, the opinions are consistent with consistent jurisprudential beliefs" and as such present little threat to the court's collegiality.

But in this case, Professor Sherry said, for conservatives "the politics and jurisprudence were in conflict." The conservative justices in the majority set aside their concern for states' rights, for judicial restraint, for limitations on standing, for their usual insistence that claims raised at the Supreme Court level have been fully addressed by the lower courts.

"There is really very little way to reconcile this opinion other than that they wanted Bush to win," Professor Sherry said. Those who oppose the decision, she said, are likely to conclude not only that it was a mistake but "a different kind of mistake, not just that they got the law wrong but that it exposed a different side of the court." ∎

ANTHONY LEWIS

A Failure of Reason

The New York Times

"How can I convince my students now that the integrity of legal reasoning matters?"

That was the despairing comment of one law professor after he read the per curiam opinion that spoke for five members of the Supreme Court. His reaction, widely shared among law teachers, points to the real failure of the decision that gave the presidency to George W. Bush.

Originally published in *The New York Times,* late ed., December 16, 2000, p. A19.

The problem is not so much that the court intervened in politics. It is that the majority's stated reasons for its decision were so unconvincing.

Courts have an obligation to persuade. Their power is legitimate only if they give reasoned arguments for what they do. By that standard, the decision in *Bush* v. *Gore* was a dismal failure.

The 5-4 majority decided that disparate standards for recounting ballots in different Florida counties denied voters the equal protection of the law and that there was no time to do a recount under a proper, single standard. Many have noted the irony in that conclusion: The Supreme Court itself, by stopping the recount on Dec. 9, helped run out the time.

But there is a further, even more damaging aspect to the Supreme Court's performance. When Governor Bush asked the Supreme Court to intervene for the first time, on Nov. 22, he raised the equal-protection question, among others. The court granted a review—but not on that question. It sent the case back to the Florida Supreme Court on Dec. 4 without a hint of the equal-protection problem, which could then have been resolved in ample time.

The Florida court could have gone ahead on its own to set a specific rule for all ballot counters, instead of using the vague statutory standard of "the intent of the voter." But if it had done so, the justices in Washington would surely have said that step was an improper change in the law.

The majority, deciding the case at 10 p.m. on Dec. 12, said time was crucial because an old federal law declares that any state certification of its electoral vote is valid if filed by Dec. 12. But states have often filed after Dec. 12, and many missed the date this year.

Would Florida give priority to filing by Dec. 12 or to making sure that its count was complete and fair? Florida statutes aim at both objectives. Which should prevail was a question of Florida law, not one to be made by the U.S. Supreme Court.

Prof. Michael W. McConnell, a legal conservative at the University of Utah College of Law, made just that point in *The Wall Street Journal*. "The Dec. 12 'deadline' is only a deadline for receiving 'safe harbor' protection for the state's electors," he wrote. "A state is free to forgo that benefit if it chooses. . . . The decision is one for the state to make."

For that reason, Professor McConnell said, it would have been better for the justices to leave the issue to the Florida court. And it would have been the wiser course politically, he said. Two dissenting justices, David Souter and Stephen Breyer, agreed that there were equal-protection problems, so a remand to see whether a recount could be carried out on a single standard by Dec. 18, when the electors are supposed to meet, would have been by a more convincing 7-2 vote.

The majority's rush to judgment has no credible explanation in the per curiam opinion. So the country is left with the impression that five justices acted as they did because they cared more about the result—ending the recount—than they did about the reasoning that would compel it.

A thoughtful British columnist, Philip Stephens of *The Financial Times,* said the ruling put "indelible stain on the court's always half-illusory reputation as honest guardian of the Constitution." Deciding a case of this magnitude with such disregard for reason invites people to treat the court's aura of reason as an illusion.

That would be a terrible price to pay. The Supreme Court must have the last word in our system because its role is essential to our structure of freedom. Preservation of the public respect on which the institution depends is far more important than who becomes president. ∎

SCOTT TUROW

A Brand New Game: No Turning Back from the Dart the Court Has Thrown

The Washington Post

When two candidates are separated by less than one ten-thousandth of the votes cast, resolution of the most minute ambiguities in the rules is likely to determine the outcome—as in fact it did in Florida. Yet despite the 24-hour-a-day analysis of the legal events as they were unfolding, the real costs to our legal system seem to have been lost in the shock of events. The wheels fell off.

Our courts, supposedly neutral institutions, lost their ability to function neutrally in the election free-for-all. In the end, even the U.S. Supreme Court jumped into the partisan fray. Surrendering neutrality will have long-lasting effects on the way the law—and judges—function. It is liable to leave a legacy of more openly political decision-making in our courts and make them less likely to fulfill their traditional role.

In some ways, American jurisprudence has been cushioning itself against this development for most of the last century. Despite the day-after denials by Chief Justice William Rehnquist and Justice Clarence Thomas that politics had any impact on the Supreme Court's decision last week, it has long been acknowledged that judges' political prejudices—both liberal and conservative—shape their decision-making. Legal Realism, the dominant school of jurisprudence in the 20th century, recognized that when judges are free to choose, they will fashion rules that mirror their own ideologies.

Given that reality, however, the Legal Realists—Justices Oliver Wendell Holmes, Benjamin Cardozo, Louis Brandeis and others—tried to erect a tradition that minimized the occasions when judges could do that. Judicial restraint, deference to legislation and strict adherence to procedural norms were some of the ways Realists sought to restrict judicial decision-making.

Legal Realism has been subject to furious debate, but for most practicing lawyers, it has been the received tradition.

The events in Florida proved how fragile the understanding about the limited role of judges could be. In the Sunshine State, partisanship in the legal process was like an infection, escalating as it grew. What resulted was a nasty series of begats: The excesses of Florida Secretary of State Katherine Harris drove the Florida Supreme Court to action, which in turn inspired the U.S. Supreme Court to step well beyond the lines it had long drawn for itself. And as the Realists had anticipated, once judges try to referee on the political battlefield, they become politicians themselves.

The path to open partisanship among legal decision-makers, while fresh, is worth reviewing. Harris, also the co-head of Gov. George W. Bush's Florida campaign, was empowered under Florida law to interpret state election code. She was called upon in this role when the Democrats demanded hand recounts in four predominantly Democratic counties after Bush's lead fell to a scant 327 votes once the automatic recount was completed on Nov. 9. Some of the decisions Harris made or endorsed, like adherence to the Nov. 14 date for counties to certify returns, had clear support in the statutes. Others, like the advice she gave to the counties that manual recounts could only take place to rectify machine errors, flew in the face of the plain language of the law. Taken together, though, Harris's actions were increasingly open to question because each had the effect of preventing the manual recounts, which the Bush campaign by then was trying to stop in federal court.

Even at that stage, the contestants on both sides were clearly counting on making allies of the courts, focusing on the venues where their party's appointees dominated. Bush went to federal court because it was the more certain path to Washington and the U.S. Supreme Court, while Vice President Gore chose the state route, counting on the Florida Supreme Court, which had a history of conflict with the Republican legislature, to stop Harris.

Watching raptly from the sideline, I felt sure that the Realist tradition would somehow prevent either of the courts from acting in ways that could be perceived as political. But when a circuit court judge in Tallahassee ruled that Harris had the discretion to ignore the hand counts in the final totals, the Florida high court was forced front and center. Should it have deferred to Harris, the politician chosen by Floridians to make these decisions? Many Legal Realists undoubtedly would say yes. But it is also a matter of fundamental fairness that an arbiter cannot have a stake in the outcome, and Harris's role in the Bush campaign was also well beyond the norm for an impartial interpreter of the law. In the end, the Florida Supreme Court unanimously overruled Harris and extended the deadline for the hand counts by five days.

Constitutional scholars of all stripes had predicted that the U.S. Supreme Court would follow the Legal Realist tradition of restraint and avoid politicizing itself by allowing the Florida high court to make the final decision about state law. They were wrong. The court in Washington accepted the case, and then, after looking over the precipice, wisely withdrew, vacating the Florida decision and asking that court to muse on various constitutional principles. But the remand carried a clear warning that the U.S. high court would not be so reluctant next time.

"Next time" unfortunately arrived on Dec. 8, when the Florida Supreme Court decided Gore's contest action aimed at forcing a hand count of undervotes. The dilemma faced by the Florida court was the institutional imperative against mixing in politics versus what six of the court's justices ultimately viewed as a clear error made by the trial judge, N. Sanders Sauls, in interpreting the law. The Florida high court decided 4 to 3 to order a count of undervotes throughout the state. Then, last weekend, the five conservative justices of U.S. Supreme Court answered Bush's call to arms.

I have no doubt that the U.S. Supreme Court's conservative majority viewed the Florida court as grossly partisan and deserving of a vigorous response, especially in light of the U.S. high court's moderation the first time. But in this dizzying tit-for-tat, the U.S. court's actions were probably the most wholly at odds with its own traditions, which are of special importance because that court, lacking any supervision, is the institution most vulnerable to charges of arrogance and abuse. I see little chance that history will not apply that judgment to the court's actions.

The court's decision a week ago to stay the hand count of undervote ballots was the most overtly politicized action by a court that I have seen in 22 years of practicing law. It was an act of judicial lawlessness that effectively terminated Gore's chance to win the presidency. It deviated so far from governing legal principles that Terrance Sandalow, a conservative legal scholar and former dean of the University of Michigan Law School, was quoted calling the decision "incomprehensible" and "an unmistakably partisan decision without any foundation in law." The court ignored the lower federal courts, which had four times rejected similar stay requests from the Bush campaign, because it could not prove that Bush would be irreparably harmed by the recounts.

Yet, Justice Antonin Scalia declared in support of the stay, "The counting of votes that are of questionable legality . . . threaten[s] irreparable harm . . . by casting a cloud upon what [Bush] claims to be the legitimacy of his election." Scalia's logic eludes me. The court itself could—and did—repair any harm by calling Bush the legitimate winner in its eventual decision. Far more important, the harm that Scalia identified—a belief that Bush did not actually win—is clearly protected by the First Amendment, which guarantees the right of Americans to think freely, especially about political questions.

By comparison, the court's oblique 5 to 4 decision last Tuesday night was more appropriate. Adhering to a more traditional role, the majority found the recount unconstitutional, mostly because there was no guidance as to what the Florida legislature meant in requiring ballot counters to discern, as the law requires, "the clear intent of the voter." But in accepting the "clear intent" argument, the court gave credence to a point it had deemed unworthy of consideration the first time Bush presented it. More important, the decision seemed the work of an angry combatant. The five justices of the majority refused to say that the Florida high court (rather than the legislature) ever had the authority to define "intent of the voter." By doing so, they prevented any eleventh-hour effort by that court to restart the recount.

And in the end, the majority emphasized that "our consideration is limited to the present circumstances." They were, in other words, not defining legal principles that could govern future disputes. Instead, they were simply deciding the election—and on the galling basis that there was not time enough to count correctly, despite the fact that it was the court itself that had held the ball while the clock ran out.

Even worse, perhaps, the court was unable to articulate any neutral principle that seems to justify Bush's victory—and that could be accepted by both sides. There was no "one man, one vote"; no "all men are equal"; not even a court declaration that our president-elect got the most votes in Florida. We were left only with, "Time's up." History will regard the past month as nothing but a raw power struggle in which Bush prevailed because he had more allies in the right places: in the offices of Florida's secretary of state and governor, in the state legislature, in the U.S. House of Representatives and in the U.S. Supreme Court.

More pressing is the problem posed by the high court's foray into politics. Even the much-maligned Warren Court never came close to picking a president. As the Legal Realists knew, such actions diminish courts, because they were not chosen for the job. I doubt the *Bush* v. *Gore* decision will seriously erode the authority of the court with average Americans. But its impact on those who live the law—lawyers and legislators—is likely to be far-reaching. Essentially, the Legal Realist compact has been shattered: We have been told that in the face of perceived political favoritism, neutral process and recognized boundaries for judicial action can properly give way to a decidedly political response.

Finally, the fiery logic of partisanship seems likely to continue in our courts. Lower courts, especially those inclined to decide in ways they believe the Supreme Court will favor, will be tempted to make decisions with a more openly political flavor. That means that we can expect reprisals whenever and wherever Democrats have their hands on the levers of judicial power. Unless there is sustained outcry from the legal profession calling for restoration of the boundaries we have known for a century, the reliability of our courts will remain uncertain for a long time to come. ▮

LANI GUINIER

A New Voting Rights Movement

The New York Times

What began as judicial overreaching may be a clarion call for major democratic reform. Some legal experts already argue that last week's United States Supreme Court decision, though heavily criticized for deciding an election, could help open the local courthouse doors to election reform.

Perhaps, given its new rhetoric about restoring citizen confidence in the outcome of elections, the conservative majority will now look closely at other suits based on the principle of equal protection—others that, like *Bush* v. *Gore*, challenge disparate treatment of voters in voting procedures. The more important effect of the court's choice of language, explicitly valuing no person's vote over another's, may be to launch a citizens' movement.

The one person, one vote language of the court under Chief Justice Earl Warren—language which the recent decision draws on—did exactly that, inspiring civil rights marchers in the 1960's. Current efforts could focus on creating new federal reforms, like financial assistance to poor counties to upgrade voting equipment and the elimination of all ways of recording votes that fail to give the voter feedback as to how his or her intent is being registered.

Also needed are meaningful assistance to semi-literate or non-English-speaking voters, 24-hour polling places and a national Election Day holiday. Enacting standards for federal elections is consistent with the Voting Rights Act, which has banned literacy tests nationwide as prerequisites for voting. That ban was passed by Congress in 1970 and unanimously upheld by the Supreme Court.

But reforms to equalize voting access, while important, are not enough. The circumstances of this election call for a larger focus on issues of representation and participation. If we are to build a genuine pro-democracy movement in this country, we cannot limit ourselves to butterfly ballots and chads.

A pro-democracy movement—needed now more than ever in the United States—would look seriously at forms of proportional representation that

Originally published in *The New York Times,* late ed., December 18, 2000, p. A27. Lani Guinier is a law professor at Harvard University.

could assure that Democrats in Florida (or Republicans in Democratic-controlled states) or racial minorities in all states are represented fairly in the legislatures themselves. The five-member Supreme Court majority allowed the interests of the Florida Legislature to trump any remedy to protect the rights of the voters. If legislatures are to enjoy such power, it is imperative for voters' voices to be reflected in fully representative legislative bodies.

That means that voters must have a more meaningful opportunity to participate in the entire democratic process—and not just on Election Day. Such an opportunity is not possible when the majority party holds a disproportionate amount of power over a heterogeneous citizenry, divided along racial and party lines, as is evident in the Florida Legislature. Recognizing the danger of majority legislative tyranny is crucial at a time when every state legislature will soon be engaged in the decennial task of redistricting.

Under current law, the members of the Florida Legislature can use their legislative authority to create winner-take-all districts to cement their power. The drawing of districts often becomes the real election. We cannot sustain the confidence of citizens to vote and participate beyond Election Day if we continue to allow election outcomes to be determined when the legislature draws districts.

A winner-take-all scheme in appointing a state's delegates to the Electoral College is similarly unfair. Florida gave all of its electors to President-elect Bush, even though, while he won a plurality of the popular vote in that state, he did not win a majority. A system that apportions a state's electoral votes based on the popular vote received by each candidate in that state would better reflect the will of all the voters.

Proportional voting—where the political parties gain seats in proportion to the actual percentage of votes won on Election Day—means everyone's vote counts toward the election of someone he or she voted for. In conjunction with other reforms, it makes voting the first step in a democratic system by which we, the people, not they—the court or the unrepresentative legislature—rule. ▌

DAVID TELL
for the Editors

The Bush Victory

The Weekly Standard

We have no trouble conceding that Al Gore's was an especially generous and gracious speech last Wednesday, in which the vice president conceded that he'd lost this year's election. All indications are, however, that Gore's supporters still cannot bring themselves to concede that George W. Bush actually *won* the election fair and square. All indications are, quite the contrary, that the any-more-than-fig-leaf legitimacy of Bush's victory is the one thing Gore's proponents remain quite intent to deny. They continue to insist, instead, that the vice president's extraordinary five-week post-election effort to thwart his opponent's claim on the White House was the soul of righteousness.

A righteousness so absolute, in fact, that in its defeat a vocal army of irredentist Goreophiles are now prepared to perceive a deep wound to the very idea of America. Their statements fill the front pages of the newspapers, and their op-eds fill the back. The manner in which George W. Bush will have acceded to the presidency is "contemptible." It is "immoral." It represents an abject "defiance of justice and common sense" and a "terrible venture away from the territory of democracy." And so forth.

In our view, this goes well beyond the merely delusional and far, indeed, into genuine irresponsibility, for many of the people making these claims are smart—smart enough to know better. As is the vice president himself. And yet he more than anyone has acted to encourage such furious derision of the nation's electoral decision-making. And so, given that the derision is being promoted on his behalf, he more than anyone should be expected to repudiate it. Which he has not done, and appears unwilling to do. For this reason, Gore's long-delayed fifteen minutes of gentle-manliness last Wednesday seems not enough to us.

It bears reviewing here, once again, what bizarre distortions of tradition and law and logic the vice president's attorneys, acting of course under his

Weekly Standard, December 25, 2000, pp. 9–10 (on sale December 18). Reprinted with permission.

authorization and direction, have proposed and accomplished in Florida these past five weeks. Gore finished second in that state's initial November 7 voting tally. Gore finished second in that state's automatic machine recount over the next few days. Gore would have finished second on November 14, Florida's statutory deadline for state certification of county-by-county returns. But three of the four counties whose election night numbers Gore had "protested" were not yet finished with their resulting recounts, so Gore's lawyers sought and secured a novel Florida Supreme Court "interpretation" of state law: The state's statutory seven-day deadline was meant to be nineteen days long.

By the time the nineteenth of these seven days arrived, Miami-Dade County had suspended its recount, Palm Beach County had still not completed its own, and the U.S. Supreme Court had unanimously vacated their deadline extension in any case—with a warning to the Florida court that it must be careful not to encroach on the state legislature's constitutionally derived plenary authority to determine how presidential electors should be chosen. Secretary of State Katherine Harris moved at last to certify the Florida popular vote. Al Gore was again in second place.

At which point he requested, and received from the Florida Supreme Court, a fifth opportunity to win. Elections in Florida work essentially as follows, David Boies informed the justices: State law requires tabulating machines to reject as invalid any ballot cast contrary to explicit instructions given every voter. State law nevertheless assumes that these machines, in the successful performance of this duty, will thereby produce an illegal result— for among the ballots they are required to reject will be ballots on which an "intent of the voter" can sometimes be magically discerned. And while state law might appear to have arranged for this "intent" to be ignored from the gitgo, way down deep the law cherishes it as necessary to democracy, and consequently hunts it to the ends of the earth. At least in a close election, that is, when the discretionary county-level manual recounts provided for by statute become mandatory, even though no one has ever realized it before.

The argument was ridiculous on its face, but a 4-3 majority of the Florida high court bought it anyway. Their earlier opinion had been entirely rejected by the U.S. Supreme Court. No matter: This subsequent ruling baldly reaffirmed, without comment, those portions of the rejected opinion most favorable to Al Gore's designs. The Florida court's earlier opinion had endorsed a construction of state law in which officially certified election tallies were accorded paramount importance in the determination of a winner. No matter there, either: This subsequent ruling rendered official certification a prac-

tical nullity—again, to Al Gore's advantage. The Tallahassee majority ordered revised tallies from three heavily Democratic counties included in
Florida's running total, though none of these numbers had ever been properly certified by the state. Results that *had* already been properly certified in
Florida's 64 other counties, the state Supreme Court now pronounced presumptively invalid, subject to a manual review of the "undervote" in each.
A review to be conducted by it doesn't really matter who, and according to
interpretive standards (a chad here, a dimple there) invented on a case-by-
case basis.

Last Tuesday, December 12, this ghastly plan, Gore's *sixth* grab for
Florida's electoral votes, was struck down by the U.S. Supreme Court, thus
ending the presidential election of 2000 once and for all. As thanks for this
piece of bravery, and as if to prove that's what it was, the High Court's majority has since been roundly excoriated by hardcore recountniks everywhere:
"partisan," "ideological," "chilling," "lawless," a "travesty," a "disgrace." But
interestingly enough, the bulk of this bitterness has not been directed against
the majority's reasoning. Seven justices concurred, after all, that the Florida
ruling warranted reversal. And none of the dissenting justices could convincingly explain how it was any longer feasible for Florida to fix its mistakes
and restart the recount—given that the Tallahassee justices had already twice
decreed that tabulation past December 12 would violate the law.

The real criticism now being leveled against the majority seems to be this:
Law or no law, the U.S. Supreme Court should have given the vice president
what he wanted *anyway.* "I cannot see," Justice Ruth Bader Ginsburg announced in her dissent, how a Gore-friendly last-minute recount, "flawed as
it may be, would yield a result any less fair or precise than the certification
[for Bush] that preceded that recount."

Needless to say, the vice president and his spokesmen and lawyers have
never acknowledged so naked a concern to "yield a result" in Florida. They
have been concerned instead, they want us to know, with principle. Gore allegedly won a plurality of the votes Floridians "intended" to cast on Election
Day. We should not conclude that their intention wasn't realized until every
last Florida ballot has been inspected by hand. For a vote is "a human voice,"
the vice president has reminded us. We "must not let those voices be si-
lenced," lest we silence "the American spirit in a very real way."

Well. Let's think about this "principle" for a moment. The vice president
and his supporters demanded a recount in just four of 67 counties in Florida.
They attempted to "yield a result," nothing more. In defense of which apparent cynicism, the Gore people respond that George W. Bush, too, could

have requested self-interested Florida recounts. But that response is actually a guilty plea, barely disguised. For what they are suggesting, if you look at it closely, is that in a tight statewide election that might determine the American presidency, the winner should be the fellow who campaigns best *after* the polls have closed—the fellow who games the system most effectively, the fellow whose agents are prepared to exploit its loopholes most unscrupulously. It should be this way just this once, at least. So that just this one Democratic candidate can win just this one presidential election.

This is no kind of "principle" at all, of course. We blame Al Gore for the fact that so many people are now prepared to pretend otherwise—and to cast aspersions on American democracy in the process. To mitigate this blame, he'll have to do even better than he did last Wednesday. ∎

JEFFREY ROSEN

The Supreme Court Commits Suicide

The New Republic

On Monday, when the Supreme Court heard arguments in *Bush* v. *Gore,* there was a sense in the courtroom that far more than the election was at stake. I ran into two of the most astute and fair-minded writers about the Court, who have spent years defending the institution against cynics who insist the justices are motivated by partisanship rather than reason. Both were visibly shaken by the Court's emergency stay of the manual recount in Florida; they felt naive and betrayed by what appeared to be a naked act of political will. Surely, we agreed, the five conservatives would step back from the abyss.

They didn't. Instead, they played us all for dupes once more. And, by not even bothering to cloak their willfulness in legal arguments intelligible to people of good faith who do not share their views, these four vain men and one vain woman have not only cast a cloud over the presidency of George

New Republic, December 25, 2000, p. 18 (on sale December 18). This article was posted online on December 14. Reprinted by permission of The New Republic, ©2000, The New Republic, Inc.

W. Bush. They have, far more importantly, made it impossible for citizens of the United States to sustain any kind of faith in the rule of law as something larger than the self-interested political preferences of William Rehnquist, Antonin Scalia, Clarence Thomas, Anthony Kennedy, and Sandra Day O'Connor.

This faith in law as something more than politics has had powerful opponents throughout the twentieth century. For everyone from legal realists and critical race theorists to contemporary pragmatists, it has long been fashionable to insist that the reasons judges give are mere fig leaves for their ideological commitments. Nevertheless, since its founding, *The New Republic* has resisted this cynical claim. From Learned Hand and Felix Frankfurter to Alexander Bickel, the editors of this magazine have insisted that, precisely because legal arguments are so malleable, judges must exercise radical self-restraint. They should refuse to second-guess the decisions of political actors, except in cases where constitutional arguments for judicial intervention are so powerful that people of different political persuasions can readily accept them. This magazine has long argued that the legitimacy of the judiciary is imperiled whenever judges plunge recklessly into the political thicket. And this has led editors of different political persuasions to oppose the judicial invalidation of laws we disagreed with as well as those we supported — from Progressive-era labor laws to the New Deal administrative state to laws restricting abortion and permitting affirmative action. In all these cases, we argued that judges should stay their hand. Our views about judicial abstinence have been those of Oliver Wendell Holmes: "If my fellow citizens want to go to hell, I will help them," he said. "It's my job." But in *Bush* v. *Gore,* as in *Dred Scott* and *Roe* v. *Wade,* the justices perceived their job differently. They foolishly tried to save the country from what they perceived to be a crisis of legitimacy. And they sent themselves to hell in the process.

The unsigned per curiam opinion in *Bush* v. *Gore* is a shabby piece of work. Although the justices who handed the election to Bush — O'Connor and Kennedy — were afraid to sign their names, the opinion unmasks them more nakedly than any TV camera ever could. To understand the weakness of the conservatives' constitutional argument, you need only restate it: Its various strands collapse on themselves. And, because their argument is tailor-made for this occasion, the conservatives can point to no cases that directly support it. As Justices John Paul Stevens, Ruth Bader Ginsburg, and Stephen Breyer wrote in their joint dissent, this "can only lend credence to the most cynical appraisal of the work of judges throughout the land."

What, precisely, is the conservatives' theory? "Having once granted the right to vote on equal terms, the State may not, by later arbitrary and disparate treatment, value one person's vote over that of another," they declare. The citation is *Harper* v. *Virginia Board of Elections,* the case that invalidated the poll tax in 1966 on the grounds that it invidiously discriminated against the poor. But there is no claim here that Florida's recount law, shared by 32 other states, discriminates against the poor. Indeed, Florida argued that its scheme is necessary to avoid discrimination against the poor, because a uniform system of recounting that treated the punch-card ballots used in poor neighborhoods the same as the optically scanned ballots used in rich ones would systematically undercount the votes of poorer voters. By preventing states from correcting the counting errors that result from different voting technologies, the conservatives have precipitated a violation of equal treatment far larger than the one they claim to avoid.

"The fact finder confronts a thing, not a person," write the conservatives in a clumsy and perverse inversion of the famous line from *Reynolds* v. *Sims,* the great malapportionment case, which noted that "legislators represent people, not trees." But things do not have constitutional rights; people have constitutional rights. It is absurd to claim that the "right" of each ballot to be examined in precisely the same manner as every other ballot defeats the right of each individual to have his or her vote counted as accurately as possible. Were this theory taken seriously, many elections over the past 200 years would have violated the equal protection clause, because they were conducted using hand counts with different standards. The effect of the majority's whimsical theory is to fan the suspicion, which now looks like a probability, that the loser of both the popular vote and the electoral vote has just become president of the United States. At least the ballots can sleep peacefully.

The conservatives can rustle up only two cases that purportedly support their theory that Florida's recount scheme gave "arbitrary and disparate treatment" to voters in its different counties: (Both were written in the 1960s by liberal activist Justice William Douglas, which must have given the conservatives a private chuckle.) The first case, *Gray* v. *Sanders,* held that Georgia's county-based scheme of assigning votes in the Democratic U.S. senatorial primary discriminated against voters in urban counties, whose votes were worth less than those in rural counties. The same logic, applied to this case, would hold that the Florida legislature could not adopt a county-based scheme for assigning votes in presidential elections. But this conclusion is completely inconsistent with the conservatives' earlier argument, the one that emboldened them to stop the manual recount in the first place: that

Article 2 of the Constitution allows the Florida legislature to structure its presidential electing system however it chooses. The second case, *Moore* v. *Ogilvie,* held that applying "a rigid, arbitrary formula to sparsely settled counties and populous counties alike . . . discriminate[d] against the residents of the populous counties of the State in favor of rural sections." That case, in other words, does not support the conservatives' claim that ballots in rural and urban counties must be counted and recounted in precisely the same manner. It suggests the opposite.

The reason the conservatives can find not a single precedent to support their equal protection theory is because the theory is made up for this case only. But the damage is not so easily limited. The Supreme Court has called into question not only the manual-recount procedure adopted by the legislature of Florida but our entire decentralized system of voting—in which different counties use different technologies to count different ballots designed differently and cast at different hours of the day. In addition to throwing the presidential election and destroying the legitimacy of the Supreme Court, *Bush* v. *Gore* will spawn an explosion of federal lawsuits after every close election, lawsuits arguing that different counties used different ballot designs and voting systems and counted the ballots in different ways.

In this way, *Bush* v. *Gore* is a ludicrous expansion of cases like *Shaw* v. *Reno,* in which the same five-member conservative majority, led by the addled and uncertain Sandra Day O'Connor, held that federal courts must second-guess each legislative exercise in state and federal redistricting to decide whether or not race was the "predominant purpose" in drawing district lines. The idea that this usurpation of our democratic electoral system by the federal judiciary has been precipitated by a group of conservatives who once posed as advocates of judicial restraint and champions of state legislatures can only be met with what the legal scholar Charles Black called the sovereign prerogative of philosophers: laughter.

But the majority asks us not to worry about the implications of its new constitutional violation. "Our consideration is limited to the present circumstances, for the problem of equal protection in election processes generally presents many complexities, the justices write. It certainly does. But a mobilized nation is now far less likely to tug its collective forelock and wait for the preening O'Connor and Kennedy to sort out the confusion on our behalf. We've had quite enough of judicial saviors.

In a poignant attempt to split the difference between the two camps, Justices Breyer and David Souter tried to prevent the Court from destroying itself. They agreed that applying different counting standards to identical ballots in the same county might violate the equal protection clause, and they proposed sending the ballots back to Florida and letting its courts apply a uniform counting standard. But their attempt at statesmanship was crudely rejected by O'Connor and Kennedy, which left Breyer and Souter with their hands extended, played for dupes like everyone else who naively believed the conservatives were operating in good faith. "Because the Florida Supreme Court has said that the Florida Legislature intended to obtain the safe-harbor benefits of 3 U.S.C. Sec. 5," O'Connor and Kennedy wrote in the tortuous punch line of their opinion, "Justice Breyer's proposed remedy—remanding to the Florida Supreme Court for its ordering of a constitutionally proper contest until December 18—contemplates action in violation of the Florida election code." With this feint at deference to the state court at precisely the moment there was nothing left to defer to, the jig was up. O'Connor and Kennedy had converted the Florida court's passing reference to the federal law telling Congress which electoral slate to count in the event that a controversy was resolved before December 12 into a barrier, now mysteriously embedded in state law, that prevented the Florida Supreme Court from completing manual recounts after December 12. And for the Court to announce this rule at ten o'clock at night on December 12, after having stopped the count two precious days earlier, only added to the gallows humor.

It will be impossible to look at O'Connor, Kennedy, Scalia, Rehnquist, and Thomas in the same light again, much as it was impossible to look at President Clinton in the same light after seeing him exposed in the Starr Report. But this time the self-exposure is also a little bracing. Conservatives have lectured us for more than 30 years about the activism of the Warren and Burger Courts. Those tinny and hypocritical lectures are now, thankfully, over. By its action on December 12, the Supreme Court has changed the terms of constitutional discourse for years to come. Just as *Roe* v. *Wade* galvanized conservatives a generation ago to rise up against judicial activism, so *Bush* v. *Gore* will now galvanize liberals and moderates for the next generation. But, unlike the conservative opponents of *Roe*, liberals must not descend to the partisanship of the current justices; they must transcend it. The appropriate response to *Bush* v. *Gore* is not to appoint lawless liberal judges who will use the courts as recklessly as the conservatives did to impose their sectarian preferences on an unwilling nation. The appropriate response, instead, is to appoint genuinely restrained judges, in the model of Ginsburg and Breyer, who will use their power cautiously, if at all, and will dismantle the federal judiciary's imperious usurpation of American democracy.

Those of us who have consistently, if perhaps naively, opposed liberal and conservative judicial activism throughout the years can now point to *Roe* and *Bush* as two sides of the same coin. (How fitting that Bush is now a dubious president and a dubious precedent.)

In his dissent in *Casey* v. *Planned Parenthood,* the abortion case that reaffirmed *Roe* in 1992, Scalia recalled the portrait of Chief Justice Taney that hangs in the Harvard Law School library. Taney had led a bitterly divided Supreme Court to strike down the Missouri Compromise; but, instead of saving the nation from its partisan divisions, his reckless intervention precipitated the Civil War:

> There seems to be on his face, and in his deep-set eyes, an expression of profound sadness and disillusionment. Perhaps he always looked that way, even when dwelling upon the happiest of thoughts. But those of us who know how the luster of his great Chief Justiceship came to be eclipsed by *Dred Scott* cannot help believing that he had that case—its already apparent consequences for the Court and its soon-to-be-played-out consequences for the Nation—burning on his mind. I expect that two years earlier he, too, had thought himself "call[ing] the contending sides of national controversy to end their national division by accepting a common mandate rooted in the Constitution." It is no more realistic for us in this litigation, than it was for him in that, to think that an issue of the sort they both involved . . . can be "speedily and finally settled" by the Supreme Court. . . . Quite to the contrary, by foreclosing all democratic outlet for the deep passions this issue arouses, by banishing the issue from the political forum that gives all participants, even the losers, the satisfaction of a fair hearing and an honest fight, by continuing the imposition of a rigid national rule instead of allowing for regional differences, the Court merely prolongs and intensifies the anguish.

Who would have dreamed that in describing Taney's portrait Scalia imagined his own? ▌

THE EDITORS

Unsafe Harbor

The New Republic

Healing? Sure. American culture requires it, and so do the careers of American politicians. But healing is also a part of the strategy of the Republican larcenists, in and out of robes, who arranged to suppress the truth about the vote in Florida and thereby to make off with the election of 2000. Having satisfied their lower impulses, they are counting on us to act on our higher impulses, and to come together. Well, we cannot come together, at least not yet, because we have just been driven apart. The rupture is real, and it demands to be analyzed. After what happened at the Supreme Court on December 12, anger is a mark of analysis.

The casuistry of William Rehnquist, Antonin Scalia, Clarence Thomas, Sandra Day O'Connor, and Anthony Kennedy—this was a 5-4 decision, not a 7-2 decision, as some Republican spinners would have us believe, on the utterly false assumption that every justice who acknowledged the chaos in the standards of counting concurred in shutting the counting down—will be exposed by scholars of the law. We will leave it to them to demonstrate, for example, that the "safe harbor" provision in Florida law has no constitutional stature, that an extension of the deadline for a fair and methodologically consistent tally of all the votes of Florida would not have violated Article 2 of the Constitution. We insist instead that the election of the president of the United States by the Supreme Court of the United States needs to be regarded not only legally, but also morally and historically. And morally and historically speaking, we have witnessed an outrage.

The Orwellian character of the majority opinion in *Bush* v. *Gore* is plain from even a cursory reading. The justices cite precedents affirming "the one man, one vote basis of our representative government," and then they proceed to nullify the votes of thousands of men and women. They castigate the contest provision of the Florida Supreme Court for failing to "sustain the confidence that all citizens must have in the outcome of elections," and then they proceed to shatter the confidence that all citizens must have in the outcome of elections. They protest that "none are more conscious of the vital

New Republic, December 25, 2000, p. 9 (on sale December 18). Reprinted by permission of The New Republic, ©2000, The New Republic, Inc.

limits on judicial authority than are the members of this Court," and then they proceed to extend judicial authority into the very heart of American politics—an extension so vast and so unprecedented that it can only be described as un-American.

Are the justices, then, hypocrites? Alas, they are not. They are—*sub silentio,* as they might say—Republicans. This ruling was designed to bring about a political outcome, and it is an insult to the intelligence of the American people to suggest otherwise. There was a basis for the suspicion about the politicization of the Supreme Court already on December 9, in the startling decision to grant the stay that George W. Bush desperately needed. That decision was 5-4; and those who clung to the fine conviction that politics stopped at this chamber's door were hoping that the partisan split would not reproduce itself in *Bush* v. *Gore,* when the integrity of the American system of government hung in the balance. But it did. Not even O'Connor and Kennedy, the most illustrious open minds in America, opened their minds.

Dissolve to Philadelphia on July 25, 1787. On that Wednesday morning the Constitutional Convention took up the question of how the executive in the American republic was to be elected. In his notes on the debates, James Madison recorded his own opinion of the matter. "The election must be made either by some existing authority under the National or State constitutions—or by some special authority derived from the people—or by the people themselves. The two existing authorities under the National Constitution would be the Legislative & Judiciary. The latter he presumed was out of the question." It now appears that he should have made no such presumption. And so it will be that George W. Bush's presidency will forever be haunted by James Madison's ghost. Constitutionally speaking, this presidency is ill-gotten. It is the prize of a judicial putsch.

Needless to say, James Madison will not keep George W. Bush awake at night. But there is something else that should trouble the vacant and victorious man's sleep. There are all those sealed metal boxes in the Sunshine State, the ones upon which the Supreme Court does not want the sun to shine, the ones that hold the dimpled and undimpled instruments of the people's will. It is very likely that those ballot boxes contain an arithmetical secret that could cast doubt upon the legitimacy of his electoral success. After all, everything that Bush and his minders have said and done since November 7 has been premised on a terror of the contents of those boxes, a frantic fear of what they might reveal, which is that George W. Bush won the election but Al Gore won the vote. And the Supreme Court of the United States has made itself a party to this dread of the democratic truth.

We disrespectfully dissent. ▌

NELSON LUND

An Act of Courage: Under Rehnquist's Leadership, the Court Did the Right Thing

The Weekly Standard

Generations of law students have learned that the U.S. Supreme Court should avoid entanglement in "political" cases in order to preserve its reputation for impartiality. Unless, of course, such cases involve certain selectively chosen constitutional principles, which invariably call for the uninhibited expenditure of this carefully husbanded political capital.

Some of the more conservative justices have bought into this excessive and asymmetrical concern with protecting the Court's reputation. The decision in *Bush* v. *Gore*, however, suggests that a majority are now willing to enforce the law more evenhandedly, even when that very evenhandedness will subject the Court to strident political attacks.

The High Court's decision at first glance looks important primarily for its effect on this one presidential contest. The holding is deliberately narrow, and seems unlikely to have significant effects on future elections. The broader significance lies in a passage near the end of the majority opinion, where the justices stress their sensitivity to the limits of judicial authority and the wisdom of leaving the selection of the president to the political sphere. Despite these considerations, they say, it sometimes "becomes our unsought responsibility to resolve the federal and constitutional issues the judicial system has been forced to confront."

The Court could easily have avoided this responsibility, and that is what many observers expected. These expectations had a real foundation. In 1992, for example, the Court reaffirmed the judicially created right to abortion, even while strongly hinting that some of those who voted to do so had serious misgivings. One important reason they gave for their decision was a fear that overruling *Roe* v. *Wade* would be *perceived* as a capitulation to political pressure.

Bush v. *Gore* rejects this beguiling logic. The majority, including two justices who had joined the 1992 abortion opinion, recognized that their de-

Weekly Standard, December 25, 2000, pp. 19–20 (on sale December 18). Reprinted with permission. Nelson Lund is professor of law at George Mason University.

cision would subject them to merciless, politically motivated attacks. But rather than take the easy way out, they courageously accepted their "unsought responsibility" to require that the Florida court comply with the Constitution.

The significance of this act of courage comes into focus when we consider the strongest argument offered by the dissenters. Justice Breyer, who admitted that the Florida court's decision was arbitrary and unconstitutional, suggested that the Twelfth Amendment assigns Congress (rather than the federal courts) the responsibility for correcting such problems. This is a plausible interpretation of the Constitution, especially if one also concludes (as Justice Breyer did not) that the Constitution authorized the Florida legislature to override the Florida court's attempted retroactive rewrite of the state election statute.

But Justice Breyer's position does not rest on a disinterested interpretation of the Constitution. Rather, it is based on the tired theory that "the appearance of a split decision runs the risk of undermining the public's confidence in the Court itself." Justice Breyer thought the risk not worth running because the majority's decision does not "vindicate a fundamental constitutional principle."

What would it mean to "vindicate a fundamental constitutional principle"? As it happens, we know what Justice Breyer means. Just a few months ago, he wrote the majority opinion in a 5-4 case that split the Court much more bitterly than this one. In that case, moreover, Justice Breyer adopted a farfetched interpretation of a state statute that contradicted the state's interpretation of its own law. The result was the invalidation of a state statute that had been drafted specifically to conform with Supreme Court precedent. And what fundamental constitutional principle was vindicated? The right to what is euphemistically called "partial-birth abortion." Now there's something worth fighting for.

If the Twelfth Amendment argument is the best that the *Bush* v. *Gore* dissenters had to offer, the worst was Justice Stevens's claim that Governor Bush irresponsibly impugned the impartiality of the Florida judges by appealing their ruling. Justice Stevens also noted that the real loser in this year's election will be the nation's "confidence in the judge as an impartial guardian of the rule of law." It is certainly true that almost no one will believe that *all* the judges who ruled in the election cases were impartial, or devoted to the rule of law. Justice Stevens, however, was entirely wrong to place the blame for that fact on his colleagues and on Governor Bush.

The blame rests squarely on Florida's supreme court, which violated the Constitution, and on the High Court dissenters, who would have let the

Florida judges get away with it. "Impartial guardians of the rule of law" are willing to enforce the law even when they know they will be excoriated for doing so. Which is why the majority decision in *Bush* v. *Gore* deserves a spirited defense. ∎

JOHN J. DIIULIO JR.

Equal Protection Run Amok:
Conservatives Will Come to Regret the
Court's Rationale for Bush v. Gore

The Weekly Standard

By custom, U.S. Supreme Court justices end even impassioned dissenting opinions collegially with the words "I respectfully dissent." That's how three dissenters, Justices Breyer, Stevens, and Souter, all signed off in *Bush* v. *Gore*. But the fourth, Justice Ginsburg, closed her opinion with a cold two-word punch at the majority: "I dissent."

Cold but correct, because Justice Ginsburg's dissent is resoundingly right on law and precedent.

Yes, on criminal law and other matters, Florida's supreme court judges too often act as ultra-liberal, activist, self-appointed legislators. They did so in their initial, disgraceful 7-0 groupthink ruling on the state's presidential vote-count controversy. No, I wouldn't rather still be listening to people debating dimpled chads. Sure, I'm glad the Court ended the Florida follies, and doubly glad that—cued by Vice President Al Gore, who was supremely patriotic and gracious in defeat—most Americans, including most of my fellow Democrats, now call George W. Bush our forty-third president-elect.

But still, to any conservative who truly respects federalism, the majority's opinion is hard to respect, and the concurring opinion, penned by Chief Justice Rehnquist and joined by Justices Scalia and Thomas, should be rejected in its entirety. The arguments that ended the battle and "gave" Bush the presidency are constitutionally disingenuous at best. They will come back to haunt conservatives and confuse, if they do not cripple, the principled conservative case for limited government, legislative supremacy, and

Weekly Standard, December 25, 2000 (on sale December 18). Reprinted with permission.

universal civic deference to legitimate, duly constituted state and local public authority.

"In most cases," acknowledge Rehnquist, Scalia, and Thomas, "comity and respect for federalism compel us to defer to the decisions of state courts on issues of state law." There are, however, "a few exceptional cases," and "this is one." Why?

Why, suddenly, do inter-county and intra-county differences in election procedures, which are quite common in every state, rise in the Florida case to the level of "equal protection" problems solvable only by uniform standards (by implication, uniform national standards) and strict scrutiny from federal courts?

How can the conservative jurists on the Court find prima facie fault with what the Bush legal team disparaged as "crazy quilt" local laws and procedures? Why, in any case, weigh the alleged problem in Florida without taking cognizance of how election procedures vary from polling station to polling station and from county to county in, say, Pennsylvania? And why, in reversing a state's highest court for not following the U.S. Constitution, and for infringing upon the state legislature's authority, does the nation's highest court substitute its own resolution of the ultimate "political question" for the Constitution's explicit, black-letter reliance on state legislatures and, if need be, the U.S. Congress?

Satisfactory answers are nowhere to be found either in the majority's opinion or in the concurring opinion. As each dissenting justice stressed, the federal questions that emerged from the Florida Supreme Court's 4-3 decision were simply not substantial enough, and the Florida majority's opinion by no reasonable interpretation renegade or recalcitrant enough, to warrant anything like Rehnquist et al.'s outright, roughshod reversal.

As Justice Ginsburg noted, the Court "more than occasionally affirms statutory, and even constitutional, interpretations with which it disagrees," even with respect to administrative agencies. "Surely," she continued, "the Constitution does not call upon us to pay more respect to a federal administrative agency's construction of federal law than to a state high-court's interpretation of its own state's law. And not uncommonly, we let stand state-court interpretations of federal law with which we might disagree." "The extraordinary setting of this case has obscured the ordinary principle that dictates its proper resolution: Federal courts defer to state courts' interpretations of their state's own law." And, even if this were truly an equal protection case, the Court's majority opinion needlessly substitutes "its own judgment about the practical realities of implementing a recount" for the "judgment of those much closer to the process."

I would like to believe there was a time when conservatives would have instinctively recoiled at the way we have all now fallen into thinking of and battling for the presidency as if it, rather than the Congress, were constitutionally the first branch of our national government. There was a time when conservatives understood that the localisms of little platoons and county governments were good and to be preserved and protected by law and custom unless proven bad by experience. There was a time when conservatives knew that legislators, our "partly federal, partly national" republic's "proper guardians of the public weal," as Madison described them—not executives or judges—were best able to decide difficult or divisive matters of great civic moment. There was even, I suppose, a time when conservatives would rather have lost a close, hotly contested presidential election, even against a person and a party from whom many feared the worst, than advance judicial imperialism, diminish respect for federalism, or pander to mass misunderstanding and mistrust of duly elected legislative leaders.

If there ever was such a time, it has now passed, and conservatives ought to do what they can to bring the country back to this future. Regrettably, *Bush* v. *Gore* does no such thing. Desirable result aside, it is bad constitutional law. ∎

MICHAEL S. GREVE

The Real *Division in the Court:*

Neither the Conservative nor the Liberal Justices Were Hypocritical. They Just Have Fundamentally Different Views of Federalism

The Weekly Standard

"So much for states' rights," *Washington Post* columnist E.J. Dionne sneered in commenting on the Supreme Court's ruling in *Bush* v. *Gore*. His comment encapsulated several weeks' worth of noisy complaints about Republican politicians. As the Gore camp portrayed it, the GOP was cynically

Weekly Standard, December 25, 2000, pp. 28–31 (on sale December 18). Michael Greve is the John G. Searle Scholar at the American Enterprise Institute and director of AEI's Federalism Project.

selling out its own commitment to federalism when it talked trash about the Florida Supreme Court, ran to federal court at the drop of a chad, and nationalized the appointment of presidential electors—a matter the Constitution explicitly reserves to the states.

Conservative Supreme Court justices, as well, were said to be hypocrites. "It is ironic indeed," the *New York Times* harrumphed on the occasion of the U.S. Supreme Court's stay of the Florida vote count, "to see the very justices who have repeatedly ruled in favor of states' rights—Chief Justice William Rehnquist and Justices Antonin Scalia, Clarence Thomas, Anthony Kennedy and Sandra Day O'Connor—do an about-face in this case."

Conservatives could easily play this same game: Why did the *New York Times* not find it "ironic" that Laurence Tribe, Gore's Supreme Court counsel, increasingly sounds like a states' rights apostle, circa 1960? But that would be to miss a larger point. Both liberals and conservatives actually have coherent conceptions of federalism, and the justices pursue those conceptions with remarkable (though not unfailing) consistency. The conservative version reflects the constitutional structure and logic. The liberal version erodes that structure and perverts its logic.

Bush v. *Gore* confirms the pattern. It would be silly to deny that partisan considerations influenced the parties' arguments before the Court, the debate over the case, and the justices' rulings. It is true, moreover, that seven justices, the five conservatives among them, embraced an equal protection argument that ought to worry constitutional federalists. But the case presents no ironic inversion of federalist positions. The parties fought, and the justices ruled, on their accustomed sides.

Two Federalisms

Every federalist system faces the challenge of ensuring national cohesion without centralizing the entire system of government. The Founders' solution was to limit the functions and powers of the national government, while ensuring its unqualified *legal* supremacy. Within its constitutional sphere of authority, the national government must be able to accomplish its purposes by acting directly upon the citizens, without the help or intermediation of the states (to say nothing of obstruction by them). National laws must have precedence over those of the states. The themes of functional separation and legal supremacy are central to constitutional federalism. They run through the records of the Constitutional Convention, the Federalist Papers, and the opinions of the Marshall Court.

This constitutional federalism is the federalism Clarence Thomas, Antonin Scalia, William Rehnquist, and (with significant reservations and qualifications) Sandra Day O'Connor and Anthony Kennedy have attempted to recapture. While their endeavor is constrained by political realities and decades of adverse precedents, the case law is beginning to reveal the basic contours of their federalist project.

In a series of decisions, beginning with the invalidation of the federal Gun-Free School Zones Act in *U.S.* v. *Lopez* (1995), the five federalist justices have reestablished constitutional limitations on the national government's power. At the same time, a long line of cases, beginning with *Seminole Tribe* v. *Florida* (1996), has reasserted the sovereign immunity of state governments against private lawsuits brought under federal statutes. In *Printz* v. *United States* (1997), the five federalists invalidated Congress's attempt to compel state and local enforcement of federal gun control requirements. Justice Scalia's far-reaching opinion in that case was explicitly based on the Founders' intention: If Congress wishes to coerce citizens, it must do so directly, not by "commandeering" the states. In all these cases, the four liberal justices (Breyer, Ginsburg, Souter, and Stevens) dissented.

In *Bush* v. *Gore,* the four liberals invoke federalism and states' rights principally against the concurring opinion signed by Chief Justice Rehnquist and Justices Scalia and Thomas. The concurrence finds the Florida Supreme Court's ruling in violation of Article II of the Constitution, which provides that state legislatures shall determine the manner of appointing presidential electors. The liberals' invocation of federalism is misplaced, though: If the supremacy of federal law means anything, it means that state courts may not do end-runs around the federal Constitution.

Still, one cannot dismiss the dissenters' objections as disingenuous or tactical. All four liberal justices have invoked states' rights with some passion and regularity. Justice Stevens in particular has been a vociferous defender of states' rights—for example, in cases concerning the federal preemption of state law (where the principle of federal legal supremacy tends to push the five conservative federalists towards a "nationalist" position).

The liberal justices, then, aren't mindless nationalists. Rather, they adhere to a "cooperative" or "administrative" view of federalism. Under that conception, the national government is unlimited, or at least has no constitutional limitations that a court could recognize. It accomplishes its purposes not through legal supremacy but through institutional cooperation with the states. The states' role lies not in governing a separate sphere of authority but in their independent authority to administer federal schemes.

Such a federalism is not intrinsically incoherent. It is the federalism of Germany, Switzerland, and Europe, as Justice Breyer observed in his *Printz* dissent. Under this view, there is nothing objectionable in the federal commandeering of state officers.

"The fact is that our federalism is not Europe's," Justice Scalia replied to Justice Breyer, and as a matter of constitutional logic and structure, Scalia is right. Cooperative federalism does, however, have a political and judicial tradition in America. Its first judicial endorsement flowed from the pen of Justice Roger Taney, in an opinion celebrating the state enforcement of (of all statutes) the federal Fugitive Slave Act. Politically, cooperative federalism can be traced to the Progressives, who hoped to harmonize national aspirations with the virtues of localism. Cooperative federalism became dominant, both as a matter of political practice and judicial doctrine, under the New Deal.

As the political pedigree suggests, the shift from constitutional to cooperative federalism is tied to the growth of government. Constitutional federalism constrains government. It limits the national government's powers, and it exposes the states, which may wish to regulate in the vast realm beyond the national government's power, to competitive discipline: Excessive regulation may induce productive citizens (or businesses) to move to other, more hospitable states. Cooperative federalism, in contrast, unleashes the national government and enables state governments, through "cooperation" with each other and with the Congress, to establish national policy cartels that preclude citizens from voting with their feet.

Some legal scholars have argued that the justices' seemingly wavering pro- or anti-federalism opinions simply mask their pro- or anti-government preferences. Among the conservative justices, however, only Clarence Thomas can reasonably be suspected of harboring libertarian sympathies, while cooperativist Justice Breyer has inveighed in books and articles (though not in his opinions) against the excesses of federal regulation. The real, much deeper divide runs between constitutional constraint and democratic aspirations, a divide that ran through the *Bush* v. *Gore* opinions.

Constitutionalism is not per se anti-democratic. It insists that "We the People" ordain and establish the Constitution. The constitutional point, though, is to break, fragment, and temper democratic impulses through a system that institutionalizes intra-governmental rivalry, jealousy, and competition. Federalism, for a prominent example.

Democrats chafe under formalistic constraints, and they like cooperative federalism because it trumps those constraints. When government institutions become partners rather than competitors, they cease to frustrate the demos and instead provide it with multiple access points. The system, to be sure, remains too messy and fragmented to satisfy Rousseauean aspirations.

Cooperative federalism, however, may be the closest possible American approximation of the European centralizing ideal.

In the course of the post-election campaign, we have been treated to relentless appeals to "the will of the people"—not as expressed through the ordinary, constitutional channels, but in the raw form of the national popular vote. The purveyors of this demagogy opened fire on institutions that embody constitutional federalism—prominently, the Electoral College—and hit bottom in the persistent demands, and the judicial attempts, to identify the voters who "intended" to vote for Gore, as distinct from those who actually did so by complying with the formality of punching a ballot.

When the Supreme Court's majority effectively halted the Florida Supreme Court's endeavor to "recover," as the Florida justices put it, the voters' true intent, Justice Ginsburg denounced the ruling as a lamentable breach with—cooperative federalism.

Of Judges and Judging

Justice Ginsburg's operative phrase, in fairness, is "cooperative *judicial* federalism," invoked twice in her dissent. Federal and state judges, no less than elected officials, are partners in a common enterprise, and that consideration bars federal interference with state adjudication in all but the most extreme circumstances. Writing in the same vein, Justice Stevens took the majority to task for endorsing the *Bush* plaintiffs' "lack of confidence in the impartiality and capacity" of the Florida judges.

Putting aside the immediate causes of that distrust, it bears emphasis that the Founders viewed state judges very much from James Baker's perspective—as partisan, parochial hacks. State courts would routinely favor their own citizens over those of other states, which is why such "diversity" cases fall in the jurisdiction of federal courts. State courts may, in the ordinary course of deciding cases, adjudicate federal causes of action. The point of that arrangement, though, is not to empower the states but to extend the supremacy of federal law. State court applications of federal law are subject to Supreme Court appeal, and Congress is empowered to establish lower federal courts to handle federal cases if state courts should prove partisan and unreliable.

The Founders considered that event quite likely. "The fitness and competency of [state] courts should be allowed in the utmost latitude," Hamilton writes in Federalist 81. But the conciliatory gesture is followed by an apprehension that "the prevalency of local spirit may be found to disqualify the local tribunals for the jurisdiction of national causes." Moreover, "state judges, holding their offices during pleasure, or from year to year, will be too little independent to be relied upon for an inflexible execution of the national laws."

As if to earn this distrust, the state courts of the young nation soon began to obstruct federal laws under the guise of interpreting their own state laws. The Marshall Court overruled them. That early case is cited as a precedent by the *Bush* v. *Gore* majority, along with two civil rights era cases that overruled segregationist state court decisions under state law. Justice Ginsburg's dissent acknowledges the precedents, but proceeds to protest that *Bush* v. *Gore* "involves nothing like the kind of recalcitrance by a state high court that warrants extraordinary action by this Court." The Florida Supreme Court, Ginsburg writes, "surely should not be bracketed with state high courts of the Jim Crow South."

Perhaps repeated judicial attempts to stack the deck in a presidential election do not compare to the moral scandal of Jim Crow. But still the Florida Supreme Court made up its own election statute, in derogation of federal law; refused to respond to the U.S. Supreme Court's exhortation to observe the federal strictures; and then repeated the exercise. Just how much recalcitrance is too much?

How much collateral damage, moreover, does it take until the obstruction of federal laws and purposes, under the guise of state law interpretation, becomes a federal issue? Why, yes, Justice Breyer concedes, "the selection of a President is of fundamental national importance. But that importance is political, not legal." As a matter of law, the Florida Supreme Court is entitled to drive the country over a political cliff, and never mind Article II and statutory safe harbors.

It is entirely fitting that this position should have been urged upon the Court by David Boies, a trial lawyer—one of a cast of characters who round up thousands of plaintiffs across the country, sue corporations for several billion dollars in some forsaken Alabama county that neither the plaintiffs nor defendants have ever entered, and then protest federal tort-reform measures on the grounds that product liability lawsuits are strictly a matter between Alabama's citizens and judges. (The national importance is economic, not legal, as Justice Breyer might say.) Ruthless transgressions by parochial state judges and juries, however, were not the Founders' idea of federalism. They were the Founders' nightmare.

The Sovereign

Having extolled cooperative federalism, Justice Ginsburg ends her disquisition on Article II by invoking the real, constitutional federalism. The concurring justices' "solicitude for the Florida Legislature comes at the expense of the more fundamental solicitude we owe to the legislature's sovereign," meaning the citizens and the State of Florida as a political entity "Were the [conservative] members of this Court as mindful as they generally are of our system of dual federalism," Justice Ginsburg chastises, "they would affirm the judgment of the Florida Supreme Court."

The serious, almost persuasive version of this argument is that the remedy for the Florida court's transgressions lay with the Florida legislature, rather than the U.S. Supreme Court. But that is not Justice Ginsburg's argument. The only hint at the Florida legislature's powers appears in the majority's per curiam opinion, not in Ginsburg's or in any other dissent. With that omission, Ginsburg's solicitude for state sovereignty collapses into an alarming embrace of judicial supremacy.

In its two decisions, the Florida Supreme Court trashed an entire structure of government. It emasculated canvassing boards by subjecting their determinations to *de novo* judicial review (excepting the boards that had manufactured additional Gore votes, which the court ordered to be certified without any review). The court twice overruled perfectly sensible determinations by the secretary of state (one made pursuant to established state law; the other, pursuant to the Florida Supreme Court's own deadline). The court twice supplanted the legislature's election laws with its own rules and deadlines.

A comparable legal action by the Florida legislature, the U.S. Supreme Court learned from Boies during oral argument, would have constituted an impermissible postelection change of the laws; coming as it did from the Florida Supreme Court, it constituted mere "interpretation." When the Florida legislature threatened to exercise its rightful authority to appoint a slate of electors, democratic (and Democratic) partisans hysterically denounced the attempt as—well, an undemocratic interference with the judiciary's recovery of the voters' true intentions. Nothing and no one, no rule and no structure, must stand between the will of the people and its vicarious interpretation by the judicial committee for public safety.

That is the sovereign to whom, in the dissenting Supreme Court justices' world, we owe solicitude and unquestioning obedience. "It is confidence in the men and women who administer the judicial system," Justice Stevens writes, "that is the true backbone of the rule of law."

The rule of law is in trouble, and *Bush* v. *Gore* provides little comfort. The justices' unanimous remand of the Florida Supreme Court's first ruling expressed concern over the state court's reckless disregard for Article II and the federal safe harbor provisions. In the end, though, only three justices were prepared to follow the constitutional argument, while seven members of the Court resorted to an unprecedented, free-floating equal protection argument that invites federal regimentation for almost any reason.

One may hope that the equal protection part of *Bush* v. *Gore* will prove a ticket for this day and train only. The deeper and true problem is the assault on constitutionalism. That assault reflects long-rampant misconceptions, and it comes itself in the constitutionalist garb of federalism, judicial restraint, and the rule of law. For that reason, it cannot be countered with facile slogans about "judicial activism," "states' rights," and the like. We will have to remind ourselves of some long-forgotten truths about what it means to live in a constitutional, federal republic. If the crisis just passed helps us to do so, it will have done some good. ∎

HENDRIK HERTZBERG

Eppur Si Muove

The New Yorker

That was a tough concession speech Al Gore had to give the other night, but people have had to give tougher ones over the years. In 1633, a prominent, well-connected member of the high-tech community of Florence found himself on the wrong end of a decision by the then equivalent of the Supreme Court. Put on trial by the Inquisition, he was found guilty of advocating a doctrine described in the Holy Office's indictment as "absurd and false philosophically, because it is expressly contrary to Holy Scripture." This was a characterization with which the defendant was known to privately disagree. But he was anxious to avoid being cast as a troublemaker and eager for the healing to begin, so he said the words the occasion required. "I, Galileo, son of the late Vincenzo Galilei, Florentine, aged seventy years," he recited, "abjure, curse, and detest the aforesaid errors and heresies, and I swear that I will never again say or assert that the Sun is the center of the universe and immovable and that the Earth is not the center and moves." Before Galileo was led away to spend the rest of his life under comfortable house arrest, however, he kicked the ground and, according to legend, muttered, "*Eppur si muove*"—"But still, it moves."

Vice-President Gore, too, offered the required pieties last Wednesday evening—about putting rancor aside, about love of country, about how "that which unites us is greater than that which divides us." He did so with considerable grace and a few touches of rueful humor. He permitted himself only the faintest of heretical intimations: a declaration that he continues to "strongly disagree with the Court's decision" (coupled, to be sure, with an assurance that he accepts it); a mention of "those who feel their voices have not been heard," which might be taken as a reference to those whose votes remain uncounted; and an explanation that he was conceding because he was concerned about "our unity as a people and the strength of our democracy"—that is to say, not because he had lost the election.

And indeed he did not, as far as science can determine, lose the election. He lost the post-election, in which the franchise, it turned out, was limited to certain members of the Supreme Court. The embarrassment of this was evident even to them. At exactly this time of year four decades ago, John F. Kennedy made up his mind that he was going to appoint his kid brother Robert Attorney General. Benjamin Bradlee asked him how he planned to make the announcement. "Well," the President-elect replied, "I think I'll open the front door of the Georgetown house some morning about 2 A.M., look up and down the street, and, if there's no one there, I'll whisper, 'It's Bobby.'" The Court last week actually did what J.F.K. joked about, except that what the Court whispered into the darkness was nothing so forthright as "It's Bush." While millions watched in bafflement, network and cable television news correspondents, many of them lawyers trained to skim judicial opinion for its gist, struggled to make sense of the majority opinion's verbiage. It's no wonder they were confused: the crabbed, ugly language had been crafted to obscure what had been decided, and even who had done the deciding. As the indispensable Linda Greenhouse noted a couple of days later in the *Times,* the opinion, which was unsigned, was styled "per curiam," meaning "by the court"—"a label used by courts almost exclusively for unanimous opinions so uncontroversial as to not be worth the trouble of a formal opinion-writing process." It took the experts the better part of an hour just to deduce that the ruling was by a five-to-four vote: to solve the mystery, they had to identify the authors of the overlapping dissents, add them up, and subtract from nine. In the text itself, the only clue to the breakdown was an innocent-sounding sentence—"Seven Justices of the Court agree that there are constitutional problems with the recount ordered

by the Florida Supreme Court that demand a remedy"—which suggested
that the opinion, or part of it, had been agreed to by all but two Justices.
This was false. But it was only a drop in the rancid bucket of the majority's
bad faith.

The in-house reviews were not kind. The Court's decision "can only lend
credence to the most cynical appraisal of the work of judges throughout the
land" (Justice Stevens). "There is no justification for denying the State the
opportunity to try to count all disputed ballots now" (Justice Souter). "I dissent" (Justice Ginsburg, omitting the customary softener, "respectfully").
The decision is "a self-inflicted wound—a wound that may harm not just
the Court, but the Nation" (Justice Breyer). The clarity of the dissenters'
prose and reasoning only makes their anger and sorrow more striking.

On the basis of the available evidence—not least the ruthless determination of the Republican Party to use all the powers at its command, from the
executive and legislative branches of the Florida state government to the five-
person Supreme Court bloc (now exposed not as jurisprudential conservatives but as ideological and nakedly partisan ones), for the single purpose of
preventing a fair count of the ballots of Florida's citizens—it may now be in-
ferred, pending the eventual recount by scholars and journalists under Florida's
freedom-of-information laws, that the President-elect (a suddenly Orwellian
honorific) lost not only the popular but also the true electoral vote. Nevertheless, the election of 2000 was not stolen. Stealing, after all, is illegal, and,
by definition, nothing the Justices of the Supreme Court do can be outside
the law. They are the law. The election was not stolen. It was expropriated. ∎

STUART TAYLOR JR.

Why the Florida Recount Was Egregiously One-Sided

The National Journal

Most of the attacks on the U.S. Supreme Court's 5-4 ruling on Dec. 12 halting Florida's statewide manual recount have proceeded from the assumption that the Florida Supreme Court had acted reasonably—or at least de-

National Journal, December 23, 2000, pp. 3932–33. Copyright 2000 by National Journal Group, Inc. All rights reserved. Reprinted by permission.

fensibly—in its stunning, 4-3 decision four days before to order the rushed recount. The assumption is wrong, as I demonstrate below, and my next column will discuss what the U.S. Supreme Court should have done about the Florida case.

The Florida court's decision was so blatantly, one-sidedly pro-Gore that but for the U.S. Supreme Court's intervention, it would have had the foreseeable effect of rigging the recount in the guise of "counting every vote." To be precise, the Florida court's decision—aside from making a hash of Florida's election laws and denying George W. Bush any semblance of due process—awarded Al Gore several hundred more "votes" than he would have gained from any fair and credible vote-recounting process. If Gore had pulled ahead of Bush by, say, 300 votes in the further recounts ordered by the Florida court, such phony "votes" would have provided his entire margin of victory, and then some.

I won't focus here on legalisms. Let's just count the votes, as the saying goes. Starting with some undisputed numbers from three counties that have received far less attention than they deserve: the Broward 567, the Miami-Dade 168, and the Palm Beach 176. These are the margins (totaling 911) by which the new "votes" generated for Gore exceeded those for Bush in the manual recounts that had already been done, before Dec. 8, by the Democratic-dominated canvassing boards in these three big, mostly Democratic counties. (Superlawyer David Boies, who represented Gore, has repeatedly put the Palm Beach number at 215. He has repeatedly been wrong.)

With no real explanation, the Florida court conclusively awarded Gore all 911 of these "votes." It added the Miami-Dade 168 and the Palm Beach 176 to Gore's statewide total—even though Miami-Dade had done only a partial recount, in heavily Democratic precincts, and even though Palm Beach had missed the Florida court's own Nov. 26 deadline for completing its recount. The Florida court also made final the Nov. 26 certification of Broward's number, 567. In doing so, it ignored Bush's pending challenge to hundreds of these Broward "votes" (and similar "votes" in Volusia County)—most of which were not votes at all, Bush's attorneys argue persuasively. Rather, they were unreasonable deductions of voter intent, from inscrutable pieces of paper, by the transparently partisan, count-every-last-dimple majority of the Broward canvassing board.

According to the Florida court's own calculations, the Dec. 8 decision thus brought Gore to within 193 votes of overtaking Bush. (This assumes the Palm Beach number to be 176, not 215.) The Florida court's new recount also gave Gore some hope—his *only* hope—of pulling ahead, by assigning hundreds of new vote-counters to search through 50,000 as-yet-unexamined "undervotes" for the 200 dimples that could make Gore President. (Undervotes are ballots on which vote-counting machines had detected no vote for any presidential candidate.)

If enough dimples could be found, it appears, the Florida courts would almost immediately have designated Gore the winner of Florida's electoral votes, and of the presidency. But even a cursory analysis suggests that this would have been a travesty, because about two-thirds of both the Broward 567 and the Miami- Dade 168 appear to have been *phony* votes—ballots that came nowhere near proving voter intent to choose Gore.

Some sixth-grade arithmetic: Officials in Broward interpreted about 25.6 percent (1,721) of the county's 6,716 undervotes as votes for either Gore (1,142) or Bush (579). The vote-to-undervote ratio in Miami-Dade's partial recount before Thanksgiving was also about 25 percent. But officials in Palm Beach County, including the estimable Judge Charles Burton, interpreted less than 8 percent (828) of the 10,604 undervotes there as real votes.

So Broward and Miami-Dade generated more than three times as many "votes" per 100 undervotes as Palm Beach. Given the similarities between Broward and Palm Beach, the magnitude of this difference is almost surely attributable to different vote-counting standards.

Other evidence bolsters this inference: Democratic officials in Broward, Palm Beach, and Miami-Dade counties had all liberalized their chad-counting standards several times during the post-election period, amid complaints from the Gore camp that the counties would put Gore over the top only if they "counted" more dimpled chads. Even the liberalized Palm Beach standard—counting a dimpled chad when a pattern of dimples on the ballot indicated voter intent—was not nearly as pro-Gore as the new standards used by Democratic officials to "count" the Broward 567 and the Miami-Dade 168.

Broward, in particular, counted virtually all dimpled chads, after Gore's attorneys produced an affidavit claiming—falsely, as it turned out—that this was what the Illinois courts had done in a case quoted approvingly by the Florida Supreme Court in its first, Nov. 21 decision. In fact, Illinois and most other states do not ordinarily count dimpled chads, with a few exceptions that Gore's attorneys misrepresented to be the rule. And until this election, no Florida court had ever suggested (let alone ordered) that dimpled chads be counted as votes. In fact, Palm Beach County had *barred* the counting of dimpled chads.

The new, liberalized Palm Beach County standard nonetheless seemed reasonably fair to Bush and Gore alike (although both maintained otherwise). Certainly there was no unfairness to Gore. It follows, as the night the day, that the standards (or nonstandards) used in Broward and Miami-Dade were *not* credible or fair to Bush.

(This seems to have eluded the Florida Supreme Court's four-member majority, which perhaps was trying to make a virtue of standardless chad-counting.)

If the Broward and Miami-Dade recounts had been fair, Gore's net gains would have been reduced by about two-thirds—by some 378 votes (567 minus 189) in Broward and some 112 votes (168 minus 56) in Miami-Dade. The combined reduction in Gore's net gain would have been about 490 votes. Subtracting these 490 from the Gore total would have increased Bush's lead from 193 to about 683. And this is without factoring in the *additional* net gain of roughly 400 to 500 votes that the Bush attorneys expected to find by recounting technically flawed but otherwise valid overseas absentee military ballots—many of which had initially been thrown out at the request of the Gore camp.

Another way of looking at it: Had the Democratic officials who ran the manual recount in Palm Beach County also been in charge of Broward and Miami-Dade, Bush would have had an apparently insuperable lead in the range of about 683 votes to 1,183 votes (if 500 more overseas ballots were counted). Conversely, had the Democratic officials who ran the Broward recount also been in charge of Palm Beach, they would have found a net Gore gain there of an additional 352 votes (176 times two) on top of the 176 credited to Gore by the Palm Beach officials. That would have put Gore some 159 votes (352 minus 193) ahead of Bush, unless Bush could pick up overseas ballots.

The bottom line is that even if one assumes that the Florida court was trying to be evenhanded, the election's outcome, under its standardless approach, would have depended not on who won more real votes, but on who was "recounting" (interpreting, really) the ballots.

It is also fairly clear that the Florida court's late-afternoon Dec. 8 decision had set the stage for the Florida courts to railroad through a Gore victory by Dec. 12 (if Gore were to pull ahead). This would have left Bush without even a fraction of the time necessary for a fair hearing on his evidence that any Gore "lead" was an illusion based on phony votes—and no time at all for appeals.

As implemented by Judge Terry Lewis, the Florida Supreme Court's decision gave short shrift to Bush's basic right to judicial review of the thousands of disputed ballot-interpretation decisions made by (among others) openly partisan Democratic officials. In a series of late-night rulings hours after the Dec. 8 decision, Judge Lewis refused to suggest (or hear evidence on) what chad-counting standard vote-counters should use; assigned hundreds of untrained counters to plunge into this world of standardless chad-interpretation, without even requiring that they be nonpartisan; refused to require that a record be kept of chad-interpretation decisions, thereby making appeals virtually impossible; ignored Bush's request for a recount of those hundreds of rejected overseas military ballots; and shrugged off claims that some Gore votes would inevitably be counted twice.

In short, Judge Lewis understood his marching orders: Damn due process. Full speed ahead. So, it seems, did a majority of the U.S. Supreme Court. ∎

RANDALL KENNEDY

Contempt of Court

The American Prospect

The U.S. Supreme Court's intervention into the presidential election was and is a scandal. Five right-wing justices used the flimsiest of pretexts to block the Florida vote recount. Chief Justice William Rehnquist and Company are typically unmoved by alleged Equal Protection Clause violations (except when the plaintiffs are whites charging so-called reverse discrimination). In *George W. Bush et al. Petitioners* v. *Albert Gore, Jr., et al.,* however, they created a new right to uniform treatment in ballot counting.

Typically, these conservative justices insist that every benefit of the doubt be accorded to state judges interpreting state law. Indeed, they are usually so deferential to state judges that they have been willing even to countenance the executions of prisoners rather than encroach even a bit on the perceived prerogatives of state courts. In *Bush* v. *Gore,* however, Rehnquist, Justice Antonin Scalia, and Justice Clarence Thomas asserted that the Florida Supreme Court's interpretation of state law lacked a reasonable basis. Joined by Justice Anthony Kennedy and Justice Sandra Day O'Connor, they further

Reprinted with permission from *The American Prospect,* volume 12, number 1, January 1–15, 2001, pp. 15–17 (on sale December 26, 2000). The American Prospect, 5 Broad Street, Boston, MA 02109. All rights reserved. Randall Kennedy is a professor at Harvard Law School.

usurped the state court's authority by preventing it from even attempting to establish the standards for uniform vote-counting that were said to be essential. True, Justice Stephen Breyer and Justice David Souter found fault of a constitutional dimension with differences in how various jurisdictions were determining voter intent in the manual recount. But while they insisted that the Florida court should be accorded the opportunity to fix this perceived deficiency—as is normally done—the Court majority took the unusual step of foreclosing this possibility. That act of judicial fiat crystallizes, more than anything else, the outrageousness of *Bush* v. *Gore*.

The Gang of Five showed themselves to be a cadre of downfield blockers committed to clearing away any last-minute impediments to the ascendancy of George W. Bush. Their opinion is a hypocritical mishmash of ideas that even some of their ideological allies—for instance, Einer Elhauge, a Harvard Law School professor who represented the Republican-dominated Florida legislature—have criticized as being poorly written and thinly reasoned.

Every Supreme Court decision is animated by capital-P Politics of a certain sort: a given conception of constitutional interpretation, or federalism, or the proper relationship of the competing branches of government. *Bush* v. *Gore*, however, is driven by small-p politics—a decisive preference by the judges for one party over another. In a talk before high school students the day after the decision, Justice Clarence Thomas declared that people ought not to apply the rules of the political world to the Supreme Court. But in light of recent events, that assertion rings ridiculously hollow.

The Gang of Five used their power to accomplish their ends. Now those who oppose them should use their power to respond.

Three tasks are essential. First, we should state forthrightly what occurred in *Bush* v. *Gore*. Some critics of the Court's intervention are sidestepping the sobering reality of the situation: that the Court majority acted in bad faith and with partisan prejudice. If the political shoe had been on the other foot—if Al Gore had been the petitioner instead of George W. Bush—the Court would have acted differently.

Second, we should inject realism into public discussions about the Court. It is a journalistic convention to state that the Republican Party now controls the White House, the Senate, and the House of Representatives, but to exclude talk of right-wing Republican control of the Supreme Court (which journalists and other arbiters of public opinion deferentially place on a different plane from the other branches of government). Such rhetorical obfuscations should be erased.

Some readers will retort that it is important to retain public confidence in the Court because, as Anthony Lewis writes, "[i]n this vast, diverse country, we depend on the Supreme Court as the final voice." But trusting the Court is good only if it is trustworthy. Because of progressive Court decisions from the 1940s through the 1960s, many liberals have come to believe that there is something peculiarly virtuous about the third branch of government, the supposedly least dangerous branch. A reconsideration of that particular dogma is long overdue. *Bush* v. *Gore* offers as good an invitation as any to rethink whether we ought to depend upon and defer to the Supreme Court as the final voice.

Third, we should begin preparing the ground to prevent another rightward lurch of the federal judiciary through the president's appointment power. The sad truth is that the Democratic Party bears a substantial part of the responsibility for permitting the Supreme Court to drift as far to the right as it has. It was, after all, a Democrat-controlled Senate that confirmed the ascension of William Rehnquist to the chief justiceship after he had given ample notice as an associate justice that he was a committed foe to the just aspirations of racial minorities, women, organized labor, and civil libertarians. Judicial nominees should have to pass certain litmus tests before they receive a senator's vote for confirmation. Their records and testimony should give us confidence that they will respect people's hard-won rights. When that confidence is lacking, nominees should be rejected. Given the powerful presence of the federal bench in the nation's life, a more rigorous process of oversight by progressives is clearly warranted.

Democrats should have blocked right-wing confirmations and demanded that Republican presidents nominate jurists who are more politically palatable. Now, Democratic senators should unapologetically refuse to confirm for judgeships individuals ideologically in line with Justice Antonin Scalia, whom President-elect Bush has repeatedly praised. We all should recognize that in a Bush administration, there will be no Larry Tribes brought to the bench. But we should also insist that there be no confirmations for Scalia-like champions of the right-wing agenda.

The Supreme Court has hurt its own reputation by wrongly intervening to ensure the victory of George W. Bush. Those who abhor what the Court did should say so and say so loudly and directly. And they should demand that the Court repair its own damaged reputation. Only when that occurs should the public repose its trust in the Court, which is now unworthy of deference. ▮

≈⟩

What We'll Remember in 2050

The Chronicle of Higher Education

We want to know now. In the aftermath of the Supreme Court's decision in *Bush* v. *Gore*, we gave nine scholars and writers a weighty mandate: predict how historians in 50 years will see this year's election and its consequences in the cold light of history. [The comments of Cass Sunstein and Harvey Mansfield are reprinted here.]

CASS SUNSTEIN

In America, the new century began with a loud bang—more particularly, with the election of George W. Bush, brought about by the extraordinary 5-to-4 decision of the U.S. Supreme Court in *Bush* v. *Gore*. Of course the court's decision resolved the post-election controversy. But the election aside, the most general importance of the court's decision lay in its remarkable effects on popular understandings of the court itself.

As hard as it is to believe, *Bush* v. *Gore* came during a long period of complaints about "liberal judicial activism"—and extremely difficult to defend in nonpartisan terms. Americans seemed grateful that the court had ended the fierce post-election struggle, which had threatened to become a crisis. But millions of Americans also believed that the court had acted in an unacceptably partisan manner, and not as a court of law at all. They were unable to look at Chief Justice William H. Rehnquist, and the Rehnquist court, in quite the same way again.

It was for this reason that the early 21st century was a period in which citizens finally recognized that "liberal judicial activism" was a brief quirk of history, limited to a short time in the middle of the 20th century. Citizens of various political stripes came to see that conservative judicial activism was both far more likely and hence far more dangerous for democracy. *Bush* v. *Gore* raised widespread doubts about the neutrality of the Supreme Court, and those doubts contributed to a period in which the court was increasingly meek, even silent. In fact, the first two decades of the 21st

Chronicle of Higher Education, January 5, 2001, pp. B15–16 (on sale December 29, 2000). Reprinted with permission of the authors. Cass Sunstein is professor of jurisprudence and political science at the University of Chicago. Harvey Mansfield is professor of government at Harvard University.

century saw a court that was increasingly likely to tell the elected branches that whatever they did would be constitutionally acceptable. The Quiet Court, as it has come to be known, may well be a direct outgrowth of the noise generated by *Bush* v. *Gore*.

Strangely, the major effect of *Bush* v. *Gore* was to reinvigorate America's interest in democracy itself, partly by producing a more limited judicial role, but much more by ensuring that all votes would be counted, and be counted equally. By discrediting itself, the Supreme Court that decided *Bush* v. *Gore* helped to draw new attention to the importance of the franchise, and to the ideals of self-government and political equality. To give just one example, the early 21st century's impressive efforts to ensure improved technology for voting, treating poor and rich alike, are directly traceable to questions raised by the election of President Bush. The last 50 years have shown fresh attention to democratic principles in America. It is ironic but true that the illegitimate, undemocratic, and unprincipled decision in *Bush* v. *Gore* deserves much of the credit.

HARVEY J. MANSFIELD

This decision saved the country from possible turmoil and a good deal of further partisan confusion. In this election, there seemed to be more partisanship after people voted than before. I heard hardly anyone agreeing with the thesis of the person he didn't vote for in the matter of the Supreme Court. So I voted for Bush, and I very much supported the final decision made by the U. S. Supreme Court. It very correctly overruled the Florida Supreme Court, which had gone much too far in the direction of judicial activism. And it took an activist majority in the U. S. Supreme Court to correct an even more activist one in the Florida Supreme Court.

I don't think it was a violation of principle by the U. S. Supreme Court. It's true they mainly support states' rights, but I don't think that's a principle that people can hold to on every occasion. I think they would have made a grave mistake and looked quite foolish if they had held to the right of the Florida Supreme Court to abuse its discretion in this matter. It would have been better if Florida had been able to decide its own affairs constitutionally, but states' rights are not an absolute—we live under a Constitution that also has a federal government. It's good for Republicans and conservatives to remember this. But it's not inconsistent or malicious of them to resort to the final constitutional power of the U. S. Supreme Court.

It was unfortunate that the majority of the court had to go to the equal-protection clause, which hasn't been applied in voting cases before this and has potential for future mischief if it comes to be supposed that equal protection requires each vote to have the same power. That would run counter to our federal system. But I think the five conservative justices agreed to using the equal-protection clause in order to get two more votes, from Breyer and Souter, and that was a reasonable and statesmanlike thing to do in the circumstances.

The two parties were very much themselves throughout. The Republicans stand for the rule of law, and the Democrats for the rule of the people. And the Democrats, because they stand for the rule of the people, believe that rule should be paramount, and that technicalities are subordinate to that will. Whereas the Republicans believe in doing things properly or legally. It really was a contest of principle between two parties. ▌

Index to Writers and Publications

The Editors

E.J. Dionne Jr. is a senior fellow in the Governmental Studies program at the Brookings Institution and a columnist for *The Washington Post*.

William Kristol is editor and publisher of *The Weekly Standard*.